CONTENTS

W9-BNT-452

PART ONE

Introduction

WHY THIS BOOK CAME ABOUT

While job hunters love the simplicity, clarity, and brevity (and, no doubt, the irreverence) of *The Damn Good Resume Guide,* I learned that people, paradoxically, have an insatiable appetite for more and more good EXAMPLES to look at. So, rather than expand the *Guide* (which would sacrifice its basic appeal), I chose to produce this SEQUEL for those hungry readers who can't get enough: a COMPANION RESOURCE BOOK with all the examples they ever wanted, and more!

HOW THIS BOOK CAME ABOUT

"Darn! I just can't think of that word!"

Even though I have worked with clients on hundreds of resumes, sometimes my mind will go totally blank when I try to think of a specific word or phrase to exactly fit the situation. Of course I have saved copies of all the resumes I've written in the past, and sometimes I'd flip through them with a client, looking for ideas and alternative ways to express a thought or illustrate a skill.

Eventually it occurred to me that it would be easier to find the right examples if I organized the resumes into groups according to their job objectives, and put them in a notebook. Then, after a year of using this informal "Resume Sample Book," I realized how valuable it was to me and to my clients, and decided that eventually I should share it with others.

I also noticed that the "juicy highlights" were a favorite source of inspiration to my clients, but they, too, needed organizing. So one day, in a burst of energy, I copied down hundreds of the best "highlight" statements from the resumes, and organized THEM into categories such as "commitment," "leadership skill," "reputation," "credentials," "special knowledge," and "experience."

Being an "organization junkie," this was still not enough for me: I had to start a card file with everybody's PAST work history, TOO. So then when a client—say, a flight attendant —came in and wanted to see what OTHER flight attendants put on THEIR resumes, well I could just quick-as-a-wink check with the card file and produce what they wanted! NOW this was beginning to look like a real System, a serious resource.

In the back of my *Damn Good Resume Guide* (selling briskly since publication in 1983, and revised in '86), I "tested the waters" by mentioning that "a supplement for career counselors" was in the works, and many readers—both career counselors AND serious job hunters—wrote back saying they were definitely interested in having a copy. So I told George Young, of Ten Speed Press, that I had some good material for another book, and that readers were already enthusiastic and asking for it. George said, "Great, let's do it."

Then people who looked at the manuscript were sure that the ordinary job-hunter would like the book just as much as the professional resume writer. So the focus was changed a bit, and now there's just one section addressed specifically to professional resume writers (rather than the whole book). However ...

Be your own Career Counselor

Here's a HINT FOR READERS who can't find (or don't need) a good professional to help them: EAVESDROP ON THE TIPS FOR CAREER COUNSELORS section, and take a do-it-yourself approach to the ideas presented there.

In case you should ask

I would like to answer a few questions that I expect may be asked of me:

1. WHY do the resumes all LOOK so much alike?
BECAUSE I worked hard to find a format and a style that worked best for most of the people most of the time. And once I got it right, I stuck to it! (But I'd be happy to see some models that look different and are equally effective.)

2. WHY aren't there more BLUE-COLLAR workers represented here? Or kids? Or poor people? Or people with little education? Or more people from the east or south or mid-west?
BECAUSE this is a book of REAL PEOPLE, all of whom were my clients, and the reality is that most of them live near the San Francisco Bay Area—and they had the motivation, inclination, and resources to hire professional help.

3. HOW do you know these resumes are any GOOD?
Many clients call me back to tell me they GOT EXCELLENT RESULTS from their resumes. And many readers write telling me how helpful *Damn Good Resume Guide* was, especially in opening their eyes to a new appreciation of their own skills and how to write about them. This model gives them a fresh new view of what a resume can be: an exciting, effective, and personally expressive document.

Thank you

I also want to say "thank you" to the 200 people who allowed their resumes to be shared with other job hunters. And "thank you" to Estelle Yancey, Roger Blair, and Liz LaCaze who contacted all those 200 people, and kept a million details straight.

Yana Parker 12/1/87

The Joy of Resume Work
by one who loves it.

Writing a resume is like creating a work of art. Like writing a poem, a haiku: given strictly limited space and conditions, you say who you are, expressively. It's a challenge.

Or like a sculpture: you keep building—chipping away here, moving this over there, trying out another word or phrase or arrangement—until, voila!, it works!

And it's like polishing silver, revealing the precious radiance hidden beneath.

Or like washing off a mirror and seeing what you look like when examined from a fresh perspective.

A resume is like a sophisticated comic strip: you draw little word sketches of yourself, taking appropriate license with the arrangement of dry "truth" to tell a <u>higher</u> truth:

> ... what makes you tick
> ... what motivates you
> ... what work your heart wants to do
> ... where your hidden or not-so-hidden talents are
> ... what you've done that makes you feel proud
> ... what calls forth your passion and competence.

And it's like a flattering snapshot: it captures you at your best, revealing your unguarded beauty.

When it's good, you've "spilled the beans" about yourself...giving an advance clue to your essence...
telling them what they really need to know:
> what's special about you.

Helping someone write a good resume is very gratifying work.   —YP

200 Sample Resumes

...arranged in 12 broad Job Categories

About Ampersands,
Anonymity,
& Phony Dates

on these resumes:

WORK HISTORY DATES

In many of the resume Work Histories here, "1985-present" or "1980-present" means "present" *at the time the resume was written.* So if you see, for example, "1986-present Manager ROYALE CAFE/RESTAURANT, Oakland" and you KNOW the restaurant, please keep in mind that this was true *at the time the resume was written,* and somebody ELSE is probably the manager by the time you read this book!

Also, you may notice that it SEEMS like most of the people in this book are currently employed because the date of their most recent employment is often listed as "1984-present," "1979-present," "1986-present." However, a fair number of those clients were NOT EMPLOYED when we did their resume (they had recently quit a job or were laid off), and their actual resume read "1984-86," or "1979-87" for the job that just ended. But we changed those dates to avoid having this book appear "dated" in only 6 months (too soon to be revising it).

THE CASE OF THE COMPROMISING AMPERSAND (&)

In this book the word "and" has sometimes been replaced with "&" for no good reason except to conserve space and conform to the margin constraints of book printing; on the original resume, in those cases, the word was probably spelled out "a-n-d."

This was the compromise that often saved us from having to cut a whole line out in order to make the resume fit on the page.

Which is to say, in real life, "When in doubt, spell it out."

ANONYMITY AND FICTITIOUS PLACES

Sometimes you'll see a reference that you KNOW couldn't be true; for example that someone has worked at Esprit Co. in Portland ME and you KNOW there's no Esprit Co. in that city. In that case the author changed the name of the city and/or the company solely to preserve the anonymity of the job hunter.

If you think you know someone in this book, and/or for some reason you want to contact them, send a message through the author, at the publisher's address, and it will get forwarded to the correct person . . . as time permits.

ALEXANDER ROGERS
2933 Broderick St.,
San Francisco CA 94115
(415) 998-3654

Objective: Position in Quality Control Management
with the Food, Drug, and Cosmetics industry

HIGHLIGHTS OF QUALIFICATIONS
- Proven track record in managing a total quality control system.
- Expert trouble-shooter in both manufacturing and packaging.
- Thorough working knowledge of the food/drug/cosmetic industry.
- Results oriented; confident in making on-the-spot decisions.
- Industry reputation for professionalism and competence.
- Eighteen years professional experience.

PROFESSIONAL EXPERIENCE

Quality Administration
- Successfully located and qualified the best contract manufacturers in the industry, consistently meeting all regulatory and corporate specifications.
- Designed and implemented effective quality/cost control systems:
  Contract manufacturing:
  -placed over 100 products with contract manufacturer, achieving a trouble-free transition from in-house manufacturing.
  -maintained a product complaint level below the industry norm.
  In-house manufacturing:
  -increased departmental productivity by 65%
  -decreased product rejection rate by 30%
- Managed a $1.3 million departmental budget.

Management/Trouble Shooting
- Restored efficiency of Component Inspection Dept. at Max Factor in 3 months:
  -retrained staff   -rewrote procedures
  -introduced time management   -automated inspection procedures.

Industry Expertise/Product Knowledge
- Wrote procedure manual detailing the requirements for qualifying contract manufacturing with Shaklee.
- Wrote procedure manuals for Quality Control program at Max Factor & Co.
- Participated actively in promoting industry technical education:
  -spoke on qualification of contract manufacturers, at both ASQC and SCC.
  -served on national Executive Committee of ASQC, FD&C section.
  -selected Publicity Chairman, 1987, ASQC, FD&C annual West Coast seminar.

EMPLOYMENT HISTORY

1979-88	**Quality Assurance Manager**	SHAKLEE HEADQUARTERS - San Francisco
1978-79	**Quality Assurance Manager**	SHAKLEE, Hayward
1976-78	**Quality Control Supervisor**	MAX FACTOR & CO. - Los Angeles
1975-76	**Quality Control Manager**	DRACKETT INC. - Los Angeles
1971-75	**Quality Control Supervisor**	CARTER-WALLACE INC. - Los Angeles
1968-71	**Quality Control Inspector**	CARTER-WALLACE INC. - Momence IL

EDUCATION
B.S., Business Administration - UNIVERSITY OF REDLANDS, CA

CHARMAINE DUNCAN
361 - 25th Ave
San Francisco CA 94121
339-4421

Charmaine's Army experience is interpreted in civilian language.

Objective: Management position in a nonprofit organization.

Highlights of Qualifications
★ Six years successful supervisory and management experience.
★ Resourceful and self-confident; get the job done, and do it well.
★ Strong interpersonal and communication skills.
★ Extensive experience in design & implementation of training programs.
★ Remain calm and work well under demanding conditions.

PROFESSIONAL EXPERIENCE

Management
- Established training programs:
  - Wrote and published yearly training calendars;
  - Located and scheduled instructors for weekly classes in military skills;
  - Coordinated training for personnel dispersed over 1.7 million miles;
  - Forecast and managed annual training budget while maximizing formal schooling.
- Planned, coordinated and conducted management conferences attended by officers from all over the country.
- Managed a small convenience store, overseeing orders and deliveries, and supervising 3 employees.

Supervision
- Exercised total supervisory responsibility for a unit of 22 security personnel:
  - Organized the unit into teams and designated the first-line supervisors;
  - Established an evaluation program, utilizing quarterly written reports;
  - Directed field operations: planning, budgeting, travel and housing arrangements.
- Successfully planned, organized and led field training missions in a "real-world" environment, ensuring adequate provisions and operational equipment, and providing direction and supervision for 30-40 trainees for up to three weeks.

Written & Oral Communication
- Made presentations to officials to get approval and funding for operations.
- Wrote & presented info briefings to peer officers to maximize use of resources.
- Effectively counseled team leaders and supervisors.
- Authored award recommendations for subordinates that consistently won approval.
- Compiled and edited comprehensive activity reports from subordinate units for national publication.

WORK HISTORY

1987-now	Administrative Assistant	ALUMNAE RESOURCES Career Center - SF
1978-86	Chief, Technical Security Branch	US ARMY - San Francisco
"	Battalion Plans & Training Officer	"
"	Chief, Collection Management Sect.	US ARMY - Germany
"	Platoon Leader	"
1976-78	Student	
1974-75	Manager	RICHLAND CORPORATION - Atlanta GA
1973-74	Admin.Asst/Bookkeeper	STATE BANK & TRUST - Atlanta GA

EDUCATION
B.A., German - Georgia State University, Atlanta GA

DIANE H. CHRISTOFARO
Health Care Management Consultant
RD1 ... PO Box120A-3
Uniondale PA 18711
(717) 909-4114

"Health Care Management Consultant" is used in place of "Objective:..." because she's looking for an independent consultant relationship rather than employee status.

Highlights of Qualifications

★ 15 years experience in health care management.
★ Recognized as an authority on managed care programs.
★ Professional credentials in nursing and health education.
★ Successfully administered joint venture for Blue Cross.
★ Developed innovative programs for major HMO, incorporating trends on the leading edge of health care delivery.

REPRESENTATIVE ACCOMPLISHMENTS

Health Management Joint Venture

Managed joint venture, Eastern Managed Care Inc., from initial start-up through full implementation as a successful and self-sustaining corporation:
• **Defined corporate goals** and objectives.
• Set up the operational **systems**, with enhancements as needed.
• Authored operational and program **policies and procedures**.
• **Recruited and trained** management staff, field staff and support staff; built staff to a national network of 40 professionals.
• Developed **budget** ($.5 million first-year, $1 million second-year) incorporating **long-term planning** and **marketing** strategies.
• **Wrote proposals** for submission to state and federal agencies, employers and HMOs.
• **Negotiated contracts** with employers, HMOs and insurance companies.
• Maintained high level of **program effectiveness**, constantly evaluating performance against industry standards.
• As recognized **authority in the field** of Health Benefits Management, addressed the National BC/BS Conference on "Psychiatric and Substance Abuse Case Management."

HMO Contract Management

Successfully obtained contract with a major HMO, being the only company that could provide the needed expertise in comprehensive managed care.
• Designed utilization **review standards** and protocols.
• Incorporated a unique component, **"Case Management,"** to ensure the most medically appropriate and cost-effective care and treatment.
• Upgraded the reporting procedures, providing accurate **measures of program success.**

Capital Blue Cross Program Development

Developed a department within Plan to provide case management services to external accounts.
• Designed customized **software program** enabling the Department to efficiently obtain, store and retrieve critical claimant information, essential for quality case management.
• **Wrote manuals** for Operations, Case Management, and Marketing Training for field staff, account reps, and administrators.
• Advised management on program **pricing, advertising and marketing** strategies.

- Continued -

PROFESSIONAL EXPERIENCE

1986-present	**Executive Director**	EASTERN MANAGED CARE INC., Wilkes Barre PA
1985-present	**Vice-President, Managed Care Services**	MOORE HEALTH MANAGEMENT INC., Oneonta NY
1984-85	**Owner/Principal**	INDUSTRIAL HEALTH DESIGNS, health care management consulting, New York State
1983-84	**Rehabilitation Consultant**	NATLSCO Rehab Management Inc., NY and PA
1981-83	**Rehabilitation Specialist**	INTERNATIONAL REHAB ASSOC., Missoula MT
1981-82	**Health Educator**	FIVE VALLEYS HEALTH CARE, Missoula MT
1980-81	**Director, Medical Services**	ONEONTA, NY JOB CORPS CENTER
1979-80	**Interim Director**	STUDENT HEALTH SERVICES, Delhi, NY Ag & Tech
1972-79	**Critical Care Nurse/Supv.**	Hospitals in New York and Colorado

EDUCATION & CREDENTIALS

M.A., Social Sciences - STATE UNIVERSITY OF NEW YORK, BINGHAMTON
B.S., Education, STATE UNIVERSITY OF NEW YORK, ONEONTA
A.A.S., Nursing (honors), ORANGE CO. COMMUNITY COLLEGE, Middletown NY
Psychology, UNIVERSITY OF COLORADO, Boulder

Certifications & Licenses
Licensed Registered Professional Nurse - New York
Certified Facilitator, National Center of Health Promotion

PROFESSIONAL DEVELOPMENT

1986 National Medical Case Management Seminar, INTRACORP, Dallas TX
1986 POCONO Conference, "The Future of Health Care," Wilkes Barre PA
1987 Annual Risk Management and Employee Benefits Conference, Las Vegas NV

PROFESSIONAL AFFILIATIONS

Institute for the Advancement of Health
National Center of Health Promotion
National Association of Executive Females
National Rehabilitation Association
American Society for Training and Development
Association of Rehabilitation Nurses

ELIZABETH WOOL

29 Ramsgate Lane
Pleasant Hill CA 94523
(415) 555-2136

**Objective: Executive/administrative position
with a broad based community services agency**

HIGHLIGHTS OF QUALIFICATIONS

★ Over 10 years administrative and management experience.

★ Practical working knowledge of every level of agency operations.

★ Solid theoretical training in management.

★ Proven record of innovative and effective staff development.

★ Strong commitment, vision and leadership.

PROFESSIONAL EXPERIENCE

Management; Organizational Development
- Provided highly effective management for a 3-yr. national demonstration research project:
  -Established cooperative spirit by developing channels for exchange of expertise and resources;
  -Built highly productive work teams, introducing many more opportunities for staff in-put;
  -Convinced skeptical manager to support the program, through effective negotiations and follow-through.
- Secured funding for 3 child development programs, writing successful grant proposals.
- Set up improved filing systems for statistical data and program record keeping.

Staff Training & Development
- Conducted teacher training sessions for private and public school teachers:
  -Implemented needs assessment of existing teaching staff;
  -Developed training program specifically for identifying and managing (in classroom) preschool and school age children with emotional and learning disabilities;
  -Trained teachers in special testing & tutoring skills for use with learning disabled children.
- Designed and conducted an innovative 6-week intensive training program for child care personnel, featuring unique opportunities for in-service training leading to college enrollment.

Promotion, Advocacy, Negotiation
- Built up an effective advocacy program for Home Start, a model federally-funded program:
  -Successfully involved all staff members in developing a comprehensive network of community services and contacts;
  -Developed a slide show presentation explaining the program to other agencies;
  -Gained the support of other organizations, to provide client services needed to achieve program goals.
- Served, by invitation of Community Council, as representative entrusted to negotiate with the university for space and financial support of child care program.

- Continued -

11

EDUCATION

M.E., Education - Northeastern University, Boston
B.A., Government - Boston University, Boston
Graduate study in Public Administration - University of Pittsburgh, PA
Training in Human Resource Development - Certificate Program, UC Berkeley Extension

WORK HISTORY

1984-present	**Community Relations Coor.**	AMERICAN RED CROSS - Richfield CA
1983-84	**Program Specialist** (consultant)	PARENTAL STRESS CENTER - Pittsburgh PA
1979-82	**Student**, part-time	UNIVERSITY OF PITTSBURGH
	concurrent parttime work as: Insurance & Sales; Census Enumerator; Researcher.	
1975-79	**Training Specialist**	PITTSBURGH CHILD GUIDANCE CENTER, PA
1973-75	**Director,** "Home Start" Project	ACTION INC. - Gloucester MA
		(National Research & Demonstration Project)
1968-72	**Director**	P.M. HASSETT DAY CARE CENTER - Boston MA

ERIN IRWIN
724 Filbert Street, Apt. 5
San Francisco CA 94123
(415) 688-7816

Objective: Management position with a health care agency, specializing in counseling, management and public relations.

HIGHLIGHTS OF QUALIFICATIONS
- Strong combination of management and clinical experience.
- Knowledgeable in health care systems and community agencies.
- Natural talent for public relations and marketing.
- Successfully developed and controlled a $1.3 million budget.
- Supervised a staff of 32 professionals and support personnel.

RELEVANT EXPERIENCE

Management & Supervision
- Developed $1 million budget covering unit's personnel, supplies and equipment.
- Audited and analyzed unit-level needs for supplies and equipment.
- Interviewed and hired personnel, both clinical and support staff.
- Facilitated staff planning meetings, promoting high level of goal achievement.
- Developed effectiveness & efficiency of clinical staff at St. Joan's nursing unit:
  -upgraded quality of training and orientation of both new and old staff;
  -instituted a unit-based management group, improving communication;
  -evaluated individual work performance and advised on career development.

Public Relations
- Followed up on a day-to-day basis with patients on adequacy of their care; identified problem issues and effectively arranged for best resolution possible.

Community Liaison/Health Care Systems
- Coordinated discharge planning with outside health care agencies.
- Developed expertise in health care systems through 17 years experience.

Counseling/Advocacy
- Counseled patients in crisis and terminal care situations; counseled staff on both personal and work issues.
- Served as advocate for clients, cutting through red tape to assure adequacy of patient care and access to health care information.
- Successfully mediated conflicts among staff members, between staff and patients, and between patients and family.

EMPLOYMENT HISTORY

1976-86	**Head Nurse**	ST. JOAN's HOSPITAL, Cardio-Vascular Surgical Unit
1973-76	**Senior Staff Nurse**	ST. JOAN's, S.F., Surgical Intensive Care Unit
1971-73	**Senior Staff Nurse**	ST. JOAN's, S.F., General Surgical Unit
1969-71	**Staff Nurse**	ST. JOAN's, S.F., General Surgical Unit

EDUCATION

M.S. Human Resources & Organizational Development - U.S.F., San Francisco
B.S.N. - U.S.F., San Francisco; Licensed California RN

FRANCES RICHARDSON

333 Twenty-third Ave.
San Francisco CA 94121
(415) 489-9000 work
(415) 233-4141 home

Objective: Management position with a hospital or HMO, related to environmental services, safety, education, marketing, development, guest relations, and/or physician relations.

HIGHLIGHTS OF QUALIFICATIONS

- 10 years professional experience, plus degree in Health Services Administration.
- A born leader; inspires others to work at their highest level.
- Proven management skills and record of accomplishment.
- Highly creative and innovative, not afraid to take risks.

REPRESENTATIVE ACCOMPLISHMENTS

Environmental Services/Safety and Education
- Reduced budget and staff costs by 30%, as Director of Housekeeping & Linen Depts. while maintaining highest quality service.
- As Safety Director, managed Workers Compensation Program and successfully reduced loss ratio from 35% to 11% in one year, resulting in major savings to the hospital.
- Served as expert advisor for a videotape on hospital disaster planning produced by Hospital Satellite Network for nationwide distribution.

Guest Relations/Physician Relations
- Researched and selected Guest Relations Program, a major hospital investment:
  ...selected most effective potential staff trainers;
  ...co-designed detailed implementation plan.
- Introduced highly successful programs, enhancing rapport between hospital and physicians:
  ...Practice Enhancement Program, which attracted personal involvement of the physicians;
  ...seminar on use of CO2 Laser, providing Continuing Education credit for physicians and increasing use of the hospital's equipment and surgery revenue.

Marketing/Special Events Coordination
- Developed innovative marketing concepts and strategies, assisting Director of Marketing in:
  ...new program identification, development and promotion
  ...research   ...advertising campaigns   ...media liaison   ...ad agency selection.
- Organized all aspects of successful major fund-raising events, benefitting:
  ...Coming Home Hospice, a subsidiary of VNA (a hospice for AIDS patients);
  ...St. Vincent de Paul Society shelters for the homeless.

EMPLOYMENT HISTORY

1985-present	**Director, Customer Relations**	HUNTINGTON HOSPITAL, San Francisco
1983-85	**Environmental Services Manager**	HUNTINGTON HOSPITAL, San Francisco
1981-83	**Director, Housekeeping & Linen**	HUNTINGTON HOSPITAL, San Francisco
1977-81	**Environmental Services Asst.**	HUNTINGTON HOSPITAL, San Francisco

EDUCATION

B.A., Health Services Administration, with honors - St. Mary's College, Moraga - 1983

HELEN BEESON, R.N.
1722 Nelson Blvd., Oakland CA 94611
(415) 801-3277

Helen lists each different position with the same employer, showing advancement within her field.

Objective: Position as Assistant Clinical Nursing Coordinator, Intensive Care Nursery at Stanford University Hospital

HIGHLIGHTS OF QUALIFICATIONS

- Thorough understanding of the nursing process, both in theory and in practice.
- Highly skilled in effective leadership techniques.
- Able to balance the needs of the staff with the priorities of the institution.
- Solid experience in staff orientation, scheduling, evaluation and development.

PROFESSIONAL EXPERIENCE

Orientation

- Coordinated and developed programs:
  -education program for professional organization's annual symposium;
  -outreach education for Level I and Level II nurseries;
  -orientation program and in-service programs on a variety of subjects:
    ...transport of sick infants ...contemporary teaching/learning theories
    ...nursing interventions with families of sick infants ...resuscitation of the newborn
- Oriented ICN staff and outreach nurses from other hospitals.
- Authored numerous policies and procedures for nursing care.

Counseling & Development

- Developed a highly effective strategy for working with "difficult employees":
  -determine whether there is potential for positive change;
  -identify and present the problem to the employee;
  -clarify and reach agreement about behavioral expectations;
  -strongly support the employee with my confidence that she can change;
  -develop a plan, including time frame for reevaluation of progress;
  -carefully document the steps taken and the results.

Staff Supervision

- Currently supervise a staff of 80 intensive care nursery nurses and 12 pediatric nurses, on a 24-hour basis.
- Served as Night Shift Coordinator for 3 years at Mount Zion Hospital and 1 year at Children's Hospital, supervising up to 45 nurses.
- Scheduled and staffed intensive care nursery and pediatric units.

EMPLOYMENT HISTORY

1985-now	**Nurse Manager**	Intensive Care Nursery
1983 6 mo	**Interim Manager**	Mount Zion Hospital - Intensive Care Nursery
1980-83	**Clinical Coordinator**	Mount Zion Hospital - Intensive Care Nursery
1979-80	**Liaison Nurse**	Mount Zion Hospital - Intensive Care Nursery
1977-78	**Shift Nursing Coor.**	Children's Hospital, Oakland - Intensive Care Nursery
1976-77	**Staff Nurse II**	Mount Zion Hospital - Intensive Care Nursery
1974-76	**Staff Nurse I, II**	Children's Hospital, Oakland - Intensive Care Nursery

EDUCATION & TRAINING

A.A., Nursing, with honors - MERRITT COLLEGE, Oakland
Specialized training: Leadership; Problem Solving, Coaching & Developing, Group Dynamics
A.A., Mathematics & Science, with honors - MERRITT COLLEGE, Oakland

HELLMUT DIETRICH
333 - 65th Street
Oakland CA 94609
(415) 699-4742

Objective: Position as Administrative Director
with a nonprofit social service agency

HIGHLIGHTS OF QUALIFICATIONS
- Experience and training in basic office systems.
- Skilled supervisor; able to motivate and handle conflict.
- Competent in programming and operating computers.
- Creative and flexible in organizing and planning.
- Diplomatic and effective in negotiations.

RELEVANT EXPERIENCE & SKILLS

Administration
- Served on Board of Directors for a nonprofit organization serving parents:
  -wrote successful grant proposals -planned annual budget
  -negotiated contracts for property rentals, insurance, apprenticeships;
  -interviewed and hired staff, as member of personnel team;
  -interpreted personnel guidelines, resolved staff conflicts, negotiated wages.
- Negotiated with speakers and artists (singers, writers, parliamentary figures,
  representatives of minority groups) and made detailed arrangements.

Supervision
- Supervised volunteer teachers and free-lance tutors at a drop-in community center
  for low-income youth.
- Supervised warehouse crew in the shipping and handling of merchandise, as
  warehouse superintendent at a large freight company in Munich.
  -initiated improvements in teamwork efficiency by clarifying areas of responsibility
  and promoting better communication.;
  -developed and updated time schedules and delivery tours for truckers.

Coordination
- Organized public educational/entertainment events, involving arrangements for
  location, insurance, contracts, security, advertising and promotion.
- Successfully coordinated community projects involving previously conflicting groups,
  overcoming hostility and mistrust by identifying common interests and goals.

Computer Skills
- Familiar with use of personal computers and printers:
  -customized commercial computer programs to meet special needs;
  -wrote complex programs in BASIC using direct disk access to retrieve lost data.

- Continued -

MANAGEMENT

EMPLOYMENT HISTORY

1987		Travel and relocation to the Bay Area.
1984-86	**Student**	University of Tübingen, Germany
1979-83	**Display Builder**	S&E Stark Promotional Display Co. - Ostfildern, Germany
1976-78	**Teacher**	Jr.High School; Elementary School - Osfildern, Germany
1973-75	**Teaching Asst.**	Pädagogische Hochschule College - Esslingen, Germany
1972-76	**Student**	Pädagogische Hochschule College - Esslingen, Germany
1970-71	**Social Worker**	City of Schwäbisch Hall, Germany
1969-70	**Warehouse Supv.**	Anton Glatz Freight Co. - Munich, Germany
1966-69	**Warehouseman**	Hohl Freight Co. - Michelfeld, Germany

VOLUNTEER WORK

1978-80	**Program Organizer**	Citizens Against Racism - Esslingen, Germany
1980-84	**Member, Board of Directors**	Parent & Child Services - Tübingen, Germany

EDUCATION & TRAINING

B.A., Social Work (German equivalent) - University of Tübingen, Germany
Teaching Credential (German equivalent) - Pädagogische Hochschule College
Classes in: Bookkeeping, correspondence, transportation, business principles, business math.

- References available on request -

> Hellmut makes sure that all his German work history is clearly described, adding a word or two where needed to explain the employer's business. In the Education section, he points out the German equivalent of US credentials.

MOLLY PETERSON
800 Marietta Drive
Los Angeles CA
(202) 141-1119

"Home management, travel and study" account for a major break in Molly's work history.

Objective: Regional office director of a national preservation organization.

Highlights of Qualifications

- Lifelong interest in and commitment to architecture and preservation.
- Four years leadership experience as president and Chairman of the Board of Los Angeles Architectural Preservation (LAAP).
- Fund-raising experience during six years chairing development committee.
- Recent completion of 18 months graduate work in nonprofit management.
- Competent in communicating the value of historic preservation.
- Ability to work creatively and effectively with staff and volunteers.

PROFESSIONAL EXPERIENCE

Public Relations, Communication, Media
- Spoke as expert in preservation issues and the history and architecture of Los Angeles:
  - conducted walking tours of residential and commercial areas for past 8 years;
  - made one-to-one and small group presentations to major donors and corporate leaders.
- Conducted demonstrations for audiences of 100-1000 people throughout the U.S.

Fund-raising/Development
- Successfully identified and cultivated major donors & significantly increased contributions;
  - brought people onto the board who themselves were excellent fund-raisers and givers;
  - increased participation, matching contributors with projects aligned with their interests.
- Conceived, organized, and implemented numerous successful fund-raising events:
  - doubled the profit of The Urban Career Center's annual luncheon, from $9,000 to $18,000;
  - netted LAAP $10,000 from a building opening and $25,000 from a restaurant opening;
  - increased, from $20,000/evening to $45,000, the proceeds of LAAP's annual Summer Ball.

Leadership, Management, Administration
- Monitored organizational budgets of $300,000 - $380,000 monthly for eight years.
- Served on the Board of Directors of LAAP and The Urban Career Center:
  - developed program and personnel policies, and organizational goals and budgets;
  - evaluated critical preservation issues, and prioritized for action.
- Directed interviews for executive and development directors, and new board members.

WORK HISTORY

Current	Graduate student	University of Califirnia, Los Angeles
1984-87	Member, Executive Committee	Los Angeles Architectural Preservation
"	Vice President, Board of Directors	The Urban Career Center - S.F.
1979-83	Chair and President of Board	Los Angeles Architectural Preservation
1966-78	Home management, travel, study	
1963-65	Teacher	Los Angeles public schools
1960-62	Home Economist	Swift & Co. - Chicago
1958-60	Teacher	Denver public schools

EDUCATION
M.P.A. graduate studies in Nonprofit Management, 1984-85 - Univ. of California, Los Angeles
B.S. - Iowa State University - Ames, Iowa

JANET CRITTENDON
4967 Neilson Blvd.
Albany CA 94706
(415) 666-3115

This resume can easily be made "generic" to fit any other office management setting just by replacing the 5 "Highlights" and dropping the last line of the resume.

Objective: Supervisory or office management position in an interior design firm.

HIGHLIGHTS OF QUALIFICATIONS

★ Over six years experience in management and supervision.
★ Reputation for excellence and high quality service to clients.
★ Highly effective in promoting a positive, productive work environment.
★ Good eye for detail; well organized, skilled in setting priorities.
★ Lifelong interest in interior design; classwork in space planning & color.

RELEVANT EXPERIENCE

Management
- Designed office procedures; developed company policy on handling customer complaints.
- Delegated responsibilities among production foremen, collaborating on daily production priorities and maintaining a smooth flow of operations.
- Developed innovative customer services, building a reputation for our company as a leader in the industry, with unique same-day service & products not available elsewhere.
- Purchased manufacturing materials and office supplies for Albany Surgical Shoes, Inc, considering production schedules, vendor delivery schedules, and cost effectiveness.

Supervision
- Successfully built a cooperative work team and promoted productive environment by:
  -delegating jobs in accordance with employees' skills and abilities;
  -treating employees with respect; maintaining a sense of humor;
  -welcoming constructive criticism and input on production improvements;
  -support morale by posting letters of appreciation from customers.
- Trained employees in developing and maintaining good customer relations, and how to effectively negotiate and resolve customer service problems.

Organizing/Record Keeping
- Organized and improved filing system for contracted accounts, resulting in substantial time saving for handling government files and mandatory quarterly report.
- Oversaw all facets of record keeping for a small manufacturing firm, involving payroll, insurance, banking, accounts receivable, accounts payable, general ledger.

EMPLOYMENT HISTORY

1980-present	**Manager, Plant & Office**	ALBANY SURGICAL SHOES, INC., Albany CA manufacturer of shoes and podiatry supplies
1978-80	**Office Manager**	"
1974-78	**Office Asst./Customer Svc.**	"
1972-74	**Assembler/Inspector**	"

EDUCATION
SAN FRANCISCO CITY COLLEGE
Business Management, Bookkeeping, Accounting, 1974-76
Interior Design, 1986-87

JANICE SPEAR
119 Hemlock Road
San Francisco CA 94115
329-6790

Objective: Management position incorporating customer support, training, and/or sales.

HIGHLIGHTS OF QUALIFICATIONS

- Ten years successful experience as a manager.
- Outstanding communication skills, both one-to-one and before groups.
- Highly effective in motivating and supervising employees.
- Well organized; strong in planning and implementing programs.
- Enjoy a dynamic and challenging work environment.

PROFESSIONAL EXPERIENCE

PR/Marketing/Sales
- Developed an improved marketing plan:
  - assembled a photographic presentation of services available;
  - changed procedure for membership sales, to include facility tour and active closing;
  - initiated a program of follow-up calls to guests to encourage membership.
- Stimulated direct involvement in social and athletic activities by communicating the excitement and fun of the event, and creating a nonthreatening environment.
- Persuaded large corporations and businesses to sponsor public events with prizes and cash contributions.

Program Development/Coordination
- Selected social and athletic activities to be offered; coordinated implementation, promoted and registered participants.
- Planned, coordinated and promoted dozens of racquetball tournaments:
  ...statewide charity events   ...celebrity events   ...in-house events   ...professional events

Supervision & Training
- Recruited, trained and supervised 15 employees, 2 assistants and an Athletic Director, and evaluated their performance.
- Authored employees' training manual, describing the facility, all operations, and detailed procedures of the athletic club.
- Maximized effectiveness and morale of staff by assigning tasks related to their interests and promoting teamwork rather than competitiveness.

Management
- Oversaw all aspects of personnel and operations of an 8-court racquetball club, including full financial accounting of $250,000 annual revenues.
- Forecasted and developed $100,000 annual operating budget for $10 million facility, covering: salaries, monthly guest fees, rentals, locker room supplies, uniforms, locks & keys.
- Cut costs by 20% through more cost-effective purchasing of supplies.

EMPLOYMENT HISTORY & EDUCATION

1985-present	**Hostess**	PRINCESS CRUISE -San Francisco
1982-84	**Operations Supervisor**	THE TEXAS CLUB athletic club - Houston
1978-82	**Manager**	WOODLAKE RACQUETBALL CLUB - Houston
1975-78	**Asst. Manager**	COURT SPORTS Racquetball Club - Houston

B.S., Elementary Education, University of Texas at Austin
Teaching Certificate, Special Education

JUDITH BROWNELLE
8686 Shellmound
Emeryville, CA 94608
644-2989 (home); 421-8744 (office)

Objective: Position as Director, East Bay Small Business Development Center

HIGHLIGHTS OF QUALIFICATIONS

- Strong background combining business, liberal arts and community experience.
- Familiar with Bay Area business, government, education and non-profits.
- Extensive experience in writing and reviewing proposals.
- Work effectively both as team member and independently.
- Knowledgeable in computer applications to program research & development.
- Enthusiastic, sharp, and well organized.

PROFESSIONAL EXPERIENCE

Program Planning
- Designed and directed a highly successful youth volunteer program later chosen as model for other programs nationwide:
  -persuaded school district to provide critical financial and staffing support;
  -coordinated joint sponsorship of City, Volunteer Bureau, and community agencies and businesses.
- Developed broad range of educational and community programs in cooperation with:
  -federal, state, local governments -public schools -community colleges and business.

Communications & PR
- Produced wide range of business and programming communications:
  -edited TELETRENDS, international newsletter on telecommunications trends in higher education;
  -wrote program proposals, summaries , evaluations and recommendations;
  -authored business plans, annual reports & status reports
- Chaired community meetings, local/regional conferences, planning meetings of college development staff, and professional association meetings.
- Trained faculty and staff in proposal writing and program planning techniques.
- Addressed groups of educators, community and business leaders and students.
- Promoted agency programs through networking and presentations at major conferences.

Research/Analysis/Evaluation
- Reviewed demographic data and labor market projections to establish program directions.
- Developed theoretical knowledge of financial analysis, budgeting, forecasting, statistics and research methods and strategic planning, through MBA case studies.
- Designed and monitored project budgets for community and educational projects.

EMPLOYMENT HISTORY

1982-present	**Resource Development Specialist**	PERALTA COMMUNITY COLLEGE DIST., Oakland CA
1979-82	**Staff Assistant/Planning & Dev't**	PERALTA COMMUNITY COLLEGE DIST.
1976-79	**Project Director**	VOLUNTEER CNTR OF ALAMEDA Co., Oakland
1975-76	**Program Coor.** (VISTA Volunteer)	VOLUNTEER CENTER OF ALAMEDA CO.
1973-75	**Administrative Assistant**	FIDELITY MUTUAL LIFE INS. CO. Philadelphia

EDUCATION

MBA, Executive Program - St. Mary's College - Moraga CA 1985
BA, Geography/Urban Studies - Millersville Univ. of Pennsylvania 1973

MARLA MOSES

78 Westwind Street
Walnut CA 95448
(707) 323-7804 or (415) 823-2929

Objective: Position as director/associate director with a public or nonprofit agency

HIGHLIGHTS OF QUALIFICATIONS

- 6 years successful experience in program management & development.
- Resourceful in solving problems and maximizing resources.
- Talent for balancing long-range vision with attention to detail.
- Effective in promoting a positive, productive work environment.
- Able to set and achieve goals, and work well under pressure.

PROFESSIONAL EXPERIENCE

Planning & Program Development

- Served on agency strategic planning committee, developing 5-year long-range plan for Circuit Rider Productions (CRP) corporation, addressing issues of:
  -current and projected financial and physical resources
  -current and proposed educational and environmental services.
- Managed implementation of the Vocational Training Div. portion of long-range plan:
  -developed time line and short-term objectives
  -delegated tasks   - revised long-term plan as needed.
- Developed and managed several pilot programs to train youths and adults, e.g.:
  -community Conservation Corps program   -VCR repair vocational program.

Personnel Management & Supervision

- Hired, supervised and trained 4 year-round staff and 12 seasonal assistants.
- Effectively managed program staff by encouraging pride in performance, supporting individual career development, and training staff in problem solving and teamwork.

Public Relations/Marketing

- Lobbied for job training programs, assisting legislators in developing first drafts of youth training bills and keeping them informed of CRP's programs and developments.
- Secured national recognition from National Arbor Foundation, for CRP's "Tree Project," named an "exemplary education project" in 1982.
- Initiated contact with potential funding sources (local, county and state governments, and community agencies) to promote training programs of CRP.

Community Relations

- Participated in community planning along with contractors, architects and other business people, serving on City of Healdsburg Design Review Commission in 1984-85.

Budgeting/Resource Management

- Developed and oversaw $350,000 budget for vocational training division with multiple funding sources:
  -consistently completed programs on or under budget while meeting program standards.
- Secured financial support for training programs from local Private Industry Council and other funding sources, through successful proposals submitted annually.

- Continued -

MARLA MOSES
page two

RELEVANT WORK HISTORY

1981-present CIRCUIT RIDER PRODUCTIONS - Walnut CA
              (nonprofit, integrating environmental management and vocational training)
              Division Manager, Vocational Training, 2 years
              Project Coordinator, 3 years
              Supervisor/Instructor, 1 year

1980   **Supervisor/Instructor**   KAIROS, human service agency - Cotati CA

1979-80   **Horticulturist**   SONOMA STATE, BOTANIC GARDEN - Cotati CA

1977-78   **Naturalist/Educator**   NATURE CONSERVANCY - Penngrove CA

EDUCATION & CREDENTIALS

B.A., Environmental Studies & Planning - Sonoma State University, 1980
Junior College Teaching Credential
California Private Post-secondary Administrator & Instructor Certification

Management Training Courses:
-Making Meetings Work   -Team Building   -Conflict Resolution   -Fiscal Management
-Visionary Leadership   -Stress Management   -Time Management   -Personnel Process

> Marla breaks down her various roles at Circuit Rider. She also illustrates a *good general principle* at 2 places in her Work History: *Briefly explain the nature of the business whenever it isn't obvious.*

MICHAEL HASSID
5029 Grizzly Peak
Berkeley CA 94708
(415) 389-6552

Objective: Position as Chief Rehabilitation Officer with City Housing Authority

HIGHLIGHTS OF QUALIFICATIONS

★ Committed to the challenge and responsibility of providing
quality and cost-effective construction for public housing.
★ Excellent professional reputation among city building inspectors,
architects, general/subcontractors, owner/builders.
★ Extensive experience with new construction, remodeling and rehabilitation,
including estimating and subcontractor scheduling requirements.
★ Competence with computer cost estimating and job control programs.

PROFESSIONAL CONSTRUCTION EXPERIENCE
(list of projects attached)

Estimating and Bidding

• Accurately and profitably estimated residential rehabilitation projects from foundation to
finish.
• Successfully estimated as a subcontractor on plumbing, heating and solar systems throughout Bay Area.

Contract Planning and Scheduling

• Developed contract language documenting agreed-upon prices, schedules, procedures
and responsibilities.
• Reviewed plans and developed schedules with architects, contractors and subcontractors
assuring proper coordination, efficiency and profitability.

Coordinating and Subcontracting

• Successfully coordinated remodeling and rehabilitation projects, each involving 7 or more
specialty subcontractors simultaneously, including:
-plumbing -heating -electrical -sheetrocking -roofing.
• Designed and installed plumbing, heating and solar systems in new construction and rehabilitation projects, both residential and commercial.

Job Control and Building Inspections

• Assured subcontractors' strict adherence to projected scheduling and costs, using computer
job control programs to monitor construction contract compliance.
• Achieved consistent high quality control in compliance with building codes and inspection standards.

Final Project Wrap-up

• Completed detailed pickup work on all projects, achieving extremely high level of client
satisfaction, consistently generating new referrals and repeat business.
• Completed all paperwork, including Notices of Completion, Lien Releases & closing
financial statements.

- Continued -

MICHAEL HASSID
page two

EMPLOYMENT HISTORY

1985 to now	**President/Managing Officer**	Hassid Construction, Inc., Berkeley
1983-85	**Owner/Manager**	Hassid Construction, Plumbing/Solar, Berkeley
1981-83	**Co-Owner/Manager**	Hassid & Brown, Plumbing & Solar, Berkeley
1979-81	**Journeyman Plumber**	Hassid Plumbing, Berkeley
1975-79	**Apprentice Plumber**	Several contractors in Colorado

SPECIALIZED EDUCATION and TRAINING

1983-84	Architectural and Mechanical Drafting classes - UC Berkeley Extension and City College, San Francisco
1979-80	Solar System & Hydronic Heating Design/Installation - Vista College, Berkeley
1975-78	Plumbing Apprenticeship Program - Red Rocks Community College, Denver

MICHEAL BLACKWOOD
1213 Hearst St.
Santa Cruz CA
(408) 229-1914

Objective: position as project director, in nonprofit housing development

SUMMARY OF QUALIFICATIONS

★ 11 years involvement with administration of nonprofit housing.
★ Served on Board of Directors of two housing co-ops.
★ Served on planning commission of a major intentional community.
★ Managed or directed:
- manufacturing business grossing $250,000/year
- work force of 60
- residential community
- environmental bookstore and business office.

PROFESSIONAL EXPERIENCE

Project Management
• Served as Personnel Manager, overseeing all labor force issues, including:
- matching individual preferences and work requisitions
- designing and maintaining work-hours accounting system
- planning and projecting labor flow
- counseling workers on career development and training options
- mediating conflicts among workers and managers
- preparing budget proposals and presenting them for membership approval
• Set up books and annual budget and process at Walnut House Co-op.
• Appointed and trained management committees, and monitored their progress.

Initiative & Innovation
• Started a worker-owned business and served as its first manager.
• Designed and implemented a comprehensive process of long-term resource and
  social planning for a residential community of 60 people.
• Helped organize an urban Limited Equity Housing Co-op conversion.

Nonprofit Housing
• Personally lived in cooperative housing for the last eleven years.
• Trained in getting DRE subdivision approval.
• Familiar with the complexities of developing Limited Equity Housing Cooperatives.
• Knowledgeable in financial management of nonprofit housing.
• Trained shared-housing participants in:
- communication skills   - cooperative assertiveness
- conflict resolution/mediation   - organizing and facilitating meetings
- personal needs assessment   - bookkeeping and financial planning

EMPLOYMENT HISTORY

1980-present	**Office Manager/Bookstore Manager**	THE ECOLOGY CENTER Berkeley CA
1974-1979	**Director, Personnel Manager &** **Planning Commissioner**	EAST WIND COMMUNITY, INC. Tecumseh MO

26

BRENDA GILBERT
49006 LaCrosse Road
Dayton, Ohio
919-7887

Objective: Position as Management Services Officer

HIGHLIGHTS OF QUALIFICATIONS

- Strong background in financial management and control using latest computer technology.
- Highly effective in space development, management and control.
- Demonstrated experience in program development and implementation, including large scale special events involving special talent groups.
- Technical knowledge in contract preparation and negotiation.
- Skilled in job structuring and resource allocation under tight budgetary controls.
- Talent for picking the right people for the job.
- Resourceful in developing contacts and information sources.

PROFESSIONAL EXPERIENCE

Financial Management & Control
- Administered $12 million budget of university Business School, with full signature control.
- Developed highly effective internal cost reporting system using front line computer technology.
- Oversaw $6 million budget of self-supporting organization, Calif. Continuing Educ. of the Bar.
- Accurately forecast short-term and long-term financial needs involving complex and speculative base of resources.
- Submitted successful grant applications for funding of numerous projects, including:
  -development of OEO funded educational program for neighborhood legal offices;
  -legal/educational project for mental health social workers.

Space Development & Allocation
- Developed new building project planning guides for CEB Program and Business School.
- Located highly desirable new locations and negotiated favorable contracts for:
  -CEB and MBA Programs -private financial institution -program locations throughout state.
- Collaborated with architects and interior designers on new facilities within Business School:
  -Career Planning and Placement Center -Computer Center -tiered classrooms
  -special events rooms   -major conference areas
- Effectively redesigned and reallocated limited classroom and office space to meet constantly changing priorities.

Programming & Special Projects
- Implemented simultaneous professional programs statewide (approximately 200 programs per year):
  -scheduled programs -selected participants   -developed program content
  -drafted brochures, program handouts, participant guidelines, presentor guidelines
  -coordinated physical logistics and staffing.
- Hosted and coordinated shipboard activities for newspaper personnel and travel agents.
- Acted as liaison between University and State Bar, monitoring operational agreement.
- Researched and produced video tape on LPS Act.

- Continued -

BRENDA GILBERT
page two

Personnel
- Recruited high caliber personnel: attorneys, editorial staff, computer operators, administrators, clerks, secretaries, non-professional support staff.
- Assessed and managed personnel needs for department of 300 professionals & support staff:
  - established organizational chart   -determined specific job responsibilities
  - allocated staff resources   -supervised sr. admin. staff   -arbitrated personnel disputes
  - hired, evaluated and terminated staff   -established personnel guidelines.

Marketing & Sales
- Sold cruise packets and hotel space via counter and phone sales; guided public tours through ships; hosted shipboard activities for newspaper personnel and travel agents.
- Set up hospitality rooms and sales promotion booths for ABA and State Bar conventions.
- Established successful business designing/selling college suspenders featuring humorous logo.

Systems Development
- Streamlined sales and enrollment accounting procedures for rapidly expanding CEB unit.
- Designed effective new packaging and promotion that increased sales of legal how-to books.
- Assessed Business School's computer application needs in major change-over to computerization.

Management Consulting Activities
- Served as management consultant to:
  - University Faculty Club: analyzed management problems and submitted recommendations.
  - Lawyer groups: set up criteria for new profession of paralegals.
  - Small business owners and tradesmen: advised on marketing of professional entertainment groups, developing professional networks, negotiating worksite contracts.

EMPLOYMENT HISTORY

1976-present	**Management Services Officer**	University Business Schools, Dayton, OH
1966-76	**Asst. to Dir., External/Internal Affairs**	Continuing Education of the Bar - Dayton
1963-66	**Legal Assistant**	Rogers, Ryan and Luce, attys - Dayton
1960-63	**Sales Representative**	Gorman Navigation Co. - Kansas City

EDUCATION

B.S., Chemistry/Psychology - Kansas State University

Additional training
Legal studies: Contracts, Torts, Property, Tax - Dayton Law School
Management, Computing & Financial Management workshops - Univ. & business training schools
ACT class, Psychology, Communication Skills

-References available upon request -

RITA L. SASAKI
1990 Norwood Street
San Francisco CA 94123
(415) 672-8111

Rita explains, in her employment history, what "Seventy-Seven, Inc." is about.

Objective: Position as Executive Assistant in an international organization focusing on trade and business development in the Pacific Rim countries

HIGHLIGHTS OF QUALIFICATIONS
- Diplomatic and tactful with professionals and non-professionals at all levels.
- Exceptional communication and interpersonal skills; effective negotiator.
- Analytical and versatile; able to maintain a sense of humor under pressure.
- Readily transcend cultural and language differences.
- Poised and competent as a professional business representative.

PROFESSIONAL EXPERIENCE

Knowledge of East/West Business
- Coordinated all elements of a high-rise construction project, dealing with:
  -American architects and construction firms   -Chinese entrepreneur in Hong Kong
  -British bankers and solicitors in Hong Kong   -American and Hong Kong brokers
  -Hawaii-based American mortgage bankers, attorneys and accountants.
- Worked in Tokyo as executive assistant to the manager of a NY based import/export firm.

Coordination/Problem Solving
- Monitored progress of a $26 million construction project in Hawaii to meet contracted completion date.
- Mediated job-site conflicts among subcontractors.
- Organized and led international group tours to China and other parts of the Orient.

Communication Skills
- Made oral and written presentations to bankers on financial status and work progress, to get approval and funding.
- Prepared and delivered briefings for sales agents and brokers.
- Presided over weekly project meetings with contractors and architects.
- Created and maintained filing systems; drafted forms, correspondence, reports.
- Wrote and recorded English text of educational radio program for Hong Kong Commercial Broadcasting Co.

EMPLOYMENT HISTORY

1985-present	**Realtor**	REYNOLDS & CO., REALTY - Hawaii
1981-85	**Project Manager**	SEVENTY-SEVEN, INC. - Hawaii, real estate development
1976-80	**Tour Manager**	CULTURAL TOURS, INC. - Hawaii, Hong Kong, Canada
1973-75	**Office Manager**	LUM AND LUM ASSOCIATES - Hawaii, architectural firm
1970-73	**Financial Sec'y**	THE HAWAII CORP - Honolulu, holding company
1968-69	**Executive Sec'y**	ORIENTAL EXPORTERS (JAPAN) LTD. - Tokyo

EDUCATION

B.A., Asian Studies - UNIVERSITY OF HAWAII, 1980, Summa Cum Laude

SANDRA HOENIG
890 Piedmont Place
Oakland CA 94611
(415) 211-5744

Objective: Management position with Winchell Retail Development Corp.

HIGHLIGHTS OF QUALIFICATIONS

- Direct, successful background in both franchise management and multi-unit operations.
- Extensive experience implementing company policy.
- Highly effective and diplomatic trainer and manager.
- Expertise in production of candy, ice cream and bakery.
- Very good communication skills; able to put people at ease.

RELEVANT EXPERIENCE

Management & Franchising
- Coordinated daily operations of optometric offices located at 5 sites, involving staffing, patient scheduling, patient records review, customer services, instructing staff in correct techniques for phone answering , patient check-in, product sales and paperwork.
- Coordinated start-up of a new retail food franchise, soliciting and reviewing bids, coordinating construction, and securing permits and licenses.
- Implemented procedures for cash handling; oversaw daily, weekly and quarterly reporting.

Personnel
- Selected, hired and scheduled a staff of 8-12 responsible part-time employees for Heavenly Cookies store, successfully running the operation with only limited supervision.
- Designed procedures for staff consistency in:
  -customer service   -product handling and stocking   -equipment and store maintenance
- Trained personnel in sales techniques and opening/closing procedures consistent with franchise operations manual.
- Evaluated employee performance; made recommendations for promotions or dismissals.

Production
- Located best suppliers of ice cream ingredients and tested their products.
- Produced ice cream in accordance with Heavenly Cookies standard formulas.
- Developed special ice cream formulas to accommodate regional customer preferences.
- Trained personnel in production of candy, ice cream and bakery specialties.
- Produced, and managed daily production of...
  ...baked goods: -giant cinnamon rolls -five muffin varieties
  ...candy: -truffles -melt-aways -turtles -clusters -fruits, etc.

EMPLOYMENT HISTORY

1985-present	**Owner/Manager**	HEAVENLY COOKIES FRANCHISE, Berkeley
1980-84	**Area Manager**	PENTA/EYECARE USA, San Diego
1979-80	**Sales Associate**	TARBELL REAL ESTATE CO., San Diego
1978-79	**Student**	San Diego State; and real estate classes
1974-78	**Computer Operator**	NAVAL DATA PROCESSING CENTER, San Diego

EDUCATION & TRAINING
Dietary studies, University of Wisconsin, Madison
Associate Sales License in Real Estate

WILLARD TOWNSEND
1990 - 87th Avenue, Oakland CA 94603
(415) 213-6567 home

Objective: Position as Executive Director, City Redevelopment Agency

HIGHLIGHTS OF QUALIFICATIONS
★ 6 years successful experience in management.
★ Professional reputation for prudent fiscal management.
★ Thorough familiarity with redevelopment law and process.
★ Exceptional skills in assessing business opportunities.
★ Involved community leader; inspires confidence and trust.

RELEVANT EXPERIENCE

Business Assessment
• Served as business consultant for the Old Oakland Project:
  -reviewed site and plans for use; researched other historic rehabilitation projects;
  -reviewed City of Oakland Redevelopment Plan for overall perspective;
  -advised general partner on minority equity participation.
• Identified an underutilized tax deferral system, enabling corporations to increase their investment profits.

Financial Planning
• Developed present and future strategies to increase clients' investment income through procedural and investment methods, including:
  -municipal bonds -real estate investment trusts -oil and gas investments
  -real estate partnerships (private and public)   -mutual funds.
• Successfully managed financial portfolios of upper income individuals.

Project Development
• Assessed ambitious business plans for a new San Francisco night club, to be the third largest in North America:
  -evaluated the site; investigated the backgrounds of potential partners;
  -met with accountants and attorneys to review and document financial projections
  -researched plans of similar ventures throughout Europe and the eastern US;
  -made extensive presentations to investors, raising large amount of capital.

Public Relations/Community Leadership
• Won support for a development project, successfully responding to complaints and convincing city agencies and community residents of its benefits to the city.
• Successfully mediated disputes and communication breakdowns between businesses and organizations, clarifying the issues and recommending effective resolution.
• Provided leadership for community service projects, including:
  -Rotary Club of Oakland, World of Work Program;
  -Oakland Parents in Action, "Just Say No" club;
  -Volunteers of America Bay Area, Inc. Board of Directors, Director of Enterprise.

EMPLOYMENT HISTORY

1981-present	**Principal**	Townsend and Associates, Investments - Oakland
1981-83	**Account Executive**	Xerox Business Machines, Inc. - Oakland
1980-81	**Life Underwriter**	Mutual Life Insurance Co. - Sacramento
1977-80	**Administrative Asst.**	Cal. State Dept. of Rehabilitation - Sacramento

EDUCATION
B.A., Political Science - University of California, Davis
College for Financial Planning, Denver CO

31

ANNE HAYWARD
1224 Colusa Avenue
Berkeley CA 94707
(415) 527-6069

Objective: Position as human resources trainer: management & supervision

QUALIFIED BY
Eight years experience in adult training,
expertise in adult learning theory:
- Designed courses and evaluation techniques.
- Monitored and trained trainers.
- Delivered over 300 hours of adult training.
- Recruited presenters and trainers for 100 programs.

RELATED ACCOMPLISHMENTS

- Designed and presented hour-long weekly orientation program for career development organization; doubled membership.
- Designed five courses, and all materials, to train over 500 adults in job search techniques.
- Monitored and evaluated 30 trainers for more than 100 programs; instituted quality control methods.
- Developed and delivered public seminars for libraries, police departments, women's organizations.
- Completed 50 hours additional course work in interpersonal communication and conflict negotiation.

PROFESSIONAL EXPERIENCE

PROGRAM DIRECTOR, Career Options, career development organization, San Francisco.   1984-present
-Designed quarterly programs of 15-20 workshops & panels.
-Wrote course descriptions for quarterly calendar of events.
-Trained trainers and monitored classes.
-Supervised volunteer and counseling staff.
-Managed public relations program.
-Presented workshops.
-Recruited employers and professionals to participate in monthly programs.

COMMUNITY ORGANIZER, Berkeley CA   1973-82
Concurrent with graduate studies at CSU/Hayward:
-President of three parent/teacher organizations.
-Appointed member of Citizens Task Force to elect a new School Superintendent.
-Researcher/Writer/Editor, Crime Prevention Newsletter
-Election campaign steering committee/school board supervisors
-Elected member, BUSD Teachers Corp. Program.
-Earned secondary teaching credential, UC Berkeley

- Continued -

HUMAN RESOURCES

ANNE HAYWARD
Page two

**PROFESSIONAL
EXPERIENCE**
(continued)

HEAD LIBRARIAN & CHILDREN'S LIBRARIAN 1966-68
Wayne County Library System, Michigan;
San Francisco Public Library

**EDUCATION &
CREDENTIALS**

UNIVERSITY OF CALIFORNIA, BERKELEY
Bay Area Writers' Project, 1982
Secondary Teaching Credential
MLS, UNIVERSITY OF MICHIGAN, 1966
BA, MICHIGAN STATE UNIVERSITY, Honors College, 1965

AWARD

Selected Teacher of the Year, 1982
Graduate School of Education, UC Berkeley

**ADDITIONAL
COURSE WORK**

- Training and Human Resource Development
  UC Berkeley Extension 1983
- Interpersonal Communications
  UC Berkeley 1982
- How to Make Meetings Work
  Interaction Associates,
  Community Training & Development, 1985
- Conflict Negotiation,
  Community Training & Development, 1985
- Assertive Communication
  Community Training & Development, 1985

CAROL WEITZELL

1912 Kains Avenue
Berkeley CA 94702
(415) 235-3980

One of three resumes for Carol. See also pages 55 and 135.

HUMAN RESOURCES

Objective: Position as Personnel Analyst

HIGHLIGHTS OF QUALIFICATIONS

- 7 years administrative and analytical experience.
- Strength in creative problem solving.
- Outstanding ability in personnel interviewing and skill assessment.
- Designed & implemented highly successful employee training programs.
- MSW degree, focusing on administration and planning.

PROFESSIONAL EXPERIENCE

PERSONNEL
Staff Development

- Developed an in-service training program for social work staff which increased their professional expertise and theoretical background:
  - Developed a form for self-assessment by workers.
  - Wrote and managed annual training budgets.
  - Contracted with trainers to provide instruction in specific issues in social work.
  - Met regularly with supervisors to evaluate the program on an on-going basis.
- Compiled and edited a comprehensive resource manual instructing social workers in services available in Boston, how to access them, & procedures for qualifying.

Skill Assessment & Supervision

- Interviewed & assessed skills of applicants for positions as Child Welfare Workers.
- Trained, supervised and evaluated a social worker, resulting in an improvement in her administrative skills and her effectiveness in a large public agency.
- Designed a project for student interns that enabled them to learn about community resources and produce a resource used by social work staff; supervised their daily work, and evaluated their performance.

ADMINISTRATION & PLANNING

- Produced a community social service needs assessment to be incorporated in the budget narrative of a Boston DSS office, synthesizing data from:
  - ... National census
  - ... Boston redevelopment survey
  - ... Child welfare worker survey
  - ... DSS computerized records.

WORK HISTORY

1985-present	Case Manager	AREA OFFICE ON AGING, W. Contra Costa Co.
1985-present	Social Worker	CONTRA COSTA COUNTY, CA
1983-85	Photographer	Self-employed
1980-83	Program Development	MASSACHUSETTS DEPT. of SOCIAL SERVICES
1979-80	Administrative Analyst	"
1978-79	Child Welfare Worker	"
1977-78	Student Intern	"

EDUCATION

MSW, Boston University - SRS fellowship in Child Welfare, 1978

SONJA MICHAELS
444 Luella Drive
Woodside CA 94602
(415) 518-2929

**Objective: Position as program and grant analyst,
with the Woodside Community Foundation.**

HIGHLIGHTS OF QUALIFICATIONS

- Committed to researching community needs and funding projects that realize the county's potential.
- Working knowledge of community issues and legislative process.
- Extensive experience in needs analysis and research, effectively applying findings to specific projects.
- Skill in handling sensitive issues with diplomacy and objectivity.
- Clear and effective writer and speaker.

RELEVANT EXPERIENCE

Research/Assessment/Evaluation

- Analyzed bills and directed advocacy efforts on state legislation pertaining to public schools, housing, church-state, and religious issues.
- Participated in fact-finding missions to Israel, Romania and Poland, to determine fund-raising and social planning needs and strategies.
- Developed policy for community action in response to Ethiopian famine and Soviet human rights issues, involving on-site research and data gathering missions.
- Identified and catalogued credible African relief organizations in California for contributor reference.

Marin County/Community Relations

- Directed county community relations committee, which serves as the public affairs liaison between the Jewish community and the community at large.
- Served as consultant to county public schools on curriculum development, minority rights, and church-state separation.
- Organized meetings with elected officials (Congresswomen Barbara Boxer, Sala Burton, Congressman Doug Bosco) to inform them of constituents' positions on national and international issues.
- Designed and implemented educational workshops on public affairs issues, overseeing: -invitations -site -speaker procurement -press releases -follow-up.

Writing/Speaking/PR

- Spoke before large audiences on a variety of domestic and international issues.
- Published articles in Northern California Jewish Bulletin (20,000+ circulation).
- Created a photographic exhibit and catalog on the refugees of Africa, viewed in the Bay Area and 7 other states.
- Appeared on numerous radio and TV programs, addressing human rights issues.

- Continued -

WORK HISTORY

1981-present	**Assistant Director**	JEWISH COMMUNITY RELATIONS COUNCIL San Francisco
1974-82	**Board & campaign work**	JEWISH COMMUNITY FEDERATION - San Francisco ...Board of Directors, 1980-82 ...Solicitor Training Chairman, 1974-76; 1982 ...Woodside Fund-raising Campaign Chair, 1979
1971-72	**Counselor**	PLANNED PARENTHOOD - San Francisco
1962-67	**Teacher**	PUBLIC SCHOOLS - Detroit, Oakland, Edwards AFB

EDUCATION

B.S., Education - BOSTON UNIVERSITY
Mortar Board Honor Society

Graduate study in English,
Dominican College and SF State University

COMMUNITY AFFILIATIONS

- Citizens Advisory Committee for the Woodside High School District 1986-present
- Education Advisory Committee of the Human Rights Resource Center,
   County Human Rights Commission 1985-present
- Martin Luther King Jr. Birthday Observance Committee 1986-present
- County Holocaust Committee 1985-present
- Alliance for the Study of the Holocaust, at Sonoma State University 1984-present

> We combined Sonja's paid jobs and her volunteer work under the title "WORK HISTORY" rather than calling it "EMPLOYMENT HISTORY," avoiding a potential conflict, and also presenting substantial community work with the respect it deserves.

JOYCE MEYERS
2400 California Street, #203
San Francisco CA 94109
702-3939

**Objective: Position as program director/coordinator/advisor
in a human services setting**

HIGHLIGHTS OF QUALIFICATIONS

- Demonstrated talent for directing and supervising staff,
  achieving balance between task needs and employee needs.
- Highly effective in analyzing work flow and communication patterns,
  to maximize effectiveness of the work team.
- Skilled and confident in organizing start-up phase of new projects.
- Degree in human relations; 12 years professional experience.

PROFESSIONAL EXPERIENCE

Staff Development & Supervision
- Directed staff of 4 -30, including counseling, support, security, and clerical personnel in
  several work environments: school, counseling center, community treatment centers, and
  business.
- Trained , supervised & evaluated staff, enabling them to improve skills and achieve work
  objectives.

Program Coordination
- Designed a highly successful and innovative parent-child relations program:
  - assessed the needs of the parents, and the staffing & housing resources available;
  - analyzed the program design to anticipate and minimize problem areas;
  - developed guidelines for participation, specifying responsibilities of the parents, the staff
    and the children's guardians;
  - evaluated results of a trial run before full implementation.
- Coordinated the complex logistics of opening two residential treatment centers, including
  hiring and training staff, supervising set-up of physical facilities, and developing programs.

Advising/Counseling
- Mediated to identify and resolve conflicts between staff members, clarifying work relation-
  ships and alleviating communication problems.
- Counseled individuals to identify personal objectives & develop strategies for attainment.
- Counseled youths and adults in group and individual sessions, focusing on problem solving
  and crisis resolution.

WORK HISTORY

1985-present	**Coor. of Volunteers**	GOLDEN GATE NATIONAL PARK ASSOC. - San Francisco
1976-84	**Superintendent**	COMMUNITY TREATMENT CENTERS - Oklahoma City
1974-75	**Counselor**	GROUP PROCESSES (counseling center) Oklahoma City
1973	**Project Director**	URBAN LEAGUE - Oklahoma City

EDUCATION
M.A., Human Relations - University of Oklahoma

LINDA JAMIESON
1200 Michigan Drive
Cortland NV
(415) 616-5003

Objective: Position as Administrative Analyst, Development Office.

HIGHLIGHTS OF QUALIFICATIONS

- Experience in planning and supervising fund-raising events.
- Ten years demonstrated ability to recruit and motivate volunteers.
- Seven years experience planning and organizing official functions for the President of University of Nevada.
- Public Relations experience.

PROFESSIONAL EXPERIENCE

Project Management

- Chaired organizing committee for a major retirement event for University Vice President.
- As Budget Assistant, interpreted policy and monitored $400,000 discretionary fund for compliance with fund guidelines.
- Revitalized a Sierra Club outings program, doubling participation by recruiting, training and motivating leaders, and initiating an effective advertising program.
- Helped define Wilderness Use Regulations at Yosemite National Park.
  - integrated data from an inventory of resources and an environmental quality study;
  - developed and implemented the park's wilderness permit system.

Written & Verbal Communication

- Conceptualized and wrote descriptive brochure on the Division of Agriculture and Natural Resources.
- Developed extensive, quality network of people resources for Division of Agriculture and Natural Resources.
- Organized and conducted numerous meetings & retreats of association boards and clubs.
- Delivered program status reports before 50-member national Sierra Club committee, successfully persuading officials to continue support of a threatened program.

Public Relations

- Participated in development of an external relations and governmental relations program for the Division of Agriculture and Natural Resources.
- Planned and organized official functions for the President of the University of Nevada at the Richards Estate and on the campus:
  - functions honored donors, Regents, awardees and executive officers on special occasions including Charter Day.
- As Information Specialist, educated general public on specific park regulations, policy regarding wilderness use, and environmental quality.
- Spearheaded planning of conferences and educational tours for Cooperative Extension.

- Professional Experience continued -

PROFESSIONAL EXPERIENCE
(continued)

Fund-raising

- For six years, organized volunteers and assisted in planning fund-raising events for the University Art Museum.
- Assisted in the identification of corporate and family foundation prospects for a $500,000 capital campaign for Cooperative Extension.
- Reviewed direct-mail solicitation copy.
- Represented the Division of Agriculture & Natural Resources, filling in for supervisor at UN Development Officers' meeting; participated in University-wide Development Study requested by the Office of the President.

WORK HISTORY

7/86-present	**Space Planning Assistant**	Budget & Space Planning, University of Nevada
1985-86	**Special Projects Analyst**	External Relations, Div. of Agric. & Natural Resources Office of the President, University of Nevada
1982-85	**Budget Assistant**	Budget & Space Planning, University of Nevada
1980-present	**Co-owner/Trip Leader**	Destinations Inc. (white-water rafting company)
1977-84	**Administrative Assistant**	President's Office, University of Nevada
1976-77	**Computer Coder/Editor**	Reilly Marketing Research Corp. - San Francisco
1974-75	**Information Specialist**	US National Parks Service, Yosemite National Park

CURRENT COMMUNITY LEADERSHIP / PROFESSIONAL AFFILIATIONS

1986-87	Elected to Board, University Art Museum Council
1984-87	Elected Sub-Committee Chair, Sierra Club National Outings
1976-87	Leader for Sierra Club National Outings
1984-86	Elected President, Cortland Horsemen's Association
1987	Special Assistant to President for Range Management, Cortland Horsemen's Association

EDUCATION

B.S., (Honors) Conservation of Natural Resources - University of Nevada, 1974

Management Training

"Mid-Management Mentorship";   "Functional Prose for Analysts and Administrators"; "Preparing For Successful Fund-raising";   "Fund-raising Techniques";   Accounting

MARILYN E. COSBY
4990 Benvenue Avenue
Berkeley, CA 94705
(415) 859-0555

Objective: Human Resources Development position which involves travel.

SUMMARY OF QUALIFICATIONS

- High energy **process** and **results**-oriented professional.
- Over 10 years experience planning and organizing creative projects.
- Successful history in manager facilitating, coaching and training.
- Extensive experience in curriculum design and delivery.
- Effective team member who is comfortable with leading or collaborating.
- Keen intuition and strong interpersonal and communication skills.
- Committed to helping managers reach their professional and personal visions.

PROFESSIONAL EXPERIENCE

Planning/Organizing

- Planned, developed and established three new human service projects for County Board of Supervisors; all three still successfully operating.
- Directed capital improvements campaigns for a municipal civic center and a community hospital; surpassed financial goals.
- Formulated and directed national marketing plan for a software product; realized profits the first year.
- Produced semi-annual regional seminars for middle managers; doubled sales in two years.
- Redesigned format for annual meeting of a national organization; facilitated processes during the meeting. Three-year outcome: greatly increased member participation.

Training - Ten years designing and delivering management training in:

- Roles and Responsibilities of Middle Managers and Executive Managers
- Team Management
- Project Management
- Supervisory Skills
- Management by Goals and Objectives
- Time Management
- Project Evaluation
- Performance Appraisal
- Stress Reduction
- Introduction to Microcomputers
- Effect of Microcomputers in the Workplace

External Consultation

- Organization Development Specialist for two year-long projects:
  ...defining mission and strategies
  ...developing executive level teams
  ...systems diagnosis, including data feedback and problem solving in six departmental groups.

- Organization Development Specialist for twelve 6-month projects, developing management information systems and introducing new technologies utilizing Action Research, leading to the following interventions:
  ...intergroup conflict resolution   ...team building   ...transition planning.

- Continued -

WORK HISTORY

1985-present	**Management Consultant**	COSBY & ASSOCIATES, Berkeley
1982-86	**Senior Associate**	CENTER for LOCAL & COMMUNITY RESEARCH, Oakland
1979-82	**Executive Director**	THE CENTER, Pleasanton Counseling, Education and Crisis Services
1977-79	**Program Director**	COMMUNITY ACTION COMMISSION, Santa Barbara Co.
1975-77	**Student Activities Coor..**	UNIVERSITY OF CALIFORNIA, Dean of Students

EDUCATION

M.A., Counseling Psychology, CALIFORNIA STATE UNIVERSITY at LONG BEACH
B.A., Sociology and Psychology, UNIVERSITY OF MINNESOTA

LOCAL & NATIONAL PROFESSIONAL AFFILIATIONS

• American Society of Training & Development   • Organization Development Network

PROFESSIONAL DEVELOPMENT

1986 **Internal Consulting Skills,** Peter Block, Block Petrella and Weisbord, Plainfield NJ

1984 **Tavistock Training: Pairing, Partnerships and Mergers,** Grex Institute, San Francisco

1980 **Gestalt Awareness Training: Group Dynamics,** Univ. of Southern California, Los Angeles

1978 **Research Evaluation and Design,** University of California, Los Angeles

1976 **Client Centered Therapy,** Carl Rogers, Western Behavioral Sciences Institute, La Jolla

HUMAN RESOURCES

MARSHA RIFENBERG
12 Sherwood Avenue
Oakland CA 94611
(415) 797-2131

Objective: Administrative position in Personnel and Human Resources

PROFESSIONAL EXPERIENCE

Human Resources Administration
- Recruited, screened and interviewed applicants for exempt positions.
- Coordinated special projects such as the United Way Campaign, Pre-Retirement Seminars and Campus Recruiting Program.
- Designed and implemented a multi-purpose orientation for newly hired employees.
- Interpreted Human Resources policies and procedures to management.

Training & Development
- Conducted corporate training needs assessments.
- Facilitated Quality Circle/Task Force meetings; trained QC leaders and facilitators.
- Provided employee awareness seminars on topics such as alcohol and drugs.
- Planned, delivered and evaluated management/employee development programs.

Negotiation/Mediation
- Successfully headed off a court battle between disputing business partners, negotiating an amicable dissolution of the business and an acceptable financial settlement.
- Mediated and arbitrated for San Francisco's Community Disputes Services.
- Conducted effective mediations in the Bay Area over the past 7 years.
- Resolved employee grievances, avoiding potential lawsuits against the company.

Employee Assistance Program Coordination
- Assessed employee problems and made referrals to appropriate treatment.
- Researched and evaluated community resources to ensure quality referrals.
- Coordinated and developed internal communications and promotion of the EAP.
- Advised managers and supervisors on the handling of troubled employees.

EMPLOYMENT HISTORY

1984-present	**Human Resources Rep.**	JENNER ENGINEERING - Oakland
1976-1984	**Partner**	DOUGH RAY ME BAKERY - Berkeley
1982	**Teacher**	PERALTA ELEMENTARY SCHOOL - Oakland
1978-present	**Mediator**	PRIVATE PRACTICE - Oakland
1976-1979	**Office Manager/Instructor**	CENTER FOR HUMAN GROWTH - Berkeley
1977-1979	**Instructor**	RE-EVALUATION COUNSELING - Berkeley

EDUCATION, TRAINING & CREDENTIALS
M.S., Educational Psychology - California State University, Hayward 1985
Chemical Dependency Studies Certificate, CSUH 1985
Arbitration/Mediation Training, American Arbitration Association 1985
Multiple Subjects Teaching Credential, CSUH 1980
B.A., English - Ohio Wesleyan University 1968

-References available upon request-

MARY EDDY
121 Paris Lane, San Mateo CA
(415) 771-6163

Objective: Position in administration or human resources emphasizing analysis, planning, writing, problem solving

HIGHLIGHTS OF QUALIFICATIONS

- Outstanding skills in analysis, strategy and planning.
- Proven ability to create and manage a results-oriented team.
- Successful liaison between departments and companies.
- Able to meet demanding time goals.
- Experience in clear and effective business communication.

RELEVANT EXPERIENCE

Analyzing & Planning
- Streamlined procedures to generate cash management document:
  -rewrote job descriptions for greater efficiency with fewer personnel;
  -retrained clerks in gathering raw data;
  -designed and implemented a system of quality control.
- Reevaluated work assignments and job descriptions for staff of 5 in Navy Educational Services office to distribute tasks more equitably.

Managing/Supervising
- Managed team of 24 federal census takers handling over 3000 forms:
  -interviewed, hired, trained and counseled all census takers;
  -broke down and assigned specific areas;
  -reviewed and approved completed census forms.
- Coordinated and supervised major project of assembling benefits information packets, and distribution to 1000 GENENTECH employees:
  -assisted manager in determining content of packets;
  -supervised two clerks assembling materials;
  -arranged for printing, Xeroxing and distribution.

Writing & Research
- Designed and produced a 100-page Procedures Manual covering personnel, training, and administrative issues for a naval reserve unit.

Liaison/Problem Solving
- Developed strong liaison network with staff in various SP departments, subsidiaries and banks, to effectively resolve financial/operational problems.
- Effectively bridged cultural and language differences:
  -integrated American and Japanese business office procedures in US-based office of Japanese financial securities firm;
  -mediated a communication breakdown between American and Latin American military representatives.

- Continued -

Mary Eddy
Page two - continued

EMPLOYMENT HISTORY

1986-present	Human Resources Assoc.	BIOTECH - San Francisco
1985	Accounting Asst.	MANPOWER - San Mateo
1981-84	Senior Supervisor of Treasury Operations	SOUTHERN PACIFIC TRANSPORTATION - S.F.
1980	Crew Leader	CENSUS BUREAU - San Mateo
1976-79	Student & PT Salesclerk	CANADA COLLEGE/I. MAGNIN
1974	Administrative Asst.	NOMURA SECURITIES INTERNATIONAL - S.F.
1970-72	Salary Allotment Clerk	EQUITABLE LIFE - San Francisco
1967-69	Educational Svcs. Officer	US NAVY - Pensacola FL
1969-85	Dept. Manager	US NAVAL RESERVE, Personnel & Admin. units

EDUCATION

B.A., Sociology - CREIGHTON UNIVERSITY, Omaha NB, 1967
Certificate in French - UNIVERSITY OF GRENOBLE, France, '1973

MARY NEWBURGH
2345 Piedmont Road
El Sobrante CA 94803
(415) 666-3267

Objective: Analyst position, targeting productivity or organizational development.

Highlights of Qualifications
- Strong analytical skills, with exceptional attention to detail.
- Successful in establishing productive work relationships.
- Thoroughly explore all avenues and options in solving problems.
- Positive, professional attitude; committed to excellence.
- Outstanding presentation skills, both written and spoken.

PROFESSIONAL EXPERIENCE

Problem Solving / Needs Analysis
- Developed wide ranging recommendations for cost-effective solutions:
  - decreased shop labor costs 21% through personnel reallocation;
  - improved inventory control through establishing optimum quantities for stock on hand, and a regular schedule for inventory;
  - improved personnel accountability by redefining responsibility for essential functions.
- Streamlined motor pool's administrative procedures, saving money, space and time by identifying and eliminating needless steps, and computerizing the process.
- Created first-ever comprehensive picture of Presidio road facilities, quantifying and consolidating historical data, maps, blueprints and past studies.

Cost/Benefit Analysis
- Saved over $ half million for government offices:
  - gathered and analyzed cost data and documentation provided by suppliers;
  - made formal presentation to upper management;
  - recommended conversion from lease to purchase of WANG word processing and other equipment.

Presentation/Communication
- Developed highly effective presentation outlining results of a work productivity study, contributing to the adoption of over 80% of my recommendations.
- Served consistently as study team's preferred presenter, delivering all team briefings to top management, using audio visual aids.
- Delivered informational talks on study results and newly adopted procedures, to:
  - employee groups - administrative units - office personnel - managers.

Organizational Development
- Developed working knowledge of evaluation techniques:
  - work sampling   - operational audit   - group timing technique
  - engineered and non-engineered standards   - technical estimate

Language
- Interpreted negotiations and translated documents regarding the marketing of an imported French soft drink.
- Provided translation for technically complex quality control meetings.

- Continued -

MARY NEWBURGH
Page two

EMPLOYMENT HISTORY

1983-present	**Management Analyst**	PRESIDIO of San Francisco (Dept. of Army)
1982-83	**Administrative Asst.**	PRESIDIO of San Francisco (Dept. of Army)
1979-81	**Interpreter/Tour Guide**	Free-lance/self-employed - San Francisco
1977-79	**Tour Director/bilingual**	HOLIDAY TOURS - San Francisco
1975-77	**Sales Assistant**	LACHMAN & EMERIC STOCKBROKERS - S.F.

EDUCATION & TRAINING

M.A., French - SAN DIEGO STATE UNIVERSITY, 1981
B.A., Comparative Literature - SAN DIEGO STATE UNIVERSITY, 1973

Management Engineering courses:

- Planning & Conducting Management Audits
- Administrative Systems Analysis & Design
- Economic Analysis for Decision Making
- Work Methods and Standards
- Organization Planning
- Work Planning & Control Systems
- Human Behavior in Organizations
- Efficiency Reviews

> Mary shifts the emphasis by detailing her
> on-the-job management training courses
> in the Army, while downplaying the French
> and Literature background.

PATRICE DuMAURIER
3667 Spruce Street, Apt.101
Berkeley, CA 94709
(415) 405-9090

Objective: Program coordinator or counseling position with a corporation, working in human resource development or EAP program.

HIGHLIGHTS OF QUALIFICATIONS

- 14 years experience integrating counseling, nursing and administrative skills in community and business settings.
- 5 years experience developing and managing successful programs.
- MFCC intern registration pending; credentials in nursing and theology.
- Specialist in relationship, drug/alcohol and career counseling.
- Sincere compassion; able to empathize with a diversity of people.

PROFESSIONAL EXPERIENCE

Counseling
- Counseled as primary and family therapist in short- and long-term treatment for adolescents, adults, couples and families using a range of methods:
  -Psychodynamic -Family Systems -Transactional Analysis -Values Clarification.
- Provided crisis intervention for suicidal and substance abuse clients and their families.
- Facilitated small therapy groups of chemically dependent adults and their families.
- Facilitated small groups for adults experiencing loss of a spouse thru death or divorce.

Program Design/Development
- Developed stress management programs for a variety of groups:
  -new parents with high risk infants;
  -epileptic patients, using biofeedback for seizure control;
  -pastoral counselors, in a burnout prevention program.
- Created a highly successful program for hospital chaplains which dramatically decreased on-the-job stress: (still in operation 5 years later)
  -identified and interviewed the potential participants located at 39 hospitals;
  -designed a program addressing 3 primary concerns uncovered in the survey, namely:
   ...training and education ...clarification of values ...burnout prevention;
  -developed a program budget and submitted it for Diocesan approval;
  -designed evaluation tools to assure staffing and program effectiveness.

Program Coordination & Supervision
- Coordinated implementation of the above chaplains' program:
  -engaged guest speakers on grief and death, drugs and alcohol, etc.;
  -scheduled and led 1-day retreats focused on clarifying values;
  -coordinated and led counseling support groups; facilitated informal networking;
  -provided opportunities for refresher courses;
  -developed a referral system covering days off and vacation.
- Created and conducted weekend workshops for individuals experiencing loss of a spouse.
- Trained and supervised peer counselors in group counseling and grief counseling skills.

-Continued -

HUMAN RESOURCES

EMPLOYMENT HISTORY

Current	**Consultant**	DIOCESE OF HOMETOWN, Hospital Ministries
1985-1987	**MFCC Intern**	FAMILY SERVICES of the North Bay, Napa/Vallejo
1985-86	**Alcohol/Drug Counselor**	ST. ROSE HOSPITAL, LifeMasters Unit, Hayward
1985	**Alcohol/Drug Intern**	VETERANS ADMINISTRATION HOSPITAL, Martinez
1983-84	**Program Manager**	UC BERKELEY, San Francisco Laser Center
1981-83	**Program Coordinator**	DIOCESE OF HOMETOWN, Hospital Ministries
1981	**Program Co-Director**	MT. ZION HOSP,SF, Biofeedback/EpilepsyProject
1979-83	**Grief Program Coordinator**	SCHOOL OF APPLIED THEOLOGY/GTU, Berkeley
1973-79	**Staff Nurse**	CHILDRENS HOSPITAL, San Francisco

EDUCATION

MFCC Intern registration pending
M.A., Clinical Psychology, 1987 - JOHN F. KENNEDY UNIVERSITY, Orinda
M.A., Applied Theology, 1983 - GRADUATE THEOLOGICAL UNION, Berkeley
California Licensed Vocational Nurse 1971

SPECIALIZED TRAINING

Interpersonal Relationships, Communication Skills, Career Development
James Institute, Lafayette CA   1980-present

PROFESSIONAL AFFILIATIONS

California Association of Marriage and Family Therapists (CAMFT)
International Transactional Analysis Association (ITAA)
Beginning Experience - an East Bay peer counseling organization

- References available upon request -

> Even though she doesn't yet have her
> MFCC Intern registration, Pat can note that
> it's pending.

STEPHEN R. HONDA
788 Manada Ave.
Oakland, CA 94612
(415) 890-6443

Objective: Position as ADMINISTRATIVE ANALYST, RELOCATION DIVISION
COMMUNITY DEVELOPMENT DEPARTMENT, CITY OF SAN PABLO

HIGHLIGHTS OF QUALIFICATIONS
★ Conducted extensive research and analysis of RE prices and availability.
★ Designed and implemented surveys on relocation needs.
★ Adept in counseling residents on relocation options and responsibilities.
★ Strength in innovative program planning, funding, and analysis.

COMMUNITY DEVELOPMENT EXPERIENCE

Research and Analysis
• Conducted survey and established vacancy rate in high density Oakland neighborhood, and presented findings to City Council and Planning Commission.
• Developed and administered a survey of business and relocation needs in redevelopment area.
• Researched and compared Concord condominium prices.
• Extensively studied and documented mortgage availability and distribution in City of Oakland via: ...personal interviews ...documents collection ...correspondence.
• Researched laws governing transfer and write-down of land from public to private ownership; and submitted detailed report advising City Attorney of contract requirements.

Relocation Counseling
• Counseled residents on timetable, options and responsibilities in conversion and eviction procedures.
• Wrote description of eligibility requirements for Concord home ownership assistance program.
• Explained above program requirements and limitations to potential home buyers.

Program Administration
• Set budget priorities for community development projects, incorporating community input.
• Completed annual CDBG performance report.
• Surveyed and compared methods of saving and leveraging city's CDBG funds.
• Applied to foundations for historic preservation funds.

EMPLOYMENT HISTORY

1984-present	**Classroom teacher**	Oakland public schools; Richmond public schools
1983	**Office Manager**	Pacific Car Rental - Oakland
1981 summer	**Administrative Asst.**	Concord Community Development Dept. - Concord
1980-1982	**Full-time grad student**	Columbia University - NYC
1980	**Researcher/Writer**	Task Force on City-owned Property - NYC
"	**Library Clerk**	UC Berkeley
1979	**Housing Advocate**	Oakland Citizens Committee for Urban Renewal
1978 summer	**Housing Intern**	Calif. Dept. of Housing & Community Development

EDUCATION
Completed graduate course work in Urban Planning, COLUMBIA UNIVERSITY, NYC
B.A. - Geography - UC BERKELEY

VERONICA SILVA

3804 College Ave.
San Francisco CA 94124
(415) 411-8785
(415) 903-7900 (messages)

Objective: Health care administrative analyst or program coordinator with an agency or firm providing health management services.

HIGHLIGHTS OF QUALIFICATIONS

★ Highly competent professional, able to work well independently.

★ Skill in accurately assessing needs and developing program criteria.

★ Dependable and hard working; get along well with colleagues.

★ Very well organized and thorough in researching information.

★ Effective trouble shooter; can be counted on to get the job done.

PROFESSIONAL EXPERIENCE

Program Coordination/Planning

Coordinated and oversaw Medical Audits program:

• Organized working committees of each medical specialty, including representatives from units' professional medical staff & ancillary services;

• Facilitated meetings to develop criteria for conducting patient care audits;

• Conducted audit research, analyzing patients' medical records, applying the above criteria;

• Trained and supervised MR technicians to analyze records;

• Produced statistical report of audit findings, identifying problem areas;

• Followed through to assure that corrective action was taken on problems.

Analysis/Evaluation

Conducted federally mandated audits aimed at cost containment, focusing on three primary criteria and making preliminary assessments of:
-appropriateness of patient admission
-quality of medical care rendered
-accuracy of hospital billing.

EMPLOYMENT HISTORY

1984-present	**Review Coordinator**	WESTERN MEDICAL REVIEW INC., Concord CA
1980-84	**Patient Abstractor**	UCLA STUDENT HEALTH SERVICES, L.A.
1979-80	**Supv., Medical Records**	CEDARS-SINAI MEDICAL CENTER, L.A.
1975-79	**Medical Records Tech.**	USC/COUNTY HOSPITAL, L.A.

EDUCATION

B.A., Health & Safety - CAL STATE UNIVERSITY, Los Angeles 1980
A.S., Medical Records - CITY COLLEGE, San Francisco

TYRA C. BEACH

687 Eucalyptus Avenue
San Francisco CA 94127
(415) 999-7790

Objective: Position as **Training Specialist** for corporate training programs

Highlights of Qualifications

★ 15 years of progressively responsible achievement in training, educating, marketing, communications.

★ Demonstrated gift for motivating people towards higher achievements.

★ Enthusiastic, high energy, and especially creative.

PROFESSIONAL EXPERIENCE

Training & Instructional Design

• Developed and implemented successful program in stress management.
• Coordinated and presented an effective program in substance abuse education.
• Introduced and facilited effective Values Clarification program.
• Trained and coached successful athletic teams.
• Trained professional staff members for CPR-Basic Life Support II certification.
• Instructed classes in: Health, Physical Education, Family Life.

Management & Program Coordination

• Initiated highly successful Wellness Program in public school system:
  - Completed a needs analysis; researched potential programs.
  - Designed program to respond to expressed needs.
  - Conducted first annual Health Fair designed to increase awareness of stress-reduction techniques.
• Conducted citywide aerobic program for teachers, with increasing participation.
• Reorganized and revitalized Human Sexuality curriculum, increasing its acceptance and effectiveness.
• Created an innovative physical education dance program; at the same time improved the teaching environment and resolved space conflicts.

Marketing & Communication

• Conducted successful public relations meetings on a controversial school subject, greatly increasing parental support of the program.
• Promoted winning attitudes in athletic teams, as well as winning teams.
• Increased student involvment, as sponsor of 100-member Pep Club.
• Lectured for open running clinics, for citywide physical education clinic and for county Alcoholism Council.

WORK EXPERIENCE

1982-now	**Instructor,** Health/Physical Education	FORD HIGH SCHOOL, Fairvale CT
	Health Fair Organizer	
	Aerobics Program Trainer	
	CPR-Basic Life Support II Trainer	
1974-83	**Instructor:**	JR. HIGH SCHOOL, Fairvale CT
	Family Life, Health, Physical Ed.	
1969-74	**Instructor,** Physical Education	JR.HIGH SCHOOL, Fairvale CT
		DOSS HIGH SCHOOL, Louisville KY

EDUCATION

B.S., Psychology , Health, Physical Education
Western Kentucky University, Bowling Green KY

40 postgraduate credits in Counseling, Psychology, and Dance

HUMAN RESOURCES

ANNE FULLHAM
2323 Blake Street
Berkeley CA 94704
540-0707

OBJECTIVE: Position as Events Coordinator

SUMMARY OF QUALIFICATIONS
★ Successfully coordinated educational seminars.
★ Thoroughly enjoy coordinating workshop programs.
★ Excellent at follow-up and detail; extremely dependable.
★ Skill in developing cooperative relationships with caterers, managers, etc.
★ Tolerant and comfortable with all kinds of people.
★ Professional in front of large groups; able to introduce speakers.

PROFESSIONAL EXPERIENCE

EVENT COORDINATING

- Set up workshop materials (books, documentation, binders, literature, name tags, pens) for seven computer applications seminars, involving from 60-180 people.
- Signed-in registrants, collected/recorded workshop fees, and prepared receipts.
- Opened seminars: introduced speaker, presented day schedule, provided general orientation.
- Acted as liaison between hotel staff and attendees; arranged for smoking/nonsmoking areas.
- Presented Certificates of Completion; collected evaluation forms and forwarded them to the sponsor.
- Updated registration records and distributed accurate Attendee List to each participant.

ORGANIZATION / COMMUNICATION

- Made detailed arrangements for annual student field trips, including transportation, scheduling, soliciting ticket contributions, and adult assistance.
- Organized annual new-teacher luncheons for 200: arranged hotel accommodations, projected costs, selected menu, prepared publicity fliers, greeted and hosted.
- Wrote detailed lesson plans for 5 daily classes, for years as a classroom teacher.
- Analyzed textbooks for content, skill development, age-level appropriateness, for an educational products testing company.
- Reviewed textbooks for school library.

WORK HISTORY

1985-present	**Seminar Coordinator**	NEW TECHNOLOGY INSTITUTE - Santa Barbara CA
1984-85	**Textbook Analyst**	EPIE INSTITUTE Educational Testing - Berkeley CA
1981-85	**Studio/Business Asst.**	COILLE HOOVEN PORCELAIN - Berkeley CA
1963-81	**English Teacher**	OAKLAND PUBLIC SCHOOL - Oakland CA
1961-63	**English Teacher**	ADAMS COUNTY PUBLIC SCHOOL - Northglenn CO

EDUCATION & TRAINING

B.A., English - University of Colorado, Boulder CO
California public school teaching credential

ADMINISTRATION

EDITH T. LEVENSON
400 Dolphin Drive
Santa Rosa CA
(707) 215-0033

Objective: Position as Public Information Officer with City of Santa Rosa

HIGHLIGHTS OF QUALIFICATIONS

- Familiar with the City of Santa Rosa; active resident for 23 years; take personal pride in representing my community.
- Impeccable reputation within the community for credibility, professionalism, and dependability.
- Energetic and highly effective leader and team member.
- Skill in public speaking and written communication.

REPRESENTATIVE SKILLS and ACCOMPLISHMENTS

Special Events Coordination
- Spearheaded highly successful Annual Community Festival for Santa Rosa, increasing attendance by 30% and income by over 20%:
  -planned, scheduled and coordinated complex details of the event including entertainment, decorations, publicity, public safety, parking and utilities;
  -recruited and coordinated nearly 300 volunteers;
  -obtained all permits and licenses;
  -coordinated with agencies to avoid schedule conflicts and assure smooth logistics involving transportation, sanitation and easy public access.
- Planned and coordinated numerous annual events, for example:
  -holiday decoration contest   -general membership meetings.

Community Promotion
- Spoke before varied audiences on behalf of local social service agencies and officially represented the Santa Rosa Chamber of Commerce.
- Successfully persuaded businesses, agencies and hundreds of individuals to donate time, talent, materials and money in support of community projects.

Public Information / Knowledge of the Community
- Advised visitors, potential residents, and employers of the opportunities and characteristics of the community, including history, demographics, cultural offerings, housing, jobs, public service agencies and general community ambiance.
- Actively participated in a wide range of community organizations and programs:

-Smith Memorial Church	-Women's Lunch Network	-Salvation Army
-Eden Express Restaurant	-Santa Rosa Socialization Center	-Santa Rosa Arts Council
-League of Women Voters	-Santa Rosa Unified School Dist.	-Bay Area Community Svc.

Media Relations
- Successfully solicited national TV coverage for community and project promotion:
  -persuaded Channel 5 Evening Magazine to choose Santa Rosa over 35 other communities for a Salute to Communities;
  -convinced Channel 2 that "The Best of Santa Rosa" board game was newsworthy.
- Achieved extensive free coverage in local press, TV and radio for community projects, composing press releases and PSAs, and conducting TV interviews, phone interviews and anchor spots.

- Continued -

ADMINISTRATION

EDITH T. LEVENSON
Page two

WORK HISTORY

1985-present	**Community Promoter and Special Events Coordinator**	SANTA ROSA CHAMBER OF COMMERCE
1985-present	**Promotion Consultant***	UNIVERSAL CUSTOM PROMOTIONS, Cupertino
1983-85	**PR/Fund-raising Rep**	SANTA ROSA PRE-VOC CENTER
1982-86	**Art Exhibit Coordinator**	EDEN EXPRESS Nonprofit Restaurant
1976-80	**Adult Ed. Art Teacher**	SANTA ROSA UNIFIED SCHOOL DIST.
1966-present	**Art Teacher for children***	Self-employed
1966-71	**Police Matron**	CITY OF SANTA ROSA POLICE DEPT.
1965-67	**Police Radio Dispatcher**	CITY OF SANTA ROSA POLICE DEPT.

*concurrent with above

EDUCATION & TRAINING

B.A., Art - UNIVERSITY of NORTHERN IOWA, Cedar Falls IA
•California Teaching Credential, Cal State Hayward   •Seminars in Promotion and Marketing

CAROL WEITZELL
1912 Kains Avenue
Berkeley CA 94702
(415) 235-3980

One of three resumes for Carol. See also pages 34 and 135.

Objective: Position as Program Specialist

HIGHLIGHTS OF QUALIFICATIONS

- Seven years administrative and analytical experience.
- Three years experience as program specialist.
- Strength in creative problem solving.
- Outstanding ability to work with community and professional groups.
- MSW degree, focusing on administration and planning.

PROFESSIONAL EXPERIENCE

COMMUNITY RELATIONS
- Liaison for community/professional Advisory Board for 3 years. Projects of the board included:
  - Community resource evaluation and coordination.
  - Budget plan development for child welfare agency.
- Compiled and edited a comprehensive community resource manual instructing social workers in services available in the city of Boston, how to access them, and procedures for qualifying.

ADMINISTRATION & PLANNING
- Produced a community social service needs assessment to be incorporated in the budget narrative of a Boston DSS office, synthesizing data from:
  - ...National census   ...Child welfare worker survey
  - ...Boston redevelopment survey   ...DSS computerized records.
- Coordinated development and production of an Internal Management Plan for a Boston DSS office.
- Developed an in-service training program for social work staff which increased their professional expertise and theoretical background:
  - Developed a form for self-assessment by workers.
  - Wrote and managed annual training budgets.
  - Contracted with trainers to provide instruction in specific issues in social work.
  - Met regularly with supervisors to evaluate the program on an on-going basis.

WORK HISTORY

1985-present	**Case Manager**	AREA OFFICE ON AGING, W. Contra Costa Co.
1985-present	**Social Worker**	CONTRA COSTA COUNTY, CA
1983-85	**Photographer**	Self-employed
1980-83	**Program Development**	MASSACHUSETTS DEPT. of SOCIAL SERVICES
1979-80	**Administrative Analyst**	"
1978-79	**Child Welfare Worker**	"
1977-78	**Student Intern**	"

EDUCATION

MSW, Boston University - SRS fellowship in Child Welfare, 1978

ADMINISTRATION

CHRISTIE KELLER
1213 Filbert Street
San Francisco CA 941123
(415) 674-5499

Objective: Administrative position with a nonprofit organization — specializing in marketing, PR, development or program coordination in the performing/visual arts.

HIGHLIGHTS OF QUALIFICATIONS

- Degree in Arts Administration; academic background in the arts.
- Coordinated highly successful PR and fundraising events.
- Strong interest and ability with the skills involved in marketing.
- Experience providing management and direction for nonprofits.
- Special talent for motivating and training volunteer staff.

REPRESENTATIVE PROFESSIONAL EXPERIENCE

Marketing & Public Relations

- Increased public awareness of the economic and political issues involving women's employment, through coordination of highly successful public rally:
  - prepared local PR releases and packets
  - channeled national PR to local media
  - represented organization on TV and radio
  - served as rally MC
  - developed successful logos and slogans for products sold nationwide.
- Prepared clear and effective press releases for San Francisco Jazz Dance Company.
- Managed media data bank and coordinated mailings for employment organization.
- Produced videotape for grant application, well received by the California Arts Council (CAC) and later incorporated into SF Jazz Dance Company's marketing.

Development

- Developed a grant proposal submitted to CAC which was instrumental in placing an arts organization on the priority list for funding consideration:
  - prepared an appropriate request, researching and consulting with CAC and staff;
  - wrote comprehensive description of the program and its goals and objectives.

Management & Administration

- Developed an in-depth working knowledge of program development and management principles, through studying 20 resource sharing programs of Bay Area nonprofits;
  - Identified the following as among the predictors of successful programs:
    ...participant consensus on goals & objectives   ...research of similar programs
    ...accurate projections of budget & staff needs   ...appropriate growth rate.

EMPLOYMENT HISTORY

1984-present	Board Member/Consultant	SAN FRANCISCO JAZZ DANCE COMPANY
1983	Arts Advisory Panel Member	SAN FRANCISCO FAIR & EXPOSITION
1978-82	Program Coor./Steering Committee	WOMEN ORGANIZED FOR EMPLOYMENT
1975-77	Development Associate	SAN FRANCISCO BALLET
1975	Aide to General Manager	SAN FRANCISCO OPERA

EDUCATION

M.A., Arts Administration - GOLDEN GATE UNIVERSITY, San Francisco
B.A., Cultural Anthropology - UNIVERSITY OF WASHINGTON, Seattle

ADMINISTRATION

DEBORAH ELSTAD

648 Crescent Street, #133
Oakland CA 94610
home (415) 653-9090
work (415) 645-4000

Objective: Administrative position directing a department or program

HIGHLIGHTS OF QUALIFICATIONS

★ Masters in Public Administration; 7 years professional experience.
★ Successful in implementing new programs.
★ Exceptional skill in personnel supervision and training.
★ Management talent for "seeing the whole picture."
★ Effective in budgeting and long-term planning.
★ Strength in problem solving and conflict resolution.

PROFESSIONAL EXPERIENCE

1979-present	**Operation Concern - PACIFIC PRESBYTERIAN MEDICAL CENTER - S.F.**
1982-present	**Assistant Director** (outpatient mental health agency)
1979-82	**Office Manager/Admin. Director**

Program Administration
• Supervised day-to-day operations of the out-patient mental health clinic:
  - assured that standards were maintained for quality of client service;
  - constantly observed overall activity in the clinic; redirected people resources as needed.
• Served as Acting Director in absence of the Executive Director.
• Implemented prompt action to resolve administrative emergencies, such as last minute budget changes, urgent maintenance or repair of equipment, and staffing shortages.
• Developed agency policy on all issues involving personnel and operations.
• Negotiated and monitored contract with Community Mental Health Services.
• Oversaw and approved selection and purchase of all office equipment and supplies.

Budgeting; Financial Planning
• Assisted Director in developing long-term financial plan.
• Oversaw agency's annual budget of $700,000:
  - conducted detailed comparison of monthly expense statements and projected revenues;
  - identified potential cost overruns and collaborated with Director to resolve the problem;
  - developed annual expense budget, and submitted quarterly financial status statements.
• Conducted complex monitoring of monthly income, in collaboration with agency's accountant, involving revenues from city, state, private foundations, client fees, grants.

Personnel Management
• Supervised clinical and administrative staff of 23 regarding all administrative activities.
• Interviewed, hired and terminated clerical and administrative staff and maintained their personnel records.
• Successfully mediated conflicts between management and staff, improving internal communications and cooperation.
• Conducted weekly staff meetings and weekly administrative task meetings.
• Negotiated personnel issues, serving as liaison with hospital Personnel Office.

- Continued -

Deborah Elstad
page two

1977-79   **RIVER QUEEN COMMUNITY CENTER - Guerneville CA**
                 Community Relations Coordinator

Fund-Raising & Public Relations
- Implemented all publicity activities, including preparation of public service announcements, fliers, newspaper articles, and monthly newsletter.
- Spoke before community groups outlining services provided at the center.
- Organized, publicized and coordinated all community fund-raising events.

Counseling
- Counseled individuals regarding AFDC and food stamp eligibility; provided crisis counseling.
- Supervised 4 CETA staff in providing counseling services.

ADDITIONAL EXPERIENCE

Teaching
- Taught "Interpersonal Criticism," applicable to conflict resolution and communication, at San Francisco State University. 1978-79.
- Taught "Changing Woman," involving women's changing role in the work world, at Sonoma State University, Rohnert Park CA. 1975-76

EDUCATION

M.P.A. (Masters in Public Administration) - Golden Gate University, San Francisco 1983
B.A., Political Science - San Francisco State University 1977

-References available upon request -

Chronological/functional combination.

ADMINISTRATION

ELLEN CUMMINGS

332 Traverse Road
Sausalito CA 94965
(415) 392-4455

Objective: Position as project manager or program coordinator, with a focus on needs analysis, creative problem solving & public communication.

HIGHLIGHTS OF QUALIFICATIONS

- Strength in anticipating problems and needs before they arise.
- Proven record of excellence and dependability.
- Confident and decisive under stressful conditions.
- Firsthand experience with worldwide range of cultures.
- Talent for getting diverse groups to work well together.

RELEVANT EXPERIENCE

Analysis/Problem Solving
- Conducted firsthand comparative evaluation of worldwide travel markets; advised individuals and organized small groups, counseling on details of:
  ...sight-seeing   ...travel accommodations   ...reputable merchants and best buys
  ...restaurants ...hotel accommodations ...skiing costs & skill-level services ...ambience.
- Redesigned food service operations, greatly increasing customer satisfaction:
  - coordinated preparation and delivery into an efficient, smooth-flowing schedule;
  - upgraded standards of food quality, aesthetic presentation and timeliness.

Organizing/Coordinating
- Directed special events for social organizations:
  - chaired membership drive event which increased club membership by 25%;
  - created and directed promotional skits involving 18-member cast, boosting public support and enthusiasm for sports events and increasing attendance to capacity.
- Organized company employees for a cost saving group membership in an athletic club, reducing expense 65% by using club facilities at off-peak hours.

Communications/PR
- Developed expertise in working with worldwide range of cultures and languages: European, African, So. & Central American, Middle Eastern, Indian, and the Pacific Basin.
- Represented Pan Am at public events and as company ski team member.
- Translated flight announcements into French.
- Trained and supervised newly hired flight attendants.
- Provided individualized services for thousands of airline customers, assessing needs and handling difficult customers effectively.

WORK HISTORY

1974-present	**Flight Attendant**	PAN AM - San Francisco Won in-flight services Recognition Award twice
1970-74	**Flight Attendant**	PAN AM - New York City
1966-70	**full time student**	BUCKNELL UNIVERSITY - Lewisburg PA
1967	**Tour Guide**	GOLD SEAL VINEYARDS - Hammondsport NY

EDUCATION

B.A., Art History - Bucknell UniversityForeign study, 1968 - Florence, Italy
Further studies in computer fundamentals & financial accounting.

HEATHER ARNOLD

1200 Circline Drive
Oakland CA 94610
(415) 388-1919

Objective: Program management position with a corporation or agency
focusing on creative program design, administration and training.

HIGHLIGHTS OF QUALIFICATIONS

- Creative flair for generating and presenting program ideas.
- Inspire and support others to work at their highest level.
- Ability to prioritize, delegate and motivate.
- Exceptional communication and interpersonal skills.
- 7 years successful experience in management.

PROFESSIONAL EXPERIENCE

Management & Supervision
- Planned $250,000 food budget and monitored expenses for Child Care Food Program, maintaining mandatory records and filing for reimbursement.
- Orchestrated complex transportation of 1800 meals per day to 22 sites, from one central kitchen in San Francisco.
- Supervised staffs of up to 90 employees:
  -interviewing and hiring   -scheduling   -attendance control   -evaluating.
- Supervised the training of university student interns.

Administration
- Coordinated all aspects of the nutrition component of Head Start programsfor 1000 children in San Francisco and Alameda, involving:
  -food service administration   -nutrition education   -program compliance.

Creative Program Design
- Revitalized newsletter of Bay Area Dietetic Association, making it the most creative such newsletter in the nation, with a redesigned masthead, new features of popular interest, and reflecting a more professional image.
- Succeeded in winning media coverage for The Body Shop program by writing dynamic proposal for a feature story on childhood obesity.
- Designed innovative promotional campaigns, as intern at New York City PR firm.
- Introduced, for the first time, the use of closed circuit TV as an effective medium for teaching hospitalized diabetic patients how to control their disease.
- Chose topics of high public interest, and located expert speakers, for hospital's community health program promotion.

Education & Training
- Initiated a 5-week nutrition education program for recovering patients in an alcohol and substance abuse treatment facility.
- Monitored parent education program for low income families, assuring appropriate focus on identified nutritional problems of anemia, obesity, high sugar intake, etc.
- Taught weekly classes for children ages 8-12, on behavior modification, self-esteem, parent support, and physical exercise, in a weight control program.
- Trained teachers in effective teaching techniques with preschool children, and monitored their use of the nutrition curriculum.

- Continued -

EMPLOYMENT HISTORY

1986-present	**Nutrition Consultant**	SAN FRANCISCO HEAD START, ALAMEDA HEAD START, and THE BODY SHOP, Oakland CA
1985	**Clinical Dietitian**	OAK CREEK MEDICAL CENTER, Arlington TX
1984-85	**Dir. Nutritional Svcs.**	RALEIGH HILLS HOSPITAL, Dallas TX
1983-84	**Food Supervisor**	ARLINGTON MEMORIAL HOSPITAL, Arlington TX
1981-83	**Food Supervisor**	SKY CHEFS/AMERICAN AIRLINES, Dallas TX
1979-80	**Admin. Dietitian**	KNUD-HANSEN MEM. HOSPITAL, St. Thomas, VI

EDUCATION & CREDENTIALS

M.S., Education - COLUMBIA UNIVERSITY, New York City
B.S., Nutrition & Food Science - SYRACUSE UNIVERSITY, Syracuse NY
American Dietetic Assoc, Reg. #676192

- References available upon request -

ADMINISTRATION

HELGA J. PERRY
67734 Magnolia Street
Albany CA 94720
(415) 709-2001

**Objective: Position as project manager and team participant
with an environmental consulting services firm.**

HIGHLIGHTS OF QUALIFICATIONS

- Effective project coordinator and team supervisor; skilled in prioritizing, delegating and motivating.
- Experienced teamworker; able to work cooperatively or independently.
- Excellent writing, communication and organizational skills.
- Diplomatic and effective working with parties of conflicting interests.
- Knowledge of urban and nonurban environmental issues.
- Experience working with municipal agencies and local government.

RELEVANT EXPERIENCE

Project Management
Directed the San Francisco Conservation Corps 1984 Summer Program, consisting of a public space improvement contract with the Office of Community Development:
- Negotiated contracts and permits with San Francisco city agencies.
- Hired, trained and supervised 75 employees and 14 staff.
- Developed site renovation plans.
- Scheduled and monitored project implementation.
- Oversaw project budget and compliance with city accounting.
- Wrote progress reports; authored final report to Mayor's office and city agencies.

Land Use & Resource Management
- Authored technical chapters of book for city planners on Third World food production, including site analysis, land and water use, soils, hydrology, and plant ecology.
- Taught botany and urban landscape design at California Academy of Sciences.
- Taught course on urban soil, plant, food, waste and water systems at UC Berkeley.
- Conducted community development and urban planning workshops in the US and abroad.
- Reviewed construction plans and conducted energy analyses.

- Relevant Experience continued on page two -

ADMINISTRATION

RELEVANT EXPERIENCE
continued

Writing/Communications
- Authored project reports and evaluations, training manuals, educational and public relations materials; developed and presented lecture/slide shows for resource-use organizations.
- Published articles and books on urban and rural resource use in US and developing countries. (Bibliography available.)
- Speak fluent French; working knowledge of Spanish.

Government Agency Liaison
- Coordinated Mayor Feinstein's Urban Tree Task Force:
- Served as central contact person for Task Force appointees, including representatives of Mayor's office, other city agencies, private developers, planners and landscape architects.
- Conducted nationwide legislative research, summarized findings, and presented recommendations.
- Coauthored ordinance promoting urban forestry management.
- Authored final report to Mayor and Board of Supervisors.

WORK EXPERIENCE

1980-present	**Consultant**	Environmental planning and land use consultant, specializing in program development and administration, project management, and communications services; Typical contracts and services described above.
1980-81	**Instructor & Project Director**	UC Berkeley - College of Natural Resources
1977-81	**Program Director**	Farallones Institute - Berkeley, CA Research and education organization focusing on resource conservation.

EDUCATION

B.S., Conservation of Natural Resources
University of California, Berkeley 1978, Highest Honors.

REFERENCES

Available upon request

ADMINISTRATION

MARDIJEAN RITCHIE
163 Vivian Street
Menlo Park CA 94025
(415) 690-1212

Objective: Position in public information services with an agency or business.

Highlights of Qualifications
- Able to plan, prioritize and implement activities.
- Demonstrated success in developing information resources.
- Perceptive and sensitive listener, skilled in assessing needs.
- Poised and self-confident in dealing with a wide variety people.

RELEVANT EXPERIENCE

Directing/Coordinating
- Initiated and currently co-leading a Career Transitions group for women:
  - developed a library of career resource materials;
  - arranged for speakers on job development subjects;
  - wrote publicity for special events; located meeting places; notified participants;
  - served on steering committee to design program responsive to participant needs.
- Supervised and reported sales activity of 23 sales reps throughout US & Europe:
  - informed and updated reps on product information and current sales materials;
  - assembled and relayed verbal sales reports;
  - maintained worldwide Telex correspondence with parts vendors.

Information Services/Networking
- Assembled wide range of current job resource materials: newspaper articles on market trends, career magazines and books, job listings, sample resumes.
- Instituted a Job Information Bulletin Board for career networking.
- Matched business executives with job seekers in related fields, for the purpose of informational interviews.

Assessing Needs
- Identified needs of individuals involved in career search:
- Developed registration cards listing special interest categories.
- Evaluated responses for use in developing speaker program.
- Conducted phone surveys to determine level of interest in proposed programs and opinions of past speakers and events.
- Led group discussions inviting participants to discuss their current needs and successes in their career exploration.

WORK HISTORY

Year	Title	Organization
1984-now	Registrar, On-call	SAN MATEO CO. CONVENTION & VISITORS' BUREAU
1985	Secretary	AMERICAN HEART ASSOCIATION, Burlingame
1984	Marketing Assistant	KAPTRON Fibre Optics Co., Palo Alto
1983	Office Mgr./Loan Processor	SECURITY INVESTMENTS, Cupertino
1982	Marketing/Promotion Rep	GLORIA MARSHALL'S SALON, Palo Alto
1981	Secretary/Receptionist	STANFORD SCIENTIFIC Medical R&D, Menlo Park
1978-80	Acting Administrator	BETHANY CONVALESCENT HOME, Livermore
1968-78	Office Manager	WOODSIDE DEVELOPMENT CORP., Burlingame

EDUCATION & TRAINING
Business Subjects; Respiratory Therapy - Foothill College, Los Altos CA
Sociology/Psychology - College of Notre Dame, Belmont CA
Nursing - San Francisco State

ADMINISTRATION

MARY QUINLAN
1290 Golden Gate Blvd.
Walnut Creek CA 94596
(415) 909-6667

Objective: Administrative position in international import trade, shipping, or telecommunications

Highlights of Qualifications

★ Successfully lived, worked and taught in China; thoroughly familiar with Eastern business practices.
★ Managed an annual purchasing budget of a half million dollars.
★ Experience in negotiating major maintenance contracts.
★ Able to oversee large projects, and follow through to completion.
★ Exceptionally well organized and highly motivated.

PROFESSIONAL EXPERIENCE

Management & Administration

• Worked within the corporate structures of business and communications industries for 17 years.
• Calculated and wrote detailed financial analysis of subsidiary operation of Exxon stations, assessing the cost-effectiveness of continuing Exxon's car wash operation.
• Coordinated and implemented a massive changeover project, from leaded to unleaded gas delivery:
  - identified and recruited appropriate maintenance contractors to modify 3000 service stations;
  - contracted with laboratory testing facilities to provide ongoing gasoline analysis;
  - wrote and managed detailed budget, and negotiated vendor rates.

Business, Trade, International Culture

• Traveled extensively throughout the Pacific Rim, including:
  - lived in mainland China (one summer)
  - taught and worked in Taipei, Taiwan
• Arranged for cost-effective shipping of consumer goods, complying with import regulations.
• Designed and presented classes in Business Communication to dept. managers at Cyanamid Taiwan.

EMPLOYMENT HISTORY

1984-88	**Full-time student**	CAL STATE UNIVERSITY, HAYWARD and DIABLO VALLEY COLLEGE
1987	**Instructor in Business Communications**	CYANAMID TAIWAN - Taipei
1977-84	**Maintenance Administrator**	EXXON CO. USA - Walnut Creek CA
"	**Administrative Assistant**	EXXON CO. USA - Dallas TX
1966-77	**Advertising Dept. Secretary**	WKY-TV - Oklahoma City OK

EDUCATION & TRAINING

B.A., magna cum laude; major: Chinese Studies. Cal State Univ.., Hayward - 1988
A.A., magna cum laude; Psychology. Diablo Valley College, Pleasant Hill CA - 1985
Intensive Chinese language program, Biejing Language Institute, Biejing, China, 1985
Student observer, auditing on-site Asian business development sessions in Taiwan

ADMINISTRATION

NANCY CHICAGO
2326 Trowbridge Rd.
Lafayette CA 94549
(415) 777-9090

Objective: Associate Director position in college admissions.

HIGHLIGHTS OF QUALIFICATIONS

★ 17 years experience in interviewing and evaluating students.
★ Self-motivated, confident, high energy manager.
★ Effective leader; able to prioritize, delegate and motivate.
★ Reputation for taking the initiative and seeing a task through to completion.
★ Excellent writing, speaking and counseling skills.
★ Committed to higher education and eager to support it.

PROFESSIONAL EXPERIENCE & ACCOMPLISHMENTS

Marketing & Sales
• Earned distinction as Top Salesperson at both Macy's and Hawaii Realtors.
  -developed substantial and profitable repeat business through extensive follow-up and customer record keeping;
  -exceeded sales goal at Macy's by 160%.
• Followed up successfully on prospect leads, as admissions counselor for Farnsworth.

Interviewing, Evaluation, Assessment
• Recruited applicants to undergraduate program:
  -visited secondary schools and community colleges, and consulted with counselors;
  -advised counselors on availability of scholarship money and financial aid alternatives;
  -interviewed students and maintained on-going communication, in person and by phone;
  -counseled students on financial aid options and academic requirements;
• Researched, evaluated and presented data before the state legislature in support of special education and ancillary services.

Management & Supervision
• Co-owned and managed 4 retail stores (gifts and needlework) in Hawaii:
  -personnel -training -sales -advertising/promotion -purchasing -bookkeeping.
• Directly supervised staff of 16-20 sales employees on a daily basis; designed and implemented incentive programs to motivate and achieve sales goals.
• Organized and chaired major fund-raising event benefitting St. Francis Hospital, overseeing the functions of all subcommittees.

RELEVANT WORK HISTORY

1986-present	**Admissions Counselor**	FARNSWORTH COLLEGE, Hawaii (mainland rep)
1970-86	**Alumni/Admissions Rep***	PINE MANOR COLLEGE, Chestnut Hill MA
1984-86	**Sales Associate**	MACY'S GIFT & CHINA DEPT., Concord MA
1979-83	**Realtor Associate**	HAWAII REALTORS Ltd., Hawaii
1972-80	**Co-Owner/Manager**	TBS, INC. (4 retail stores), Hawaii
1965-72	**Inventory Auditor**	Independent contractor for major retailers

*part time, concurrently with positions below

EDUCATION

B.S., Education - UNIVERSITY OF IDAHO, Moscow ID
A.A., Liberal Arts, Pine Manor College

ADMINISTRATION

GRACE FLANDERS
390 Forest Blvd.
San Francisco, CA 94115
(415) 214-6771

"Family management" is used to fill in the gap in Grace's 'employment history'; in this case we changed it to "work history."

Objective: Position as development officer or fund-raiser

Highlights of Qualifications
- Understanding of the philosophy of philanthropy.
- Special talent for organizing and motivating volunteers.
- Committed to and experienced in work that furthers the development of nonprofit organizations.

PROFESSIONAL EXPERIENCE
Planning
Annual giving
- Created first-ever annual giving campaign for Crowell Daycare Center, successfully persuading parents and other supporters to contribute to their maximum capacity;
Chaired CDC Board's sub-commitee on fund-raising.
- Chaired Phone-a-Thon for Bayside Primary School which surpassed projected goal; introduced and implemented several new and successful fund-raising techniques.

Events planning & evaluation
- Organized "Book Week" for Bayside Primary School, developing and monitoring the time line, recruiting committee chairs, and greatly improving the record-keeping process.
- Chaired committee for Sunrise Day School Auction, a major fund-raiser, projecting staffing and scheduling needs.
Evaluated in detail the impact of the auction, and submitted recommendations to the board.

Implementation
- Identified and adapted successful fund-raising techniques for a phone-a-thon event:
   -targeted donor groups and developed appropriate techniques for soliciting each group
   -recruited/trained volunteers -accurately tracked pledges -immediately acknowledged gifts.
- Transformed school's "Book Week" from a relatively minor and disorganized event into a successful annual fund-raiser by developing a disciplined, workable organizational structure.
- Identified, trained and scheduled staff of 30 for Sunrise Day School Auction.

Solicitation
- Solicited donations on a one-on-one basis, with a consistently high level of success:
   -raised more money than any other phone solicitor, for 3 consecutive years working on the
     Sunrise Day School's annual giving campaign;
   -successfully persuaded merchants, service providers and professionals to contribute
     goods and services to auctions for 3 private school fund-raisers;
   -surpassed goals in personally soliciting major contributions from parents for the first-ever
     capital campaign for Sunrise Day School.

WORK HISTORY

1983-present	**Residence Manager**	Supervising unique home for students of S.F. Ballet School
1979-82	family management	
1976-78	**Job Placement Counselor**	ENTERPRISE FOR HIGH SCHOOL STUDENTS - San Francisco
1975-76	**Coor. of Volunteers**	COMMON CAUSE - San Francisco
1973-74	**Assistant Teacher**	MONTESSORI SCHOOL - LaCrosse, WI
1970-72	travel in Asia	
1964-69	**Assistant Teacher**	Schools in Michigan, New York and California

EDUCATION & TRAINING
B.A., English Literature , UNIVERSITY OF MICHIGAN • THE FUND-RAISING SCHOOL, San Francisco 1986

ADMINISTRATION

MS. GELIA THORNTON
6788 Virginia St.
Oakland CA 94602
(415) 990-3255

Objective: purchasing and inventory control manager

HIGHLIGHTS OF QUALIFICATIONS

- 10 years experience in purchasing and inventory control.
- Proven ability to transform a chaotic department into a smooth running efficient operation.
- Skill in maintaining optimum stock levels within budget allowances.
- Successfully managed several automotive parts departments.
- Work effectively with a wide variety of people.

RELEVANT EXPERIENCE

Management & Supervision
- Supervised and streamlined a shipping/receiving department:
  -identified and corrected the operational problems undermining efficiency;
  -greatly increased the number of orders shipped daily;
  -minimized the backlog of open orders.
- Set up an efficient parts department for a new Mazda dealership, starting with an empty room, a very large stock order, and a packing list in Japanese.
- Developed a variety of check-and-balance systems to reduce errors in inventory record keeping; achieved high accuracy (well under 1% loss) on annual inventory.

Inventory & Purchasing
- Requested bids from vendors for awarding of annual purchasing contracts, and compared bids submitted, considering price, quality and shipping terms.
- Determined minimum and maximum stock levels for 6,000 line items.
- Conducted on-going reviews and updates of stock level figures, considering:
  -expected and actual usage figures   -seasonal fluctuations
  -planned equipment phase-out and replacement.
- Monitored invoices for accuracy of account coding; tracked expenditures for comparison with budgeted figures.

EMPLOYMENT HISTORY

1981-present	**Senior Parts Technician**	SHORELINE SHIPPING Inc. - Richmond International cargo shippers
1980	**Foreman, Shipping/Receiving** (temp. layoff from Shoreline)	ARMICO Inc. - Oakland Wholesale/Retail Automotive Parts
1977-80	**Senior Parts Technician**	SHORELINE SHIPPING Inc. - Richmond
1976-77	**Administrative Assistant**	DREISBACH EXPORT PACKING - Oakland
1973	**Parts Manager**	LONG BEACH MAZDA - Long Beach NY
1972	**Parts Manager**	VARS BUICK - Glen Cove NY

EDUCATION
English major - STATE UNIVERSITY of NEW YORK, Plattsburgh

ADMINISTRATION

ROBERTA SWAN
115 Versailles Ave.
El Granada CA 94018
(415) 224-4443

**Objective: Position in program management/administration
with a social service agency.**

HIGHLIGHTS OF QUALIFICATIONS
★ Experience in program planning and coordination.
★ Strong motivation to help others live life fully.
★ Skilled in handling the public with professionalism and sensitivity.
★ Thrive on organizing complex projects and following through to completion.
★ Excellent written, verbal, and listening skills.
★ Special talent for assessing and improving office systems.

RELEVANT EXPERIENCE

Program Planning & Coordination
• Established and implemented a system for assigning credentials to convention staff and guests at
1984 Democratic National Convention.
  - negotiated with national committee chairperson to upgrade staff credentials;
  - made group presentations to staff, explaining complex credentialing procedures.
• Analyzed office paperwork flow in an AV studio and devised more efficient procedures.
• Developed a system for maintaining accurate record of financial transactions for a nonprofit
workshop sponsored by Elisabeth Kubler-Ross Center.

Management & Training
• Assessed appropriate duties for a new position in billing department, and trained the new
employee for monitoring rental equipment location, pricing job orders, and paperwork processing.
• Researched and documented correct procedure for hiring free-lance union studio talent, reducing
hiring expense and office chaos.
• Delegated daily job assignments to 20-25 employees, and resolved logistics problems relating to
timely delivery, setup and operation of audio-visual equipment.

Community Resources
• Located wide range of services for out-of-town convention production company:
  ...costumes   ...props   ...caterers   ...audio-visual equipment.
• Conducted extensive research to locate appropriate site for weekend workshops supporting
teenagers and children in effectively handling profound life crises.

EMPLOYMENT SUMMARY

1979 to present:
Free-lance Production Services (conventions, film/TV, communications)

Administrative Assistant	UNITED WAY PRODUCTIONS - El Granada
Workshop Coordinator	ELISABETH KUBLER-ROSS CENTER - San Francisco
Asst. Production Manager	FM PRODUCTIONS (Demo. National Convention) - SF
Office Services/Trainer and	McCUNE AUDIO VISUAL - San Francisco
Equipment Rental Coordinator	" "
Production Coordinator	CREATIVE ESTABLISHMENT (convention production)

EDUCATION

B.A., Sociology, Univ. of Colorado • Legal Assistant Program, Univ. of San Diego

ADMINISTRATION

69

ROSE ELLINGTON
2773 Middletown Avenue
Alameda CA 94501
415-366-8447

OBJECTIVE: Member Relations Manager for a large Health Maintenance Organization.

HIGHLIGHTS OF QUALIFICATIONS

★ Extensive experience with patient advocacy.
★ Supervisory background in agency and retail environments.
★ Demonstrated competence in coordinating programs.
★ Excellent mediator, moderator and facilitator.
★ Inspires and supports others to work at their highest level.
★ Licensed Marriage and Family Counselor.

Supervision
• Managed staff of 25 youth in retail establishment.
• Supervised up to 5 assistants in a career development program.
• Supervised peer counselor trainees at San Francisco State career center.
• Taught and supervised 12 student teachers.
• Supervised 2 employees in my own public relations business.

Patient Advocacy and Counseling
• Served as patient advocate for 2 years, at a community health agency.
• Mediated domestic conflicts as marriage and family counselor for 9 years.
• Handled grievances as customer service rep in telecommunications.
• Developed training presentations for medical students on patients' rights.
• Acted as counselor and grievance liaison at mental health agency.

Program Administration
• Managed my own businesses for 8 yrs, as a private therapist and as a publicist.
• Developed and coordinated numerous training programs.
• Prepared reports for state & county agencies, and for local agency directors.
• Participated in hundreds of staff meetings and planning sessions.
• Coordinated statistical research and analysis for grant proposals.
• Developed extensive marketing experience as owner of a public relations business.

PROFESSIONAL EXPERIENCE

1982-now	**Publicist/owner**	Out There!, a public relations firm, Alameda CA
1981-82	**Career Counselor**	Self-employed, Berkeley CA
1979-81	**Coordinator, Career Program**	Woman's Resource, San Rafael CA
1977-78	**Manager**	MacDonald's Restaurant, Mill Valley CA
1975-81	**Marriage & Family Counselor**	Self employed, SF bay area
1972-75	**graduate school**	San Francisco State
1969-72	**Teacher/trainer**	San Mateo Co. Mental Health Assoc, Daly City CA Parent-Child Communication Program
1966-70	**Counselor/Grievance Liaison**	San Mateo Co. Mental Health Assoc, Daly City

EDUCATION & CREDENTIALS
M.A. San Francisco State University - San Francisco CA
Marriage, Family & Child Credential (MFCC)
Adult School Credential - communication skills

ADMINISTRATION

SHIRLEY E. KRENZ
12 Bruenner Square
North Oakfield CA
(415) 777-1313

Objective: Project management position in Marketing, Public Relations or Customer Service

HIGHLIGHTS OF QUALIFICATIONS

★ Enthusiastic, committed, resourceful; can be counted on to get the job done.
★ Outstanding record in recruiting, training and motivating employees.
★ Successful in negotiating and winning cooperation and support.
★ Poised and professional with both top management and support staff.
★ Able to pull together and manage all aspects of a complex project.

PROFESSIONAL EXPERIENCE

Management & Supervision
• Managed implementation of sales office automation:
  - Met with national management, as local office rep reporting on field requirements
  - Hired personnel to operate two computer stations
  - Selected and purchased work station furnishings
  - Arranged for both in-house training and local tutoring of new staff
• Hired clerical and temporary sales support staff for regional operations office.
• Supervised daily work flow & allocated clerical tasks, as business office manager.

Project Design & Coordination
• Coordinated relocation planning of western regional office, Taylor Instrument Co:
  - Researched locations, developing a criteria graph of variables between locations:
    ...costs per square foot   ...tenant improvement costs
    ...restaurant/hotel facilities   ...proximity to airports and customer base
  - Planned physical layout of new offices, working with building architect
  - Acted as liaison between company management and real estate representatives.

Presentation/Public Relations/PR
• Successfully negotiated for hard-to-get facilities, with sales and catering directors of major hotels.
• Found HMO speakers to make presentations to employees on the best health plan options available.

EMPLOYMENT HISTORY

1980-present	**Regional Administration Manager**	TAYLOR INSTRUMENTS, Oakfield CA
1975-80	**Office Manager**	"
1970-75	**Regional Secretary**	"
1966-69	**Executive Secretary**	MANPOWER INC. - Oakfield CA

EDUCATION

A.A. Supervision - Chabot College, Hayward CA
Training in: Peak Performance Training; Assertiveness Training;
Presentation for Professional Women; Time Management

ADMINISTRATION

SUSANNAH HOLT

346 Walpert Street
Hayward CA 94541
(415) 980-6774

Objective: Position as Volunteer Coordinator for Marin Humane Society

HIGHLIGHTS OF QUALIFICATIONS

★ Demonstrated talent in assessing skills and making appropriate volunteer placements.
★ In-depth experience with pet therapy programs.
★ Established and managed a successful pet care business.
★ Supervised volunteers at local humane organizations.
★ Over 10 years of effective public relations experience.

PROFESSIONAL EXPERIENCE

Pet Therapy Programs; Volunteer Work

• Implemented a new pet therapy program at The Latham Foundation for Human Education, thoroughly researching other programs and selecting the most appropriate features.
• Introduced pet therapy program to nursing homes:
 -made initial contacts and described the program benefits
 -scheduled visits to nursing homes
 -coordinated efforts with Oakland SPCA
• Served as a volunteer at three area humane organizations.

Communication & Public Relations

• Worked directly with hundreds of pet care clients, advising and assessing their pet care needs.
• Effectively handled emergencies and customer inquiries, as BART train operator, earning commendation for outstanding service to patrons.
• Mediated between volunteers and staff to maintain harmonious working relationships, and maximize volunteer job satisfaction within the limitations of the program.

Management, Supervision & Training

• Started a pet care business from scratch, on my own:
 -interviewed job applicants, assessed their skills, placed, trained and supervised;
 -wrote all the contracts, generated billings, followed up on billings.
• Trained new BART train operators.
• Trained new volunteers at Latham Foundation and at Oakland SPCA.

WORK HISTORY

1978-present	**Train Operator**	Bay Area Rapid Transit - Oakland
1983-85	**Owner/Manager**	Dog's Best Friend, pet care - Albany
1980-83	**Humane Educator** (volunteer)	Latham Foundation, and Oakland SPCA
1975-78	**Owner/Operator**	Collins Trucking Co. - Albany
1970-72	**Kennel Aide**	Berkeley/East Bay Humane Society

A.S. Degree, Biology - Laney College, Oakland

ADMINISTRATION

TONYA THURBER
1919 Thirteenth Avenue #2
San Francisco CA 94122
(415) 191-0887'

Objective: Program assistant/coordinator in education or human services, focusing on program analysis, evaluation and planning.

HIGHLIGHTS OF QUALIFICATIONS

★ Successful in designing and implementing educational programs.
★ Five years professional experience in program coordination.
★ Committed to work that furthers the growth and wholeness of individuals.
★ Masters Degree; special study in human behavior.

PROFESSIONAL EXPERIENCE

• Managed the development of educational programs for preschool children, elementary age children, adolescents, and adults, involving 500-2000 families.

• Coordinated the planning and implementing of programs for college students:
-retreats -films and speakers -social events.

• Supervised 7 to 30 volunteer teachers, including:
-recruiting -training -supporting -evaluating

• Advised and consulted with parents, including advising on course content, class scheduling and teacher/student expectations; and arranging for special tutoring and scheduling as needed.

• Served on grad school Admissions Committee and on alumni association steering committee.

• Operated computer terminal for information storage and retrieval.

EMPLOYMENT HISTORY

1985-present	**Director of Religious Education**	ST. MATTHEW's PARISH - Santa Rosa
1984	**Religious Education Coordinator**	ST. ANN CHAPEL - Palo Alto
1981-84	Full-time Student	GRADUATE THEOLOGICAL UNION, Berkeley
1983	**Religious Education Coordinator**	CATHOLIC CHAPLAIN, Treasure Island, San Francisco
1982	**Director, House Church**	UNITAS CAMPUS MINISTRY, UC Berkeley
1981	**Data Entry Operator**	CRAFTWAYS Mail Order, Berkeley
1980	Student	German language study, in Bonn, West Germany
1979	**Program Coordinator**	NEWMAN CENTER - Fullerton

EDUCATION

M.A. Theology, GRADUATE THEOLOGICAL UNION - Berkeley 1984

ADMINISTRATION

73

CAROL A. PARKER
2330 Baker Street
Berkeley, CA 94704
834-8425

JOB OBJECTIVE

Position as Bookstore Clerk at Avenue Books

QUALIFICATIONS

★ Thorough knowledge of bookstore layout, shelving books, finding books through reference books and use of microfiche.

★ Have inventoried, organized and shelved materials for retail store.

★ Ability to help customers in a professional, concerned manner.

★ Personal appreciation for books.

★ Familiar with operating a cash register.

★ Experienced in ordering and receiving materials.

EMPLOYMENT HISTORY

1987-1988	Clerical Worker. Western Temporary Service. Berkeley, CA
1986	Senior Clerk. Personnel Office, University of California. Berkeley, CA
1984-1985	Retail Clerk. Lacis, Antique Lace Store. Berkeley, CA
1979-1983	Librarian's Assistant. Burling Library, Grinnell College. Grinnell, IA
1973-1979	Librarian's Assistant. Town School for Boys Library. San Francisco, CA

EDUCATION

B.A. Spanish, Grinnell College - Grinnell, IA   1983
A.A. Wood Technology, Laney College - Oakland, CA   1983-84

DARLENE JACOBSON
1219 Colusa
Berkeley CA 94707
(415) 891-6500 Ext.888, ans. svc.
(415) 351-2828, home

Objective: Position as program assistant/administrative assistant

HIGHLIGHTS OF QUALIFICATIONS
★ Able to take responsibility for implementing a project.
★ Strong commitment to cooperative teamwork.
★ Excellent skills in facilitation, communication, presentation.
★ Readily transcend educational/cultural/language barriers.
★ Effective teacher and innovative designer of learning projects.

RELEVANT EXPERIENCE
Program Implementation
• Developed and implemented art programs for 3-5 year olds at an Oakland Montessori school:
  - designed and presented student projects coordinated with teaching themes;
  - supervised 3 teenage teaching assistants, focusing on job skills and goals;
  - served as liaison to parents; organized their participation in field trips.
• Taught English As a Second Language to adults.

Administrative Support
• Assisted owners to remodel building for use as a produce market and ice-cream store involving light construction, plumbing, moving, ordering, pricing, advertising.
• Served as teaching aide in preschool and grade K-6 classrooms.
• Reported on the development of children's skills at weekly teachers' meetings.
• Facilitated meetings: political action committees, business collectives, school staff.

Public Relations
• Created and presented educational slide show on refuges for women victims of domestic violence: - took photos - wrote script
  - organized speaking engagements - facilitated public discussion
  - provided referral information on community resources.
• Greeted, oriented and scheduled clients, in several office settings:
  ...doctor's office   ...social service hot line   ...massage studio   ...answering service.

EMPLOYMENT HISTORY
1987-present	Masseuse	BERKELEY MASSAGE STUDIO - Berkeley
1985-86	Assistant Teacher	MONTESSORI CHILDREN'S COMMUNITY - Oakland
1983-84	Phone Operator	BABYLON ANSWERING SERVICE - Berkeley CA
1982	Asst. Manager	PRODUCE STORE, BOONT BERRY FARM - Boonville CA
1981	Asst. Editor	CAREER CENTER FOR WOMEN - Santa Cruz CA
1980	ESL Teacher/Tutor	Free-lance - Paris, France
1975-80	Student	UCSC (spent 1977-78 in France, field study)
1974-75	Teaching Assistant	BECKNOLL DAY SCHOOL - Santa Ana CA

EDUCATION
B.A., Community Studies - University of California at Santa Cruz, 1980

ELIZABETH DELOIT EMERY
990 Twentieth Ave.
San Francisco CA 94121
(415) 399-2878

Objective: Administrative Assistant position in fashion/design business

HIGHLIGHTS OF QUALIFICATIONS
★ Able to see a demanding project through to the end.
★ Work effectively in collaboration with others.
★ Thoroughly enjoy working with clothing design and color.
★ Outgoing and poised in dealing with the public.
★ Strong organization and planning skills.

RELEVANT EXPERIENCE

Project Organization & Planning
- Synthesized large amount of data to produce accurate and complete lists and records:
  - developed guest/mailing list for major university event, the President's Inauguration;
  - updated catalog of paintings in permanent collection of Whitney Museum of Amer. Art.
- Organized meetings and planned agendas for academic and social events.
- Researched and planned detailed itinerary for several trips within Europe and United States; kept accurate and detailed expense records, and daily log of activities.

Fashion Sales /Promotion /Public Relations
- Assisted and directed customers in petites clothing department.
- Merchandised clothing as assistant to Macy's sales manager.
- Designed successful promotional campaign that increased attendance at athletic events:
  - thought up catchy, motivational slogans; planned and performed in humorous skits;
  - designed posters and wearable/edible souvenirs advertising the events.
- Led tours of private school campus, describing the school's advantages, features and facilities.

Leadership & Supervision
- Developed schedules for students working as cooks and salespeople in school cafeteria and lounge.
- Cofounded a new student performing arts organization (Dance Club):
  - made a presentation which convinced the administration of the need for the new organization;
  - found a faculty advisor for the club.

WORK HISTORY

1985-present	**Salesperson**, Petites Dept	MACY'S of CALIFORNIA - San Francisco CA
1978-85	**Full-time student**	MIDDLEBURY COLLEGE & Garrison Forrest School
1985 summer	**Inauguration Coor. Asst.**	LONG IS. UNIVERSITY Grants Dept. - Greenvale NY
1985 spring	**Waitress**	MIDDLEBURY (VT) COLLEGE DINING SERVICE
1983 winter	**Clerical/Research Intern**	WHITNEY MUSEUM OF AMERICAN ART - New York NY
1982 summer	**Server/Cashier**	JACK'S ICE CREAM - Falmouth MA
1981 spring	**Clerical/TV Intern**	CHANNEL 13 Public TV - New York NY

EDUCATION
B.A., German - MIDDLEBURY COLLEGE - Middlebury VT, May 1985
- References available upon request -

ESTELLE HAVENS
3744 Thirty-fifth Ave., Oakland, CA 94605
Telephone 443-9090

Objective: Part-time clerical position in a bank or other business, assisting management with bookkeeping, filing, and light typing.

HIGHLIGHTS OF QUALIFICATIONS

- Dependable; can be counted on to get the job done.
- Committed to a career in office work; motivated to learn and grow in responsibility and business skills.
- Good with figures; experience in bookkeeping and general office support.
- Excellent references from past employers and teachers.
- Well groomed; get along well with others.

RELATED SKILLS & EXPERIENCE

General Office Support
Assisted store manager in orienting and assigning employees:
- Prepared new employee personnel folders; called in substitutes as needed.
- Monitored minor's work permits to assure they were still valid.
- Filed personnel records and managers' test results.
- Posted and filed official documents.
- Typed correspondence; answered phone; scheduled interviews; made reservations.

Assisted local author in assembling material for new book:
- Contacted over 100 persons by phone and letter, successfully getting their permission to use personal data in new publication.
- Kept detailed records of results of contacts; updated client files.
- Mailed brochures and review copies of author's book.
- Accurately prepared subject cards for cross-indexing new book.

Assisted candidate running successfully for office of County Supervisor:
- Called registered voters describing the candidate's position on political issues.

Bookkeeping
- Accurately completed bookkeeping tasks at MacDonald's in half the usual time.
- Recorded daily sales:
  - tallied total items sold and computed total daily revenues
  - recorded totals of wasted food and paper products
  - audited the cash register records for each employee and reported errors.
- Earned an Outstanding Achievement raise at MacDonald's for consistently accurate money handling and good relationships with customers.
- Assisted in computing employee hours and verifying accuracy of vendor statements.
- Balanced family checkbook statements and paid bills.

WORK HISTORY

summers	1986-87	**Office Assistant**	DAMN GOOD RESUME SERVICE - Berkeley
Nov.1984-Apr.	1985	**Bookkeeper**	MAC DONALD'S - Oakland
Oct.1983-Nov.	1984	**Cashier**	MAC DONALD'S - Oakland and Hayward
summer	1983	**Clerk**	HAVENSCOURT COMMUNITY CHURCH - Oakland
weekends	1981	**Cashier/sales asst.**	CERAMIC TILE CO. - Oakland

EDUCATION & TRAINING
Freshman, CHABOT COLLEGE, Majoring in Entrepreneurship & Accounting
Completed courses in: Accounting, Law, Typing, Journalism

JOY HOLLAND
660 Pinebluff Ave.
Vallejo CA 94590
(707) 888-2557

Joy maximizes the impact of her business training by spelling out the relevant courses she took.

Objective: Project Coordinator or Administrative Assistant position,
involving personnel services, training, supervision, and/or payroll and bookkeeping.

HIGHLIGHTS OF QUALIFICATIONS

- ★ Enthusiastic, personable; professional in appearance and manner.
- ★ Reputation for dependability and credibility.
- ★ Demonstrated skill in supervising an efficient, well-run department.
- ★ Take pride in doing a good job and achieving results.
- ★ Extensive experience in personnel and office administration services.

RELEVANT EXPERIENCE

Project Coordinating
- Oversaw start-up of a new unit, Executive Credit Card, at Wells Fargo Bank:
  -interviewed and hired employees to develop a staff of 10;
  -set up initial Accounts Receivable ledgers for monthly posting;
  -conducted credit investigations and developed profiles on new credit card applicants.

Personnel, Payroll & Bookkeeping
- Served as Group Benefits Coordinator at California Rubber (CR) and General Electric (GE).
- Processed Accounts Payable and Receivable; reconciled bank accounts at CR and GE.
- Processed payroll: calculated hours, taxes and deductions, and prepared special checks.

Training/Supervising
- Trained new employees at Wells Fargo Bank in bookkeeping and use of calculators, adding machines and typewriters.
- Trained employees of California Rubber on use of Burroughs bookkeeping machine.
- Supervised 10 clerical employees in the Accounting unit at Wells Fargo.

EMPLOYMENT HISTORY

1978-present	**Bookkeeper/Admin. Assistant**	CALIFORNIA RUBBER MFG. CO., Vallejo
1976-78	**Financial Representative**	GENERAL ELECTRIC CO, Oakland
1967-76	**Credit Asst./Unit Supervisor**	CROCKER BANK; WELLS FARGO BANK, S.F.

EDUCATION & TRAINING

Heald Business College, Laney College, College of Alameda
Business Coursework

- Small Business Management
- Introduction to Business Law
- Principles of Accounting
- Business Math

- Word Processing
- Business English
- Payroll Accounting
- Income Tax Accounting

- References available upon request -

LORI W. VERNON
(415) 982-9065

97 Del Mar Blvd.
Oakland CA 94611

OBJECTIVE: Position as Administrative Assistant

HIGHLIGHTS OF QUALIFICATIONS

- Special gift for getting along with all levels of staff.
- 5 years responsible experience in administrative work.
- Bachelor's Degree in Education.
- Can be counted on to get the job done, without supervision.

RELEVANT EXPERIENCE

Computer Use & Data Processing

- Entered all data for Levi Strauss employee contributions to United Way on an IBM-PC, retrieved data, and ran spreadsheet reports.
- On WANG word processor, composed correspondence and reports, merged letters, addressed envelopes.
- Edited reports and correspondence on IBM Displaywriter documents.

Administrative Support Projects

- Managed office for 6 weeks while all other staff worked at Olympics.
- Compiled complex financial computations and verified eligibility for "matching funds" for over 400 nonprofit agencies throughout the country.
- Coordinated accurate placement of thousands of pieces of office furniture and equipment in major corporate relocation project.
- Arranged transportation for United Way agency visits for 400 employees.

Supervision & Training

- Trained new employees in equipment use, cashiering, food preparation.
- Monitored attendance of student teacher aides.
- Oriented substitute teachers on school policies and schedules.
- Advised coworkers on various procedures of WANG word processing.

EMPLOYMENT HISTORY

1984-present	Admin. Coor., United Way Campaign	ALDOUS CORPORATION, SF
1983-84	Admin. Asst., Olympic Marketing	LEVI STRAUSS & CO., SF
1982-83	Counter Salesperson	CALIF. BAKING CO, Piedmont
1981-82	Levi Plaza Relocation Team Asst.	LEVI STRAUSS & CO., SF
1979-81	Assistant to Principal	Piedmont Unif. School Dist.

EDUCATION

B.S., University of Texas, Austin TX - Elementary Education

OFFICE SUPPORT

MARYANNE HAIN
790 Martinez Ave.
San Francisco CA 94127
(415) 867-3522   (415) 733-9097

Objective: Executive Assistant in an international organization focusing on trade and business development in the Pacific Rim countries.

Highlights of Qualifications
- Young, enthusiastic, committed to professional growth.
- Liberal arts background, with high academic achievement.
- Traveled extensively, and often independently, on the Mainland.
- Studied Mandarin Chinese intensively in Hong Kong and Taiwan.
- Keen awareness of regional politics; strong analytical skills.
- Readily transcend cultural and language differences.

RELEVANT EXPERIENCE

Knowledge of Chinese Customs and Culture
- Lived with local family in Taiwan, speaking Chinese exclusively in the home.
- Lived and studied with Chinese students in Hong Kong:
  -took part in a wide range of university activities;
  -participated in The International Club, encouraging cultural exchange and social interaction, as cultural liaison between Americans and Chinese students;
  -studied Chinese international relations and Chinese literature;
  -completed supervised historical research on relations between China and the West;

Knowledge of East Asian Politics and Economy
- Attended extra-curricular events sponsored by Yale-China Association, e.g.:
  -speeches by diplomats -political/social events on the future of Hong Kong.
- Participated in a series of conferences analyzing the difference between Chinese and Western law, regarding impending transition of Hong Kong in 1997.
- Tutored Vietnamese refugees in English; greatly increased my political awareness.

Management Responsibility
- Worked up to increasing levels of responsibility with Hotel Group of America, starting out as desk clerk at Hotel Union Square:
  -trained newer desk clerks in computer use, guest relations, billing & reservations;
  -earned opportunity for advancement to position as sales representative.

WORK HISTORY

current	**Desk Clerk***	DUBUQUE HOTEL, San Francisco
1984-85	**Desk Clerk***	HOTEL UNION SQUARE, San Francisco
1983-84	**Cashier***	VIE DE FRANCE Restaurant, San Francisco
1983 summer	**Cashier**	SOURDOUGH PUFF CO, bakery, San Francisco
1982 summer	**Office Assistant**	LEOUNOUDAKIS & FORAN law firm, San Francisco

* full-time summers, half-time during school year

EDUCATION

B.A. History - UNIVERSITY OF CALIFORNIA, BERKELEY
1985-86 study abroad:
CHINESE UNIVERSITY OF HONG KONG and YALE-CHINA LANGUAGE CENTER
Summer 1986, National Taiwan Normal University, Mandarin Training Center

OFFICE SUPPORT

ALVINA MORENA
587 South Stewart Street
Santa Fe, New Mexico 87504
(505) 212-6969

Objective: Administrative/client service position in a health/medical setting

HIGHLIGHTS OF QUALIFICATIONS
★ Strength in program management, organization and follow-through.
★ Twelve years experience dealing effectively with the public.
★ Personable, articulate and professional in appearance.
★ Expertise in interviewing, counseling, and training.
★ Outstanding written and oral communication in both English & Spanish.
★ Lifelong interest in and dedication to promoting health.

PROFESSIONAL EXPERIENCE

Interviewing/Orienting
• Interviewed, assessed and selected support staff; developed detailed files.
• Reported to coworkers on results of personnel interviews and assessments.
• Trained and supervised volunteers and aides in program design and presentation.

Health Services
• Advised individuals of all ages on resources available for preventive health care.
• Taught hatha yoga to adults in bilingual cultural center.
• Treated clients as massage therapist (shiatsu and oil massage) for 7 years.

Project Management & Organizing
• Designed strategy for implementing educational projects and PR events.
• Managed and coordinated all aspects of bilingual parent counseling program:
  - scheduled and set up appointments by phone and letter, and met with parents
  - followed up with feedback to parents on changes in child's performance and behavior.
• Managed small business office of a mail-order recording company:
  - maintained bookkeeping records of accounts payable and receivable;
  - wrote text and laid out brochures and fliers; arranged for printing;
  - developed mailing list for product promotion.

WORK HISTORY

1983-present	**Office Mgr**, part-time	ENTERPRISE RECORDING CO. - Berkeley CA
1981-85	**Bilingual Teacher**	THOUSAND OAKS SCHOOL - Berkeley CA
1980-81	**Teacher, ESL**	COLUMBUS JUNIOR COLLEGE - Seville, Spain
1979	**Resource Teacher**	RICHMOND, CA. UNIFIED SCHOOL DISTRICT
1978	**Student**	Graduate work in health education
1972-77	**Bilingual Teacher**	RICHMOND, CA. UNIFIED SCHOOL DISTRICT

EDUCATION & CERTIFICATION

B.A., Comparative Literature - University of California, Berkeley
Graduate work in Health Education - JFK University, Orinda CA
State Certified Massage Therapist

STEPHEN P. PARKER
1038 Shattuck Ave.
Berkeley CA 94707
(415) 566-3421

Objective: Office Assistant for the Nature Company headquarters.

SUMMARY OF QUALIFICATIONS

- Self-motivated; able to learn anything on my own initiative.
- Excellent record of dependability and reliability.
- Lifetime interest in nature and nature studies.
- Wide range of manual skills.

WORK HISTORY

1980-present   **Nature Photographer**   Free-lance, part-time, NY and West Coast.
- Published photos in national and regional magazines; agency represented.

1984-86   **Maintenance Worker**   **SOUTHSIDE MALL**, Oneonta NY
- Repaired and maintained plumbing, door hardware, grounds-keeping equipment.
- Light carpentry as needed.
- General cleaning, building security, opening and lock-up.

1984 season   **Bicycle Mechanic**   **ALL-AMERICAN SPORT SHOP**, Oneonta NY
- Repaired and maintained all types of bicycles.
- Fabricated parts as needed.

1979-83   **Auto Mechanic**   **VAN'S AUTO SERVICE**, Oneonta NY
- Repaired and maintained all makes of automobiles and light trucks.
- Developed expertise in brakes, suspension, exhaust, tune-ups, tire repair, mounting and balancing.

1975-79   **Dept. Mgr./Stock Clerk**   **GREAT AMERICAN FOOD STORES,**
Cooperstown NY
- Ordered and rotated stock; generally supervised dairy department.

STEPHEN M. SCOTT
9065 Hillegass Ave.
Berkeley CA 94705
(415) 898-3099

Objective: Entry level position in office support or sales/customer service.

SUMMARY OF QUALIFICATIONS

- Excellent telephone communication skils.
- Friendly, courteous and articulate.
- Take pride in doing a good job; willing to learn.
- Familiar with computer database and word processing.
- General working knowledge of business machines.

RELEVANT EXPERIENCE

Office Experience
- Typed letters, envelopes, labels, and invoices for student publications office.
- Ran copies on Xerox machine; refilled paper and toner.
- Waxed camera-ready copy in preparation for layout of newspaper.
- Completed basic accounting class; familiar with use of calculator.
- Worked as Administrative Assistant at Computers!Computers!:
  -answered phones   -enrolled students in IBM-PC courses.
- Worked on architectural space planning project at City Hall, measuring and recording furniture and work areas on each floor and each department.

Telephone & Communication Skills
- Sold computer training courses by phone for Computers!Computers!
- Filled in as receptionist at Center for Independent Living, handling a heavy load of incoming calls and relaying messages to staff.
- Made over 100 PR calls to businesses for Great Scott Productions.
- Took incoming calls for campus newspaper staff at University of Houston.

Computer Knowledge
- Completed introductory training courses at Computer!Computers! covering...
  -disk operating system   -database   -WordPerfect
- Input 1000 names and addresses into database for Great Scott Productions.

WORK HISTORY

1987 part-time	**Office Assistant**	COMPUTER!COMPUTERS!, SAN FRANCISCO
1986 part-time	**Office Assistant**	Short term jobs (up to 2 weeks) assisting in various PR assignments for ADMARK Corp. and CENTER FOR INDEPENDENT LIVING, Berkeley
"	**Carpentry assistant**	HAL HOWARD FLOOR REFINISHING, Berkeley
1986 1 week	**Inventory Clerk**	BERKELEY CITY HALL, Health & Human Svc. Dept.
1981-85*	**Office Assistant**	STUDENT PUBLICATIONS office* Univ. of Houston

* summer jobs assisting in my father's newspaper publication office

EDUCATION

Completed High School at Bellaire Senior High, Bellaire TX, 1987

SUZANNE WILLOUGHBY

1919 Ward Street
Berkeley CA 94704
(415) 303-7888

**Objective: Embassy administrative support position with Pacific
Architects & Engineers, working in Moscow.**

HIGHLIGHTS OF QUALIFICATIONS

- Degrees in Russian Language/Literature, and International Relations.
- Well versed in Russian culture and proficient in the language.
- Creative and resourceful in planning social activities aimed at welcoming and orienting people to a new community.
- Special talent for analyzing situations and resolving problems.
- Extremely interested in the opportunity to explore, firsthand, the politics and culture of the Soviet Union.

RELEVANT EXPERIENCE

Project Planning and Implementation
- Planned and organized social events for incoming students at Tufts University:
  -identified social and personal needs of students;
  -planned events to address those needs (stress reduction, orientation, etc.);
  -located and contracted with specialists to deliver talks;
  -coordinated with campus facilities to arrange logistics of events.
- Organized and maintained administrative data in a consistent form (food price lists, recipes/menus), minimizing waste and simplifying planning in the dining services unit.
- Successfully established a small business with 4 others, handling vendor licensing, staff scheduling and purchase of equipment and supplies.

Problem Solving & Communication
- Served as vice president of college's Center Board, encouraging communication between campus groups and promoting collaboration in planning activities.
- Mediated between residential staff and university administration over pay and job duty disputes and conflicts, as chair of Residential Advisory Board.

Knowledge of Russian; Language Skills
- Developed a strong historical understanding of the Soviet Union; studies in...
  -Tolstoy and Dostoevsky   -Historical and Political Writings of the Soviet Union
  -World War II   -19th and 20th Century Russian Literature.
- Studied language in classes conducted entirely in Russian; able to converse comfortably in Russian; read and understand Pravda.

WORK HISTORY

1986-present	**Waitress**	BIRKENSTOCK RESTAURANT - Berkeley CA
1981-85	Full-time student	TUFTS UNIVERSITY - Medford MA
1983*	**Research Intern**	CENTER FOR SPACE POLICY - Somerville MA
1982-85*	**Administrative Asst.**	DINING SERVICES, Tufts University
1983-85*	**Resident Assistant**	DEAN OF STUDENTS, Tufts University
1984 summer	**Partner**	JUMBO ICE CREAM, entrepreneurial venture
1979-82*	**Swim Instructor**	PARKS & RECREATION DEPT. - Newtown CT

*parttime

EDUCATION

B.A., Russian Language & Literature/International Relations - 1985
TUFTS UNIVERSITY, Medford MA

SYLVENE PIERCY
390 Wayne Place
Oakland CA 94606
(415) 178-6663

Objective: Office or customer support position involving
project coordinating, problem solving and/or bookkeeping.

HIGHLIGHTS OF QUALIFICATIONS

- Highly reliable self-starter; can be counted on to complete assignments without supervision.
- Sincerely enjoy helping people.
- Creative in cutting costs and solving problems.
- Work well in a busy office handling a wide variety of tasks.

RELEVANT EXPERIENCE

Project Coordinating & Supervising
- Prepared conference rooms for training and administrative sessions: -ordered audio-visual & catering equipment -assembled supplies packets.
- Coordinated large office parties: -prepared guest list and menu -set schedule -ordered furniture & supplies -coordinated set-up/clean-up.
- Oriented new employees; allocated jobs and monitored distribution of work load among clerks working on drafting/engineering team.

Problem Solving/Cost Saving
- Designed efficient reporting form and desk procedure for an engineering firm.
- Researched and found alternative source of needed typewriter for president's secretary, saving the cost of a new purchase.
- Submitted cost-saving ideas implemented by Bechtel Corporation, such as: -proposed reclaiming/recycling desk supplies abandoned by relocated staff; -designed more efficient time sheet which included space for overtime data.

Technical Skill
- Experienced using: -Displaywriter3   -WANG word processor   -Ten-key
- Performed light bookkeeping; monitored records, such as: -reviewed invoices for accuracy -processed invoices and time sheets.
- Completed training in Introduction to Computers.

Customer & Client Services
- Advised customers in selecting and installing ceramic tile.
- Advised employers on choice of fabric, colors, and styles for employee uniforms.

EMPLOYMENT HISTORY

1986-present	**Student, business courses**	Laney College - Oakland
1985	**Data Processing**	EQUITEC Financial Group - Oakland
1982-85	**Work Order Clerk**	BECHTEL CORP. - San Francisco
1979-82	**Manager/Weekends**	CERAMIC TILE SALES - Oakland
1974-78	**Support Group Leader**	BECHTEL CORP. - San Francisco
1971-74	**Manager Trainee**	DUQUETTE KNITS dress mfg. - Oakland

ANDREA GRAHAM
333 San Jose Ave.
San Francisco CA 94110
(415) 689-2468

Objective: Entry level auditing position with a national CPA firm.

HIGHLIGHTS OF QUALIFICATIONS

- Ten years experience in accounting and taxation.
- Highly successful in establishing, streamlining and automating accounting systems.
- Strength in recognizing, analyzing and solving problems.
- Thrive in a dynamic and challenging environment.

PROFESSIONAL EXPERIENCE

Assessment of Financial Records

- Evaluated financial statements for a wide range of clients, both as a staff accountant in a CPA firm, and as a self-employed bookkeeper:
  -conducted thorough examination of clients' financial source documents to assure that proper accounting treatment was applied, and that records were complete;
  -investigated account balances to verify their accuracy and actual existence;
  -generated adjusting journal entries to provide accurate financial statements.

Accounting Systems Design & Implementation

- Assessed the efficiency of small business internal accounting systems, implementing procedures to improve financial accuracy and operating cost-effectiveness. Specific results included: reduced staffing, automated manual records, improved cash collections, trained personnel and developed budgets.

Client Relations/Communication

- Interpreted financial statements for clients, explaining variances in budget analyses and discrepancies in annual comparative statements.
- Maintained excellent client relationships, securing trust and confidence through providing complete, accurate and timely financial services.

EMPLOYMENT HISTORY

1984-present	**Accountant**	LARSONN MANAGEMENT CO., San Francisco
1981-84	**Self-employed Accountant**	A.GRAHAM ACCOUNTING SERVICES, S.F. & S.B.
1980-83	**Staff Accountant**	RICHARD A. BERTI, CPA, Santa Barbara
1979-80	**Full Charge Bookkeeper**	INTERNAT'L TRANSDUCER CORP, Santa Barbara
1976-79	**Staff Accountant**	GUNTERMANN, BALL et al, CPAs, Santa Barbara

EDUCATION

B.A. due 4/88, **Accounting** - GOLDEN GATE UNIVERSITY (3.63 GPA in accounting)

ANTHONY GABRIELLE
2399 Blake Street
Berkeley CA 94704
(415) 313-6602

**Objective: Entry position in financial analysis or customer services
with a major international corporation.**

HIGHLIGHTS OF QUALIFICATIONS

- Expertise in current issues of international economics,
  reinforced by field studies at University of Edinburgh.
- Proven organization, communication and problem solving skills.
- Special aptitude in integrating diverse concepts.
- Natural flair for generating creative, innovative ideas.
- Lifelong interest in researching geography and demography.

RELEVANT EXPERIENCE

ECONOMICS, GEOGRAPHY, DEMOGRAPHY

- Completed extensive course work integrating international economics and politics:
  - International Trade & the EEC
  - Comparative Economic Systems
  - Politics of Global Resource Scarcity
  - US Foreign Policy
  - Middle East & Global Perspective
  - Urban Geography of Great Britain
  - Europe in Crisis (history 1914-1945)
  - Thesis Seminar in International Relations
  - Government and the Economy
  - Third World Politics
  - Soviet Foreign Policy
  - British Public Policy
  - World Military Policy
  - Comparative Political Systems
- Conducted 10 year independent research in geography and demography, acquiring a professional
  level of knowledge in both areas.

RESEARCH

- Conducted long term in-depth research on Western European security issues, using libraries,
  World Affairs Councils, international publications, the Hoover Institution, governmental archives,
  as primary resources.
- Organized, documented and successfully defended a policy-oriented thesis.
- Broadened my understanding of current international issues in history and political economy
  through extensive independent research at National Library of Scotland.

CREATIVE PROBLEM SOLVING

- Greatly improved the effectiveness of merchandise displays at Emporium's Department Store by
  creating more attracive and space-efficient arrangements.
- Devised more cost-effective, safe, and timesaving methods of packing extremely fragile merchandise, for a fast-paced mail-order service.

WORKING UNDER PRESSURE & RESPONSIBILITY

- Successfully integrated the many demanding priorities of a high-pressure, fast-paced restaurant,
  working quickly, efficiently and cooperatively as bus-person.
- Entrusted with daily delivery of highly sensitive and valuable materials (bank statements, deposits, credit cards, vitally important computer print-outs), serving as courier between hospital &
  medical building; maintained spotless driving record.

Continued

ANTHONY GABRIELLE
page two

DIPLOMATIC & LANGUAGE SKILLS

• Played key role in successful negotiation of an international security issue, as member of model UN Security Council, at UC Berkeley:
  -drafted a compromise   -presented it to the Council   -rallied support
  -effectively persuaded reluctant parties to accept the solution.
• Conversational competence in Italian; course work in French and German.

WORK HISTORY
concurrent with fulltime education

1986 summer	Overseas study	in Great Britain
1985	**Warehouse & Delivery**	Kelly Temporary Service assignments
1984 winter	**Stock & Display**	EMPORIUM, via Kelly Temporary Services
1984 summer	**Packing/Shipping**	EMPORIUM - 10th St. Distribution Center, SF
1983	**Busperson/Maintenance**	HARRIS'S RESTAURANT - San Mateo
1981-82	**Delivery/Maintenance**	THE MEDICAL CORP - San Francisco
1980 summer	**Dishwasher/Maintenance**	BIG RIVER CAMP - Sebastopol

EDUCATION

B.A., International Affairs; Minor in History - UNIVERSITY OF CALIFORNIA, Berkeley
5 months overseas study in Great Britain, on political economy.

-References available on request-

Tony makes it clear that all this work history was concurrent with his schooling.

CLAUDIA PETERSON
577 Steiner St.
San Francisco CA 94117
(415) 911-0808

"Maternity leave" and "family manage-ment" present her past priorities and leave no gaps.

Objective: Position as service representative for accounting software firm, specializing in conversions.

HIGHLIGHTS OF QUALIFICATIONS

- Excellent teacher/trainer; patient and effective with a wide range of personalities.
- Successful in identifying and solving computer related problems.
- Project oriented, sticking to a task until completed.
- Sharp in learning and comprehending new systems and methods.
- College level training in accounting, with 3.8 GPA.

RELEVANT EXPERIENCE

Bookkeeping
- Reconciled loan payment records between servicing company &100 lending institutions.
- Reconciled cash records to computer records for over 100 accounts on a monthly basis.
- Prepared monthly payroll, paid bills and processed tuition payments for private preschool.

Teaching/Supervising
- Trained 8 people in investor accounting, most of whom had no previous experience.
- Wrote a step-by-step instruction manual on the daily, weekly and monthly reporting requirements for 50 investors, minimizing training time for new employees.
- Maintained cordial working relations, while explaining and clarifying others' clerical errors.
- Interviewed and hired 4 clerical staff members.

Computer Usage
- Learned and mastered accounting clerk job and computer use in only 2 weeks.
- Worked with computer analyst in development of computerized specialty reports.
- Assisted in implementation of new program on a PC, for accounts payable.
- Input monthly account records on a PC and generated trial balance.

Problem Solving
- Successfully reconstructed investor accountant job from evidence found in desk and files, although no one remaining with the company had any knowledge of this position.
- Balanced 7 months of critical reports for a loan servicing company, involving 350,000 loans in their 6 major accounts, which had been neglected for 5 months.
- Designed an account coding system to eliminate dual coding and to avoid confusion and time wasted correlating reports.
- Reviewed company procedures, identifying sources of high error frequency, and submitted recommendations to supervisors.

EMPLOYMENT HISTORY

1985-86	**Treasurer/Bookkeeper,** part time	FIRST PRES. CHURCH PRESCHOOL, Newark
1984-present	Family management	
1982-83	**Investor Accountant**	FIRST DEED CORP, Walnut Creek
1977-82	Maternity leave	
1976-77	**Acct. Reconciliation,** part time	BALDWIN & HOWELL, San Francisco
1973-76	**Investor Acctng/Supervisor**	MASON-McDUFFIE CO, Berkeley
1971-72	**Cashier/Clerk,** part time	SIERRA COLLEGE BOOKSTORE, Rocklin

EDUCATION
Accounting & Business - ARMSTRONG COLLEGE, Berkeley; SIERRA COLLEGE, Rocklin
Selected as Bank of America Business Award student at Sierra College

DAVID DOUGLAS
245 Central Ave.
San Carlos, CA 94070
work: (415) 372-2000

> David lists each position at the hospital, showing the range of job titles.

Objective: Position as financial analyst, senior accountant, assistant controller, or cost accountant

HIGHLIGHTS OF QUALIFICATIONS
- Strong analytic and problem solving abilities.
- Thorough and well organized in completing projects.
- Thrive on opportunities to assume responsibility.
- Committed to professionalism.
- Academic background in accounting, with 10 years experience.

PROFESSIONAL EXPERIENCE

Accounting
- Completed monthly financial statements.
- Documented restricted funds to clarify amount available and responsibility for distribution.
- Developed strong working knowledge of shared data processing system, and enhanced it:
  - improved accessibility of financial and statistical data for reporting purposes;
  - allowed easier access for non-accounting managers, and for project information.
- Used Lotus 123 on an IBM-XT for a wide variety of applications.

Project Management/Supervision
- Successfully filled in for accounting manager on short notice:
  - assembled work papers for year-end audit and responded to auditors' inquiries;
  - supervised payroll, accounts payable, data processing, cashiering & financial statements.
- Served as Assistant Supervisor in accounts receivable department.

Financial Analysis
- Implemented a new program to develop accurate costs for hospital diagnostic categories, enabling the hospital to develop an equitable reimbursement scheme for contract negotiations:
  - interviewed department heads to establish financial value of procedures;
  - coordinated statistical and financial data from various sources;
  - designed appropriate format, using work sheet program on a PC.

EMPLOYMENT HISTORY

1980-present	**Cost Analyst**	MIDDLETON HOSPITAL, Middleton CA
1978-80	**Financial Analyst**	" " "
1977-78	**Accountant**	" " "
1976-77	**Budget Analyst**	" " "
1975-76	**Accounts Receivable Supv.**	" " "

EDUCATION & PROFESSIONAL AFFILIATION

B.A., Economics - San Francisco State University, 1974
Additional graduate work, and classes in Accounting
Member/Board of Directors, National Association of Accountants

HANNAH CORTLAND
1990 Grand Avenue
Berkeley CA 94703
(415) 220-1990

Objective: Bookkeeper/receptionist position, with emphasis on accounts receivable, office coordination, scheduling, computer data entry

Highlights of Qualifications

- Exceptionally responsible, diligent and thorough.
- Fast learner with a wide range of practical skills.
- Special talent for office organization.
- Excellent verbal and written communication skills.
- Thrive on challenging tasks in a busy office.

RELEVANT EXPERIENCE

Bookkeeping
- Computed and prepared monthly billings for over 100 employment agency clients, achieving a record of exceptional accuracy.
- Maintained records of daily income, and prepared agency's bank deposits.
- Calculated payroll deductions: state/federal taxes, disability, social security.
- Developed monthly Financial Report for Board of Directors of Athena House.

Office Coordination/Scheduling
- Created an efficient filing system for Here's Help Employment Agency, transforming haphazard records into readily retrievable form.
- Coordinated wide range of logistics for office functions:
  -supervised repairs of office equipment   -performed minor repairs & maintenance
  -researched sources/selected new office equipment   -ordered supplies.
- Scheduled screening interviews of job applicants; filled in for Office Manager.
- Responded by mail to employer requests for insurance related information; devised form letter for responding to inquiries from potential job applicants.
- Designed and produced promotional brochure for employment agency:
  -edited text -arranged for typesetting -laid out graphics.

Computer Data Entry
- Accurately entered personnel data for over 1000 applicants, using customized computer program; updated and maintained each applicant's records.
- Taught myself computerized word processing and basic spread sheet, and taught other employees to use business programs.

EMPLOYMENT HISTORY

1985-present	**Receptionist/Bookkeeper**	HERE'S HELP INC. employment agency, San Francisco
1980-84	**Housekeeper**	Self-employed - East Bay clients
1978-80	**Bookkeeping trainee**	ATHENA HOUSE residential treatment, Santa Rosa
1977	**Accts.Payable/Cashier**	COMMUNITY MARKET COOPERATIVE, Santa Rosa
1976	**Produce Buyer**	OUR SMALL PLANET RESTAURANT, Santa Rosa

EDUCATION

Interdisciplinary Studies - Sonoma State University 1974-77

KATHERINE LAWRENCE
1490 Acton Street
Berkeley CA 94702
(415) 488-1546

OBJECTIVE: Position as Full Charge Bookkeeper

SUMMARY OF QUALIFICATIONS
★ Can be counted on to get the job done.
★ Five years accounting experience, including automated general ledger.
★ BA degree plus 2 years education in Basic Accounting.
★ Thoroughly familiar with all general accounting procedures.
★ Highly valued and effective supervisor as well as co-worker.

PROFESSIONAL EXPERIENCE
Automated Accounting
• Analyzed financial statements, produced reports, input data on an on-line computer system, for a retail business.
• Posted to a general ledger and generated monthly and annual reports.
• Converted a manual payroll system (NCR posting machine) to a computer system.
• Operated an automated accounts payable system covering approximately 120 accounts, paid weekly, bi-weekly and monthly.

General Accounting
• Mastered a variety of accounting systems such as owner's draw system, merchandise invoice system, report-on-demand system, shared expenditure schedule, and individual store inventory audits.
• Accomplished all accounting activities for a small retail glass business, including financial statements, accounts payable, accounts receivable and payroll.
• Reconciled bank statements for both retail and wholesale businesses, involving over $1 million a month.
• Maintained materials inventory and handled purchasing for a retail outlet.
• Monitored payroll system for approximately 60 factory workers in 4 unions.

Supervision & Management
• Supervised 3 junior accounting clerks and audited their accuracy.
• Trained 12 junior accounting clerks and 2 managerial trainees in retail accounting.
• Organized and taught classes, including development of class materials; assisted in teaching an elementary accounting course.
• Researched and organized documents of manual payroll system going back 7 years.
• Monitored for full data accuracy in an automated payroll system covering 32 retail outlets.

EMPLOYMENT HISTORY
1980-now	**Senior Accounting Clerk**	Southland Corp., Corte Madera CA
1978-1979	**Payroll Clerk**	Lawley Manufacturing Co., Emeryville CA
1978-1980	**Bookkeeper & Instructor**	Stained Glass Garden Inc., Berkeley CA
1977-1978	**Inventory & Sales Clerk**	New Renaissance Glass Works, Oakland
1976-1977	**Teaching Assistant**	Napa College, Napa CA
1973-1975	**Supply Clerk**	US Army, Monterey CA

EDUCATION & TRAINING
B.A. in Linguistics, 1974   University of Michigan
Accounting Program, Napa College   COBOL Programming, University of California
Technical Skills: Ten Key, Keypunch, BASIC, COBOL, FORTRAN, NCR posting machine

LORNA BURLINGAME
1835a Broderick St.
San Francisco CA 94115
(415) 122-6754

Objective: Financial Consultant with an investment advisory company

HIGHLIGHTS OF QUALIFICATIONS
- Thrive on challenge, new opportunities for accomplishment and success in helping others achieve their objectives.
- Readily inspire the confidence and trust of clients.
- Extensive knowledge of financial instruments.
- Sharp analytic, problem solving and presentation skills.
- Legal background and training.

PROFESSIONAL EXPERIENCE

Financial Planning
- Developed customized financial plans for Merrill Lynch clients:
  -clarified their most immediate objectives and longer term goals;
  -assessed their financial resources and tolerance for risk;
  -explored various investment options and structured plans consistent with their experience, obligations, resources and risk temperament.
- Implemented and periodically updated financial plans, keeping clients appraised of the status of their investments.

Research, Analysis & Evaluation
- Researched and analyzed various investment instruments:
  -stocks -bonds -convertible bonds -mutual funds -CDs -insurance products.
- Researched market conditions affecting clients' current & future financial strategies.
- Developed a sharply defined, critical mode of evaluating clients needs and analyzing investment instruments/strategies, as a result of legal experience and training.

Communication/Presentation
- Delivered presentations on various retirement plans and on mutual funds to professional associations and private investment groups.
- Successfully mediated and guided individuals with divergent interests to reach agreements, thus avoiding litigation.
- Generated a high level of referrals from previous investment clients.

EMPLOYMENT HISTORY

1986-present	**Attorney**	DAVIS & ROWAN, attys - San Francisco
1985-86	**Financial Consultant**	MULHADY, PRUITT & PRICE, attys - San Francisco
1984-85	**Law Clerk**	PARKER, ACACIA, BLAIR & HOWARD - SF
1984	**Mediator/Arbitrator**	COMMUNITY DISPUTE SERVICES - SF
1983-84	**Judicial Extern**	SAN JOSE SUPERIOR COURT - San Jose

EDUCATION
J.D., UNIVERSITY OF SANTA CLARA LAW SCHOOL, 1984
B.A., Psychology, UNIVERSITY OF CALIFORNIA, at SANTA CRUZ, 1980

LICENSES & AFFILIATIONS
Series 7 Brokerage Securities License
State Bar of California, License & Membership • Amer. Bar Assoc.: Family Law Section
San Francisco Chamber of Commerce • Junior League of San Francisco

LYNNE JOUSSART

299 Oakland Avenue #102
Oakland CA 94610
453-2104

Lynne didn't complete her degree work, but she does tell what her academic major was.

OBJECTIVE: Part-time position in business management, financial planning and full-charge bookkeeping

HIGHLIGHTS OF QUALIFICATIONS

★ Strong grasp of accounting; experienced in all phases of accounting.
★ 10 years experience in the business world .
★ Successful in translating long-range organizational objectives into effective financial plans.
★ Set up 4 businesses and designed their bookkeeping systems.
★ Worked with nonprofit fund accounting.

PROFESSIONAL EXPERIENCE

Financial Planning

• Produced budgets and cash flow projections for several nonprofit organizations.
• Developed detailed financial plans for 2 businesses.
  - assisted management in refining their corporate goals.
  - generated the financial data to complete a business plan.

Bookkeeping & Accounting

• Performed full charge bookkeeping through financial statements:
  - payroll and payroll taxes   - cash receipts and disbursements
  - accounts receivable & billing   - bank reconciliations
  - accounts payable   - inventory control
• Prepared corporate and property tax returns for 3 nonprofits.
• Generated financial statements for small businesses on a Northstar computer.

Business Management

• Set up the initial books for 4 new businesses, and filed their incorporation papers.
• Extensively analyzed financial statements for small corporations.
• Filed periodic financial reports to supporting foundations.

EMPLOYMENT HISTORY

1984-present	**Financial Consultant**	URSA INSTITUTE & affiliates - San Francisco
	(large nonprofit firm in business consulting and social research)	
	Financial Consultant	NATIONAL ALLIANCE AGAINST VIOLENCE, Inc. - Oakland
1982-1985	**Business Manager**	LIVE OAK INSTITUTE - Oakland
		(training programs in nursing homes)
1982-1984	**Full Charge Bookkeeper**	BERKEY & ASSOC. - Berkeley
		(bookkeeping and consulting service)
1979-1981	**Part-time & Consulting Bookkeeper** - for 5 Boston area firms	
1977-1979	**Grain Buyer**	NEFCO - Cambridge MA (coop. regional warehouse)
1975-1976	**General Manager/Founder**	BUFFALO MOUNTAIN COOP - Hardwick VT

EDUCATION
Accounting - Northeastern University 1980
Liberal Arts - Goddard College 1974-75

MS. MUNANA FEHRESHTA

335 Turling Boulevard
El Cerrito CA 94530
(415) 771-1212 home
(415) 773-6984 work

Objective: Entry level staff position in a public accounting firm.

QUALIFICATIONS & ACHIEVEMENTS

- Excellent team worker; function well under pressure.
- Deeply committed, professional attitude.
- Turned a $5,000 loss into a $10,000 net profit for a retail coffee business.
- Set up a second business which was immediately profitable.
- Passed all 4 parts of the CPA examination at first sitting.

PROFESSIONAL EXPERIENCE

Auditing
- Conducted a review of lending institution's records:
  -selected random sample of transactions;
  -conducted compliance testing;
  -drafted final report for the client.

Accounting & Taxes
- Prepared quarterly payroll and sales taxes for over 50 individuals.
- Filed corporate taxes for 3 corporations.
- Reconciled bank statements to clients' books.
- Reconstructed accounting records from clients' checks and cash receipts.

Computer Use
- Posted clients' journals to computer, made adjusting journal entries, and created general ledgers.
- Generated financial statements and accountant compilation and review notes.
- Worked with a variety of computers: Apple, Radio Shack, Osborne and Astrow.
- Currently customizing a Multiplan program for two small businesses.

Research
- Researched in CCH for small business tax planning.
- Searched out-of-state tax codes relevant to client's income tax.

Business consultation
- Advised 2 retailers on:
  -most advantageous timing of major equipment purchases;
  -cash flow alternatives and comparative sources of investment capital;
  -options for minimizing federal tax.

EMPLOYMENT HISTORY

Current	**Junior Accountant**	TOM DREYER, CPA - Pleasant Hill CA
1982-86	**Manager**	EL CERRITO COFFEE MILL - retail coffee
1986	**Manager** (concurrently)	TOM SHAMSI SERVICE - office machines servicing

EDUCATION
B.S., Accounting, 1985 - ARMSTRONG UNIVERSITY, Berkeley

PREM SIRI KAUR KHALSA
59912 Le Conte
Berkeley CA 94709
(415) 888-6867

Objective: Accounting position, including financial consultation and training

HIGHLIGHTS OF QUALIFICATIONS

- 12 years experience in bookkeeping for small businesses and corporations.
- Thrive on consulting with clients, helping them get what they want.
- Commitment to professional growth and development in financial services.
- Outstanding talent for assessing clients' needs and developing individualized financial systems.
- Extremely dependable in completing projects accurately and on time.

RELEVANT EXPERIENCE

Bookkeeping & Accounting
- Served as full-charge bookkeeper and financial manager for several businesses:
  -general ledger   -cash disbursements journal   -cash receipts journal
  -payroll and payroll taxes -accounts payable -accounts receivable
  -bank reconciliation -budgeting -financial statements.
- Consulted with CPAs on behalf of businesses, presenting all financial materials to prepare for end-of-year taxes.

Needs Assessment/Advising
- Successfully advised & counseled small business clients on financial strategy, employing effective counseling methods:
  -developed trust and rapport through attentive listening, showing interest;
  -combined candid assessment of current status with proposals for improving profitability.
- Counseled individuals and couples on family and health issues.

Organization/Administration
- Trained and supervised novice bookkeepers in bookkeeping skills.
- Advised on and implemented start-up procedures for small businesses in the State of California, involving business license, bank account, fictitious name statement, resale number, state and federal employer ID number, etc.
- Served as financial officer on committees and boards of both profit and non-profit organizations.
- Established my own financial bookkeeping service.

EMPLOYMENT HISTORY

1985-86	Owner/Consultant	FINANCIAL STRATEGIES, Berkeley (serving 8 small business clients)
1983-86	Co-Owner/Financial Mgr.	ORIENTAL BEAUTY SECRETS, Berkeley
1981-85	Financial Manager/Counselor	G.R.D. CHIROPRACTIC, Albany
1979-81	Chiropractic Asst./Bookkeeper	JANET RUEGER CHIROPRACTOR, Berkeley
1978-79	Bookkeeper	HOWARD TRAVEL AGENCY, Oakland
1975-86	Financial Advisor	K.W.T.C. SUMMER CAMP, New Mexico
1974-86	Treasurer/Bookkeeper	SIKH DHARMA and 3HO ORGANIZATION

EDUCATION & TRAINING
B.A., Communication Arts & Sciences - QUEENS COLLEGE, New York City 1973
M.S. candidate, Clinical Psychology - JFK UNIVERSITY, Orinda CA
Class in General Accounting - VISTA COLLEGE, Berkeley 1986

SUZANNE CHEW

Campus Address:
2230 Haste St., Apt. 999
Berkeley, CA 94704
(415) 523-7867

Alternate Address:
226 Calamari Court
Concord, CA 94521
(415) 907-0742

OBJECTIVE: ENTRY LEVEL POSITION IN AUDIT DEPARTMENT

HIGHLIGHTS OF QUALIFICATIONS

★ Dedicated to professionalism, highly motivated toward goal achievement.
★ Successful in mastering accounting theory and technical skills.
★ 3 years demonstrated effectiveness in interpersonal communications.
★ Experience in coordinating projects involving people and activities.

EDUCATION & TRAINING

B.S., Accounting - University of California, Berkeley - May 1988
Honor student since Fall semester 1985
Accounting G.P.A. 4.0 - Overall G.P.A. 3.685

AFFILIATIONS

U.C. Berkeley Honor Society
Professional Women's Association
Undergraduate Business Association

EXPERIENCE & SKILLS

Technical and Business Knowledge

• Developed solid theoretical grounding in financial accounting; able to set up balance sheets and income statements, and analyze clients' assets and liabilities.
• Studied laws relevant to accounting and other business applications.
• Edited market research interviews; entered coded data into computer and generated reports.

Leadership/Coordination

• Developed the confidence of owners of market research firm, and was invited to assume more responsibility through a supervisory position.
• Coordinated focus group studies for a market research firm: invited prospective group members by phone; provided refreshments and study materials.
• Organized participation in a soccer team: contacted prospective players and got commitment to participate; maintained attendance records, statistics at games, medical/equipment inventory.

Communications and Interpersonal Skills

• Persuaded shoppers to volunteer time for in-person market research interviews.
• Solicited phone interviews from random samples, consistently convincing participants of the legitimacy of the project and the importance of their opinions.
• Gave oral evaluations of market research interviews, to clients from ad agencies.
• Collaborated with co-workers to assure consistent coding of research materials.
• Currently advise students on problems in accounting classes; grade homework.

WORK HISTORY

1987 fall	**Reader**	UC BERKELEY BUSINESS SCHOOL - Berkeley CA
1986 summer	**Sales Clerk**	SHOE CITY - Cornwall CA
June'85-Aug'86	**Interviewer**	PDQ MARKETING RESEARCH - Walnut Creek CA
Apr'83-Mar'85	**Interviewer**	WESTERN QUICK SEARCH - Cornwall CA

SONIA MORENA
69 Sixth Avenue
San Francisco CA 94109
411-2675

Sonia describes the US equivalent of her Guatemalan degree.

OBJECTIVE: Position managing an Accounts Receivable/Payable Department

SUMMARY OF QUALIFICATIONS

★ Over 10 years experience in Accounting.
★ Can adapt immediately to any accounting system.
★ Outstanding talent in problem solving.
★ Ability to work independently.
★ Competent with computers: IBM system 3 & 34
  Hewlett-Packard, Marketron, and others.

PROFESSIONAL EXPERIENCE

Accounting Analysis

• Made transitions from hand-operated systems to computerized systems, and from one computer system to another.
• Set up initial accounting systems for 5 small businesses and trained their staff to maintain it.
• Reconstructed accounting records lost in a fire, analyzing and reorganizing materials from vendors' files in several different states; the company was able to recover all the monies due.
• Competence in all accounting aspects:

-accounts payable	-personnel	-credit management
-accounts receivable	-payroll	-expense reports audit
-general ledger	-sales commissions	
-financial statements	-capital accounts (assets)	

Communication & Client Relations

• Established cooperative relationships with institutions (banks, credit associations) to get credit information quickly.
• Reduced bad debts from 33% to 1.5% by finding ways clients could clear up old debts and reinstate their credit with the company.

EMPLOYMENT HISTORY

1987-now	**Accountant**	Temp. assignment, Reed Advertising, San Francisco
1983-86	**Accountant**	KXYZ Radio, San Francisco
1979-82	**Accountant**	KBHK-TV44, San Francisco
1970-79	**Accountant**	KSFO Radio, San Francisco
1969-70	**Accounts Receivable**	Swank-Bechelli Leather Wholesaler, San Francisco

EDUCATION

B.S. equivalent - Business Administration - Escuela de Comercio, Guatemala
Postgraduate study: Accounting - Boston University
Bilingual in Spanish & English; US citizen

CHRISTINE GADE
998 Vincente Ave
Reno NV
(702) 615-6755

Objective: Project Supervision & Purchasing for new construction or remodeling of a multi-unit hotel, casino, office or apartment complex.

HIGHLIGHTS OF QUALIFICATIONS

- Highly skilled in purchasing, and fine-tuning of FF&E* specifications.
- Proven record for maintaining schedules; never missed a deadline.
- Effective negotiator and decision maker; direct, clear and confident in managing multi-million dollar expenditures.
- Building Dept. background; broad knowledge of building and fire codes.
- Dedicated professional attitude, committed to getting the job done.

REPRESENTATIVE SKILLS & ACCOMPLISHMENTS

Coordination/Supervision

- Successfully coordinated elements of interior finish work, maintaining project schedules with minimal impact on hotel operations and revenues.
- Coordinated complex interfacing of subcontractors for complete guest room finishing: ie, carpet layers, painters, electricians, furniture movers, drapery installers, etc.
- Served as emergency project trouble-shooter, interpreting blueprints and making decisions on last minute design details and changes.

Purchasing

- Purchased guest room, office and public area furnishings:
  -furniture for guest tower, lobby, casino and convention center;
  -carpeting, wall coverings, lighting fixtures, drapes, bedspreads.
- Researched and found excellent cost-effective alternatives to specified draperies and bedspreads for the new Benson's Casino 350-room guest tower:
  -identified inherently flameproof fabric, not requiring annual FR treatment;
  -met aesthetic and maintenance criteria, greatly reducing cost of upkeep.
- Located best vendor for wall covering materials, reducing the complexity of purchasing and increasing the value-per-dollar, with no sacrifice to aesthetics.

Contract Negotiation/Compliance

- Authored and rewrote specifications, as needed, for bidding purposes.
- Protected owner's financial interests during the bidding process:
  -maintained the integrity of bidding procedures, with equitable access to information;
  -warned prospective bidders of the consequences of unethical practices.
- Enforced contract compliance for installation of fixtures, furnishings and equipment, carefully monitoring quantity and quality of both labor and materials.

Knowledge of Codes

- Reviewed specs in detail, identifying items potentially not in compliance with codes.
- Submitted alternative finishing materials for approval of State Fire Marshal.
- Negotiated with State of Nevada officials to clarify code standards in absence of established guidelines.

- Continued -

EMPLOYMENT HISTORY

1986-present	**FF&E* Administrator**	BENSON'S RESORT HOTEL/CASINO, Reno NV
1985	**Project Assistant**	BENSON'S RESORT HOTEL/CASINO, Reno NV
1981-84	**Administrative Assistant**	BUILDING DEPT., DOUGLAS COUNTY, Minden NV
1975-80	**Office Manager**	BILOTTI TRUCKING CO., Stockton CA

(*Fixtures, Furnishing & Equipment)

EDUCATION

B.A., English - UNIVERSITY OF OREGON, Eugene OR

- References available on request -

CORONET GIBSON-BLAIR

1416 Acton Street
Berkeley CA 94702
(415) 838-6755

Objective: Position as Coordinator of Research Services for CSPP

HIGHLIGHTS OF QUALIFICATIONS

- 5 years experience as data manager using CMS and SPSSX at UC Berkeley.
- Outstanding teacher; taught several RAs to use the UC computer.
- Background in psychology.
- Skill in refining and translating researchers' goals into computer languages.
- Dependable and conscientious; accurate at detail work.
- Easy to work with; a cooperative and supportive colleague.

RELEVANT EXPERIENCE

Data Management
- Created and maintained highly accurate social science database for UC Psychology
  Department's Stress & Coping Project, directed by Richard Lazarus:
  -assisted researchers in phrasing questions to assure useable data;
  -supervised interviewers' field work;
  -designed coding manuals and supervised coding and data entry;
  -cleaned data; prepared code books for documentation and ready access to data.

Teaching/Training
- Successfully taught computer logic to Research Assts. who had no previous experience.
- Trained psychology students in editing and file management under CMS operating system.
- Taught RAs the detailed use of SPSSX software, including:
  -how to translate research goals into concrete commands
  -how to de-bug their own programs
  -how to effectively use the SPSSX manual.
- Assisted faculty in establishing research goals consistent with the data available.

Use of UC Computer Services
- Effectively consulted with UC Computer Center's technical consultants to resolve a wide
  range of problems.
- Opened and renewed CMS accounts on the UC system, including faculty approval and
  allocation of disk space.

Related Skills
- Working knowledge of UNIX system, and SAS & BMDP software packages.
- Used Lotus 1-2-3 on the IBM-XT as consultant for UC faculty.

EMPLOYMENT HISTORY

1980-present	**Staff Research Associate,** Stress & Coping Project	PSYCHOLOGY DEPT., UC Berkeley
1972-80	**Research Assistant**	SOCIAL ACTION RESEARCH CENTER, San Rafael CALIFORNIA CONNECTION, Berkeley INST. FOR RESEARCH IN SOCIAL BEHAVIOR, Berkeley
1967-74	**Research Assistant**	Prof. P.W. Sperlich, UCB Political Science Dept.

EDUCATION & TRAINING
B.A., Psychology - UC BERKELEY
Graduate studies: Clinical Psychology, UCB - Elements of FORTRAN, UC Extension

NORMAN WHITMORE
1717 Rutgers Avenue
Oakland CA 94602
(415) 657-3201

Objective: Scientific/technical writing position with a corporation or university.

HIGHLIGHTS OF QUALIFICATIONS

★ Highly effective in communicating with engineers and technicians, and translating scientific information into everyday language.
★ Drafted user and features guides for technical products and systems.
★ Analyzed corporate telecommunications needs and wrote customized proposals.
★ Successfully managed and developed major telecommunications accounts.
★ Published writer; 7 years experience in university teaching.

PROFESSIONAL EXPERIENCE

Writing
• Produced reports and business plans for management, and proposals for clients.
• Wrote users' guides and feature summary sheets for electronic equipment.
• Authored book, articles and reviews; edited textbook series.

Technical Analysis and Presentation
• Diplomatically identified and integrated the diverse telecommunications needs of senior management and their engineering, legal, financial and marketing support staff. Followed up with oral and written presentation of customized proposals for their consideration.
• Analyzed the capabilities and features of new electronic equipment and products for their marketability to distributors and the buying public.

Project Management
• Independently developed successful marketing plans for telecommunications manufacturer, which quadrupled sales in the western U.S.
• Reported to corporate management, summarizing opportunities and problems with new products and recommending marketing and technical improvements.
• Supervised and trained sales representatives.
• Trained client staffs and sales teams in the use of new technical equipment.
• Discovered and developed profitable new market of previously unaffiliated independent phone companies, through extensive field research.

EMPLOYMENT HISTORY

1983-present	**Manager-Distribution Sales**	BRUENER COMMUNICATIONS, San Mateo CA
1982-83	**National Accounts Executive**	BEAM CORP, Digital Telephone Systems Div., San Mateo CA
1981-82	**Major Account Executive**	ULTRA DYNAMICS COMMUNICATIONS CO., Foster City CA
1979-81	**Senior Sales Representative**	XEROX CORPORATION, San Carlos CA
1971-79	**Lecturer in History**	UNIVERSITY OF SYDNEY, Sydney, Australia

EDUCATION

Ph.D. - German History - University of Wisconsin
M.A. - Economic History - University of California, Berkeley
B.A. - Economic History - Rutgers University

MARK EBRAHIMI
89 Twelfth Street, Apt. 144
Oakland CA 94607
(415) 575-0734

Mark presents a smooth blending of work history and education in Iran and the US.

TECHNICAL & COMPUTERS

Objective: Position in Telecommunications

HIGHLIGHTS OF QUALIFICATIONS

- Extensive knowledge of repair problems for both old and new telephone systems.
- Sincerely enjoy the challenge of providing high quality direct service to clients.
- Personally committed to supporting the institution of the University.
- Can be trusted to handle end-user complaints diplomatically and efficiently.

PROFESSIONAL EXPERIENCE

Customer Service
- Received and successfully handled thousands of repair calls from university departments:
  -screened calls and made preliminary technical assessment of the problems;
  -referred calls to appropriate vendors...
    ...Pac Bell for line problems ...AT&T for set problems ...new vendors for new electronic sets
  -followed through aggressively with vendors to assure that good service is delivered.
- Reduced university time and expense on repair orders by:
  -minimizing time spent on each incoming call;
  -providing increased level of technical advice to telephone users on appropriate use of features of their new electronic sets.

Technical Skills
- Researched technical information using:
  -CENPAC computer terminal to identify line features;
  -technical manuals to assist in diagnosing line problems.
- Implemented new comprehensive record keeping system, documenting the repair history of each phone line, as well as their disposition codes, to increase the quality of service.
- Referred data line problems to appropriate vendors.
- Inspected pagers, making preliminary diagnosis, and referred repairs to vendors.

EMPLOYMENT HISTORY

1985-present	**Telecommunications Rep**	Univ. of Oregon, Telecommunications Dept.
1984-85	**Tech. Clerk/Telecommunications**	Univ. of Oregon, Telecommunications Dept.
1983	**Teacher** of English as a 2nd Lang.	Iran/America Society - Tehran, Iran
1975-83	**Translator/Interpreter**	Bureau of Translators - Tehran, Iran
1973-75	**Telemedia Supervisor/Teacher**	Bell Helicopter - Tehran, Iran
1971-73	**Teacher** of English as a 2nd Lang.	Air Force Language Academy - Tehran, Iran

EDUCATION & CREDENTIALS

B.A., Psychology 1978 - Teacher Training University - Tehran, Iran
California Community College Teaching Credential 1984
Completed programming course in BASIC, Univ. of Oregon Extension
Tri-lingual in English, Spanish, Persian

JOHN BRIDGES
97 Foothill Lane
Berkeley CA 94705
(415) 990-3466

Objective: Research Associate position with a biotechnology firm / basic research lab focusing on immunology and product development.

HIGHLIGHTS OF QUALIFICATIONS
- Highly inquisitive, creative and resourceful.
- Excellent skills in communication and collaboration.
- Skilled in all phases of hybridoma production.
- Good working knowledge of immunology.
- Excited by the challenge of research and experimentation.

RELEVANT SKILLS and ACCOMPLISHMENTS

Applied Research
- Successfully developed new antibodies for use in breast cancer research & therapy:
  -experimented with antigen preparation and immunization routines, resulting in the desired immune response;
  -carefully monitored the antisera to ensure presence of desired B-cell population;
  -tailored screening strategies using ELISA, RIA and Immunoblot techniques, to effectively isolate the desired hybridomas.
- Developed, in collaboration with others, a novel assay which identified the antibodies' ability to bind to live, intact tumor cells.
- Delivered periodic presentations of results and works in progress, to staff of Cancer Research Institute.

Innovation/Exploration
- Pursued unique opportunities for experimentation, for example:
  -researched and worked out procedures for in vitro immunization of human lymphocytes;
  -explored and experimented with hybridoma production, using lymph node cells of a cancer patient;
  -experimented to induce animals' immune system to respond to a weak antigen.

Lab Skills
- SDS-PAGE Electrophoresis
- Radiolabeling of Antibodies
- Tissue Culture
- Affinity Chromatography
- Immunoblot Strip Assay
- Hamster Egg Penetration Test
- Electroblotting
- Lyophilization
- Isotyping

EMPLOYMENT HISTORY

1984-present	**Lab Technician**	SCHILLING CANCER RESEARCH INST., Berkeley
1980-84	**Full time student**	UC Santa Barbara
'83 summer	**Research Asst.**	UC Santa Barbara Biology Dept.
1979	**Youth Counselor**	RAINBOW RIVER DAY CARE PROGRAM, Los Angeles
1978	**Emergency Med Tech**	SEALS AMBULANCE, Costa Mesa
1977	**Teaching Asst.**	ALTA VISTA ELEM. SCHOOL, Redondo Beach

EDUCATION
B.A., Cell Biology & Physiology - UNIVERSITY OF CALIFORNIA, SANTA BARBARA, 1984
Related coursework: **Immunology & Lab, Biochemistry, Virology, Microbiology**

- References available upon request -

LARRY B. ELTON
2330 Blake Street.
Berkeley CA 94704
(415)437-4288

Objective: Senior position in engineering management

HIGHLIGHTS OF QUALIFICATIONS

- Business oriented; able to understand and execute broad corporate policy.
- Strength in analyzing and improving engineering and administrative methods.
- Effective in facilitating communication between management and project team.
- Proven ability to manage both large and small groups and maintain productivity.
- Successful in negotiating favorable design and construction contracts.

PROFESSIONAL EXPERIENCE

Management
- Developed innovative, cost-effective concept in project management of specialty chemical plant, assigning the design engineering to outside contractors.
- Supervised recruitment and staffing of over 40 project team professionals.
- Wrote detailed execution plans for major design and construction projects, involving:
  -project staffing   -preliminary schedule   -preliminary cost estimate
  -engineering drawings-construction contractor selection -definitive cost estimate
  -approvals of contractor construction plans.
- Wrote comprehensive summary for senior level management, incorporating monthly reports from specialty engineering, project engineering, and construction management.

Construction Management
- Wrote 800-page Construction Management Guide documenting standardized construction procedures and reporting.
- Increased productivity 12% by introducing a popular 4-day/48-hour workweek alternative.
- Successfully headed off loss of over a million dollars, due to potential business failure of primary contractor, by negotiating directly with subcontractors.

Engineering / Product Development
- Conceived and patented highly profitable design for a Refrigerant Recovery System which realized a profit of over $15 million in a period of 5 years.
- Trained 25 skilled salespeople to effectively demonstrate patented equipment to various industries.

EMPLOYMENT HISTORY

1979-present	**Project Manager**	ATLANTIC RICHFIELD CO - Walnut Creek CA
1977-79	**Project Manager**	ALLIED CHEMICAL CO (now Allied Signal) - Morristown NJ
1974-76	**Project Engineer**	SUN OIL CO - (now Sun Co) - Philadelphia PA
1967-74	**Engineer**	PENNWALT CORP - Philadelphia PA
1964-67	**Captain**	U.S. Army Infantry

EDUCATION

B.Sc. Ch.E., Chemical Engineering - UNIVERSITY OF WASHINGTON, Seattle WA
Graduate studies - PENNSYLVANIA STATE UNIVERSITY and TEMPLE UNIVERSITY

LYDIA SILVERS

912 Blue Mountain Rd.
San Ramon, CA 94583
(415) 783-6221

**Objective: Position as a developmental or applications engineer,
for new plastics products or packaging**

HIGHLIGHTS OF QUALIFICATIONS

- Strong education and training in plastics engineering.
- Goal oriented, creative and resourceful.
- Proven effectiveness in coordinating and teamwork.
- Communicate equally well with technical and business staff.
- Enthusiastic and quick learner.

PROFESSIONAL EXPERIENCE

Design/Development

- Custom designed an innovative package for a new product which was more effective and had more commercial shelf impact, at a cost savings over proposed alternatives.
- Developed effective interim solution to packaging problem which could be applied immediately without disrupting ongoing marketing.
- Designed 6 packaging/advertising label options that provided needed billboard effect, and which were both commercially feasible and cost-effective.

Teamwork/Communication

- Improved working communication among technical center departments by organizing a product/package compatibility Task Force, which was able to predict, solve and avoid problems by pooling their knowledge.
- Acted as technical liaison, coordinating package development with product development, process development, marketing research, advertising, analytical, regulatory, quality assurance, legal, buying, manufacturing, contract packers, and outside suppliers.

Project Administration

- Successfully organized a packaging project in record time to meet a marketing deadline:
  -developed project time line   -researched materials   -wrote specifications
  -located suppliers   -coordinated in-house departments and outside vendors
- Supervised, trained and evaluated:
  -summer intern   -technical assistant   -temporary technicians
- Qualified materials, suppliers and contract packers; and wrote specifications.

-Continued-

LYDIA SILVERS
page two

WORK HISTORY

1982-present	**Packaging Engineer**	THE CLOROX CO - Oak Hill CA
1977-82	graduate student	University of Lowell - Lowell MA
1977-79	**Teaching Assistant**	PLASTICS MATERIAL TESTING LAB - Univ. of Lowell
1975-77	undergrad student	University of Lowell - Lowell MA
"	**Office Assistant**	Offices of REGISTRAR & ENGINEERING DEPT.
1972-75	full-time parenting	
1968-71	undergrad student	Lowell Technological Institute - Lowell MA
1971	**Night Manager** part time	CAMPUS SANDWICH SHOP - Lowell MA
"	**Building Manager**	CAMELOT COURT apartment complex - Lowell MA
1970 summer	**Supervising Inspector**	SAUNDERS ASSOC., electronics - Nashua NH
1969 summer	**Electronics Assembler**	RAYTHEON CO - Lowell MA

EDUCATION & AFFILIATIONS

M.S., Plastics Engineering - University of Lowell 1982
B.S., Plastics Engineering - University of Lowell 1977
Member, Society of Plastics Engineers
Graduate courses:
-Polymer Structure, Properties and Applications
-Product Design   -Adhesives and Adhesion
-Plastics Processing Theory   -Coatings

Fulltime parenting and student status are spelled out here, to present a no-gaps work history.

MICHAEL HAYAKAWA

345 Thornhill Drive
San Francisco CA 94141
(415) 212-4444

Objective: Position as Director of Imaging Services

HIGHLIGHTS OF QUALIFICATIONS

- Special talent for establishing rapport with both management and support staff.
- Highly effective in developing a positive and productive work environment.
- Ability to get the job done, hold expenses down, and increase profitability.

REPRESENTATIVE SKILLS AND ACCOMPLISHMENTS

Supervision and Employee Relations
- Upgraded staff skill level and productivity, and minimized staff turnover:
  -designed more effective in-service and cross-training programs;
  -demonstrated a strong personal interest in individuals' skill development.
- Increased staff morale and built team spirit through strong support of productive staff members.
- Served actively as Board member of employee Credit Union, contributing financial and managerial expertise.

Marketing and Profitability
- Steadily increased contribution margin of radiology department.
- Increased outpatient referral rate 15% by providing same-day diagnostic report.
- Introduced mammography screening to the spectrum of department services; developed a marketing/pricing strategy resulting in immediate increase in referrals.

Planning and Development
- Installed new GE 9800 Quick CT Scanner:
  -evaluated all options and selected the GE for its diagnostic capabilities;
  -oversaw installation, working with architects and construction crews;
  -coordinated and arranged for interim CT service during installation;
  -designed and implemented in-service training on new scanner.
- Advised on the installation of a new radiology department computer system, and the subsequent in-service training for staff.

EMPLOYMENT HISTORY

1981-present	**Radiology Dept. Manager**	SPAULDING MEMORIAL HOSPITAL, Oakland
1979-80	Full-time student	UCLA
1974-78*	**Evening Supervisor**	LOS GATOS-SARATOGA COMMUNITY HOSPITAL
1974-78*	**Evening Supervisor**	SANTA TERESA COMMUNITY HOSP., San Jose
1973	**Staff Technologist**	BROADWAY HOSPITAL, Vallejo
1969-72	**Asst. Chief Technologist**	DAVID GRANT MEDICAL CENTER, Travis AFB
	*concurrently	

EDUCATION

M.B.A., Management - UNIVERSITY OF CALIFORNIA, BERKELEY
B.S., Business Administration - UNIVERSITY OF CALIFORNIA, LOS ANGELES

PROFESSIONAL AFFILIATIONS

•American Hospital Radiology Administrators •Calif. Society of Radiologic Technologists
•Certified Radiologic Technologist •American Registry of Radiologic Technologists

PAMELA DREYFUSS
5670 Forrest Ave.
Oakland CA 94609
(415) 888-53311

Note the easy-to-scan overview of Pamela's instrument knowledge.

Objective: Position as chemist in an analytical or research lab
applying my expertise with gas chromatography, specializing in hydrocarbon analysis.

HIGHLIGHTS OF QUALIFICATIONS

★ Extensive experience in gas analysis in quality control labs; quality control chemist for data acquisition systems.
★ Strongly self-motivated, enthusiastic, and profit oriented.
★ Conscientious and creative; willing to assume responsibility.
★ Exceptional talent for innovative problem solving.
★ Committed to maintaining quality and efficiency.

LAB EXPERIENCE & ACCOMPLISHMENTS

Quality Control/Project Management
• Supervised production of Data Acquisition Systems, a computerized instrument package:
  -hired employees and delegated job duties
  -consulted directly with the customer to clarify specifications
  -supervised production to assure customer specs were maintained
  -resolved production problems
  -conducted on-site start-up and testing of the system.
• Trained employees in operation of instruments and quality control checks of the system.

Analysis/R&D
• Developed new techniques in gas analysis, significantly increasing accuracy.
• Improved procedures of hydrocarbon analysis.
• Set up a well organized filing system for analysis data.

Instrument Knowledge
•Perkin Elmer Sigma 2100, 2000 (FID, TCD,HW) •Perkin Elmer Sigma 3-B: FID
•Antek 320D HID •Gow Mac 550: TCD •Gow Mac 550: HW •Gow Mac 20-150: HW
•Teledyne 306 •MEECO •Horiba PR2000 (Infra Red) •Beckman 400A
•Line LDI: Trace Oxygen •Beckman E2: Oxygen Analyzer •Taylor Servomax: Oxygen
•Beckman 865 - CO2 •Teledyne 235, 326 •Beckman Methanator •Delphi A & D
•Panametric System I •Thermoelectron •IBM Computer/WordStar & DBase III

EMPLOYMENT HISTORY

1985-present	**Chemist**	BYRON ENGINEERING, software design, Oakland CA
1982-84	**Sr. Lab Technician**	UNION CARBIDE, Linde Specialty Gas Lab, Houston TX
1979-81	**Lab Technician**	UNION CARBIDE, Linde Specialty Gas Lab, Houston TX

EDUCATION & TRAINING

B.S., Chemistry (30 hrs to complete) - TEXAS WOMAN'S University, Denton TX
• Introduction for Sigma 3B, PERKIN ELMER   • Logical Troubleshooting, HEWLETT-PACKARD
• Capillary Techniques in Gas Chromatography VARIAN INSTRUMENT GROUP

PROFESSIONAL AFFILIATION - ISA / Instrument Society of America

TECHNICAL & COMPUTERS

PETER CURRAN
4667 Marlborough Road
Oakland CA 94610
(415) 918-7889

Objective: Position as Senior Engineer in non-destructive testing development.

HIGHLIGHTS OF QUALIFICATIONS

- 7 years professional engineering experience in non-destructive testing development.
- 2 years applying International Imaging System's (I^2S) digital image processing system to improve machine (microscope) vision.
- Experience presenting scientific data to engineers, scientists and end-users.
- Outstanding problem solving skills.
- Government top secret (DOE Q) clearance.

PROFESSIONAL EXPERIENCE

TECHNICAL

- Conceived and implemented improved vision of the Scanning Laser Acoustic Microscope (SLAM) unit, using an I^2S Model 75 Image Processor. Designed total system which included a DEC computer, disc drives and a Matrix camera.

- Completed basic applications course for users at International Imaging Systems, Milpitas CA.

- Designed, built and tested electro-mechanical handling system to feed material to process chamber.

- Developed a new technique to improve the sensitivity and speed of a Computer Aided Tomography (CAT) scanner for metals.

- Designed feasibility study to develop industrial CAT scanner in cooperation with Los Alamos Scientific Laboratory.

- Designed and built custom laser optical system for measuring surface deformations in an inaccessible cavity.

COMMUNICATION, PRESENTATION, LIAISON

- Designed detailed technical presentation illustrating specific digital image processing techniques which improved the detection sensitivity of the SLAM unit ten-fold.
  -Programmed I^2S system to show sequentially improved images using various techniques: (averaging, histogram equalization, Fast Forier Transform, etc.)
  -Structured the presentations so they could be seen by 300 people in one day.

- Wrote definitive volume on plant designs for laser isotope separation systems.
  -Acted as liaison between engineers & scientists of various disciplines from Lawrence Livermore National Labs, Martin Marietta, Westinghouse Electrical Corp., Bechtel, and Stone & Webster Engineering Corp.
  -Coordinated the work of 8 engineers and scientists.

- Conceived and successfully presented a unique non-destructive testing system which resulted in a $330,000 DOE contract.

- Continued -

PETER CURRAN

WORK EXPERIENCE

LAWRENCE LIVERMORE NATIONAL LAB **Sr. Engineer & Laser Expert,** 1984 -present
Stone & Webster/Westinghouse Team
Atomic Vapor Laser Isotope Separation Project

BETTIS ATOMIC POWER LABORATORY **Engineer, Nondestructive Testing** 1978-1984
Development
Westinghouse Electric Corp.
Core manufacturing, process development,
and quality assurance group.

DAS/SOLAR SYSTEMS, Brooklyn **Installation Manager/Assoc.Engineer** 1977-1978

EDUCATION

B.S. Physics - Stevens Institute of Technology - Hoboken NJ - 1978
Graduate study in Computer Science - University of Pittsburgh - Pittsburgh PA
Graduate study in Mechanical Engineering - City College of New York

Westinghouse Electrical Corp: continuing education in Nuclear Physics
Application, Digital Systems, Laser Optics, Nondestructive Testing.

PUBLICATIONS & PATENTS:
Numerous technical works on nondestructive testing methods related to nuclear technology.
5 patent disclosures in nuclear technology.

PROFESSIONAL AFFILIATIONS:
Laser Institute of America
American Society of Nondestructive Testing (officer)
Institute of Electrical & Electronic Engineers, Inc.

TECHNICAL & COMPUTERS

ROCHELLE NORMANDY
PC Support Specialist
Specialist in PC support services for large and small businesses.
1256 Richlieu Drive
San Jose CA 95129
(408) 577-3665

Rochelle's intent is very clear.

HIGHLIGHTS OF QUALIFICATIONS

- Know computers inside and out; 12 years experience in the field, directed PC training and support for 11 National Computer stores.
- Infectious enthusiasm for computers; gifted and inspiring PC trainer.
- Expert trouble-shooter and problem solver.
- Proven ability to design systems for quick access to vital information.
- Committed to excellent service and customer satisfaction.

REPRESENTATIVE ACCOMPLISHMENTS

Training
- Trained thousands of individuals at all levels, in computer literacy:
  -corporate executives, accountants, sales people, clerks.
- Developed and presented trainings for clients throughout the western U.S., e.g.: manufacturing, service agencies, banking, telecommunications, government, etc.
- Managed the design and implementation of customized hands-on classroom trainings and computer labs:
  -met with department heads to clarify specific training and scheduling needs;
  -provided software and hardware for hands-on training in computer fundamentals, word processing, spreadsheets, relational databases, communications, graphics, macro programming, labs in customizing spreadsheets and databases.

Systems Design and Implementation
- Designed computerized workstations for cost-effectiveness use of existing hardware, scheduling for multiple-user access and coordinating related functions.
- Designed and computerized an inventory system for 6 National Computer stores, increasing inventory turnover by 60%.

Maintenance Contracts
- Provided field service maintenance on a 24-hour basis, including telephone hot-line support and routine testing and maintenance for all major computer products:
  -IBM -Compaq -Apple -Epson -AT&T -Okidata.
- Successfully identified service problems in initial service call 90% of the time.

EMPLOYMENT HISTORY

1983-present	**Director of Training Operations**	NATIONAL COMPUTERS, San Francisco
"	**Sales Manager**	NATIONAL COMPUTERS,, San Francisco
"	**Customer Support Manager**	NATIONAL COMPUTERS,, Silicon Valley
"	**Service Manager**	NATIONAL COMPUTERS,, Monterey
1978-82	**Senior R&D Technician**	MONARCH SYSTEMS, San Jose
"	**Production Supervisor**	MONARCH SYSTEMS, San Jose

EDUCATION & TRAINING

Business Administration - San Jose State University
Dale Carnegie Sales and Management courses
•IBM Service School •Apple Service School •Compaq Service School

SUSAN PIEPER
3680 Alcatraz Ave.
Oakland CA 94602
(415) 777-1224

Objective: Position in software support for a computer or software retailer.

HIGHLIGHTS OF QUALIFICATIONS

- Exceptional ability to quickly master new software and apply its full range of capabilities.
- Accurately interpret customers' problems and offer the best resolution.
- Outstanding telephone communications; patient, personable and receptive.
- Four years experience with personal computers.

RELEVANT EXPERIENCE

Training
- Trained 7 magazine publishers in computer application to their industry:
  - introduced them to elementary computer use;
  - taught them how to use Remote Copy Input program, designed by my company;
  - advised on which parts of the program applied to their current needs;
  - assisted them on an on-going basis to use increasingly more components of the program.

Troubleshooting / Problem Solving
- Advised <u>clients</u> on what is technically possible or impossible and how to achieve particular printing effects.
- Successfully resolved timing problems between client, production and printer.
- Saved important photo-history data for a client by effectively backtracking to the source of the problem and correcting the original file.
- Reorganized user-areas on customer's hard disk, restoring compatibility of file locations so they were retrievable by the program.

Software Development & Program Application
- Assisted programmers in design of a program to translate computer generated ads into full-page compositions by advising on how typesetting works.
- Identified specific applications for a new program as the package grew.
- Tested newly written programs for any bugs and documented them for the programmer.
- Reported to programmers customer feedback on program weaknesses & strengths.

WORK HISTORY

1980-present	**Production Manager**	SYSTEMS DEVELOPERS, Oakland CA
1979-80	**Asst. to Director of Production**	HOMES & LAND PUBLISHING CO, Tallahassee FL
1977-79	**Mail Clerk**	STATE OF FLORIDA, Tallahassee FL

113

CHARLES D. LaBUZ

Until June 30   **home: (717) 419-5665** - RD1, Box 120A-3, Uniondale PA 18470
                 work: (607) 901-6688 Ext.234
After July 1   579 North Bloomfield, Tuscon, Arizona 85710

Current objective: Position as a Secondary School Counselor.
Available also as coach for wrestling and football.
Future objective: Director of Guidance Services or Career Center Director

Future objective included.

Highlights of Qualifications
- Nine years experience in teaching and counseling.
- Sincere commitment to the welfare of the student.
- Special talent for assessing individual needs.
- Work supportively with colleagues and administration.

- PROFESSIONAL EXPERIENCE -

GUIDANCE & COUNSELING
1982-present   **Junior High School Counselor** -   WINDSOR JUNIOR/SENIOR HIGH SCHOOL, Windsor, NY

-Individual Counseling
- Counseled students on a wide range of issues:
  -physical, sexual and emotional abuse/neglect -stress due to divorce, separation and death
  -drug and alcohol abuse -suicide intervention -runaway intervention -dropout prevention

-School Counseling
- Advised special-need students, e.g., learning disabled, gifted students, athletes.
- Developed individual education programs, coordinating intervention with Committee on Special Education (previously called Committee on Handicapped).
- Maintained accurate up-to-date academic records, including:
  -general counseling information -standardized testing information
  -report cards -academic information -correspondence.
- Originated "Parents' Night," to explain academic programs to parents.
- Designed and coordinated orientation program for incoming students in Grade 7.
- Competent in using and revising Master Schedule, and in applying NY State Regents Action Plan academic requirements to scheduling.
- Assembled current college catalog and microfiche library.

-Career Development
- Created and taught "Life and Career Skills" course for junior high students, focusing on decision making skills, values clarification and communication skills.
- Counseled potential drop-out students in career options.
- Introduced students to the use of computer programs for college search, and library resources on career decision making.

-Measurement & Evaluation
- Administered and interpreted a full range of instruments, including:
  -Iowa Test of Basic Skills -Stanford Achievement Test -California Achievement Test
  -Orleans-Hanna Algebra Prognosis Test -Otis-Lennon Mental Abilities Test
  -Differential Aptitude Test -Career Decision Making System
  -Strong-Campbell Interest Inventory -Gessell School Readiness Screening Test.

-Coordination of Resources
- Initiated consultations with parents, faculty, and appropriate professionals.
- Referred students to community resources when necessary.
- Coordinated the intervention services of the Department of Social Services, Office of Mental Health, community agencies and health care professionals, to assure appropriateness to students' needs.

-Continued -

EDUCATION

114

GUIDANCE & COUNSELING (cont)

1982   **Advising Assistant/Grad Student** UNIVERSITY OF MONTANA
            • Counseled undergraduate students on academic and personal problems.
1981   **Counselor Intern** BIG SKY HIGH SCHOOL - Missoula, Montana

TEACHING

1981-82   **Substitute Teacher** MISSOULA COUNTY HIGH SCHOOLS - Missoula, Montana
1979-80   **Elementary Science Teacher, Grades 4-6** DARBY SCHOOLS - Darby, Montana
1975-79   **Elementary Science Teacher, Grades 1-6** DARBY SCHOOLS - Darby, Montana
            • Coordinated science program for elementary grades.

COACHING

1973-86   **Coach** for a variety of sports including: -wrestling -football -track

MILITARY SERVICE

1963-67   **Personnel Specialist** - UNITED STATES AIR FORCE

- EDUCATION & TRAINING -

M.Ed. Guidance and Counseling - UNIVERSITY OF MONTANA 1982
B.S., Elementary Education - STATE UNIVERSITY OF NEW YORK at ONEONTA 1973
Minor in Physical Education - NORTHERN MICHIGAN UNIVERSITY 1975
Completed 30 additional graduate hours for permanent New York certification 1986

Professional seminars and workshops:

1987   "All in the 'Blended' Family: About Step Families' Attitudes, Behavior and Parenting Skills"
1987   ACT-Discover Program: "Linking Professionals and Technology to
        Strengthen Career Planning"
1986   Region VIII Workshop, "Home & Career Skills"
1986   Occupational Education Regional Conferences of
        Administrators, Counselors and Teachers
1986   New York State Association for Counseling & Development Convention
1986   New York State Association of College Admission Counselors,
        "Hands Across the Border"
1986   "Students, Spirits and the Schools"
1985   National Diffusion Network Awareness Program
1985   Middle States Association of College and Schools,
        Evaluation Committee; Chair of Personnel Committee
1984   New York State Association for Counseling & Development Convention
1984   "Bank Street Writer," Computer Literacy
1984   "Career Counseling Strategies: Changes in the 80's"
1984   "Grief, Mourning and Transition"
1983   "New Directions for Education in a Technical Society"
1983   "The Parachute Process"

CURRENT PROFESSIONAL AFFILIATIONS

New York State Association for Counseling & Development, New York
Broome Tioga Counselors' Association, New York
National Coaches' Association

CERTIFICATIONS

Arizona	School Counselor (K-12)
New York State	School Counselor (K-12)
	Elementary Education (N-6)
Montana	Guidance & Counseling (K-12)
	Elementary Education (K-9)
	Physical Education & Health (K-12)
Washington State	School Counselor (K-12)

EDUCATION

CHRISTIANE LLOYD
980 Forty-Third Ave.
San Francisco CA 94121
(415) 459-6906

Here's a layout trick that makes an elaborate Job Objective look simple and clear. Note in the Education, "equivalent to masters."

Objective: Position as language instructor in German - preferably including
-academic counseling   -design of teaching materials
-curricula development   -course evaluation.

HIGHLIGHTS OF QUALIFICATIONS
- 5 years experience teaching German at all levels to many different target groups.
- Strong practical and theoretical background in developing and selecting appropriate teaching materials.
- Successful and self-confident in classroom presentation and team teaching.
- Proven effectiveness in program design and administration.
- Certified trainer for student teachers.

PROFESSIONAL EXPERIENCE

Classroom Teaching
- Taught German as a Second Language in a variety of settings:
  -beginning, intermediate and advanced students
  -male offenders in a correctional institute
  -female Spanish-speaking residents of Germany
  -foreign laborers in employment advancement courses.

Counseling/Training
- Trained student teachers in the classroom, and conducted seminars focusing on didactic issues.
- Advised adult immigrant students on complex personal and academic issues:
  -immigration and employment regulations   -housing and landlord concerns
  -health and medical resources   -entrance exams and class level placement

Curricula Development & Course Evaluation
- Improved existing curriculum on German as a Second Language, incorporating more diversity to respond both to needs and interests of students and to knowledge gained from academic research (focused on rules of grammar and on speaking/reading/writing/listening comprehension).

EDUCATION & CREDENTIALS
German equivalent of **Masters Degree**
Credentials to teach students through 10th grade
(First examination for intermediate school teachers, through 10th grade)
Relevant coursework: German, Pedagogic, Politics

EMPLOYMENT HISTORY

1983-87	**Teacher/Language Instructor** German as a Second Language Dept.	HAMBURG VOLKSHOCHSCHULE, Germany
1981-82	**Nurse Substitute/Driver**	ANSCHARHOHE EPPENDORF NURSING HOME, Hamburg, Germany
1974-81	**Full-time student;** Substitute Nurse, part-time	UNIVERSITY OF HAMBURG, Germany

EDUCATION

116

ELIZABETH S. WOOLSEY, Ed.D.
Consultant in Computer Education Program Development
9880 Atlantic Avenue
Oakland CA 94609
(415) 107-8776

HIGHLIGHTS OF QUALIFICATIONS

★ 20 years experience in education: teaching,
research, and program design.
★ Management and administrative experience.
★ Written and spoken communication skills.
★ Graduate degrees in philosophy and education.

PROFESSIONAL EXPERIENCE

Educational Program Development and Presentation
- Designed and led workshops for:
  ... inner-city teachers   ... college of education students
  ... community college faculty   ... women re-entering job market
- Consulted in schools at all levels, on program development and evaluation.
- Developed curriculum materials for, and taught:
  ... English as a Second Language   ... East-West comparative philosophy

Writing and Lecturing
- Wrote abstracts of evaluation reports on federally funded school programs.
- Wrote facilitator's manuals for workshops in education.
- Edited and produced employee handbook and procedures manual for a computer industry company.
- Currently under contract for book on computer learning.
- Lectured, as guest of educational institutions, in the U.S. and Asia.

Management and Administration
- Served as Executive Director of nonprofit organization incorporated in 30 states:
  ... recruited, trained, and coordinated activities of 10,000 volunteers
  ... managed fund-raising and a $300,000 budget
  ... planned and led two national conferences for regional and local coordinators.
- Managed operations/supported management during startup phase of four diverse corporations.
- Managed education department in national training corporation:
  ... planned and led educator workshops in six major U.S. cities
  ... organized local committees to support workshops
  ... published report on the department's work in education.

Computer Literacy
- Experienced in operation of personal computers:
  ... Apple IIe   ... IBM PC   ...Commodore 64   ... Eagle IIe   ... Compaq
- Trained and experienced in the use of word processing software:
  ... Spellbinder   ... WordStar
- Trained in simple program writing in BASIC and LOGO.
- Evaluated educational software.

- Continued -

WORK HISTORY

1982-present	**Educational Consultant**	RICHFIELD ENTERPRISES - Petaluma CA
		EDUCATION NETWORK, INC. - Santa Rosa CA
	Operations Consultant	COMPUTER SOLUTIONS - San Jose CA
		HEALTH RESOURCE NETWORK - Chevy Chase MD
		GROWING OLDER, INC. - Chevy Chase MD
1980-82	**Executive Director and President**	PEOPLE-TO-PEOPLE PROJECT, Richmond CA (organizing volunteer visits to institutionalized people on holidays)
1978-80	**Travel and study**	in Europe and Asia
1976-78	**Educational Consultant, Workshop Leader**	UNIVERSITY OF MARYLAND, Baltimore MD
1974-76	**Program Manager**	INSIGHT EDUCATIONAL CORP, Richmond CA
1967-74	**Teacher, Researcher, Graduate Student**	UNIVERSITY-WITHOUT-WALLS - Berkeley CA

EDUCATION and TRAINING

Ed.D. Education, 1974 - University of Maryland, College Park MD

M.A. Philosophy, 1967   "   "

B.A. Philosophy, 1962 (with honors)   "

National Computer Training Institute 1985
Women's Computer Literacy Workshop 1984
Original Computer Camp 1983

- References on request -

We don't leave a gap even in this impressive work history...filling in with travel and study.

EDUCATION

FERESHTEH (Frances) ASHKANI
89 Twelfth Street, Apt. 144
Oakland CA 94607
(415) 575-0734

Fereshteh points out that she has a B.A. *equivalent*, and also that she's *eligible* for US teaching credentials.

Objective: Position in child care or teaching
with a private school or day care center

HIGHLIGHTS OF QUALIFICATIONS

- Successful with the challenge of teaching groups of children.
- Patient, confident, and committed in working with children.
- Teaching credentials in Iran; eligible for equivalent U.S. credentials.

RELEVANT EXPERIENCE

Teaching

- Taught junior high age children in all mathematics subjects.
- Taught math to primary age students.
- Tutored teenagers in natural science subjects.

Child Care/Day Care

- Supervised four- and five-year-old children, teaching them basic skills in reading and drawing.
- Currently raising my own two children, ages two and four.

EMPLOYMENT HISTORY

1984-present	Family care	
1974-84	**Jr. High Mathematics Teacher**	JEAN d' ARC SCHOOL - Tehran, Iran
1974,1975, summers	**Nursery School Teacher**	GOLESTAN NURSERY SCHOOL - Tehran, Iran
1973-75	**Primary School Math Teacher**	NASEH PUBLIC SCHOOL - Tehran, Iran

EDUCATION

B.A. Economics (equivalent) NATIONAL UNIVERSITY OF IRAN - Tehran, Iran
Graduate training in education - MINISTRY OF EDUCATION -Tehran

EDUCATION

JAMES WORCESTER

1181 Spruce Street
Berkeley CA 94707
home (415) 572-1121
work (415) 539-6677

• •

**Objective: Position as High School or Middle School Teacher in a public school
teaching Social Science, American History, Civics, Economics**

HIGHLIGHTS OF QUALIFICATIONS

- Master classroom teacher who loves teaching.
- Specialist in using discussion and writing to develop students' effectiveness in forming and analyzing concepts.
- Adept in holding students' interest.
- Skilled in adapting curriculum to respond to students' needs.
- Developed teaching materials currently used in Oakland schools.
- Trained and experienced in helping other teachers as a Mentor.

PROFESSIONAL EXPERIENCE

Curriculum Development

- Co-authored comprehensive lesson plans for 11th grade American History, now being used throughout the Oakland Unified School District.
- Prepared District final exams in American History for grades 8 and 11.

Classroom Presentation

- I approach classroom teaching as a facilitator of student learning, by:
  -establishing a clear goal or objective for each lesson;
  -noticing students' reactions to material presented and checking for understanding;
  -emphasizing development of students' critical thinking skills;
  -creating a balance between my teaching goals and the students' learning needs,assuring that the students feel supported as they learn.
- Earned commendation on presentation skills from site administrators, district administrative staff, staff of Mills College and Lincoln University and University of California.

Training & Mentoring

- Taught secondary school teachers to improve student thinking by asking them better questions, in workshops presented at:
  - Oakland School District   - E.Bay Council of Social Studies   - Mills College
  - Lincoln University   - Bay Area Writing Project
- Successfully served as a mentor to four teachers at different school sites in Oakland.

- Continued -

EDUCATION

EMPLOYMENT HISTORY

1964-present	**Teacher, Montera Junior High:** -American History, 8th Gr. -Civics & Economics, 9th Gr. -Spanish	OAKLAND UNIFIED SCHOOL DISTRICT (serving as Mentor Teacher since 1984)
1985 spring	**Teacher Trainer**	MILLS COLLEGE, OAKLAND UNIFIED SCHOOL DISTRICT, and LINCOLN UNIVERSITY (SF)
1969-70	**Workshop Presenter,** -Case Method for teaching Constitutional Law	OAKLAND UNIFIED SCHOOL DISTRICT - Oakland & San Leandro secondary schools
1963-65	**Adult Education Teacher:** -English for Spanish speaking	RICHMOND ADULT EDUCATION PROGRAM
1962-64	**Teacher,** 5th and 6th grades	CASTRO VALLEY ELEM. SCHOOL DISTRICT
1962	**Salesman**	JOHN HANCOCK LIFE INSURANCE CO. - Oakland
1960-61	**Supervisor**	BURNS DETECTIVE AGENCY - San Francisco

(Previous employment as stevedore, ship rigger, fisherman, security guard)

EDUCATION & TRAINING

A.B., History - UNIVERSITY OF CALIFORNIA, BERKELEY - Minor in Spanish

Additional Special Training:
1969 - UCLA, Constitutional Law Project
1971 - National Science Foundation, Institute on Juvenile Delinquency
          (focus on Parson's Guided Self-Analysis)
1980 - UCB Bay Area Writing Project, Open Summer Institute
1984 - Special training as Mentor Teacher
1985 - Marin Office of Education - Staff Development:
          -Models of Teaching: Inquiry, Concept Formation, Skynectics
          -Mastery of Teaching, including Madeline Hunter "Instructional Skills"
          - Cooperative Learning
1985   UCB Bay Area Writing Project, Invitational Program, - Teaching Fellow

- References available on request -

EDUCATION

Jim loves teaching and SAYS so! He also shows the reader that he knows what it takes to be an outstanding facilitator of learning.

He merely mentions his job roles from many years ago, without detailing them, since he's already presented more than enough recent, relevant experience.

MARIANA KADISH
667 Vermont Ave.
San Francisco CA 94107
(415) 342-6112

Objective: Position as freelance translator and interpreter in Spanish.
for an agency, professional office, or nonprofit organization.

QUALIFICATIONS

- Sharp insight into the subtleties of both Spanish and English, with extensive background in two cultures.
- Analytic and versatile thinker, effective in developing and carrying out ideas.
- Self-motivated, creative professional; able to work independently and also coordinate with others.
- Exceptional communication and interpersonal skills.

RELEVANT EXPERIENCE

Bilingual and Bicultural Communications

- Taught English as a Second Language for Spanish speakers.
- Edited and translated literature, business correspondence, and project proposals for Salvadorean United Editors, a nonprofit literary organization.
- Interpreted at international conferences: presented simultaneous technical papers for audience of professionals; facilitated dialogue among educational conference participants.
- Served as coordinator for featured guests at business meetings, cultural programs, symposiums, and fund-raising events.

Leadership and Administration

- Represented Spanish speaking residents in legal and medical offices, insurance companies, and in municipal and criminal court.
- Administrative assistant to Rehabilitation Counselor in labor court cases for non-English speaking clients.
- Prepared petition for residence, citizenship, and political asylum on behalf of nonresidents at immigration law firm.
- Established, managed, and promoted an on-going owner-operated business for the sale of fine marbled papers and fabrics.

Public Relations

- Generated positive business response and community support for fund-raising in the arts and on behalf of cultural events, including a literary association, MEA dance company, and university programs (specific list available).
- Initiated ideas for PR in various fields; spokesperson for individuals and organizations, presenting programs to large audiences.
- Coordinated administrative projects in business and volunteer activities; business manager for Deborah Valoma, Couture Art to Wear and MARIANA Fibers; office manager of Editores Unidos Salvadorenos.

- Continued -

EDUCATION

EMPLOYMENT HISTORY

1986-present	**Staff Assistant**	SALVADOREAN UNITED EDITORS - San Francisco
1983-present	**Owner/Operator**	MARIANA FIBER (paper & fabric production) - SF
1984-86	**Sales Agent**	DEBORAH VALOMA, DESIGNER - Berkeley
1981-83	**Counselor in Training**	CORYELL & CO., Rehab Counselors - Oakland
1980	**Paralegal**	W.M. STAHL, ESQ., IMMIGRATION LAW - Oakland
1979	**Translator/Co-Owner**	LANGUAGE SERVICES - San Clemente

EDUCATION

San Francisco State University, 1987
Pacific Basin School of Textile Arts, Berkeley 1983-85
Fiberworks Center for Textile Arts, Berkeley 1984-85
UC Berkeley, 1981 - B.A., Latin American Studies
Emphasis in Anthropology, Literature, and Political Science

PROFESSIONAL AFFILIATIONS

- American Translators Association, Associate Member
- California Court Interpreters Association, Member
- Fiberworks Center for the Textile Artist, Member
- University of California Alumni Association

MARTHA JUPITER

219 Prince Street
Berkeley CA 94705
Home (415) 556-8907
Mssg (415) 455-7676

Travel and fulltime student status fill in the work history, leaving no gaps.

Objective: Teacher/counselor in children's mental health services

HIGHLIGHTS OF QUALIFICATIONS

★ Over four years of experience teaching children and preschoolers.
★ Degree in psychology with emphasis in Child Development.
★ Teaching background enriched by overseas positions and travel.
★ Experience with children and parents from varied cultures.
★ Successfully organized and managed a summer day care program.
★ Communicate with children and parents with warmth and diplomacy.

PROFESSIONAL EXPERIENCE

Teaching
- Team taught children, age one to five years, in UC Berkeley Child Care system;
  -provided warm, supportive environment for developing emotional and social growth;
  -worked with small groups consisting of children of similar developmental levels.
- Taught English as a Second Language, on a one-to-one basis, to native children in Greece; originated and publicized this program to serve families in the city of Athens.
- Co-organized with six families a summer day care program to bridge the interim period not covered by UC Berkeley system; served as sole teacher, rotating site weekly to different homes.

Planning & Supervision
- Planned, as member of staff team, a full range of activities to assist children in advancing their social and motor development:
  -art -cooking -story telling   -music -excursions -supervised play.
- Assisted Children's Librarian at city library in organizing reading materials and supervising children in book selection.

Parent Contact & Staff Relations
- Participated in staff meetings, addressing problems including family relations, staff cooperation, community support, and problem issues with individual children.
- Met with parents at parent/staff meetings, inviting their input into all phases of program planning and generating a cooperative atmosphere.

WORK HISTORY

1984-present	**Teacher**	self-employed as English Teacher in Athens, Greece, U.S.
1982-83	Travel and research	in Greece and northern Europe
1979-82	**Teacher**	Univ. of California Berkeley Childcare System - Berkeley
1973-79	**Secretary**	California Farmer Publishing Co. - San Francisco
1971-73	**Library Aide**	Children's Room, Grace A. Dow Library - Midland MI

EDUCATION

B.A., Psychology/emphasis in Child Development - graduated with high honors
UC Berkeley 1982

EDUCATION

124

MICHELLE OLSON
322 Beverly Place - Piedmont CA 94611
Home: 302-5867   Business: 685-1990

Objective: AHP conference presenter, for workshops in career development.

HIGHLIGHTS OF QUALIFICATIONS
- Masters in Career Counseling and Development.
- Outstanding teacher, specializing in creativity in business.
- Extensive background in counseling, instructing and program development.
- Highly creative and intuitive problem solver.
- Special talent for drawing people out, and clarifying their problems and needs.

PROFESSIONAL EXPERIENCE

CONSULTANT	Michelle Olson & Associates - Oakland CA	1980 to present

Counseling
- Counseled and motivated individuals to recognize and understand personal needs, problems, alternatives and goals, using a combination of practical problem solving skills and a transpersonal approach to counseling. Clients report that this combination of Eastern philosophy and Western psychological systems allows them to move to new levels of understanding with consistent and visible results.

Consulting
- Designed and presented seminars on conflict resolution for business and government agencies, increasing the number of employees utilizing EAP counseling services.

Instructing
- Prepared and presented lectures for the Creativity in Business course for the MBA programs at Stanford School of Business and California State University, Hayward. This course has consistently been ranked as one of the most outstanding courses offered by the Schools of Business.
- Developed and implemented courses and workshops for Piedmont Adult Education classes: -Effective Listening   -Managing Anger   -Making Good Decisions attracting new students to the Adult School and increasing my private clientele.

Facilitating
- Co-facilitated and collaborated on "Creativity in Business" seminars for:
  - Stanford School of Business Alumni Association, Hawaii
  - Young Presidents' Organization, Portland
- Created and led ongoing "Getting Clear" group for women, focused on improving their interpersonal relationship skills.

OWNER/DIRECTOR	Aerobic Exercise Studio - Oakland, CA	1979-83

Business Management
- Founded, developed and managed Oakland's first aerobic exercise studio.
- Trained and supervised 8 aerobic instructors, serving more than 300 clients.

Program Development
- Designed and presented workshops on stress management.
  The workshops evolved into a private practice, Michelle Jurika & Associates.

EDUCATION
M.A., Career Counseling & Development - John F. Kennedy University, Orinda CA
B.A. - Marymount College, Tarrytown, NY
Secondary Teaching Credential, University of California, Berkeley

EDUCATION

NABIL T. RAMA
(415) 663-9144

677 Williams Lane
Castro Valley CA 94546

Objective: Position as Translator, Arabic/English

HIGHLIGHTS OF QUALIFICATIONS
- Excellent command of both English and Arabic languages.
- Working knowledge of several Arabic dialects.
- Familiar with European and Middle Eastern culture, politics and economy, through study, extensive travel, and lifelong native residence in the Middle East.
- Interest in world affairs, travel and professional development.

RELEVANT EXPERIENCE

Language Skills
- Graduated from American high school and American university in Iraq, both instructed in English.
- Scored 610 on TOEFL test in July 1986.
- Effectively prepared written reports and delivered presentations in English to management.

International Education
- Developed extensive knowledge of several Arabic dialects, including Iraq, Lebanon, Egypt, Arabian peninsula, etc.
  -born and lived in Iraq for 27 years;
  -worked in United Arab Emirates for 8 years, with exposure to many Arabic nationalities with different dialects, in a cosmopolitan society.
- Acquired knowledge of Middle Eastern and European affairs:
  -vacationed in the Middle East, parts of US, and several European countries, learning of the respective cultures, traditions, history, political structures;
  -as Middle East native resident, took an active interest in political, social and economic events.
  -worked and socialized with Europeans and Americans as engineer employed by Abu Dhabi National Oil Co. in the United Arab Emirates.

Project Management/Coordination
- Successfully managed the planning and implementation of numerous projects:
  -prepared feasibility and economic studies of engineering projects in the oil industry, for presentation to management;
  -coordinated five functional units or working teams (technical, commercial, projects, construction, contracting) in executing industrial projects.
- Developed technical and economical analyses and made recommendations to management, considering:
  -cost and budget factors -technical specifications -scheduling and planning.

EMPLOYMENT HISTORY

1985-present	**Project Developer**	Free-lance financial consultant, East Bay USA
1977-85	**Project Engineer**	ABU DHABI NATIONAL OIL CO, Abu Dhabi, UAE
1976-77	**Resident Engineer**	GATI CONTRACTING CO., Iraq
1972-76	**Civil Engineer**	AIR FORCE, Iraq

EDUCATION
B.S. degree in Engineering - 1972
Courses in Management, Planning/Scheduling, Economics

EDUCATION

SANDRA DIETZ
222 - 51st Street
Oakland CA 94609
(415) 151-3423

Objective: Position as substitute teacher:
teaching mathematics, science or health education, elementary or junior high level.

HIGHLIGHTS OF QUALIFICATIONS

★ Two years successful teaching experience.
★ Firsthand knowledge of cultural differences; traveled and
   lived in Africa, Asia and Europe.
★ Sensitive to racial issues; patient and caring.
★ Strong leadership skills; able to direct and make decisions.
★ Deeply committed to high quality education for children.

RELEVANT EXPERIENCE

Teaching
• Taught General Science to junior high school students in Swaziland:
   -generated high level of enthusiasm among students;
   -overcame language barrier through creative use of visual aids.
• Taught English as a Second Language to students age 7-50 in Japan.
• Tutored Japanese student in American customs and language.

Planning & Organizing
• Developed lesson plans geared to the comprehension level of junior high students.
• Prepared, administered and graded special trial exams for junior high students, preparing
   them to qualify for entrance into high school.

Expertise in Math, Science, Health
• Studied and excelled in college level math: Algebra, Calculus, Trigonometry, Geometry.
• Completed coursework in Chemistry and Biology; degree in Health Science.
• Worked as Lab Technician for City of San Leandro.

Cultural/Racial Exposure
• Worked cooperatively with professionals in a racially mixed agency.
• Lived and worked for two years in Africa and Asia.
• Traveled under challenging circumstances, throughout India and Nepal.

EMPLOYMENT HISTORY

1986-present	**Administrative Asst.**	AMERICAN RUBBER CO. and ADIA AGENCY, East Bay
1985	**Teacher, ESL**	MAGNOLIA ENGLISH School, Shizouka City, Japan
1983-84	**Science Teacher**	US PEACE CORP - Swaziland
1982-83	**Attendant for Disabled**	JEANNIE LOJO - Hayward
1979-82	**Lab Assistant**	WASTE WATER TREATMENT PLANT, City of San Leandro

EDUCATION & TRAINING

B.S., Health Science - HAYWARD STATE UNIVERSITY
Language & Cultural Training - Peace Corp, Swaziland

EDUCATION

SARAH WHITAKER
13247 Colby Street
Berkeley CA 94705
(415) 809-4245

Objective: Position as Adult Education Teacher
•Arts and Crafts •Painting and Drawing •Creative Expression
•Drama •Physical Fitness •Physical Skills and Sensory Motor
•Communication Outlet •Current Events •Other Subjects

Also available to teach/counsel adults with handicaps,
developmental disabilities, or psycho-social problems.

HIGHLIGHTS OF QUALIFICATIONS

★ Credentialed and experienced adult education teacher.
★ Talent for incorporating 10 years background in art and drama
  into an adult education curriculum.
★ Creative skill in getting students involved.
★ Sensitivity to the needs of adults with physical and emotional
  problems, through 6 years experience as a certified body therapist.

RELEVANT EXPERIENCE

Teaching

Taught in 3 adult education programs sponsored by the Oakland Unified School District:

- **"Older Adult Program"** - Held classes for adults 65+, at Senior Citizens Centers, Hospitals and
  Retirement Homes;
  Subjects covered ...Painting and Drawing   ...Physical Fitness ...Ceramics.

- **"Older Adults In Care Facilities Program"** - Taught adults 65+, at intermediate and long-term
  care nursing facilities:
  ...Drawing and Painting ...Arts and Crafts ...Communication Outlets ...Physical Fitness.

- **"Adults With Exceptional Needs Program"** - Taught developmentally disabled adults in a
  program sponsored jointly with local community-based organizations:
  ...Physical Skills and Sensory Motor ..Painting and Drawing.

Counseling

- Counseled bodywork/massage therapy clients in areas of nutrition, stress reduction and
  therapeutic exercise. Made referrals to other professionals, as appropriate.

- Served as on-call counselor for emotionally disturbed older adults, at Rypin's residential
  psychiatric halfway house in San Francisco.

- Counseled older adults, as outreach counseling intern at Home for Jewish Parents, Oakland.

- Counseled seniors on general health issues and stress reduction, as health practitioner at
  South Berkeley Senior Center.

- Continued -

EDUCATION

WORK HISTORY

1986-present	**Adult Education Teacher**	OAKLAND PUBLIC SCHOOL SYSTEM, Pleasant Valley Adult School
1986	**On-Call Counselor**	RYPINS' psychiatric residential halfway house for adults over 65, San Francisco
1981-present	**Bodywork Practitioner**	PRIVATE PRACTICE, Oakland
1982-83	**Health Practitioner**	SOUTH BERKELEY SENIOR CITIZENS CENTER, Berkeley
1982	**Salesperson**	THE CLASSIC SHOP, women's wear, Oakland
1979-84	**Actress**	MILL VALLEY CENTER FOR PERFORMING ARTS, and other Bay Area theatres
1971-80	**Artist/Painter/Printer**	Free-lance, concurrent with above

EDUCATION, TRAINING & CREDENTIALS

B.F.A., Fine Arts/Painting - UNIVERSITY OF OKLAHOMA, Norman OK ,1976
1987 Masters Program in Counseling - SAN FRANCISCO STATE

Performing Arts Training
•Jean Shelton School of Acting   •Drama Studio/Berkeley   •Playwright's Festival/Mill Valley
Classes in: ...Scene Study ...Improvisation ...Movement ...Speech ...Script Analysis

Counseling Training
Counseling Intern, Home for Jewish Parents, Oakland (Counseling Masters program, SF State)
Counseling Orientation, Rypin's Halfway House
Art Therapy, San Francisco State

Credentials
Adult Education, Preliminary Designated Subjects Credential through 1991
Certified Clinical Masseuse

> Sarah has little paid teaching experience, so she emphasizes OTHER experience applicable to the objective AND expands fully on the experience she does have.

EDUCATION

SHARON ZIMMERMAN
788 Alameda
San Francisco CA 94122
(415) 990-3132

Objective: Position teaching Studio Art, Art History and/or Aesthetics.

EDUCATION & CREDENTIALS

Ph.D., Aesthetics & Art History (with honors), UNIVERSITY OF PARIS 1, Pantheon-Sorbonne
D.E.A., Aesthetics & Ethnology (with honors), UNIVERSITY OF PARIS 1, Pantheon-Sorbonne
M.A., Aesthetics & Ethnology (with honors), UNIVERSITY OF PARIS 1, Pantheon-Sorbonne
D.S.A.P., BFA equivalent, L'ECOLE NATIONALE Superieure des Beaux-Arts, Paris

HIGHLIGHTS OF QUALIFICATIONS

- Doctorate in Fine Arts; solid academic background, through both field research and studying under great artists and scholars.
- Broad artistic perspective resulting from extensive travel and education on 3 continents.
- Active artist, personally attuned to the world of art.
- Talent for creating a stimulating, challenging learning environment.
- Demonstrated success in establishing art classes and programs.

PROFESSIONAL EXPERIENCE

Teaching
- Taught painting and sculpture in a variety of settings:
  -community centers in Toronto, Paris and Madagascar
  -special education programs in Canadian public schools
  -private art school in Italy.
- Designed and taught an Ethno-Aesthetics course on Malagasy funeral art for art history students at the Pordenone Civic Center in Pordenone, Italy.
- Taught a course in Aesthetics at the Santa Rosa Arts Center, Pordenone, Italy.
- Presented a lecture series on Judaism and Art, sponsored by St. George Church, Paris, for theologians and scholars.

Curriculum/Program Development
- Established a Studio Art program at the American Cultural Center in Madagascar:
  -introduced creative arts to adults who had never held a paintbrush;
  -presented new concepts and media to students not previously exposed to the imaginative and creative processes.
- Directed Wallaceburg Community Cultural Center, the first of its kind in the area, stimulating community interest in both art theory and studio art:
  -wrote a grant proposal successfully winning funding from Canadian government;
  -taught painting, photography, sculpture, and drawing; lectured on art history.

- Continued -

EDUCATION

PROFESSIONAL EXPERIENCE, continued

Research
- Led a research program for university students and scholars interested in exploring Malagasy funeral art, familiarizing students with the ethnology and anthropology of the areas and populations under study.
- Conducted a unique research project exploring the relationship of Judaism and art featuring a fresh, new approach to this familiar subject; developed a valuable bibliography and information network on the subject.

WORK HISTORY

1986-87	**Graduate Student**	PhD program, University of Paris
1985	**Lecturer in Art**	ST. GEORGE CHURCH, Paris
1983-84	**Art Program Coordinator**	JEWISH COMMUNITY CENTER, Oakland CA
1981-82	**Art History Instructor**	SANTA ROSA GALLERY, Pordenone, Italy
1981-82	**Lecturer**	PORDENONE CIVIC CENTER, Pordenone, Italy
1980	**Asst. Professor, Art**	UNIV. of MADAGASCAR (on contract)
1979	**Art Program Director**	AMERICAN CULTURAL CENTER, Madagascar
1978	**Lecturer, English**	UNIVERSITY OF PARIS, Paris
1973-77	**Fulltime student**	L'ECOLE NATIONALE, Paris

Sharon shows that her "D.S.A.P." is equivalent to the B.F.A. degree in the US. Then in the "Highlights" she points out her "broad artistic perspective resulting from extensive travel and education on 3 continents."

TUDY LARKSPUR
1219 Snowcrest Road
Pleasant Hill CA 94523
(415) 141-6559

Tudy generalizes about her prior years of work, having already detailed the most recent 10-year period.

Objective: Career counseling position with St.Elizabeth's College career center.

HIGHLIGHTS OF QUALIFICATIONS

★ Graduate degree in Career Development from JFK University.

★ Sensitivity and empathy for people in career exploration, based on my own personal experience with this challenge.

★ Experience in counseling both students and graduates.

★ Enthusiastic and committed to professional excellence.

PROFESSIONAL EXPERIENCE

Counseling/Interviewing

• Counseled individuals at JFK University Career Center for nine months, covering:

   ... test interpretations   ... job search skills

   ... resume preparation   ... interviewing techniques

   ... networking skills   ... researching potential employers

• Administered testing and evaluation instruments, such as Strong-Campbell Interest Inventory, Values Card Sort, Myers Briggs Type Indicator.

• Counseled groups and individuals at University Y's Turning Point Career Center:
-assessed needs of drop-in participants, providing informal counseling and guiding them to appropriate resources;
-led Job Search Support Group and workshop on Goals and Decision Making.

Resource Development

• Conducted in-depth research of a corporation to determine its desirability as a potential employer:
-visited libraries and read annual reports; visited company headquarters to observe working conditions, relationship to community and potential career path; learned history of organization.

• Located and directed clients to career library resources, such as professional publications, labor market information, college catalogs, Bay Area job outlook reports, information on special populations (handicapped, refugees, etc.).

• Attended Employer Information Series at Turning Point, increasing specific knowledge of entry requirements and working conditions in various career fields.

WORK HISTORY

1986-present **Counseling Extern**.....Univ. YWCA/Turning Point Career Center, Berkeley
1983-86   **Student**.....John F. Kennedy University, Orinda CA
1981-82   **Part-time paralegal**.....Moraga law firm
1979-80   **Paralegal intern**.....Walsh, Morton, Meaden law firm, Moraga CA
1979-80   **Student**.....St. Mary's College, paralegal studies
1976-78   **Receptionist**.....Women's Career Center, Diablo Valley College, Pleasant Hill

Prior years: variety of positions as medical assistant, receptionist, secretary, followed by 20 years of family management.

EDUCATION & TRAINING

M.A. Career Development - John F. Kennedy University, Orinda
Paralegal Certificate - St. Mary's College, Moraga
B.A. Liberal Arts - UC Berkeley

EDUCATION

VERONICA LONDON

543 West Grand Ave. #8
Oakland CA 94612
(415) 877-4010

Veronica trimmed her over-long list of jobs from 11 down to 8 by dropping one (child-care) and combining 2 similar jobs (Eligibility Worker).

Objective: Teaching position for primary grades or preschool with a private school or government funded program

HIGHLIGHTS OF QUALIFICATIONS

- Committed to high quality education for young children.
- BA in Anthropology; elementary teaching credential pending.
- Well organized, efficient and a quick learner.
- Effective and knowledgeable in working with cultural/social differences.
- Skilled in resolving conflicts and promoting harmonious relationships.
- Strong sense of responsibility as a professional team worker.

RELEVANT EXPERIENCE

Classroom Teaching
- Implemented curriculum featuring age-appropriate activities for children of ages 2-5 at Lombard Nursery School.
- Employed age-appropriate and child-initiated activities in directing learning experiences for children 2-7 in a day-care setting.

Effective Teaching Methods
- Provided wide range of optional play and learning materials to appeal to all children's interests, maximizing participation and enjoyment.
- Carefully observed and communicated with children to develop activities relevant to their immediate interests and needs.
- Promoted the development of social skills by helping children learn to communicate their feelings and to hear each other.

Teamwork
- Co-facilitated program planning meetings of political action organization:
  -promoted full and effective participation and follow through, by making sure that all members' primary concerns were heard and considered;
  -resolved conflicts by identifying points of agreement.

WORK EXPERIENCE

1984-present	Cook/Substitute Teacher	LOMBARD NURSERY SCHOOL - Oakland
1980-present	Part-time art student	LANEY COLLEGE; MERRITT COLLEGE
1981-83	Assistant Potter	BLUEBIRD FINE POTTERY, Richmond
1980-81	Child Care	Mrs. KRISTIN ORDWAY - Berkeley
1979-80	Certification Technician	CETA PROGRAM - Richmond
1977-79	Distribution Clerk	US POSTAL SERVICE - Berkeley
1972-77	Eligibility Worker	L.A. and ORANGE CO. WELFARE DEPTS.
1971-72	Substitute Teacher	HOWTHORN SCHOOL DISTRICT - L.A.

EDUCATION, TRAINING & CREDENTIALS

B.A., Anthropology - CALIFORNIA STATE UNIVERSITY, Long Beach

Additional Relevant Studies
Overview of Early Childhood Studies - Cal State Hayward
Currently enrolled for Early Childhood Education studies, CSH
Partial Elementary Credential issued 1973

EDUCATION

KATHLEEN WEBSTER
8022 Pine Street
Oakland, CA 94606
(415) 909-4334

Objective: Position as a Library Assistant

HIGHLIGHTS OF QUALIFICATIONS

- Over six years working in library settings.
- Smart and personable; interact easily with the public.
- Strong and precise clerical skills.
- Capable in research and reference work.

RELEVANT EXPERIENCE

Library Skills

- Worked six years in the public library system...

   ... interacting with the public in all aspects of library work

   ... processing applications and working in the registration file

   ... answering simple reference questions   ... retrieving reserve books

   ... typing book orders ... processing new books   ... repairing damaged books

   ... shelving and shelf reading.

Administrative Support Skills

- Operated APPLE Macintosh computer and LaserWriter printer, as Instructional Assistant for Mills College graduate course in Technical Communications.
- Inventoried, ordered and stocked merchandise for national greeting card company, interacting with personnel at 3 store locations.
- Tabulated regional statistics; organized and dispatched census forms.
- Performed clerical duties and acted as Relief at the Fire Control Dispatch Center.
- Dispatched fire fighting equipment from a warehouse distribution center.

EMPLOYMENT HISTORY

1980-present	**Library Aide**	Downtown Public Library	So. Hayward, CA
1987	**Instructional Asst.**	Mills College	Oakland, CA
1983-present	**Store Merchandiser**	Gibson Card Co.	Oakland
1980	**Census Worker**	U.S. Census Bureau	Oakland
1979	**Library Assistant**	Feather River College	Quincy, CA
1979	**Fire Control Clerk**	U.S. Dept. of Forestry	Quincy, CA

EDUCATION

BA English (with honors) Mills College, Oakland, CA 1987
AA Social Sciences (with honors) College of Alameda, Alameda, CA 1985

EDUCATION

134

CAROL WEITZELL

1912 Kains Avenue
Berkeley CA 94702
(415) 235-3980

One of three resumes for Carol. See also pages 34 and 55.

Objective: Program Development position working with the elderly population

HIGHLIGHTS OF QUALIFICATIONS

- Case management experience with elderly population.
- Three years experience as program specialist.
- Strength in creative problem solving.
- Outstanding ability to work with community and professional groups.
- MSW degree, focusing on administration and planning.

PROFESSIONAL EXPERIENCE

ELDERLY SERVICES

- Case manager for the West Contra Costa County Office on Aging:
  -Assisted elderly population in using community resources, care planning arrangements, and support in dealing with issues of aging.
- In-Home Supportive Services Social Worker, Dept. of Social Services, West Contra Costa County.
  -Implemented County Homemaker/Chore program.

COMMUNITY SERVICES

- Compiled and edited a comprehensive community resource manual instructing social workers in services available in the city of Boston, how to access them, and procedures for qualifying.
- Liaison for community/professional Advisory Board for 3 years.
  Projects of the Board included:
  ...community resource evaluation and coordination.
  ...budget plan development for child welfare agency.

ADMINISTRATION & PLANNING

- Developed an in-service training program for social work staff which increased their professional expertise and theoretical background:
  -Developed a form for self-assessment by workers.
  -Wrote and managed annual training budgets.
  -Contracted with trainers to provide instruction in specific issues in social work.
  -Met regularly with supervisors to evaluate the program on an on-going basis.
- Produced a community social service needs assessment to be incorporated in the budget narrative of a Boston DSS office.

WORK HISTORY

1985-present	**Case Manager**	AREA OFFICE ON AGING, W. Contra Costa Co.
1985-present	**Social Worker**	CONTRA COSTA COUNTY, CA
1983-85	**Photographer**	Self-employed
1980-83	**Program Development**	MASSACHUSETTS DEPT. of SOCIAL SERVICES
1979-80	**Administrative Analyst**	"
1978-79	**ChildWelfare Worker**	"
1977-78	**Student Intern**	"

EDUCATION

MSW, Boston University - SRS fellowship in Child Welfare, 1978

DONNETTE C. FROST
6241 Park Blvd.
Oakland CA 94602
(415) 514-2777

Objective: Internship in Chemical Dependency Treatment Unit, working with individuals, families and groups

HIGHLIGHTS OF QUALIFICATIONS

- Special strength in educating and treating families of chemically dependent clients.
- Solid understanding of addictive and compulsive disorders.
- Sensitivity and knowledge of cultural/ethnic issues in addiction.
- Professional background in both counseling and nursing.
- Effective in balancing professionalism with sincere empathy.

PROFESSIONAL EXPERIENCE

Clinical Counseling
- Conducted long and short-term psychotherapy for 3 years with:
  -individual adults -adolescents -groups -families -couples.
- Provided crisis intervention, problem solving and brief therapy in two mental health clinics and city employee assistance program.
- Counseled chemically dependent individuals and families.
- Served as outreach counselor for Community Senior Centers.

Assessment
- Conducted assessment, brief therapy, referral and follow-up for employees.
- Performed investigative intake interviews and diagnostic evaluation.
- Developed diagnostic profiles and treatment plans to address patients' therapeutic needs.

Supervision and Administration
- Evaluated and advised clinical team on psychological needs and appropriateness of services for potential clients.
- Supervised and/or trained counselor trainees, interns and community organization staff.
- Conducted educational and informational presentations on Mental Health and Chemical Dependency for community organizations.
- Coordinated and supervised an alternative disciplinary action program for students experiencing academic and emotional difficulties.

Cross-Cultural Skills
- Provided counseling services to clients from a wide range of ethnic backgrounds.
- Lived and worked with people of various cultures and social strata in Europe and the United States.

- Continued -

THERAPY & SOCIAL WORK

DONNETTE C. FROST
Page two

WORK HISTORY

1986-present	**Counseling Intern**	EMPLOYEE ASSISTANCE PROGRAM, City of Oakland
1986-present	**Research Assistant**	INSTITUTE OF BLACK FAMILY LIFE & CULTURE, Oakland
1985-86	**Psychotherapist Intern**	BERKELEY MENTAL HEALTH CLINIC, City of Berkeley
1984-85	**Psychotherapist Intern**	J.F.KENNEDY COMMUNITY COUNSELING CNTR, Concord
1982-84	**Sr.Head Resident Counselor**	ST. GEORGE HOMES INC., Berkeley
1979-82	**Special Tutor/ Instructional Assistant**	SAN DIEGO UNIFIED CITY SCHOOL DISTRICT
1975-78	**Staff Student Nurse**	BRONX LEBANON HOSPITAL & CALVARY HOSPITAL, NYC
1973-74	**Adolescent Activity Counselor**	NEW YORK CITY YOUTH CORP PROGRAM

EDUCATION

M.A., Clinical Psychology, 1987 - JOHN F. KENNEDY UNIVERSITY, Orinda CA
Certificate in Chemical Dependency, 1987
M.F.C.C. candidate, J.F.K.U. - anticipated April 1988
B.A., Psychology, 1981 - United States International University, San Diego CA
LPN (Vocational Nursing Diploma), 1976 - MORRIS SCHOOL OF NURSING, New York

HONORS

National Dean's List of American Universities and Colleges
Selected candidate for the 1979-81 Annual Encyclopedia
Who's Who Among Students in American Universities and Colleges
Selected candidate for annual Encyclopedia, based on academic standings,
community service, leadership ability and future potential, 1980-81.
New York Association of Nurses
Merit scholarship award.

PROFESSIONAL AFFILIATIONS

California Association of Marriage & Family Therapists
Association of Black Psychologists, Bay Area Chapter

- References available upon request -

EILEEN T. SCHULMAN
1412 California St., Apt. 206
Francisco CA 94109
(415) 262-3977

Objective: Social work position with University of California Medical Center

HIGHLIGHTS OF QUALIFICATIONS

- Genuine concern for and sensitivity to clients.
- Excellent problem solving and counseling skills.
- Enjoy the challenge of assisting clients in time of crisis.
- Work well as member of an interdisciplinary health team.
- Thorough familiarity with S.F. community resources.

PROFESSIONAL EXPERIENCE

Counseling
- Successfully engaged resistant clients in counseling.
- Co-developed a unique Bereavement Counseling Program for group counseling of individuals facing recent loss of a loved one.
- Served as practitioner in wide range of situations, utilizing skills in:
  -short/long-term counseling -crisis intervention -phone counseling
  -family counseling -bereavement counseling.

Interviewing & Needs Assessment
- Conducted psycho/social assessments of individuals and families.
- Developed individualized needs assessments for homebound patients, providing:
  -case management -counseling -supervision of care attendants
  -home care hours -sickroom equipment -home care supplies
  -appropriate referrals to community resources -case conferences.
- Monitored home care plans for indigent homebound cancer patients.
- Provided comprehensive discharge planning, identifying adequate placement resources for hospitalized patients.

Administration
- Administered Home Health Program which won award for Service to the Community during my tenure.
- Coauthored a popular and effective bimonthly Newsletter for Home Care Attendants, providing career information, training opportunities and professional support.
- Codeveloped Attendant Training Workshops, Rap Sessions and Annual Attendant Recognition Dinner.
- Prepared annual budget and biannual Program Report, including all statistical program information.
- Organized an information network and referral system on health care in the Bay Area to provide highest quality referrals.

- Continued -

EILEEN T. SCHULMAN
page two

EMPLOYMENT HISTORY

1984-present	**Program Coordinator**	MILLER-BUNTING PROGRAM of the American Cancer Society, S.F.
1983-84	**Program Social Worker**	MILLER-BUNTING PROGRAM, ACS/SF
1982-83	**Social Work Intern**	PACIFIC PRESBYTERIAN HOSP. - S.F.
1981-82	**Social Work Intern**	DEPT of SOCIAL SERVICES - S.F. Children's Protective Services
1976-83	**Licensed Vocational Nurse**	ST. LUKE'S HOSPITAL - San Francisco Adult Medical/Surgical; Pediatrics
1975-76	**Licensed Vocational Nurse**	VETERANS' ADMIN. HOSPITAL - S.F. Cardiology/Neurology

EDUCATION

MSW - San Francisco State University 1983
Additional Training: Oncology Social Work, Memorial Sloane-Kettering Cancer Center 1985
LVN - College of California Medical Affiliates, San Francisco 1975

PROFESSIONAL AFFILIATIONS

National Association of Social Workers
Bay Area Social Workers in Health Care (Executive Committee 1983-85)
San Francisco Grief Care-Givers Network

GREGORY ACKERMAN
7 Captain Drive
Emeryville CA 94608
(415) 511-2323

**Objective: Position as Mental Health Treatment Specialist/Intern
at Contra Costa County Jail.**

HIGHLIGHTS OF QUALIFICATIONS

★ Deeply committed to gaining experience and expertise in psychotherapy.
★ Interested in the challenge of working with the jail population.
★ Masters degree, and working toward MFCC License.
★ One year clinical experience with a diverse population in an outpatient
counseling center.

PROFESSIONAL EXPERIENCE

Interviewing & Assessment
• Interviewed and counseled men at Center for Men's Health and Education, providing education and emotional support for partners of women having abortions.
• Conducted intake interviews and performed assessments of outpatients at Pathways,
a general counseling center.

Treatment Planning & Implementation
• Developed individualized therapeutic treatment plans, applying short and long-term
strategic psychotherapeutic methods.
• Conducted successful psychotherapy with a suicidal, agoraphobic client; no longer
suicidal, and currently enrolled in a paraprofessional program.

Reporting
• Maintained records of therapeutic activities and client progress.
• Delivered weekly verbal reports to counseling supervisors.
• Reported diagnoses and prognoses to Dept. of Rehabilitation, as needed.

EMPLOYMENT HISTORY

1986-present	**Counselor, MFCC Intern**	LIGHTHOUSE COUNSELING CENTER, Walnut Creek
1984-85	**Counseling Student Trainee**	LIGHTHOUSE COUNSELING CENTER, Walnut Creek
1983	**Full time student**	JOHN F. KENNEDY UNIVERSITY, Orinda
1980-82	**Owner/Manager**	FIRE AND ICE, jewelry store, San Francisco
1973-80	**Gem Cutting/Sales**	SELF-EMPLOYED, San Francisco

EDUCATION

M.A., Clinical Holistic Health Education - John F. Kennedy University, Orinda, 1985
M.S., Pharmacology - University of California, San Francisco, 1973
Additional coursework: Psychology , San Francisco State College, 1966
B.A., Biophysics - University of California, Berkeley, 1965

WILLIAM ERNEST
Clinical/Psychiatric Social Worker
2432 Santa Maria Avenue
San Francisco CA 94110
(415) 590-3936

Objective: Professional psychotherapy position
with a public or private agency, clinic or hospital

HIGHLIGHTS OF QUALIFICATIONS
★ Licensed clinical social worker; 10 years professional experience.
★ Strong practical and theoretical foundation in a number of
  therapeutic and intervention models.
★ Integrated, flexible, and appropriate approach.
★ Outstanding skills in assessing clients' needs.
★ Committed to bringing about real, practical results in people's lives.

PROFESSIONAL EXPERIENCE

Counseling & Interviewing
• Managed large caseload comprised of voluntary and involuntary outpatient clients through
  Department of Health Continuing Care Services program:
  - individual and group counseling with voluntary clients.
  - casework follow up of involuntary clients involving home visits and referrals to other agencies
    providing support services.
  - implementing a model independent community halfway house for selected higher-
    functioning clients to supervise their development of independent living skills.
• Maintained a small private practice for two years.
• Conducted individual, group and family therapy at the Indian Health Project.

Cross-Cultural Experience
• Trained native American paraprofessionals in basic psychotherapy concepts as applied to
  their unique cultural heritage.
• Served as liaison with Black, Asian-American, Latino, Chinese and Samoan community
  groups as research associate in NIMH cross-cultural needs assessment study of the minority
  elderly.
• Counseled at a Latino heroin addiction treatment facility.

EMPLOYMENT HISTORY

1985-present	**Real Estate Agent**	CLASSIC PROPERTIES - San Francisco
1983-84	**Retail Management**	MACY'S - Menlo Park
1982	**Counselor/Supervisor**	THE INDIAN HEALTH PROJECT - Eureka CA
1979-81	**Psychotherapist**	Private practice - San Francisco
1976-78	**Psychiatric Social Worker**	CALIFORNIA DEPT. of HEALTH - San Diego
1974-76	**Research Associate**	SCHOOL OF SOCIAL WORK, SDSU - San Diego
1973-74	**Psych. Social Work Intern**	VA HOSPITAL, Outpatient MH Clinic - San Diego
1972-73	**Substance Abuse Counselor**	NARCOTICS PREVENTION & EDUC. SYSTEMS - "

EDUCATION & CERTIFICATION
MSW, Clinical Social Work - SAN DIEGO STATE UNIVERSITY
BA, Economics/Political Science - UC BERKELEY
LCSW - 1978

KARAM JOT SINGH KHALSA
FAMILY MEDIATOR - DIVORCE MEDIATOR
7644 Cragmont Ave, Berkeley CA 94709
Telephone 991-0333

Professional title replaces "objective" for an independent consultant.

Summary of Qualifications

- Graduate degree in clinical psychology; training in family mediation.
- Deep compassion and commitment in helping families under stress.
- 15 years leadership responsibility in human relations and personal growth.
- Objective, supportive and trusting attitude in working with people.
- Creative and effective in dealing with fear, anger, sadness, passivity.

Professional Experience

Conflict Resolution

- Mediated marital disputes about parenting, couple relations, and other family concerns.
- Mediated tenant-landlord disputes as real estate property manager.
- Negotiated issues and programs between yacht club, UC Administration and City.
- Mediated hundreds of disputes between individuals and groups in a religious organization on individual needs, programs, relationships, financial planning, group policies, goal setting:
  -developed ground rules for discussion   -clarified major issues and needs of individuals
  -evaluated and summarized conflicting ideas   -generated options and alternatives
  -aided in getting understanding and structuring agreements.

Counseling & Interviewing

- Counseled individuals, couples and families,
  -as a student and therapist intern, over the past 4 years;
  -as a minister, for the past 4 years, involving issues of educational, career and spiritual goals; marital and premarital concerns; physical, mental and emotional issues.
- Conducted over 30 therapy and communications groups.
- Interviewed over 150 applicants for membership in a residential community, for in-depth assessment of their personal interests, needs, attitudes and beliefs.
- Screened potential employees and subcontractors for real estate/building company.

Teaching & Education

- Lectured at college and university level, and to private and public groups.
- Taught classes; trained hundreds of students and teachers; and tutored in:
  -communication skills   -men and women relationships   -personal growth and self-care
  -yoga/meditation   -preventing burnout   -stress management   -health and hygiene
- Developed and led workshops in communications, human relations and marriage/family issues, for the past 10 years.
- Motivated people to learn, grow and achieve in self-help oriented classes and workshops.

Relevant Employment History

1983-present	MFCC Registered Intern	MICHAEL MAYER PhD, PSYCHOLOGIST - Berkeley
1981-82	Manager	PROPERTY MANAGEMENT CO. - Orinda
1981-82	Counselor in Training	JFK UNIVERSITY COUNSELING CENTER - Orinda
1978-81	Supervisor	REAL ESTATE/BUILDING COMPANY - Orinda
1977-78	Chairman	NATIONAL COUNCIL, SIKH DHARMA, Religious Org.
1971-77	Teacher & Director	3HO NORTH REGION - Northern California
		-Director, Drug Rehabilitation Program
		-Director, National Park Program, Yosemite
1972-present	Ashram Director	3HO/SIKH DHARMA - Berkeley

Education & Special Training

M.A., Clinical Psychology - JFK UNIVERSITY, Orinda CA 1982
Emphasis: Marriage, Family and Child Counseling
•TEAM BUILDING (business & personal use)   •FAMILY MEDIATION (with Isolina Ricci, Palo Alto)
•PARENT EFFECTIVENESS TRAINING (10 weeks, Gary Sugarman, trainer)

BENJAMIN FARBER, MFCC
Licensed Psychotherapist
30566 Hillegass Avenue
Berkeley CA 94705
(415) 909-7866

PROFESSIONAL SUMMARY

★ Extensive experience assessing and treating issues related to workplace relationships, family relationships, and stress disorders.
★ Skilled in working as member of a professional treatment team.
★ Demonstrated effectiveness in issues of alcoholism and recovery.
★ Specialist in developing self-worth and self-esteem.
★ Demonstrated effectiveness in assisting clients to identify weaknesses and reframe them into strengths.
★ Able to instill confidence in a positive treatment outcome.

EXPERIENCE

Alcoholism & Recovery
• Treated identified alcoholics, referred by alcohol treatment programs and other therapists, at early stages of recovery:
  - educated clients on the predictable course of early recovery (depression, loss of control, etc.)
  - identified clues for potential relapse to design more effective coping styles related to their social support system, job-related stresses, family relations.
  Assessed potential alcoholics in the workplace, and recommended appropriate treatment.
• Effectively employed disease model of alcoholism, combining abstinence with adjunct treatment: e.g., Alcoholics Anonymous; family therapy.
• Diagnosed and treated co-alcoholics, adult and adolescent children of alcoholics.

Workplace Relationships
• Facilitated the resolution of workplace problems with employees of school, government, military and industry:
  - advised supervisors having difficulty asserting authority
  - empowered employees to successfully identify and effectively resolve conflict with supervisors and coworkers, teaching assertiveness and communication skills.

Stress Disorders / Stress Reduction
• Assessed and diagnosed burnout and other stress related disorders.
• Taught relaxation techniques, self-hypnosis, exercise programs, development of self-worth, in the context of individual psychotherapy.

Couple & Family Relationships
• Assisted couples in:
  - identifying their issues of conflict
  - articulating individual needs within family/couple context
  - developing skills in communicating anger/uncomfortable feelings, negotiating and problem solving
  - accepting differences as normal in healthy relationships.
• Successfully applied structural family therapy techniques to assist step-families as well as intact families to develop clearer and more cooperative generational roles.

- Continued -

THERAPY & SOCIAL WORK

WORK EXPERIENCE

1984-present	Co-Director	Oakley Counseling Associates, Oakland and Berkeley
1981-84	Psychotherapist	Richfield Counseling Associates, Alameda
1979-81	Psychotherapist	Family Service Agency, Walnut Grove
1977-79	Primary Therapist	Crown Home, residential treatment facility ,SF
1976-77	Counselor/ Treatment Coor.	Parkhurst Places Inc., psychiatric halfway house, SF

CONSULTANT & TRAINER EXPERIENCE

1985-86	Supervisor	Graduate Training Program, Bay Graduate School of Marital & Family Therapy, Oakland
1981-84	Chairman	School Attendance Review Board, Oakley School Dist.
1980-84	Consultant	Special Education Dept., Berkeley High School
1980-83	Consulting Instructor	Greer College, Hayward

PROFESSIONAL EDUCATION & DEVELOPMENT

Ph.D., anticipated 1988, Clinical Psychology - Saybrook Institute, San Francisco
M.A.,Clinical Psychology - John F. Kennedy University, Orinda
B.B.A.,Industrial Psychology - City College of New York

Relevant Specialized Training

Alcoholism Treatment 1982-present, seminars with:
Matthew Skinner, M.D.
Corrine Williamson, Ph.D.
Bay Graduate School of Marital & Family Therapy

Group Therapy Training
Gestalt Institute of New York 1969-71
Gestalt Institute of San Francisco 1974-75

Marriage & Family Therapy
Bay Graduate School of Marital & Family Therapy
- Karl Greenbaum, Ph.D.
- Trevor Howard, M.D.
- Leroy Russ, M.D.
- Jane Holland, M.A.

Psychotherapy Training
Ego Psychology/Object Relations Theory & Techniques
Solano Center for Psychological Services - Albany
Control Mastery Theory & Techniques
Roger Pritchard, M.D.

Hypnotherapy, Stress Reduction & Meditation Techniques
UC Berkeley and George Solis, Ph.D.
Yoga Societies of New York & San Francisco

Professional Credentials

Licensed Marriage, Family and Child Counselor, MF909099
Community College Instructor Credential, California No. YS 4557
Hypnosis Certification No. 11Z22

PATRICK D. ENRIGHT
1919 Shaeffer Ave.
Walnut Creek CA 94596
(415) 635-9798

Objective: Position as **therapist, social worker and/or program coordinator**
working with individuals & groups using a public therapy/social rehabilitation model.

HIGHLIGHTS OF QUALIFICATIONS

★ 5 years experience counseling individuals, couples and families.
★ Outstanding skill in assessing clients' needs for clinical and social
  rehabilitative services.
★ Effective in developing programs and reaching project goals.
★ Authored curriculum and training manuals for health and safety.
★ Deeply committed to my clients' well being.

PROFESSIONAL EXPERIENCE

Counseling
• Counseled both voluntary and involuntary clients, using a range of therapy modes:
  ...psychodynamic ...social rehabilitative ...gestalt ...humanistic ...behavior modification.
• Conducted intake interviews in community mental health agencies, selecting clients appropriate
  for the program.
• Conducted couple, group and family therapy sessions using MRI Systems approach which
  provided for clients' maximum potential for growth.

Program Coordination & Management
• Developed a unique group therapy format for developmentally disabled adults;
  -increased their enthusiasm, involvement and sense of empowerment by incorporating
    opportunities for choice and recognition of their achievements.
• Organized a parent support group for families of developmentally disabled/mentally disturbed
  clients, supporting their independent living by improving family dynamics.
• Coordinated with other mental health and social service agencies to develop individualized
  program plans, for example:
  - referred clients for job training, medical care and additional therapy;
  - found alternative funding for client's medical and dental needs;
  - served as an advocate to psychiatrists, psychologists and social workers, to assure highest
    quality services for my clients.

EMPLOYMENT HISTORY

1985-present	**Counseling Intern,** Cooperative Apartments Program	ELMWOOD HOMES - San Francisco
1981-84	**Counselor/Instructor**	COMMUNITY HOME HEALTH CARE - Seattle
1979-80	**Teacher/Tutor**	DEARBORN PARK SCHOOLS - Seattle
1979	**Counseling Intern**	OPEN DOOR CLINIC (walk-in clinic) Seattle

EDUCATION & TRAINING
M.A., Counseling Psychology - JFK UNIVERSITY, Orinda 1986
Rehabilitation & Training Center, University of Oregon at Eugene
Licensed Massage Therapist, Seattle Massage School, Seattle WA
B.A., History - MARQUETTE UNIVERSITY, Milwaukee WI. 1973

ROSLYN MARCUS
409 Acadia Way
Oakland CA 94602
(415) 350-2123

Objective: Clinical Social Worker in the Dept. of Psychiatry of a large HMO.

HIGHLIGHTS OF QUALIFICATIONS

- Licensed clinical social worker; 16 years professional experience.
- Demonstrated success in reaching treatment goals, with a special focus on short-term therapy.
- Strong practical and theoretical foundation in a number of therapeutic and intervention models.
- Excellent skills in group, couple, family and individual counseling.
- Cooperative and supportive colleague.

RELEVANT PROFESSIONAL EXPERIENCE

Assessment & Diagnosis
- Conducted hundreds of psycho-social evaluations and in-depth interviews of individuals and families.
- Assessed needs of patients involving a great diversity of issues:

-crisis intervention	-adolescent acting-out
-family role disruption	-destructive relationships
-child abuse	-families divorcing; children's adjustment
-loss and grief counseling	-adjustment to chronic illness
-acceptance of aging	-"empty nest" syndrome.

Treatment
- Counseled wide range of individuals and families at time of significant family crisis:
  -assessed personal strengths and coping mechanisms of patients and families;
  -developed and implemented treatment plans in keeping with the priorities and focus of the patients' and families' needs and resources.

Group Counseling
- Led long-term psychotherapy groups for both mixed groups and women-only.
- Designed and led unique time-limited therapy group, called "New Beginnings," for widows and widowers.
- Led highly successful weekly support/therapy groups for spinal cord injury, stroke and cancer patients.
- Collaborated effectively with many different colleagues to co-lead therapy groups.

EMPLOYMENT HISTORY

1986-present	Dir. of Medical Social Work	WESTCOAST CENTER Health Plan, Oakland
1976-85	Social Worker	KAISER HOSPITAL, Vallejo CA
1973-76	Group Work Supervisor	CNTR FOR PERSONAL/SOCIAL CHANGE, Berkeley
1971-72	Social Worker and Mental Health Consultant	INDIAN HEALTH SERVICES, Arizona
1970-71	Child Protective Svcs Worker	SAN FRANCISCO COUNTY

EDUCATION, CREDENTIALS, AFFILIATIONS

M.S.W. - HUNTER COLLEGE SCHOOL OF SOCIAL WORK, NYC • **LCSW** No. LH 099998
B.A., English - cum laude, Phi Beta Kappa - HUNTER COLLEGE, New York City
National Association of Social Workers

HARRIET BLOOM
5720 Hillegass Ave.
Berkeley CA 94705
(415) 622-5917

Objective: Position as Health Educator/Nutritionist.

HIGHLIGHTS OF QUALIFICATIONS

- Proven successful in managing simultaneous projects.
- Talent in designing systems for smooth program operation.
- Skilled teacher and trainer, able to inspire others.
- Excellent counseling and interviewing skills.
- Strong commitment to promoting wellness and preventing disease.

PROFESSIONAL EXPERIENCE

ADMINISTRATION

- Revamped and managed the Health Education Program of HealthAmerica, restoring and expanding programs that had been neglected.
- Developed administrative systems to handle all details for implementing program for both the health education department and the WIC program, at HealthAmerica.
- Won federal funding for a unique WIC program, integrating medical care with a supplemental food program, maximizing the effectiveness of the programs.

SUPERVISION & TRAINING

- Trained paraprofessionals in basic nutrition concepts and group leadership skills.
- Supervised WIC staff of 3; supervised Health Education Assistant.
- Served as preceptor for UC Berkeley and SF State graduate students.
- Coordinated in-service programs for physicians:
  ...smoking cessation counseling ...latest developments in the management of obesity.

NUTRITION COUNSELING & HEALTH PROMOTION

- Counseled a very wide range of patients in preventive nutrition and chronic disease.
- Developed an effective approach to weight management, matching patients to programs with highest probability of success.
- Promoted self-care classes to increase patients' knowledge and skills and their involvement in health care decisions.

PROGRAM DEVELOPMENT

- Developed and implemented both patient and practitioner surveys to assess health education needs.
- Evaluated patient education materials, adapting and altering as needed.
- Developed a variety of evaluation tools to assess patient knowledge and behavior change.

PUBLIC RELATIONS & COMMUNITY LIAISON

- Collaborated on design of brochure and fliers for health education classes and programs.
- Organized and chaired a community-based Health Advisory Committee for Alameda Head Start.
- Set up a monthly Health Education Advisory Committee at HealthAmerica.

- Continued -

HEALTH

EMPLOYMENT HISTORY

1985-present	**Health Education Coordinator**	HEALTHAMERICA - Oakland
1980-85	**WIC Project Director/Sr.Nutritionist**	HEALTHAMERICA* - Oakland
1978-present	**Senior Nutritionist**	HEALTHAMERICA* - Oakland
1979-81	**Nutrition Consultant**	Westinghouse Health Systems - SF
	(concurrent with above)	
1976-78	**Health/Nutrition Coordinator**	ALAMEDA HEAD START - Alameda
1977-78	**Nutrition Consultant**	DEVELOPMENT ASSOCIATES - SF
		(concurrent with above)

* earlier called Rockridge Health Care Plan

EDUCATION & CREDENTIALS

M.P.H., Nutrition - University of California, Berkeley -School of Public Health
Dietetics course work, University of California, Berkeley
B.A., Psychology - Vassar College, Poughkeepsie NY

Registered Dietitian (R.D.) 1976
California Community College Instructor Credential

HARRIET BLOOM
5720 Hillegass Ave.
Berkeley CA 94705
(415) 622-5917

**Objective: Position with Highland Hospital as
Project Coordinator, Breast Feeding Support Project Study**

HIGHLIGHTS OF QUALIFICATIONS

- Experienced in developing systems essential to the smooth operation of a program.
- Proven successful in managing simultaneous projects.
- Skilled teacher and trainer, able to inspire others.
- Excellent counseling and interviewing skills.
- Strong commitment to promoting the benefits of breast feeding.

PROFESSIONAL EXPERIENCE

ADMINISTRATION
- Revamped and managed the Health Education Program of HealthAmerica, restoring and expanding programs that had been neglected.
- Developed administrative systems to handle all details for implementing program for both the health education department and the WIC program at HealthAmerica.
- Won federal funding for a unique WIC program, integrating medical care with a supplemental food program, maximizing the effectiveness of the programs.
- Developed an effective method for highlighting entries in medical records to assure timely exchange of important information between doctors and WIC program staff.

SUPERVISION & TRAINING
- Trained paraprofessional Nutrition Education Assistant in basic nutrition concepts and group leadership skills.
- Trained paraprofessionals (family advocates) in a home-based Head Start Program in basic nutrition and child development.
- Supervised WIC staff of 3; supervised Health Education Assistant.
- Served as preceptor for UC Berkeley and SF State graduate students.

BREAST FEEDING PROMOTION
- Initiated a successful program which doubled the incidence of breast feeding in a low income minority population (WIC):
  -greatly increased acceptance by identifying barriers (concerns, fears, myths);
  -added group education and individual counseling to program requirements;
  -developed interdisciplinary team immediately available to resolve early problems.

NUTRITION COUNSELING
- Counseled a very wide range of patients in nutrition:
  -prenatal -infant and pediatric -adolescent -midlife -geriatric

PUBLIC RELATIONS & COMMUNITY LIAISON
- Organized and chaired a community-based Health Advisory Committee for Alameda Head Start.
- Set up a monthly Health Education Advisory Committee at HealthAmerica.

- Continued -

HEALTH

EMPLOYMENT HISTORY

1985-present	**Health Education Coordinator**	HEALTHAMERICA - Oakland
1980-85	**Project Director/Sr.Nutritionist**	HEALTHAMERICA* - Oakland
1978-present	**Senior Nutritionist**	HEALTHAMERICA* - Oakland
1979-81	**Nutrition Consultant**	Westinghouse Health Systems - SF
	(concurrent with above)	
1976-78	**Health/Nutrition Coordinator**	ALAMEDA HEAD START - Alameda
1977-78	**Nutrition Consultant**	DEVELOPMENT ASSOCIATES - SF
		(concurrent with above)

* earlier called Rockridge Health Care Plan

EDUCATION & CREDENTIALS

M.P.H., Nutrition - University of California, Berkeley -School of Public Health
Dietetics course work, University of California, Berkeley
B.A., Psychology - Vassar College, Poughkeepsie NY

Registered Dietitian (R.D.) 1976
California Community College Instructor Credential

KEN SIRCHUK

Ken's real name. It's ok to call, he says.

INTEGRATED EDUCATIONAL BODY THERAPY
3111 Telegraph Ave., Berkeley CA 94705
(415) 548-3541

Objective:
Professional affiliation with a health practitioner, health care center , or related service, providing body therapy and/or educational services, in-house or out-call referrals.

HIGHLIGHTS OF QUALIFICATIONS
★ Advanced certification in educational body therapy from the Institute for Educational Therapy.
★ Certification in massage by National Holistic Institute.
★ Commitment to professional development.
★ Sensitivity and responsiveness to the needs of clients.
★ Self- motivated; experience in managing a successful practice.

PROFESSIONAL EXPERIENCE AND APPROACH

Educational Body Therapy
- I apply an educational approach to helping clients with mind/body health issues, increasing their self-help skills and their cause-and-effect awareness, using:
...deep tissue massage ...peripheral joint articulation ...spinal articulation ...movement therapy ...repatterning restrictive and inefficient movement habits ...postural and structural alignment through body awareness ...balance of tone ...stress release through awareness of breath.

Bodywork/Massage
- Worked with hundreds of individual clients in private practice, applying a wide range of therapeutic techniques: ...Swedish ...Acupressure ...Polarity ...Sports Massage.

EMPLOYMENT HISTORY

1985-present	**Massage Therapist**	PRIVATE PRACTICE, Berkeley
1982-87	**Banquet Waiter**	VOLUME SERVICE CO., caterers - Oakland
1982-87	**Music Instructor**	ACME MUSIC, Oakland; and J&A MUSIC, El Cerrito

RELEVANT EDUCATION & TRAINING

He details his professional approach.

INSTITUTE FOR EDUCATIONAL THERAPY, Berkeley - 200-hour Body Therapy training, 1986
Instructor, Jim Spira
NATIONAL HOLISTIC INSTITUTE, Oakland -100-hour Massage Certification, 1985
Polarity Therapy Center of San Francisco - 40-hour Polarity Therapy training, 1986
Sports Massage Workshop - 30 hours, Jesse Vargas, Oakland, 1987
Developmental Movement and **Experiential Anatomy** - Marghe Mills, Sausalito, 1986
Movement Workshop, Bartenieff Fundamentals -8th St. Studios, Berkeley
Betsy Kagan, instructor, 1986
Movement and Sound Workshops - Nina Wise and Bob Ernst, instructors, 1983-84
Skinner Releasing Techniques; Contact Improvisation (Movement Therapies)
8th St. Studios - Robert Funk and Catherine Duncan, instructors, 1986
Music, CAL STATE UNIVERSITY, Northridge CA
Music Improvisation, PASADENA CITY COLLEGE

KURT NIVER
FITNESS CONSULTANT

309 Mallorca Circle
San Francisco CA 94110
(415) 467-0200

HIGHLIGHTS OF QUALIFICATIONS

- Successfully developed and implemented programs for all levels, beginners through world class athletes.
- Strong, credible model through personal accomplishments as Mr. California and State Olympic Weight Lifting Champion.
- Proven ability to get any individual into the best shape of their life.
- An "athlete's coach"; currently active as both athlete and coach; 13 years professional experience in fitness training.

PROFESSIONAL EXPERIENCE

Athletic Training
- Trained wide range of individual athletes to achieve specific goals and benefits:
  -Olympic weight lifters, for strength training and muscular endurance;
  -football players, to improve speed, strength, agility, stamina; and to gain muscular body weight;
  -competitive body builders, to develop muscular size, symmetry, and definition; to diet and to minimize body fat;
  -nationally ranked swimmers and runners, to strengthen & condition overall body.
- Trained individuals, applying programs of diet & exercise to achieve various goals:
  -weight reduction   -body fat reduction   -weight gain.

Individual Consultations
- Successfully motivated many hundreds of people to participate in fitness training, by living what I teach and offering proven past experience.
- Personally instructed individuals in custom designed fitness programs, showing a personal interest and offering strong support for each individual.
- Adjusted and updated individual programs as goals were achieved & new goals set.

Fitness Program Design/Implementation
- Developed a basic fitness program for working the whole body, based on:
  -study of the body and how it works   -my own personal experience
  -results achieved in effectively training hundreds of others.
- Tailored basic program to the varying achievement levels of individuals, and to their specific goals, such as weight loss, weight gain, increased overall fitness.
- Constantly monitored clients' progress:
  -maintained records of weights handled, exercises done, number of sets/repetitions;
  -assessed degree of difficulty and improvement, and made adjustments accordingly.

Personal Accomplishments
- Achieved status of Nationally ranked Olympic weight lifter.
- Won title of 1986 AAU "Mr. California"; competing for current AAU "Mr. America."
  (Detailed list of titles won, on page two)

- Continued -

"Fitness consultant," immediately beneath Kurt's name, replaces the "Objective" in this case.

TITLES and AWARDS

BODY BUILDING

1985 AAU "Mr. Northwestern America" (novice)
      -first place Short Class   -first place overall   -most muscular overall
1985 AAU Pacific Association Body Builder of the Year Award: best newcomer
1986   AAU "Mr. Northern California"
      -first place Medium Class -first place overall   -most muscular overall
1986 AAU "Mr. California"
      -first place Short Class   -first place overall   -best poser overall

OLYMPIC WEIGHT LIFTING

National
1980 American Olympic Weight Lifting Championships - 4th place
1981 American Olympic Weight Lifting Championships - 3rd place clean and jerk
1982 American Olympic Weight Lifting Championships - 3rd place
1983 American Olympic Weight Lifting Championships - 5th place

State
1981 California State Olympic Weight Lifting Champion
1983 California State Olympic Weight Lifting Champion

Regional & Local
Pacific Association Olympic Weight Lifting Champion - 3 times
Northern California Open Olympic Weight Lifting Champion - 3 times
Golden West Open Olympic Weight Lifting Champion - 3 times
Pacific Coast Open Olympic Weight Lifting Champion - 2 times
San Francisco Open Olympic Weight Lifting Champion - 2 times
Sports Palace Belt Buckle Open Olympic Weight Lifting Champion

Junior National
1978 Junior Olympic Weight Lifting National Championships - 4th place
1979 Teenage National Olympic Weight Lifting Championship and
      Junior World Team Tryouts - 3rd place

EMPLOYMENT HISTORY

1980-present   **Manager; Strength & Conditioning Coach**
                        SPORTS PALACE - San Francisco
1977-80   **Manager; Head Nutritional Consultant**
                        JACK LaLANNES European Health Spa - Sacramento, Palo Alto

EDUCATION

American River Junior College, Sacramento
Business Administration; Nutrition

MARGO SEGALL, R.N.
2131 Blackhawk Rd.
Berkeley CA 94707
(415) 275-2347

Objective: Medical investigator/counselor position with Irwin Memorial Blood Bank

HIGHLIGHTS OF QUALIFICATIONS

- Skill in dealing with sensitive populations in a professional and concerned manner.
- Able to work independently and as a cooperative team member.
- Experienced and competent phlebotomist.
- Thorough understanding of the protocols of human research and data collection, through 11 years experience as a research clinical nurse.

PROFESSIONAL EXPERIENCE

Counseling
- Conducted crisis intervention and long-term counseling with individuals of diverse backgrounds, dealing with issues of confinement, illness, and institutional group living.
- Advised prospective research volunteers of positive test results indicating presence of venereal disease, TB, high blood pressure or abnormal blood values.
- Directed disqualified volunteers to appropriate referral agencies as necessary for medical follow-up.

Phlebotomy
- Drew blood samples for high volume health screenings in over 40 human nutrition research studies.
- Performed venipunctures and/or IVs throughout each study, as specified by research protocol.
- Prepared blood samples for analysis or transport.

Management/Supervision
- Served as head nurse over 6-month period, supervising support staff, research volunteers and graduate students, for a UC Berkeley nutrition-related study.
- Authored procedure on blood/body fluid precautions, and delivered in-service training talk to staff.
- Taught data collection techniques to research participants.
- Assembled final report data at conclusion of studies.

Knowledge of AIDS
- Familiar with "Guidelines for HLV Antibody Testing in the Community," as provided by the State of California.
- Completed three continuing education workshops on AIDS :
  "AIDS: Fears, Facts, and Fantasies" - Letterman Hospital and Shanti Project.
  "AIDS: The Spectrum of the Acquired Immune Deficiency Syndrome" - Letterman Hospital
  "AIDS: Infection Control for Health Workers" - San Francisco Dept. of Public Health

EMPLOYMENT HISTORY

1974-present	**Research/Clinical Nurse II**	Univ. of California /USDA - Berkeley/San Francisco
1981-84	**Health Consultant**	Berkeley Unified School Dist. (concurrent w/above)
1966-70	**Teacher, Special Educ.**	Richmond Unified School District

EDUCATION
B.A., English & Art - UC Berkeley, 1964 • Teaching Credential, 1965
R.N. - MERRITT COLLEGE, 1971;   **CPR** Certified - 1985

PATRICIA RAINES, B.S., R.N.
Specialist in Stress Reduction & Biofeedback
960 Los Cerros Ave.
Alameda CA 94598
(415) 111-5760

HIGHLIGHTS OF QUALIFICATIONS

★ Demonstrated success in facilitating clients in resolving the physical and emotional symptoms of mishandled stress.

★ Personal and professional commitment to the empowerment of clients; creative, intuitive approach, allowing them to tap into their own solutions.

★ Skill in providing a safe, supportive, and nonjudgemental environment.

★ Unique background combining 15 years in nursing, degree in psychology, and 8 years in motivational management.

PROFESSIONAL EXPERIENCE

Individual Consulting & Philosophy
Effectively consulted with hundreds of individuals, facilitating them in discovering new solutions to immediate or chronic upsets, applying these proven principles:

• Created a safe, supportive, attentive and nonjudgemental atmosphere.
• Identified the issue and the immediate goal for the session.
• Encouraged them to explore feelings, as opposed to thoughts about the issue.
• Kept them on track; persistently restored the focus; surrendered my own judgements.
• Validated & acknowledged them in a loving atmosphere that allowed them to look within.
• Supported them in going beyond what they previously thought possible, to find their own answers within.

Teaching/Motivational Training
Served as program coordinator, trainer and leader with Motivational Management Service:

• Trained and coordinated Workshop Facilitation Teams for the duration of 3-month periods; training them to work one-to-one with participants and support the workshop leaders.
• Co-led workshops on self-esteem; led the follow-up 6-week Integration Support Series
• Led Self-empowerment, a 2-month series of weekly meetings.
• Coordinated 3-month training series, Consultants Training, assisting participants to define and actualize goals.

Relevant Medical Experience
• Developed a broad understanding of medical conditions and illnesses, as nurse in all units at Alta Bates Hospital: ...Medical ...Surgical ...Orthopedic ...Neurology ...Oncology ...Obstetrics & Gynecology ...Intensive Care ...Coronary Care.
• Designed a comprehensive in-service training program for nurses at St. Joseph's Hospital.

- Continued -

EMPLOYMENT HISTORY

1976-present	**Staff Nurse**	ALTA BATES HOSPITAL, Berkeley
1965-75	Family management	
1962-64	**Nursing Supervisor**	UNIV. of CALIFORNIA MEDICAL CENTER , San Francisco
1961-62	**Asst. Dir. of Nursing**	ST. JOSEPH'S HOSPITAL, Denver CO
1958-59	**Staff Nurse**	PRESBYTERIAN HOSPITAL, New York City
1959-61	**Head Nurse**	PRESBYTERIAN HOSPITAL, New York City

EDUCATION & TRAINING

B.A., Psychology - WILSON COLLEGE, Chambersburg PA
B.S., R.N., COLUMBIA UNIVERSITY, New York NY

Motivational Management Training:
• Group Consulting, Mediation, and Partnership
• Leadership Training Programs
• Self-esteem Workshop
• Consultants Training

Biofeedback Institute, San Francisco

Patricia indicates that she's looking for a professional affiliation rather than employee status in the way she presents herself at the top of the resume.

PAULINE MASTERSON, MPA/HSA
457 Hathorn Court, San Francisco CA 94117
(415) 204-6906

Objective: Administrative management position, directing nursing services of a hospital or health care delivery organization.

HIGHLIGHTS OF QUALIFICATIONS
- Special strength in promoting an atmosphere of professionalism in nursing.
- Committed, enthusiastic, people-oriented leader.
- Highly successful in developing collaborative practice.
- Concerned with balancing quality nursing and cost containment.

RELEVANT EXPERIENCE

Administration/Management
- Managed a 45-bed medical teaching unit on a 24-hour/7-day basis, including long/short-term planning, hiring, interviewing and orienting new staff.
- Developed a management style emphasizing professional responsibility:
  -delegated authority for problem solving;
  -involved staff in decision making at every opportunity;
  -held staff accountable for their actions;
  -supported staff in resolving interpersonal issues on their own.
- Raised Quality Assurance Scores by incorporating staff input into planning process.
- Developed and implemented cost containment proposals, for example:
  -decreased staff sick time use by involving them directly in the scheduling;
  -informed staff of materials costs and encouraged ideas for economizing.
- Analyzed fiscal trends in terms of budget goals.

Staff Development
- Encouraged creativity and professionalism of the nursing staff, resulting in their taking initiative to form a unique self-governance Nursing Practice Committee.
- Upgraded the employee performance evaluation process to incorporate criteria reflecting increased individual accountability in nursing.

Promoting Professionalism
- Expanded and strongly supported high school student apprenticeship programs by authorizing one-on-one preceptorships with staff nurses.
- Provided staff nurses as preceptors for student nurses during clinical rotation.
- Serve as active bureau speaker and CPR instructor for American Heart Association.
- Conducted research, and incorporated findings, on perceptions of leadership styles and its relationship to professional autonomy and accountability of staff nurses.
- Served as on-site investigator for Stanford Research Consortium, developing more effective care for decubiti.

EMPLOYMENT HISTORY

1984-present	**Nurse Manager**	MEMORIAL HOSPITAL & MEDICAL CENTER, San Francisco
1981-84	**Clinical Care Coor**	MEMORIAL HOSPITAL & MEDICAL CENTER, San Francisco
1976-81	**Staff Nurse II**	MEMORIAL HOSPITAL & MEDICAL CENTER, San Francisco
1973-76	**Staff Nurse I & II**	SANTA CLARA VALLEY MEDICAL CENTER, San Jose

EDUCATION & LICENSURE
MPA/Health Services Administration - UNIVERSITY of SAN FRANCISCO, 1986
BS, Nursing - CALIFORNIA STATE UNIVERSITY, SAN JOSE, 1973
Registered Nurse, State of California

RICHARD JENNINGS
8009 Mountain Blvd.
Oakland CA 94602
(415) 111-6887

Compare this with Richard's other resume on page 242.

Objective: County Field Supervisor, Emergency Medical Services

HIGHLIGHTS OF QUALIFICATIONS

- Proven ability to respond immediately and confidently in emergencies.
- One year experience in staff supervision.
- Excellent relations with the public and the community.
- Able to function at top performance throughout a 24-hour shift.
- 3 years experience as a paramedic; 5 years as EMT.
- Mature lifestyle, compatible with emergency work.

RELEVANT EXPERIENCE

Crisis Evaluation & Response
- Effectively evaluated thousands of emergencies.
- Adapted immediately to changing circumstances in medical emergencies, setting priorities and constantly reevaluating them.

Supervision
- Led pre-hospital-care team, as Crew Chief for BMS, serving as liaison between paramedics, hospitals and fire department:
  -provided monthly training updates for the firemen I worked with;
  -mediated communication problems among professionals;
  -provided follow-up medical information on cases jointly handled.
- Supervised warehouse staff at Sausalito Design:
  -trained and guided personnel;
  -monitored safe and accurate filling of orders and thoroughness of paperwork,
  -researched customer complaints to identify source of error and resolve problems

PR, Community Relations
- Educated the public on the role of emergency medical services, through demonstrations, lectures and small group talks.
- Taught public CPR classes; served as volunteer medic for public events; trained nurses and hospital employees in trauma skills at Eden Hospital.

Medical Skills
- Highly skilled in medical emergency techniques:
  -taking blood pressure and pulses   -wound management
  -splinting fractures   -CPR
  -applying oxygen   -patient assessment
  -advanced life support

Training & Quality Assurance
- Selected for and served on Paramedic Peer Review Committee at Eden Hospital, monitoring paramedic response to improve treatment of patients.
- Trained new paramedics in the field portion of their state-required training time, focusing on communication and decision making skills in medical emergencies.
- Wrote draft of training manual for new medics at Bay Medical Services.
- Helped upgrade the skills of weak paramedics, providing retraining and evaluation.

- Continued -

RICHARD JENNINGS
page two

EMPLOYMENT HISTORY

1985-present	**Paramedic Crew Chief**	BAY MEDICAL SERVICES, Berkeley/Oakland
1984	**Paramedic**	KING AMERICAN AMBULANCE, San Francisco
1982-84	**EMT-1A**	ALLIED AMBULANCE, Oakland
1977-81	**Warehouseman/Driver**	GOOD GUYS; SAUSALITO DESIGN; PACIFIC FLOORING
1976-77	**Clerk Typist**	PMI MORTGAGE INSURANCE, San Francisco
1974-76	**Day Care Driver**	EASTER SEAL SOCIETY, San Francisco

EDUCATION & SPECIALIZED TRAINING

B.A., Sociology - SAN FRANCISCO STATE UNIVERSITY
A.A., Criminology - San Joaquin Delta College, Stockton

Paramedic Training; EMT-1A Training - City College of San Francisco
Basic Life Support & Advanced Cardiac Life Support Certificates - Amer. Heart Assoc.
Ambulance Driver's License - Advanced Airway Management Training
Additional courses in Anatomy, Physiology, Chemistry, 1985-86

TONY FOOTE
1992-C Parker Street
Berkeley CA 94704
(415) 399-0102

Objective: Position as Physical Therapy Aide

HIGHLIGHTS OF QUALIFICATIONS
- Compassionate, professional approach and commitment to service oriented work.
- Experienced and effective in assisting people with medical disabilities.
- Interest and knowledge in the field of physical therapy;
- Long-term goal to practice as a registered physical therapist.
- Degree in biology; course   work in human anatomy & human physiology.

RELEVANT EXPERIENCE

Physical Therapy Related
- Served as a physical therapy aide working with seriously handicapped children
  -performed basic physical therapy routines to facilitate physical development;
  -positioned children to minimize pathology.
- Performed basic occupational therapy tasks with young children.
- Implemented adaptive aquatic routines with a physically handicapped adult.

Experience with Other Disabilities
- Assisted in supervising recreation activities of mentally handicapped children and adults, as volunteer at city-sponsored specialized recreation program.
- Formulated the speech therapy program for a language delayed student under direction of a speech therapist.
- Assisted with speech therapy in a classroom for language impaired children, both as a volunteer and paid employee.
- Instructed basic academic subjects in classroom for learning delayed children.
- Developed behavioral and academic strategies for emotionally handicapped adolescents, as support staff for special education teachers.

Record Keeping
- Maintained records of medicines taken and relevant observations of physically handicapped and frail elderly residents in a senior retirement facility.
- Recorded academic performance of special education children.

EMPLOYMENT HISTORY

1984-present	Assistant Teacher	HARWOOD DAY SCHOOL, Oakland
1982-84	Personal Care Attendant	SATELLITE SENIOR HOMES, Oakland
1980-81	Instructional Assistant	PUBLIC SCHOOLS, Eugene & Springfield OR
1978-79	Developmental Aide	EASTER SEAL SCHOOL, Eugene
1977	Bus Driver	PEARL BUCK SCHOOL for mentally handicapped, Eugene

EDUCATION & TRAINING
B.A., Biology - UNIVERSITY OF OREGON, Eugene OR
Human anatomy, human physiology, massage, psychology,
abnormal psychology, language acquisition, statistics.

JULIA MILLHOUSE
68809 Steiner Street, San Francisco CA 94117
(415) 302-6113 home   (415) 815-6609 messages

Objective: Middle management position in a geriatric extended care facility, involving staff development, education, and direct supervision of patient caregivers.

HIGHLIGHTS OF QUALIFICATIONS
★Clinical expertise and experience in all aspects of geriatric care.
★Committed to highest standards of care for the geriatric population.
★Proven skill in teaching and supervising professional nurses.
★High energy leader who inspires and challenges others to excellence.

RELEVANT EXPERIENCE

Supervision
* Coordinated and supervised nursing team responsible for 24-hour care of geriatric patients, at King Medical Center Nursing Home Care Unit:
  -expanded program of preventive care, minimizing need for hospitalization;
  -upgraded anecdotal reporting on nursing care, assuring that reports were adequate for judging staff advancement potential;
  -provided personal support of staff in bettering themselves through education;
  -assured that family members were very well informed and involved.
* Successfully filled in as charge nurse during the absence of head nurse.

Teaching
* Taught in-service programs for floor staff, on geriatric care issues:
  ...diabetes ...psycho-social care needs ...infection control ...physiology of aging.
* Facilitated Wives' Support Group discussion on current trends in the care of diabetes.
* As Teaching Assistant for expert in Geriatric Care Delivery at Livermore General Hospital:
  -wrote and graded exams; evaluated written assignments;
  -arranged for guest speakers and their technical support;
  -prepared syllabus; selected reading lists; coordinated audio-visual support;
  -advised students on academic and clinical issues; coordinated & presented test reviews.

Planning/Problem Solving
* Cochaired joint committee on Infection Control and Product Evaluation, involving nurses from throughout hospital, responsible for assessing staff adherence to policy standards:
  -effectively represented the unique interests and priorities of the nursing home staff;
  -voluntarily continued as an active committee member while part-time employed.
* Took the initiative to develop a plan responding to pending JCAH requirements, showing how computers could be used in developing mandatory multidisciplinary care plans. Currently involved in the ongoing development of this plan.

EMPLOYMENT HISTORY

1986-present	**Staff RN,** part time	KING Med Cntr, Nursing Home Care Unit, Livermore CA
1986-87	**Teaching Assistant**	SCHOOL OF NURSING, Livermore General Hospital
1985-86	**Staff RN/Team Leader**	ST. GEORGE. MEDICAL CENTER, Livermore CA
1984-85	**Staff RN**	DANE MEMORIAL MEDICAL CENTER, Reno NV
1983-84	Full-time student	Univ. of Nevada, Reno, Orvis School of Nursing
1983 summer	**Student Nurse Tech.**	DANE MEMORIAL MEDICAL CENTER, Reno NV
1976-82	**Resort Supv./Waitress**	SO. LAKE TAHOE RESORTS, NV
1981-82	**Teaching Assistant**	SO. LAKE TAHOE UNIFIED SCHOOL DISTRICT, CA

EDUCATION
B.S., Nursing - UNIVERSITY OF NEVADA, RENO 1984
B.A., History - UNIVERSITY OF CALIFORNIA, LOS ANGELES 1976

ANDREA HUGHES
3945 - 20th Street
San Francisco CA 94114
(415) 628-0108 (office)
(415) 271-0055 (home)

Objective: Representative in a public relations/marketing department or agency

SUMMARY OF QUALIFICATIONS

★ Highly competitive, and thrive in challenging situations.

★ Maintain a sense of humor under pressure.

★ Extremely sharp at quickly assessing needs & priorities.

★ Diplomatic and assertive in dealing with people.

★ Three years experience in public relations and marketing.

PROFESSIONAL EXPERIENCE

Public Relations
• Promoted Spanish products and tourism to Spain:
  - organized conferences and group programs for travelling professionals;
  - participated in trade shows, informing media representatives and members of the travel industry on Spain's travel offerings;
  - advised media representatives and members of the travel industry on tourist attractions, cultural activities, living conditions, and political climate;
  - wrote press releases directed to West Coast media on up-coming travel industry conventions.
• Developed contacts in Spain for American media producing features for US audiences; also coordinated their travel arrangements to, and within, Spain.

Marketing & Sales
• Successfully made cold-calls to most Bay Area real estate developers, generating new business for local architecture firm.
• Wrote proposals and assembled information packages describing architectural services for potential construction projects.
• Developed graphic design & coordinated production of firm's promotional brochures.
• Advised boutique retail customers on fashion and merchandise selection.

Organization/Administrative
• Developed ideas for creating new business, prioritized work projects, designed and implemented follow-up procedures, resulting in more efficient & profitable work flow.

EMPLOYMENT HISTORY

1984-88	**Public Relations Rep**	NATIONAL TOURIST OFFICE OF SPAIN - San Francisco
1983	**Marketing Coordinator**	FEE + MUNSON Architects - San Francisco
1982	**Administrative Assistant**	CROWLEY MARITIME CORP -San Francisco
1980-81	**Salesperson** (summers)	DAYTIME DELIGHT clothing store - Martha's Vineyard

EDUCATION

B.A., Anthropology/Spanish Culture - DREW UNIVERSITY - Madison, NJ - 1981
Special studies in Anthropology, Universidad de los Andes - Bogota, Colombia -1980
Extensive travel in Western Europe, North Africa and South America
Fluent in Spanish

CLAUDIA GISELLE
5002 Forty-Fifth Ave.
San Francisco CA 94116
(415) 699-4104

MARKETING

Objective: Position in marketing, PR and/or promotions.

HIGHLIGHTS OF QUALIFICATIONS
- A "born promoter," able to generate enthusiasm in others.
- Proven successful in increasing sales and customer base.
- 10 years experience in public relations and promotions.
- Extremely well organized; follow through to the last detail.
- Committed to producing results above & beyond what's expected.

RELEVANT PROFESSIONAL EXPERIENCE

Marketing & Public Relations
- Developed customer service procedures and training program for managers & staff.
- Originated and implemented marketing strategies to bolster sales at unprofitable store locations.
- Set up an advertising department for a restaurant in Eugene OR, successfully initiating its new image as a community cultural center.
- Designed a successful marketing and PR dept. for Bay Area restaurant franchise.
- Established and maintained cooperative working relations with radio and print media, resulting in free advertising and free air time.

Promotion
- Successfully demonstrated gourmet food items and fine cookware in department stores and markets; educated public on its use; reported public reactions to manufacturers.
- Developed outstandingly effective network of resources and support for Community Arts Festival, resulting in a lavish, "smash hit" fund raising event.
- Delivered product presentations to corporate employees during work hours, increasing customer base of nearby store.

Customer Service/Needs Assessment
- Assessed clients' specific needs for catering services: handled initial inquiry, developed initial and final bids, visited site of affair, consulted with client to set desired menu and ambiance, proposed alternatives based on seasonal availability and unforeseen circumstances (e.g., weather).
- Managed all aspects of large & small catered affairs, setting hosts totally at ease; oversaw food preparation; coordinated staffing, entertainment, setup, cleanup.

WORK HISTORY

1985-present	**PR/Promotions Director**	CYBELLE'S PIZZA RESTAURANTS - SF & East Bay
1983-present	**Sales Rep & Partner**	CREATIVE MARKETING VENTURES - SF
1980-84	**Caterer/Sales Rep**	LET THEM EAT CAKE self-employed, Oregon & Calif.
1980-84	**Product Demonstrator**	Free-lance for West Coast manufacturers.
1980-83	**Fund-raiser/PR Asst.**	KAREN WHITTMAN PR/ADVERTISING CO. - Portland OR
1976-80	**PR/Promotions Director**	COMMUNITY CENTER RESTAURANT - Eugene OR

EDUCATION

B.S., Education - Temple University - Philadelphia
Graduate studies in Education and Administration - University of Oregon

163

CYNTHIA MICHAELS MAYER

2127 Twentieth Street - Apt. 6
San Francisco CA 94114
(415) 329-6667

Objective: Position in Marketing, Sales, or Client Services

HIGHLIGHTS OF QUALIFICATIONS

★ Diplomatic and tactful in dealing with clients.

★ Exceptionally patient and effective in training new staff.

★ Thoroughly enjoy coordinating and managing projects.

★ 6 years professional business experience.

PROFESSIONAL EXPERIENCE

Marketing Support/Client Services

- Assembled customized marketing packets used in presentations to potential clients.
- Calculated and formatted data on firm's investment performance for marketing use.
- Oriented bank clients on services, management agreements, & account procedures.
- Successfully collected interest due to clients, previously lost through brokerage firm errors.
- Advised clients on tax questions, investment fees, bank statements.

Supervision and Training

- Supervised daily activities of staff, quickly shifting priorities as market fluctuated.
- Ensured that stock wasn't overbought/ versold for accounts involving $600 million.
- Reviewed and approved reports to clients summarizing their account performance.
- Trained inexperienced Portfolio Assistants in complex administrative and operational procedures for handing clients' investment accounts, specifically how to:
  - set up and maintain portfolio activity on the computer system;
  - analyze the performance of an account;
  - resolve stock delivery problems and bank statement discrepancies;
  - analyze client's accounts, identifying sources of ready cash or tax benefits;
  - produce and process all legal documentation related to a client's portfolio.

Organization/Project Management

- Streamlined the process of gathering stock trading information and reduced costly errors, by designing better forms and procedures.
- Developed and coordinated complex stock buy-and-sell programs, involving accurate allocations of large sums of money, to achieve the Portfolio Manager's investment objectives.
- Managed 3-month computer conversion project, communicating detailed specifications to programmers and supervising final transfer of data.

WORK HISTORY

1988	**Project Assistant (part-time)**	ALUMNAE RESOURCES Career Center, S.F.
	concurrent with relocation and career transition work	
1987	**Manager, Portfolio Operations;**	SNYDER CAPITAL MANAGEMENT CO., NY
1985-86	**Sr. Portfolio Asst./Back-up Trader**	"
1984	**Portfolio Assistant**	"
1982-83	**Customer Service Representative**	METROPOLITAN TRUST CO. - Cambridge MA

EDUCATION

B.A., Urban Studies - Hobart and William Smith Colleges

ELIZABETH JULIAN
1224 Seymour Ave.
Berkeley CA 94709
(415) 345-6789

Elizabeth mentions her current graduate studies because that's more directly relevant than her completed degree.

Objective: position as publicist with an arts organization

HIGHLIGHTS OF QUALIFICATIONS

★ Personable; works effectively with wide range of personalities.

★ Experience in writing press releases and PSAs.

★ Extensive contacts in the arts/entertainment field.

★ Works well under pressure.

★ Practical talent for seeing what needs to be done, and doing it.

RELEVANT EXPERIENCE

Public Relations

• Composed press releases and public service announcements publicizing Bay Area musical benefits.
• Developed cooperative relationships with entertainment columnists from Bay Area news publications, resulting in successful coverage of musical events.
• Organized a calendar of advertising deadlines for several community organizations.

Project Organizing

• Compiled Directory of Bay Area Editors and publishers for use of literary agents.
• Organized educational workshop on publishing for writers and authors, involving:
  -soliciting speakers   -participant mailing list   -space rental   -advertising

Writing

• Edited technical and literary book manuscripts, using word processor and WordStar program.
• Wrote and recorded copy for use as spot advertising on local radio station.
• Published poetry.

Technical Skills

• Filmed & edited 8mm film of a new, experimental music performance at Stanford Center for New Music Research (later transferred to video for use as instructional feedback).
• Videotaped and edited classes in multimedia performance, for instructional feedback.
• Designed and produced flyers to advertise benefits.

EMPLOYMENT HISTORY

1986-present	**TAP Admin. Assistant**	UC BERKELEY, Music Dept.
1980-85	**Editorial/PR Assistant**	BARRET INC., LITERARY AGENTS - San Francisco
1979-80	**Film maker** (Video/8mm)	Free-lance - Bay Area
1977-79	**Benefits Organizer**	Free-lance assignments for agencies - Bay Area

EDUCATION

B.S., Environmental Planning - UC BERKELEY, 1977
Graduate studies in expressive arts, in progress - JFK UNIVERSITY

MARKETING

ELIZABETH LEONARD
340 California Street
Sacramento CA 95818
(916) 881-7213

Objective: Position in public relations, public affairs or promotions

HIGHLIGHTS OF QUALIFICATIONS
- 5 years successful experience in public relations.
- Special talent for persuasion and problem solving.
- Ability to relate easily with all kinds of people, in acting as company representative.
- Skilled in writing PSAs and promotional material.
- Well organized and self-motivated.
- Creative, energetic, positive and hard working.

RELEVANT EXPERIENCE

Public Relations/Problem Solving
- Successfully handled PR problems for cable TV company, gaining the cooperation of previously resistant homeowners, for installations on their property:
  -established friendly communication and identified homeowners' specific objections;
  -negotiated creative solutions acceptable to both our company and homeowners.
- Resolved restaurant's PR problem involving customer injury, demonstrating genuine concern for the customer, taking responsibility for medical costs, and successfully retaining the good will and business of the customer.

Promotion
- Promoted campus entertainment events: -wrote PSAs and ads -implemented creative promotional ideas -designed and distributed fliers.
- Sold program advertising space for a fund-raising musical event, raising money for Stanford Children's Home.
- Promoted special seasonal offerings for a gourmet vegetarian restaurant:
  -proposed new entrees -designed menu -designed & distributed discount coupons.
- Currently developing a 60-second TV spot to raise funds for a local charity.

Project Management/Organization
- Coordinated programming and scheduling for a live radio talk show on KGNR:
  -contacted public figures and ordinary citizens to set up specific schedule;
  -wrote up biographical material and proposed questions, for radio anchorman;
  -followed up to confirm appointments just prior to show time.
- Managed Mum's in Sacramento, an 80-seat restaurant:
  -hired, supervised and scheduled employees -monitored customer satisfaction.

EMPLOYMENT HISTORY

1985-present	**Construction Coordinator**	SACRAMENTO CABLE TV - Sacramento
1983-85	**Restaurant Manager**	MUM'S RESTAURANT - Sacramento
1983-84	**Producer Intern** (concurrently)	KGNR RADIO - Sacramento
1984 spring	**Public Relations Intern**	STANFORD CHILDREN'S HOME - Sacramento
1980-84	**Student**	CAL STATE UNIVERSITY, SACRAMENTO

EDUCATION

B.A., Communication Studies - CALIFORNIA STATE UNIVERSITY, SACRAMENTO

FRAN MORGAN
1598 Waverley Avenue
Berkeley CA 94709
(415) 523-3635

Again, consistent layout goes a long way in bringing clarity to a complicated work history.

Objective: Position in sales/marketing, promotion or public relations, dealing with consumer services or high quality consumer products

HIGHLIGHTS OF QUALIFICATIONS

★ Personable and persuasive; able to build instant rapport.
★ Aggressive, enthusiastic and energetic self-starter.
★ Effective working both independently and as a team member.
★ Successful experience in sales, marketing and promotion.

RELEVANT EXPERIENCE

Sales/Customer Relations
- Successfully sold expensive video-dating club memberships (min. $1250) to men and women.
  -interviewed, screened, selected prospects   -advised on affordable financial arrangements
- Sold custom-made jewelry at the Whole Life Exposition, KPFA Crafts Fair, Women's Center Fair, etc., advising potential customers on appropriate colors, designs and gift purchases.
- Recruited top caliber applicants to graduate programs of UC Berkeley Optometry School, involving correspondence, phone interviews, school tours, faculty introductions and financial aid advice.

Promotion/PR
- Promoted Bike-a-thon for Cystic Fibrosis Foundation:
  -assisted fund-raiser in contacting potential sponsors; distributed fliers and announcements
  -greeted participants at the event, collected contributions, distributed tee-shirts.
- Designed brochures, announcements and proposals to promote various activities:
  -gathered and edited data for brochure describing research activities for state legislature
  -wrote text of announcement advertising programs at School of Optometry
  -edited grant proposals involving more than $500,000
  -assisted PR speech writer with idea development and editing for addresses by VP of Public Relations for the University.

Marketing/Display
- Designed and set up artistic displays of merchandise at annual arts and crafts fairs.
- Demonstrated boutique clothing and accessories at off-site locations (restaurants, student gatherings).
- Contracted with jewelry designer as sales rep to better department stores and boutiques.

EMPLOYMENT HISTORY

1977-present	**Administrative Asst.**	SCHOOL OF OPTOMETRY, UC Berkeley
1985 part-time	**Sales Representative**	MATCHMAKERS Video Dating - Pleasant Valley
1975-present	**Sales Rep, part-time**	KATYA JEWELRY - Oakland
1973-75	**Administrative Asst.**	VP PUBLIC RELATIONS Office, UC Berkeley
1972 part-time	**Model/Marketing Asst.**	RAGS LIMITED Women's Clothing Boutique - Madison WI
1971 part-time	**Social Worker Intern**	VA HOSPITAL, Madison WI
1969-72	full-time student	University of Wisconsin
1969	**Office Assistant**	CHANCELLOR'S OFFICE, Univ. of Wisconsin - Milwaukee WI

EDUCATION & TRAINING
B.S., Psychology - University of Wisconsin, Madison WI
Additional training: Graphic Design, Interior Design
Affiliation: National Association of Professional Saleswomen

MARKETING

167

GARY ROSEKRANS
3500 Derby Street
Berkeley CA 94705
(415) 292-7860

Objective: Position as accounts executive with an ad agency or design firm

Highlights of Qualifications

- Five years successful experience in sales/marketing/advertising, with a special emphasis on point-of-purchase and display.
- Conceptual talent and hands-on experience in sales driven projects.
- Able to elicit the trust and confidence of clients.
- Proven record in effectively handling major accounts.
- Creative and resourceful in generating new ideas and solving problems.

PROFESSIONAL EXPERIENCE

Sales
- Developed successful sales strategy for Plastic Works' display products:
  - researched and selected effective placement of advertising in national publications;
  - coordinated all the design elements and directed image, content and copy of ads.
- Sold custom designed point-of-purchase programs and standard display products:
  - researched target area and developed leads;
  - made sales presentations to potential customers, outlining Plastic Works' design and manufacturing capabilities.
- Organized and participated in trade shows selling Plastic Works products.

New Product Strategy
- Designed and produced innovative displays for the video software industry:
  - researched the video industry and determined what products were needed for effective retail store displays, specifically:
    ...display fixtures for retail stores
    ...point-of-purchase displays provided by major manufacturers.
  - co-designed with industrial designer, compact & effective videotape display units;
  - served on R&D team for manufacture of fixtures, and monitored production.
  - marketed and sold the fixtures to stores and manufacturers.
- Currently researching the potential of developing displays for the emerging video rental market in convenience stores and supermarkets; developed fixtures for that specific retail environment.

EMPLOYMENT HISTORY

1980-present	**Sales & Product Manager** Marketing/Advertising	PLASTIC WORKS - Berkeley
1976-present	**Owner**, sign & graphics co.	SIGNAGES CO. - Oakland clients: banks, savings & loans
1974-76	**Sign Fabricator/Installer**	THOMAS SWAN SIGN CO. - San Francisco architectural signage

EDUCATION
SAN FRANCISCO ART INSTITUTE, Photography/Design
Additional Studies - UC Berkeley Extension:
•Marketing & New Product Development •Advertising Strategy

GARY BRADLEY
1717 East Street
Concord CA 94521
(415) 881-3637

Objective: Marketing or Sales Management

HIGHLIGHTS OF QUALIFICATIONS

- A born leader; effectively handled positions of major responsibility on a continuous path of professional dvancement.
- Naturally creative; able to see the overall picture from initial concept through successful completion.
- 15 years senior management experience in transportation and travel services.
- Hands-on knowledge of virtually all positions within the industry.

PROFESSIONAL EXPERIENCE

MARKETING & SALES

Promotions
- Conceived and developed creative product promotions in travel and transportation:
  -chartered Hornblower Yachts as site for highly successful presentation to 850 travel agents attending the Travel Age West convention;
  -rented Playboy Club, attracting 1000 LA travel agents to sales presentation; scripted and delivered the presentation.
  -led 250 travel agents in promotional excursion to Portugal, marketing golf packages.
- Directly implemented all phases of promotional programs:
  -locale -product -visuals -catering -giveaways -delivery of presentation.

Creative Advertising & PR
- Designed unique advertising with innovative placements, such as:
  -aerial advertising of Hawaiian tour packages, at major sports events;
  -BART station billboards promoting London and Paris charters;
  -multicolor ads in trade publications.
- Administered million-dollar advertising budget for Suntrips of California.
- Represented Suntrips, World and TAP in presentations to both industry and media.

Sales
- Attained revenue quota of $56 million with World, exceeding revenue goal by 37%, where all other regions failed to achieve target.
- Set annual sales record for Suntrips in 1985, with revenues of $46 million.
- Established and administered $133 million sales budget for World Airways.

MANAGEMENT & ADMINISTRATION
- Reorganized Suntrips of California, largest wholesale charter operator in the western United States achieving No. 1 position in sales, with revenues of $50 million:
  -designed and wrote new policy manuals and job descriptions for all departments;
  -streamlined the delegation of responsibilities to existing managers;
  -trained staff and managers in implementing more productive policies;
- Successfully directed both large and small field sales forces, consistently attaining revenue projections: - TAP-Air Portugal -World Airways -Suntrips of California.

- Continued -

MARKETING

EMPLOYMENT HISTORY

1985-present	**Executive Vice President**	SUNTRIPS OF CALIFORNIA - San Jose
1985	**VP, Marketing & Sales**	SUNTRIPS OF CALIFORNIA
1982-84	**VP, Marketing & Sales**	WORLD AIRWAYS, Western - Oakland
1980-82	**Director, Agency Marketing and Sales**	WORLD AIRWAYS
1977-80	**Area Sales Manager, Western US**	TAP Air Portugal - San Francisco
1969-76	**District Sales Manager**	TAP Air Portugal - Cleveland
1965-69	**Customer Services**	AMERICAN AIRLINES - Cleveland
1963-65	**Delivery & Dispatch**	UNITED PARCEL SERVICE - Cleveland

EDUCATION & TRAINING

Graduate, US Navy Dental Technology

Marketing & Management Training:

Incentive Sales
International Sales & Marketing
Domestic Sales and Marketing
Telemarketing
Domestic & International Tariffs
Management and Administration
Passenger & Cargo Sales

GERALD DAVIS
7600 Miracle Road
Napa CA 94558
(707) 899-6000 , work
(707) 899-4710 , home

Objective: Position in Sales & Marketing, focusing on management, Supervision, sales and product development.

HIGHLIGHTS OF QUALIFICATIONS

- 12 years experience as Vice President of Sales & Marketing.
- Successful in generating new business and increasing sales volume.
- Effective in persuading others through my enthusiasm.
- Thrive on the challenge of setting and meeting goals.
- Highly reliable; proven ability to get the job done.

PROFESSIONAL EXPERIENCE

Marketing & Product Development
- Developed new markets for leather, expanding from shoes and handbags to a wide range of other related products, significantly increasing sales.
- Researched clothing and shoe market in field trips to Europe; designed and created wide range of new colors to coordinate with current trends.
- Introduced new weights of leathers which increased our company's share of the market in heavy-weight leather products.

Management & Supervision
- Developed and supervised 5 sales agencies throughout the country:
  -traveled to each territory regularly   -trained sales reps   -visited major accounts.
- Coordinated and supervised production, overseeing quality control and scheduling.
- Monitored overall profitability, accurately projecting manufacturing costs and product pricing.

Sales
- Increased leather sales from $7 million to $18 million during first 6 years, closing many difficult sales by effectively overcoming objections.
- Introduced new and existing lines of leather all over the U.S., making fashion presentations to marketing directors of major manufacturers.
- Opened up several major profitable new accounts on the East Coast:
  -introduced our products to companies previously unaware of us;
  -overcame distance barrier by offering persuasive advantages such as
   ...modern facilities ...high quality service   ...personalized attention.

EMPLOYMENT HISTORY

1974-present	**VP Sales & Marketing**	CALNAP TANNING CO - Napa CA
1970-74	**Product Manager**	PHILIP A. HUNT CHEMICAL CORP - San Francisco
1967-70	**Technical Sales Rep**	EASTMAN KODAK CO - Los Angeles

EDUCATION & TRAINING

B.S., Business Administration - UNIVERSITY OF CALIFORNIA at Sacramento
- Graduate, Dale Carnegie Sales Course • Industrial Psychology workshop

BETSY EMORY
32 Center Street
Oneonta NY 13820
(607) 402-7442

> Betsy's work history illustrates both the variety of her roles AND her increasing level of responsibility.

Objective: Project director or public relations officer with a public service agency

HIGHLIGHTS OF QUALIFICATIONS
★ Experienced manager; effective in delegating and developing staff skills.
★ Successful in generating good will and restoring confidence.
★ Sincerely enjoy the challenge of working with people.
★ Respond effectively and creatively to change.
★ Able to focus on specific tasks, keeping overall project goals in mind.

RELEVANT PROFESSIONAL EXPERIENCE

Managing/Directing
• Managed a sales/marketing staff of 5: 2 account managers covering eastern and western national regions; 2 part-time telemarketing employees; art director.
• Oversaw and evaluated the effectiveness of national distribution network.
• Monitored sales/marketing budget for base of $7 million product sales.

Public Relations
• Represented company on extended sales trips: met with clients, promoted good will with retailers, presented new products.
• Organized and planned convention displays and strategy.
• Designed and developed a telemarketing program for Briarpatch Natural Foods:
  - researched needs of the natural foods marketplace;
  - placed new products in areas not previously serviced.

Project Development
• Conceived promotional graphics ideas (ad, posters, point-of-purchase material, newsletters), and oversaw completion of the projects in coordination with company art director.
• Developed and delegated direct retail monthly mailing program: promotional calendars, promotional fliers, and product samples.

WORK HISTORY

1985-present	**National Sales Manager**	BRIARPATCH NATURAL FOODS , Oneonta NY
1983-84	**Northeast Account Manager**	" " "
1980-83	**Customer Service Coordinator**	" " "
1979-80	**Asst. Accounting Manager**	" " "
1977-79	**Accounts Payable Clerk**	" " "
1976-77	**Computer Operator/Receptionist**	" " "

EDUCATION & TRAINING
B.A., Political Science; Art - State University of New York, Albany
Numerous marketing seminars, through American Marketing Association
Literate in computer use.

- References available on request -

JEAN BOGART
#7 Sassoon Drive
San Francisco CA 94132
(415) 225-8735

Objective: Position as Client Services Rep with Metropolitan Medical Center

HIGHLIGHTS OF QUALIFICATIONS
★ Twenty years successful experience in direct sales.
★ Proven effective in public relations targeted to the medical community.
★ Superior knowledge in use of chemical dependency treatment programs.
★ Strong public presentation skills.
★ Able to start up a program from scratch.

PROFESSIONAL EXPERIENCE

Sales & Client Base Development
• Built and maintained client bases for four service-oriented businesses:
  [funeral services, group travel, stock brokerage, training and development]
  - identified the market via a demographic survey and developed needs analysis
  - designed a sales presentation to fit identified needs of clients
  - maintained follow-up program involving newsletters, seminars, personal contact.
• Developed sales from zero and one location, to million-dollar annual sales and three locations, in 13 years.
• Opened a brokerage office and built it to $10,000/month revenues in 6 months.

Presentation & Health Education
• Facilitated week-long courses on Substance Abuse Prevention for US Navy.
• Presented employee workshops: Listening, Managing Assertively, Self Awareness.
• Spoke before numerous community groups on family mental health issues.
• Designed and delivered marketing presentations on financial planning to business & service groups.

Marketing & Public Relations
• Designed highly successful marketing program for municipal Employee Services.
• Collaborated in the design and evaluation of a training program for UC Berkeley certificate program in Training and Human Resource Development.
• Defined the desired public image goals of hospital, church, and educator groups, and designed effective marketing & sales presentations consistent with their goals.

WORK HISTORY
current	**Employee Services Intern**	CITY OF OAKLAND, CA
1983-85	**Independent Consultant, Training & Human Resource Development**	Bay Area
1980-82	**Stock Broker**	E.L. TRUMBUL & SONS, member NY stock exchange
1963-80	**VP, Personnel/Sales**	BAY FUNERAL SERVICES, Oxnard, SF, San Diego
1978-80	**Owner/Operator**	PRIMO TOURS, Camarillo, CA

EDUCATION
B.A., Psychology - UC Santa Barbara
Certificate, Training & Human Resource Development - UC Berkeley
Certificate, Alcohol and Chemical Dependency - JFK University, Orinda

JOANNE SIMPSON
1609 Walnut St., Apt.3
San Francisco CA 94123
(415) 377-2882

Objective: Entry level position in a market research firm, leading to account management.

HIGHLIGHTS OF QUALIFICATIONS

- High level of enthusiasm and commitment to a marketing career.
- Strong leadership qualities; able to take charge and get things done.
- Broad perspective of people and markets, based on extensive travel.
- Background experience in retailing and wholesaling.
- Degree in Business with concentration in Marketing.

RELEVANT EXPERIENCE

Sales

- Sold Clinique cosmetic products in three major retail stores:
  -demonstrated the product to individual customers, advising on colors and use of skin care products;
  -displayed merchandise in cases and throughout the department.
- Represented Clinique during promotional events at Bay Area retail stores, advising customers and doing product demonstrations.
- Prepared monthly sales reports, wrote purchase orders, and maintained stock control book.

Management

- Developed an understanding of group dynamics, individual motivation and interpersonal communication skills, in classes on Management and Human Behavior in Organizational Settings.
- Managed Clinique counter at Bullock's and The Crescent, involving supervision of two sales employees, staff motivation, and achieving sales goals.

Promotion and Advertising

- Developed a media plan as a component of an advertising campaign for a food product (class assignment), addressing three explicit marketing objectives:
  -obtain greater distribution   -increase market share   -increase sales by 5%.

WORK HISTORY

1985-present	**Retail Sales**	MACY'S Clinique Counter, San Francisco
1984	**Promotional Assistant**	CLINIQUE COSMETICS, Bay Area
1983-84	**Asst. to Office Manager**	MARKETING VP of Bremworth Carpets, San Francisco
1979-83	**Counter Manager**	BULLOCK'S Clinique Counter, San Francisco
1978-79	**Counter Manager**	CRESCENT Dept. Store, Clinique Counter, Spokane WA
1977-78	**Flight Attendant**	NORTHWEST ORIENT, Minneapolis MN

EDUCATION

B.S., Business, concentration in Marketing - SAN FRANCISCO STATE UNIVERSITY

- References available upon request -

MARKETING

174

JoANNE FINE
220 Georgetown Street
Albany, CA 94706
(415) 529-0620

Travel, research and self-employment round out her work history, leaving no gaps.

Objective: Professional affiliation with Holbrook Associates
assisting in international marketing expansion.

HIGHLIGHTS OF QUALIFICATIONS

- Successful generalist, with specialties focusing on:
  ...development of third world countries   ...agricultural economics
  ...social, political and economic factors of nutrition
  ...natural resources management.
- Fluency in French and Spanish gained from living in France, Belgium and Mexico.
- Special talent for relating well with people of diverse interests.
- Well organized, creative & resourceful in generating new ideas & solving problems.
- Degree in Conservation and Resource Studies.

PROFESSIONAL EXPERIENCE

Marketing / Public Speaking
- Successfully marketed and expanded EIP/No. California program, exceeding project goals by 50% and increasing project income by 75% .
- Competed successfully, via written proposals (RFPs) for projects with state & local governments.
- Spoke before numerous professional groups, introducing my organizations' programs; appeared on many panel discussions on careers in the environmental field.
- Established projects with diverse organizations such as:
  ...nonprofits   ...corporations   ...government agencies.

Project Development
- Assessed needs of potential EIP project sponsors, determining specific personnel requirements, cost and length of project, work objectives, and expected results.
- Recruited and screened hundreds of potential short-term employees, matching their skills and potential for professional growth, with sponsors' identified needs.
- Followed up with on-site visits to ascertain that both sponsor and employees were satisfied with the implementation of the project; negotiated with both parties when needed, to resolve problems.
- Handled all administrative requirements of the project: ...payroll ...taxes ...insurance.
- Originated special "Minority Urban Environmental Program" to encourage minority professionals to enter environmental occupations; accepted for funding by the San Francisco Foundation.

EMPLOYMENT HISTORY

1984-present	**Regional Director**	EIP/Northern California (Environmental Intern Program) - S.F.
1983	**Travel**	Europe
1980-82	**Full-time student**	UC Berkeley, Conservation and Resource Studies
1965-80	**Admin. Assistant** and **Exec. Sec'y**	UC BERKELEY - Dean of Letters/Sciences FEDERAL GOVERNMENT - including Dept. of Labor, US Courts, Small Business Admin., US Marshals, etc. - San Francisco
1963-85	**Free-lance Artist**	Architectural renderings, book illustrations (concurrently)
1963-65	**Office Manager**	NAT'L DEMOCRATIC COMMITTEEMAN, Louisiana, New Orleans

EDUCATION

B.S., Conservation and Resource Studies, UC Berkeley - Phi Beta Kappa, 1982

JOYCE STROEBECH

578 Willow Drive
Walnut Creek CA 94598
(415) 902-1228

One of two versions of Joyce's resume: this one focuses more on marketing. For another, see page 204.

Objective: to be a member of the creative team
managing, marketing and expanding ESPRIT retail operations.

HIGHLIGHTS OF QUALIFICATIONS

- Enthusiastic team member whose participation brings out the best in others.
- Extensive background in many areas of retail and wholesale.
- Strong visual sense and talent for coordinating colors, fabrics and accessories.
- Resourceful problem solver who is good at details.
- Highly committed to the ESPRIT philosophy and eager to support it.

MARKETING AND SALES

- Established national market for my original gift line, expanded wholesale accounts from 4 to 22 stores.
- Displayed, exhibited and merchandised clothing, gifts and textile art at retail stores, private sales, and fiber art shows.
- Increased sales in several departments of fabric store by combining merchandise to create fashion jewelry display.
- Sold clothing, gifts, cosmetics and fabrics at retail level.
- Sold my gift line directly to individuals and interior designers.
- Shipped and delivered products.

ADMINISTRATION AND MANAGEMENT

- Managed gift shop and supervised 8 employees. Maintained inventory, sales records and deposits for gift shop and for my own business.
- Handled retail and wholesale customer relations.
- Administered wholesale buying co-op for 150-member textile artists' guild.
- Ordered and distributed fabric and notions. Increased sales and variety of merchandise.
- Ordered wholesale supplies, processed purchase orders and invoices.
- Contracted assistants at peak seasons.
- Planned and directed meetings, activities and field trips for community organization of 180 parents and children. Increased membership by 50%.

DESIGN AND PRODUCTION

- Developed and produced wholesale line of fabric gifts and decorator accessories. Teamed with interior designers in clients' homes and decorator showcases.
- Created and manufactured children's clothing, soft sculpture toys and fabric jewelry.

WORK HISTORY

1979-present	**Designer/Owner/Wholesaler**	FIBER DESIGNS - Walnut Creek
1986-present	**Fabric & Craft Sales**	FABRIC HEAVEN - Pleasant Hill
1976-78	**Assistant Cosmetician**	RUNYON'S DRUGS - Walnut Creek
1974	**Assistant to Decorator**	MOBILIA FURNITURE - Houston TX
1969-71	**Gift Shop Manager**	FYNELINE GIFTS INC. - Warren, OH

EDUCATION

B.A., Home Economics: Interior Design & Textile Art - UNIVERSITY OF HOUSTON

MARKETING

LESLIE ROSE BOWMAN
990 Mystic Mountain Dr.
Mill Valley CA 94941
(415) 278-5772

**Objective: Production Coordinator for Fashion Special Events
and Public Relations, with I. Magnin**

HIGHLIGHTS OF QUALIFICATIONS

★ Outstanding stylist with a passion for art and clothing.
★ Effective as both project director and in cooperative teamwork.
★ Lifelong exposure to couture fashion and retailing.
★ Portfolio of current, forward, innovative fashion photography.
★ World travelled; worked with international photographers.

PROFESSIONAL EXPERIENCE

Special Events Coordinating & PR
• Coordinated a successful, major fashion show for SOFTWEAR art-to-wear gallery:
  conceived the idea of bringing together 2 award-winning weavers with a leading
  San Francisco fashion designer in a successful collaborative showing.
• Implemented a highly effective showing of a relatively unknown but talented weaver,
  greatly enhancing her visibility and professional opportunities.

Management & Production
• Ran a retail clothing store specializing in artistic one-of-a-kind items:
  - bought and sold all the clothing and accessories; set up all the displays.
  - established a better financial arrangement with artists which compensated them immediately,
    benefitting both parties and improving production.

Fashion Styling
• Produced 3 ads for Diet Center that appeared in Vogue, Harpers Bazaar, Woman's Day, Working
  Woman, McCalls and Glamour.
• Styled wardrobe for Levi Strauss video, publicizing shirts.
• Advised private clients on wardrobe for evolving career and fashion images.

Artistic Creativity
• Managed production of 6 album cover photographs: hired photographer; engaged makeup & hair
  stylists; found location; assembled props; styled the cover and back.
• Originated a unique pants design adapted from traditional Moroccan pattern, now in widespread use.
• Designed stage costumes for famous entertainers which helped create appropriate public image.

WORK HISTORY

1984-present	**Wardrobe/Fashion Consultant**	Free-lance - San Francisco
1984	**Manager**	SOFTWEAR & ARTWORKS - San Francisco
		art-to-wear clothing, accessories, artifacts
1983	**Saleswoman**	KEBAYA Co. imported clothing - Sausalito
1975-82	**Tours Coordinator**	Part-time, while raising children
1968-69	**Chief Docent/ Asst Curator**	ISABELLA S. GARDNER MUSEUM - Boston

EDUCATION & TRAINING

Theater lighting design, stage makeup, stage costume design - College of Marin
Painting, sculpture, and photography classes - San Francisco Art Institute
Painting, sculpture, art history - Philadelphia College of Art

LINDA MacKINNON
7907 Broderick Street
San Francisco CA 94115
(415) 994-4521

Objective: Client services representative, promoting the programs/services of a hospital, clinic or health services association.

HIGHLIGHTS OF QUALIFICATIONS

- Outstanding record of success in outside sales.
- Persuasive and knowledgeable in health services presentation.
- Communicate well with business professionals, easily establishing rapport and gaining client confidence.
- Experience in marketing health services and products.

SALES/MARKETING EXPERIENCE

Direct Sales
- Successfully persuaded major SF employers to sponsor blood drives:
  -convinced them of the community service value of participation;
  -explained the advantage to employees of accumulating blood bank credit;
  -significantly increased employee participation over previous drives.
- Made cold calls to physicians and laboratory directors of hospitals and clinics, to market reference laboratory services.

Product Presentation/Demonstration
- Explained wide range of test methodologies to doctors and lab technicians.
- Made presentations to administrators of HMOs, IPAs and medical laboratories, on the advantages of Keller's outpatient and lab management programs.

Client Services
- Serviced client accounts as sales rep for Sebring Sales, Inc:
  -made follow-up visits, inviting feedback on satisfaction with services;
  -responded quickly to resolve clients' problems;
  -maintained rapport by showing personal interest in clients and their business.
- Assisted company sponsors in coordinating logistics of on-site blood drives:
  -prepared publicity -supervised staffing -gave educational talks to employees.

EMPLOYMENT HISTORY

1985-present	**Sales Rep**	KELLER BIOMEDICAL LABORATORIES, Sacramento
1985	**Field Recruiter**	IRWIN MEMORIAL BLOOD BANK, San Francisco
1981-85	**Sales Rep**	SEBRING SALES (mfg. reps), San Francisco
1980-81	**Planner/Print Buyer**	D'ARCY MacMANUS Ad agency, San Francisco
1979-80	**Executive Secretary**	MJB COMPANY, San Francisco

EDUCATION
Biology minor, University of California, Santa Barbara

- References available on request -

SANDRA CERRITO

P.O. Box 1213A
San Francisco CA 94126
(415) 808-5772

OBJECTIVE: Marketing Manager in the medical products industry.

PROFESSIONAL EXPERIENCE

Marketing Management

- Participated in strategizing sessions to identify growth product lines:
  - -conducted market segmentation studies
  - -developed analysis of our resources and strengths compared with competitors
  - -recommended to management whether to enter this market area.
- Analyzed field experience with specialty industrial drilling chemical; compared laboratory data; made recommendations on product development and marketing; outlined sales promotion program.
- Chaired regional conference on field marketing strategy, resulting in recommendations to corporate officers.

Professional Sales

- Won top award at Pfizer Company for sales volume increase in metropolitan Chicago area.
- Reestablished professional relationship and trust with 50-60 neglected pharmaceutical accounts, tripling sales volume for my territory, and increasing profits by many thousands of dollars.
- Trained new salespeople in the field.
- Consistently achieved top ranking in district sales competition.

Communication

- Wrote sales training bulletins on better customer relations, effective communication, and sales strategy, which were distributed to 6-state regional area.
- Researched and wrote, at Sales Manager's request, an overview of company hiring practices and made recommendations to VP of Personnel, to improve company record of hiring women.
- Participated in Manager's Roundtable on effective marketing to key accounts.

EMPLOYMENT HISTORY

1984-present	**Staff Assistant**	AD VENTURES INC.(venture capital company), San Francisco
1983	**Marketing Consultant**	Independent contractor; working with ECKART CO. - Houston TX, implementing sales campaign for executive benefits.
1981-82	**Product Manager**	NL INDUSTRIES (oil field services) - Houston TX
"	**Sr. Business Analyst**	"
1980	**Regulatory Analyst**	AMERICAN HOSPITAL ASSOC. - Chicago IL
1972-79	**Sr. Sales Rep**	PFIZER CO. - Chicago IL
1970-71	**Pharmaceutical Chemist**	ELI LILLY & CO. - Indianapolis IN

EDUCATION & TRAINING

B.S. Biology - Washington University, St.Louis MO, 1969

Seminars & Conferences:

- Product Management Conference - American Marketing Association, 1982
- New Product Development, and Direct Mail Marketing - UC Berkeley 1984
- Strategic Market Planning - Braxton Associates 1981
- Sales Forecasting - University of Houston 1981

...ch position in consumer products/manufacturing, ...raphics, market surveys, and needs/trends analysis.

HIGHLIGHTS OF QUALIFICATIONS

- ...motivated and dependable in achieving set goals.
- ...alent for making creative ideas successful and profitable.
- Two and a half years experience in marketing; background in research.
- Consistently take the initiative to solve problems.
- Extensive experience with IBM-PC and spreadsheet software.
- Strong organizational skills; attention to detail.

RELEVANT EXPERIENCE

Trends Analysis/Strategy & Planning

- Projected sales potentials by analyzing sales figures from current and past years.
- Gathered pricing and scheduling information on competitors and reported on changes needed to maintain a competitive edge.
- Increased the efficiency of Pacific Tours' direct mail promotions by creating a program to consolidate passenger information, allowing for targeted mailings.
- Identified areas of customer satisfaction and motivation for repeat business, and successfully initiated changes to improve marketing program accordingly.

Demographics/Data Collection

- Input consumer data generated from questionnaire mailings and on-site surveys of Pacific Tour passengers.
- Assembled and input market data on potential customers having appropriate demographic characteristics.

Computer Software Skills

- Charted and graphed wide range of data in Lotus 1-2-3, for example...
  -customer surveys and questionnaires   -sales demographics.
- Composed correspondence using Multimate word processing program on IBM-PC.
- Knowledge of DisplayWrite III.

EMPLOYMENT HISTORY

1986-present	**Research Analyst Assistant**	PACIFIC TOUR LINES, San Francisco
1984-86	**Assistant Coordinator/Marketing**	PACIFIC TOUR LINES, San Francisco
1979-83	**Training Program Coordinator**	UNIV. OF FLORIDA Hospital & Clinics
1975-78	**Research Assistant**	UNIV. OF FLORIDA Marine Inst., Sapelo Is.

EDUCATION

B.A., Biology & Chemistry - CAL STATE UNIVERSITY, SONOMA
Graduate School, Biology - WESTERN WASHINGTON STATE COLLEGE

ARLENE FORD
115 Grand Avenue
Oakland CA 04612
(415) 468-2688

Objective: Position in sales or marketing with Digital Equipment Corp.

HIGHLIGHTS OF QUALIFICATIONS
★ Thrive in a competitive, challenging environment.
★ Ability to analyze and solve problems in a constantly changing
  work environment.
★ Competitive, efficient, hard working, articulate, enthusiastic.
★ Special talent for relating well with all types of people.
★ Able to represent my company with dignity and professionalism.

RELEVANT EXPERIENCE

SALES & PROMOTION
• Promoted World Airways & sold travel packages through visits to travel agencies.
• Developed itineraries and solved travel related problems for airline passengers.
• Sold reservations for domestic and international flights, hotels, car rental services.
• Negotiated airline and hotel discounts for international and domestic travel.
• Completed telemarketing training for World Airways, & implemented sales campaign.

COMMUNICATION & PUBLIC RELATIONS
• Represented World Airways and promoted good will with contracting foreign governments.
• Provided in-flight services to people of diverse international cultures:
 -European   -Southeast Asian   -Middle Eastern
• Developed rapport and cooperation with airline travelers: assessed their needs,
  provided accurate and timely information, responded effectively to high pressure emergency
  situations.
• Conceived and introduced new curriculum in physical education classes for high school students.
• Assessed athletic skills and taught new techniques to improve physical abilities.

ORGANIZATION & COORDINATION
• Coordinated in-flight functions to maximize the quality and efficiency of services.
• Supervised catering activities on aircrafts, and monitored inventory of supplies.
• Developed and coordinated work schedules of restaurant employees.

EMPLOYMENT HISTORY

1979-present	Flight Attendant	WORLD AIRWAYS - Oakland, Baltimore, Newark
1985-present	Telemarketing Rep	WORLD AIRWAYS - Oakland
1983-present	Sales Representative	WORLD AIRWAYS - Washington DC, Oakland
1978-79	Teacher, Physical Ed	ACALANES SCHOOL DIST. - Lafayette CA
1976-79	Asst. Beverage Manager	EPPAMINONDAS RESTAURANT - Lake Tahoe & SF
1973-77	Competitive Swim Coach	LIVORNA SWIM CLUB - Walnut Creek CA

EDUCATION
B.A., Physical Education, California Teaching Credential
University of California, Los Angeles (UCLA) & University of the Pacific, Stockton

DEBORAH RICHARDSON
3445 Mariposa Ave.
San Mateo, CA 94403
(415) 446-9133

Objective: Corporate sales representative position in hotel sales/catering

HIGHLIGHTS OF QUALIFICATIONS
★ 8 years successful experience in both inside and outside hotel sales; special talent for recapturing lost accounts.
★ Professional and self-confident in handling corporate accounts.
★ Exceptional success in establishing rapport with clients.
★ Working knowledge of major corporations in the bay area.
★ Able to work independently.

PROFESSIONAL SALES EXPERIENCE

Sales
• Successfully regained Dunfey Hotel's largest account, as first sales assignment:
  -opened a good line of communication by persistent contact;
  -determined the cause of the problem;
  -assured that the hotel knew and could meet the client's needs.
• Consistently exceeded sales and profit goals for corporate bookings.
• Created a new sales incentive program that effectively kept existing accounts, featuring attractive gift certificates for trips, meals, and hotel accommodations.

Project Coordination
• Planned and directed all aspects of a party for 600 clients, creating a theme, designing costumes and invitations, developing mailing list and party menu, and acting as emcee and overall hostess.
• Organized and implemented a highly effective 3-week door-to-door "sales blitz" involving 10 sales reps:
  -researched 400 accounts to update reps on background info and likely problems;
  -conducted strategy meetings; assigned territories and objectives for each rep;
  -reviewed all incoming reports and submitted final analysis to management.

PR/Customer Relations
• Produced and published a promotional newsletter for corporate clients:
  -wrote articles introducing their new rep and informing them of upcoming special events and discounts   -took photographs   -designed layout.
• Delivered presentations to groups of corporate executives, outlining hotel services available and conducting question-and-answer sessions.

EMPLOYMENT HISTORY
1985-present	**Account Representative**	CALIF. FURNITURE RENTAL, Foster City CA
1982-85	**Account Executive**	DUNFEY HOTEL, San Mateo CA
1981-82	**Food/Beverage Restaurant Mgr.**	DUNFEY HOTEL, San Mateo CA
1978-81	**Exec. Sec'y/Meeting Coor.**	RODEWAY INTERNATIONAL, Omaha NE
1975-78	**Legal Secretary**	H. NEUHAUS, Atty., Omaha
		(account recovery)

EDUCATION
Liberal Arts, IOWA STATE UNIVERSITY, Ames IA

SALES

DENISE WALTERS

2330 Forty-third Ave.
San Francisco CA 94121
(415) 233-2054

**Objective: Position as Sales Rep with the Eastman Kodak Company
Graphics Imaging Division.**

HIGHLIGHTS OF QUALIFICATIONS

- Education and talent in the field of Graphic Arts.
- Resourceful and committed; can be counted on to get the job done.
- Self-motivated and well organized; enjoy the challenge of outside sales.
- Effective in delivering presentations that generate new business.
- Sharp, poised, able to convey a warm yet professional image.

RELEVANT EXPERIENCE

Direct Sales/Account Management

- Called on established key accounts (corporate and insurance):
  - -identified clients' needs and problems, assuring them of a personal representative they can count on;
  - -demonstrated a personal interest in clients, taking them to lunch and remembering personal details;
  - -resolved service problems, billing problems and misunderstandings.
- Delivered effective sales presentations to business groups and individuals:
  - -introduced and promoted our product/service to leading Insurance Companies;
  - -identified appropriate corporate officers and made introductory calls to establish new accounts.
- Increased account base by 50% at two locations, through assertive salesmanship and consistent follow-up.

Planning/Organizing

- Developed monthly sales plans: set goals; identified account maintenance needed; targeted special problems requiring attention; set up schedule of appointments.
- Forecasted sales goals by dollar amount as well as by specific referral sources.
- Maintained detailed daily sales logs and referral logs.
- Wrote extensive monthly sales reports, including calls made, problems identified, and plans for the coming month.
- Conducted detailed market analyses and monthly surveys of competition throughout the Bay Area, and submitted reports to regional manager.

EMPLOYMENT HISTORY

1983-present	Sales Representative	SUPERIOR RENT-A-CAR - Oakland
1981-82	Sales Representative	PERSONNEL POOL temp service - San Mateo
1981	Sales/Service Manager	CERTIFIED TEMPORARY PERSONNEL - San Bruno
1979-81	Sales Representative	GRANTREE FURNITURE RENTAL - San Mateo
1978-79	Leasing Agent	LINCOLN PROPERTY CO. - San Bruno
1977-78	Salesperson	TOPS & TROUSERS - San Francisco

EDUCATION

ACADEMY OF ART COLLEGE, San Francisco 1975-79
Major: Graphic Design

SALES

DONNA COLE
1776 Twelfth Ave.
San Francisco CA 94118
(415) 212-6822

Objective: Sales position with a company marketing medical products

HIGHLIGHTS OF QUALIFICATIONS
★ Professional appearance and manner.
★ Versatile and adaptable; thrive on opportunities to solve problems.
★ Experience communicating with professionals in medical field.
★ Very strong presentation skills.

PROFESSIONAL EXPERIENCE

Sales and Promotion
- Made cold calls and field visits to medical wholesalers, significantly increasing accounts.
- Increased sales thru effective demonstrations of fabricating techniques.
- Visited and serviced existing accounts to assure continued product sales.
- Advised clients on options available to meet a wide variety of patient needs.
- Acted as technical liaison between doctors and prosthetists.
- Followed up by phone on dealers' requests for information and samples.

Project Management
- Successfully assumed emergency interim management of production department following sudden loss of staff; maintained production schedules thru prioritizing and rescheduling.
- Researched competition's design, fabrication materials and marketing techniques by visiting American Cancer Society facility and interviewing patients and staff.
- Maintained good customer relations by assisting clients in identifying technical and administrative problems, analyzing patient needs and developing solutions.

Business
- Set up a small business bookkeeping system:
  - acquired necessary licenses - handled accounts payable and accounts receivable
  - consulted with accountants - processed payroll and disbursed commissions
- Entered and retrieved computerized data.
- Recruited and supervised staff of 15 clerical and sales personnel.

WORK HISTORY

1982 to present	**Prosthetic Technician/Asst.Manager**	GRIFFHEIMERS - San Francisco
1978-1982	**Prosthetic Technician/ Sales Mastectomy Products**	HOSMER-DORRANCE CORP - Campbell
1978	**Bookkeeper**	ALEX'S PORSCHE HOUSE - Campbell
1977-1978	**Office Manager**	SAVE ON SOLAR, Inc. - San Jose
1976-1977	**Bookkeeper**	PAUL COLE WRECKING - San Jose

EDUCATION
Small Business Management classes - Contra Costa College & San Jose City College
Registered Technician* - American Board of Prosthetics and Orthotics
(*one of six women currently registered in the country)

SALES

ELLEN METCALFE
1912 Twelfth Avenue
San Francisco CA 94118
212-6755 home; 494-0091 work

Objective: Position as sales representative or manufacturer's representative

HIGHLIGHTS OF QUALIFICATIONS
- 8 years successful experience in retail and business sales.
- Ability to establish instant credibility.
- Confident, professional business communicator.
- Special talent for identifying clients' needs and presenting effective solutions.
- Skilled in the techniques of closing a sale.

RELEVANT EXPERIENCE
Effective Sales Techniques
- Established highly effective relationships with potential clients at all levels, from support staff through management, employing a natural conversational style:
  -created immediate rapport by establishing a commonality of interest;
  -probed for an overview of business operations to assess client needs;
  -maintained control of the situation by asking questions to elicit positive response;
  -skillfully closed sale by gaining agreement on the benefits of the product.

Market Development
- Conducted high-energy cold calling campaign, averaging 10-20 calls per day and successfully opening up new sales territory for a start-up business.
- Transformed a list of serious problem accounts, with a long history of nonpayment and potential litigation against our company, toward acceptable solutions:
  -restored relationships by reestablishing supportive contact;
  -solved 20% of the problems by upgrading and selling additional equipment;
  -renegotiated the terms of payment, effectively reducing receivables by 40%.
- Researched and developed markets to build a client base:
  -built a network of other professionals within my field and shared sources;
  -stayed abreast of industry developments through newspapers and trade journals;
- Discovered a void in the home and office furnishings market, and created a successful business solving storage problems created by new technology.

Presentation/Communication
- Made on-site presentations at residential and business locations to evaluate site requirements and provide customized space planning services.
- Addressed large and small groups, at major trade shows and at product seminars.
- Demonstrated features and benefits of computer products to corporate decision makers, and successfully negotiated closing contracts.

EMPLOYMENT HISTORY

1985-present	**Communications Manager**	HOME DESIGN CONSULTANTS - San Francisco
1983-85	**Owner/Manager**	GREGG WALL COVERINGS - Boise, Idaho
1982-83	**Branch Manager/Sales**	BAYLIN Personnel Service - San Francisco
1980-82	**Sales Representative**	CROWN COMPUTERS - San Mateo
1978-80	**Sales Representative**	G.L.W. OFFICE SYSTEMS - Palo Alto

EDUCATION
B.A., English, PENNSYLVANIA STATE UNIVERSITY

SALES

HOLLIS ANN POPE
6778 Grand Avenue
Oakland, CA 94609
(415) 699-2121

Holly includes her middle name to head off confusion over whether "Hollis" is a man or a woman.

Objective: Position as associate in merchandise sales or buying,
with special emphasis on client services, needs assessment and negotiations.

HIGHLIGHTS OF QUALIFICATIONS
- Outstanding people skills: sensitive in assessing needs.
- Readily inspire the trust and confidence of clients.
- Committed to professional excellence.
- Successful, varied experience in buying and negotiating.
- Ambitious, adventurous, goal- and profit-oriented.

RELEVANT EXPERIENCE

Buying
- Researched and located potential overseas wholesale suppliers of high-quality leather clothing:
  -reviewed wide range of designs, selected best combination of style, quality price, and on-going availability;
  -set up trade and banking operations between Turkish co. and my business.

Sales
- Sold specialty clothing to retail store buyers, initiating contacts and making direct sales.
- Developed substantial and profitable repeat business, delivering high-quality service to restaurant customers:
  -completed course in wines; offered expert advice on selections;
  -observed customers' needs/wants and personalized service accordingly.

Negotiating
- Bargained assertively and effectively with foreign merchants.
- Negotiated diplomatically with customers in an exclusive, limited-seating restaurant, maintaining both capacity seating and customer satisfaction.

Counseling/Needs Assessment
- Completed training in counseling skills at UC Berkeley Dept. of Education, and developed expertise in helping individuals communicate needs and problems.
- Helped students assess problem situations and develop practical plans for achieving positive change.

EMPLOYMENT HISTORY

1985-present	**Asst. Manager & Maitre d'**	BLUE DANUBE CAFE - Oakland
1984-86	**Waitress**	THACKERAY'S RESTAURANT - Oakland
1984-85	**Sales Assistant**	MYRA TREVOR IMPORTS - Berkeley
1983-85	**Owner/Manager**	POPE & LEWIS Importers - Berkeley
1977-82	**Fulltime Student**	UC BERKELEY
1977-78	**Librarian**	AMERICAN SCHOOL of ISFAHAN - Iran

EDUCATION

B.A., Psychology - UNIVERSITY of CALIFORNIA, BERKELEY, 1982
Honors: Phi Beta Kappa

SALES

JERRY WILCOX
Montecito Ave.
Pleasanton CA 94566
(415) 943-0104

Jerry had an uncomfortable "image" problem: people's surprised reaction to "truck-driver" on his resume. We sacrificed consistency in form and changed the job-title to "transportation."

Objective: Outside sales rep with a manufacturer or distributor, involving direct sales, account management.

HIGHLIGHTS OF QUALIFICATIONS

- 7 years successful experience in direct outside sales.
- One of top salesmen nationwide with Coca Cola.
- No. 1 in sales with Smith Corona Marchant's western US region.
- Highly motivated; an achiever who sets and reaches his goals.
- Proven skills in problem solving and customer relations.

SALES EXPERIENCE

Direct Sales & Account Management
- Trained new sales reps for developing new and existing territories, at both Smith Corona and Coca Cola.
- Achieved status of top salesman nationwide with Coca Cola:
  -sold more Coca Cola coolers than any prior salesman;
  -personally called on every customer on a weekly basis, maintaining good public relations and reviewing customers' needs;
  -designed customized exterior and interior signs featuring customers' products.

Problem Solving & Customer Service
- Increased SCM's territory sales by 120%, identifying clients' specific needs and designing cost effective alternatives:
  -demonstrated opportunities to save time and money in office billing procedures;
  -completely revised and automated clients' billing systems;
  -sold new SCM copying equipment required for the newly installed system.

Community Service
- Served actively in a wide range of community service organizations & commissions.
- Ran for City Council in 1982 and 1984.
- Appointed as Commissioner for prestigious Alameda Co. commission, responsible for:
  -allocating $800 million in retirement fund investments;
  -presiding at monthly hearings and making final judgements on disability cases.

EMPLOYMENT HISTORY

1968-present	**Transportation**	WOODLAKE MANUFACTURING, Oakland
1967-68	**District Sales Rep**	SMITH CORONA MARCHANT (SCM), Oakland
1962-67	**District Salesman**	COCA COLA Co., Hayward

EDUCATION & TRAINING
Sales training course with Smith Corona

SALES

JERRY D. PARKHURST
803 Azalea Drive
El Cerrito CA 94530
(415) 296-7566

Objective: Position in merchandising display, with a manufacturer, distributor or advertising agency

Highlights of Qualifications

- Three years experience in merchandising display.
- Self-motivated, honest and dependable.
- Skill in setting up creative, effective displays.
- Working familiarity with the Bay Area.
- Successful in maintaining rapport with retailers.
- Well groomed and professional in manner.

RELATED EXPERIENCE

Display
- Set up effective retail displays of beverages in supermarkets, liquor barns, liquor stores, and package stores on military bases.
- Inventoried and reordered display materials, and maintained warehouse, for Glenmore Distilleries.

Customer Relations
- Developed cooperative working relationships with retail owners and managers:
  - introduced myself as merchandising representative;
  - advised manager of available promotional themes;
  - advised on the benefits of the promotions, such as increased sales, and secured approval for displays.

Servicing Existing Accounts
- Assured that products were priced, positioned in proper location, and that adequate stock was on hand.
- Maintained accurate route sheet with return dates, and refurbished displays on a regular two-week schedule.
- Serviced existing accounts in Contra Costa, Alameda, Solano, and Napa Counties.

WORK HISTORY

1985-present	**Apprentice Mechanic**	SKYTREADS, - San Francisco (aircraft wheels and brakes)
1983-85	**Merchandiser**	GLENMORE DISTILLERIES - Richmond
1982-83	**Merchandiser**	BEVERAGE DISPLAY - San Mateo
1979-82	**Mechanical Assembler**	SYNMED, INC, optometry machine mfg. - Berkeley
1978	**Service Attendant**	JOHN HARRIS MOBIL SERVICE STATION - Emeryville
1976-77	**Carpenter Helper**	HOYER TERMITE CO. - El Cerrito
1968-76	**Variety Butcher**	McDERMOTT MEAT CO. - Berkeley

SALES

JUDITH R. LIPPETT
1403 Acacia Road
Oakland CA 94610
(415) 213-4646

Objective: Position as Sales Representative with Gallo Sales Co.

HIGHLIGHTS OF QUALIFICATIONS
★ Sincere enthusiasm and enjoyment of sales.
★ Successful record in securing repeat commitment from clients.
★ Easily communicate and develop rapport at all levels of interaction.
★ Designed & managed direct mail & phone campaign that raised $100,000.
★ 3 years increasingly responsible professional experience. College degree.

SALES RELATED EXPERIENCE

Customer Relations Skills
• Developed a strategy for maximizing new and repeat commitments from donors:
  - Identified donors' values, interests and priorities through personal contact and research.
  - Collaborated with volunteer solicitors to develop effective presentations.
• Developed long-term relationships with donors, increasing contributions:
  - Maintained project reports, and ensured continued donor satisfaction.
  - Resolved client problems related to staff and procedural errors.

Sales and Promotion
• Developed promotional material:
  - written brochures   -two video tapes   -monthly newspaper articles.
• Planned and organized public relations events: concerts, dinners, receptions.

Project Management
• Successfully maintained the continuity and direction of a $7.4 million fund raising project under several changes of management style.
• Recruited 25 fund-raising volunteers by persuading them of the value and satisfaction of participation.
• Facilitated biweekly planning meetings on campaign strategy and progress, to reaffirm volunteers' commitments.
• Trained and supervised small office staff in general support procedures.
• Supervised and coordinated 88 individual local fund-raising campaigns throughout the Bay Area.

WORK HISTORY

1982-present	**Administrative Director**	EPISCOPAL DIOCESE OF CALIFORNIA, San Francisco
	Asst. Campaign Director	"
	Campaign Coordinator	"
1981-82	**Admin. Law Paralegal**	CONTRA COSTA CO. LEGAL SERVICES, Pittsburg CA
	" "	WELFARE RIGHTS ORGANIZATION, Chico, CA

EDUCATION
B.A., Political Science, with highest honors - CSU, Chico
Minor: Business Administration

SALES

JUDY ROGERS
392 St. George Ave. #11
Alameda CA 94501
(415) 335-2445

Judy's work history is complex and needed a lot of explaining. This was our best compromise.

Objective: Sales/Marketing Position

HIGHLIGHTS OF QUALIFICATIONS

- Over 15 years professional experience with the public.
- Personable and persuasive in communicating creatively with thousands of customers from all cultures and economic levels.
- Proven skill in persevering to solve customers' problems.
- Self-motivated and confident in making independent decisions.
- Very well organized and able to meet deadlines.

RELEVANT EXPERIENCE

Sales & Marketing
- Made direct presentations to Bay Area retail store owners and buyers, marketing Christmas ornaments and gift items imported from the Philippines.
- Co-hosted sales seminars for potential real estate partnership investors:
  - oriented customers by answering questions regarding project details;
  - followed up by phone to verify their commitment to invest in the partnership.
- Canvassed by cold calling for contributions to a nonprofit organization.
- Consistently surpassed sales quotas in retail clothing and houseware departments.
- Co-led voter drive and personally persuaded 2000 citizens to sign the petition in support of placing a community improvement initiative on the ballot.

Organization & Customer Service
- Resolved wide range of customer problems, applying diplomacy and assertiveness to: delivery delays, fee and budget problems, property management decisions, airline emergencies and in-flight problems, and culture/communication barriers.
- Organized the logistics of speaking engagements and investment seminars:
  - location - catering - seating - literature - speakers - travel - RSVP calls.
- Maintained extensive financial records regarding individual and corporate clients.
- Successfully collected thousands of dollars in overdue or unbilled fees by thoroughly auditing billing records and persevering in telephone collection follow-ups.

EMPLOYMENT HISTORY

1985-present	**Office Manager/Bookkeeper**	OLSON LIGHTING CONSULTANTS, San Francisco
1983-85	**Office Manager/Bookkeeper**	GROTHE & ASSOCIATES, San Francisco
	(Real Estate Limited Partnerships, NonProfit organization, author/lecturer)	
1980-81*	**Philippine Import Sales**	SELF-EMPLOYED, selling to Bay Area stores
1978-80*	**Neo-Life Vitamin Sales**	SELF-EMPLOYED, selling to flight attendants
	* part-time, concurrent with airline employment)	
1971-83	**International Flight Attendant**	TRANSAMERICA AIRLINES, Oakland
1970-72	**Editorial Coor./Sales Sec'y.**	PSYCHOLOGY TODAY TEXTBOOK DIV., San Diego
1969	**Emergency Room Receptionist**	KAISER HOSPITAL, Hayward
1964-68	**Retail Sales**	MACY'S, ROOS ATKINS, part-time during college

EDUCATION

B.A., Speech/Theatre Arts - UNIVERSITY OF CALIFORNIA, SANTA BARBARA, 1968

SALES

LINDA MOWRY
348 Somerset Road
Hayward CA 94541
(415) 666-7995

Objective: Position as Sales Coordinator, Sales Rep or Account Executive
including project coordinating and good customer relations.

HIGHLIGHTS OF QUALIFICATIONS

- 10 years successful experience in direct sales.
- Enthusiastic and motivated; sincerely enjoy developing
  and maintaining good client relations.
- Professional in appearance and presentation.
- Effective working alone and as a cooperative team member.

RELEVANT EXPERIENCE

Sales & New Account Development
- Promoted and developed new distribution outlets for a special interest magazine:
  -made cold-call and follow-up visits to retail outlets throughout Northern California;
  -organized and maintained detailed routebooks and all related financial records;
  -succeeded in increasing readership by 40% over a two-year period.
- Increased advertising revenue by researching publications and by bulk-mail promotion.
- Sold dairy delivery services to both retail and wholesale customers, as co-owner of a small
  business involving a staff of five.

Customer Relations
- Served as vendor representative for Jana Imports:
  -promoted giftware products at trade shows, greeting new and old customers;
  -coordinated product information and distribution for 75 field reps and major accounts.

Advertising & Marketing
- Developed mock-up and organized details for effective photography for 20-page giftware
  product catalog.
- Coordinated production of advertising to appear in major trade publications.

Order Processing/Distribution
- Handled all aspects of order taking and order processing , at both Bill's Dairy and Jana's.
- Maintained current inventory status reports, summarizing computerized data.
- Coordinated shipping documentation for imported products, and maintained files on foreign
  manufacturers and custom brokers.

EMPLOYMENT HISTORY

1985-present	**Sales Coordinator**	JANA IMPORTS, Oakland (imported giftware)
1982-84	**Distribution Coor.**	DEJA VU PUBLISHING CO., San Rafael (magazine publisher)
1976-81	**Co-Owner/Manager**	BILL'S DAIRY PRODUCTS, Livermore (retail/wholesale milk)

EDUCATION
Health studies, BAY CITY COLLEGE, San Francisco

SALES

MARK S. FLEETWOOD
1299 Bruenner Avenue
Castro Valley CA 94546
(415) 335-9009

Objective: Position as Electronic Sales Rep

HIGHLIGHTS OF QUALIFICATIONS

★ Number One ranked salesman for 4 straight years.

★ Strong product knowledge from 5 years experience in the field.

★ Enthusiastic about both the product and the role of sales rep.

★ Able to handle large territories effectively.

★ Experience serving wide range of OEM industries.

PROFESSIONAL SALES EXPERIENCE

Account Relations/Customer Service
- Established and maintained good rapport with over 200 accounts in the electronics service industry:
  -Followed through promptly to resolve customer complaints.
  -Found hard-to-find parts for customers, by whatever means necessary.
  -Located detailed product info for customers to facilitate accurate parts ordering.
- Currently servicing retail and OEM accounts, visiting each account weekly.

Direct Sales & Product Demonstration
- Set sales record, surpassing all salesmen for any given month in company history.
- Held down company's largest territory; exceeded quotas & greatly increased sales.
- Increased average monthly sales to Pacific Stereo from $1,500 to $13,000.

Product Analysis & Forecasting
- Reviewed potential new products applicable to electronics industry:
  -Tested products on various applications
  -Introduced products to customers for their evaluation.
- Projected likely success rate of new items, computing results of customer surveys conducted by phone and mail.

Marketing/Promotion
- Effectively demonstrated to customers the benefits of quantity purchases and incentive programs.
- Organized customized accessory racks for display in retail outlets.
- Researched industry trade journals to identify potentially popular and profitable items, and locate products requested by accounts.

EMPLOYMENT HISTORY

1981-present	**No. Calif. Field Sales Rep**	PARNASSUS ELECTRONICS, Oakland CA
1980-81	**Full-time student**	DIABLO VALLEY COLLEGE
1980	**Warehouseman**	BILLINGS PRECISION box mfg., San Leandro CA
1976-78 (summers)	**Warehouseman**	BILLINGS PRECISION box mfg., San Leandro CA

EDUCATION

Business Administration & Sales, Diablo Valley College, Pleasant Hill, CA 1980-81

SALES

MELINDA SAILOR
222 Billings Drive
San Francisco CA 94132
(415) 122-6795

Objective: Position in fine jewelry sales and customer service
with a quality jewelry store or contemporary design gallery.

HIGHLIGHTS OF QUALIFICATIONS
- Successful experience in sales and customer service.
- Knowledge of fine gems and jewelry.
- Widely varied, well rounded background in art and design.
- Excellent communication skills; fluent in Spanish.
- Sincere commitment to professional growth in the field.

RELEVANT EXPERIENCE

Sales & Customer Service
- Successfully developed a combination of retail selling skills:
  -greeted customers and determined their specific needs;
  -demonstrated jewelry and advised about style;
  -handled problem customers with patience and sensitivity;
  -utilized "suggestion selling" techniques leading to effective closing;
  -followed up, encouraging customers to return, generating repeat business.

Knowledge of Fine Jewelry & Design
- Learned to identify a wide variety of gems, pearls and precious metals, from direct experience handling and cataloguing gemstones.
- Assisted gemologist in documenting appraisals of estate and period jewelry.
- Developed a keen appreciation for basic design principles, as a student and teacher in the art field. (Professional classes listed below.)

Display
- Set up jewelry displays for Richards' Jewelry Department previews.
- Prepared displays and fine arts exhibits at local museums.

Record Keeping
- Entered data on computer for catalogue descriptions written with specific gemology terms of the industry.
- Maintained detailed paperwork for retail sales inventory control.

EMPLOYMENT HISTORY

current	**Preview Staff**	RICHARDS Auctioneers/Appraisers, New York
1985	**Exhibit Technician**	TRITON MUSEUM OF ART, Santa Clara CA
1984-85	**Sales Clerk**	EMPORIUM CAPWELL, San Francisco
1981-84	**Sales Associate**	MACY'S OF CALIFORNIA - San Mateo CA
1979-81	**Teacher, art & adult ed.**	Los Angeles, CA and Miami, FL
1976-78	**Arts & Crafts Teacher**	PEACE CORPS, El Salvador, Central America

EDUCATION & TRAINING
B.A., Teaching Credential, Fine Arts, Immaculate Heart College, Los Angeles 1973
Certificate for completion of professional jewelry workshops:
•Design & Rendering •Repair & Fabrication •Basic Goldsmithing

SALES

193

NOREEN MacLAUGHLIN

1201 Genner Street, Apt. 12
San Francisco, CA 94111

Home: (415) 577-0121
Bus: (415) 439-6897

Objective: Professional sales position

HIGHLIGHTS OF QUALIFICATIONS

★ Confident, poised, well presented and competent sales professional.
★ Successful background in sales, sales training, and sales management.
★ Outstanding communication/listening skills, achieving client confidence.
★ Record of high profitability in sales and marketing promotions.
★ Strong decision-maker; goal- and profit-oriented.

PROFESSIONAL EXPERIENCE

Promotion & Communication
• Created sales and marketing programs that increased residential rent revenue by 20% per unit, and increased shopping center profits by 33%.
• As Director of Resident Relations, successfully increased resident retention rate through greatly improving customer relations and applying acute listening skills.
• Made presentations to merchants on the use of print, radio, coupons and raffles.

Direct Sales
• Developed strong pattern of repeat sales and client loyalty; provided accurate and honest product information, and help in assessing client needs.
• Consistently surpassed companies' sales records; was promoted to sales management.
• Conducted cold calls to business neighbors of shopping center, significantly increasing business and shopping center profits.

Sales: Motivation & Training
• Interviewed and hired top sales people, achieving low turnover.
• Trained over 25 assistants and sales personnel:
  -created a safe, comfortable learning environment with constructive feedback, resulting in professionally trained staff.
  -taught mastery of effective basic selling techniques:
  ...selling benefits ...handling objections ...cold calls ...demonstrations ...closing.

EMPLOYMENT HISTORY

1972-present	Assistant Administrator	HILLARY APARTMENTS - San Francisco
"	Director of Resident Relations	"
"	Sales Supervisor	"
1971	Sales Director	GILBERT GALLERY - Ghirardelli Sq, SF
1970	International Hotel Sales	SHERATON PALACE HOTEL - S.F.

EDUCATION
B.A. Humanities - San Francisco State University
UC Berkeley - Humanities
Niagara University - Nursing

Professional Associations
National Association of Professional Saleswomen
Northpoint Merchants Association

SALES

PAMELA SWISS

1930 Atlantic Avenue
San Francisco CA 94115
(415) 688-0131

Objective: Position as outside sales representative for a manufacturer, specializing in fashion, cosmetics, and/or accessories

HIGHLIGHTS OF QUALIFICATIONS

★ Strongly self-motivated, enthusiastic and profit oriented.
★ Outstanding communication and presentation skills.
★ Readily project a professional, fashionable image.
★ Extremely sociable, able to put clients at ease.
★ A decision maker; well organized, resourceful, work well independently.

RELEVANT EXPERIENCE

Sales, PR, Marketing
• Sold advertising to major SF corporations for a special newspaper supplement in support of the SF symphony: -coordinated with other sales team members
-worked independently -sold to influential business leaders -met deadlines.
• Represented Western Airlines at public relations events.
• Demonstrated manufacturers' products at trade shows and conventions.

Client Services
• Supervised direct services to thousands of airline clients, assuring that individualized needs were met, remaining calm and effective under stressful conditions.

Fashion & Design
• Conceptualized and implemented unique and artistic contemporary designs for residential environments:
-incorporated the client's personal preferences and tastes;
-researched products available, consistent with client's budget and priorities;
-collaborated with architects, construction subcontractors, upholsterers;
-prepared and submitted detailed monthly reports to clients on budget & expenses.
• Studied Interior Design at Cañada College.
• Completed courses in Fashion Coordination, Self-image, Basic Elements of Design.
• Advised businesswomen on fashion coordination, image development and personal style.

EMPLOYMENT HISTORY

1966-present	Flight Attendant	WESTERN AIRLINES, San Francisco
1963-85	Owner/Designer	PAMELA SWISS INTERIOR DESIGN, San Francisco

EDUCATION & TRAINING

Liberal Arts & Design, CALIFORNIA STATE UNIVERSITY, San Luis Obispo
Interior Design, CAÑADA COLLEGE, Redwood City

SALES

SHERRIE E.VALENCIA

378 Cornell Street - Apt. 409
San Francisco CA 94109
(415) 178-2323

Objective: Position in sales / marketing

SUMMARY OF QUALIFICATIONS

★ Honest; straightforward; respected and trusted by clients who keep coming back.
★ Equally effective working in self-managed projects and as member of a team.
★ Results-oriented professional who doesn't take No for an answer.
★ Outstanding communication, analytical and presentation skills.
★ Sharp, innovative, quick learner; proven ability to adapt quickly to a challenge.

PROFESSIONAL EXPERIENCE

Marketing, Sales Presentation
• Planned successful strategies to target and develop new accounts.
• Consistently expanded customer base by at least 50%, and increased revenues from current clients by 25%.
• Made oral presentations to upper management of major corporations, such as Bechtel, Union Carbide, Chevron, Lockheed.

Planning/Organizing
• Assessed and evaluated market conditions to identify sources for potential new client base.
• Developed and revised daily, weekly and monthly plans of sales strategies.
• Organized No.California sales territory to maximize efficiency of calling pattern.

Communications
• Wrote evaluations, problem analyses, and daily plans.
• Wrote timely reports and forecasts to management on past and projected sales volume.
• Composed product information letters and quotations for clients.
• Restored and maintained good working relations with clients:
  - maintained daily telephone contact with current accounts;
  - made field visits and discussed customers' problems;
  - researched problem areas and provided detailed information;
  - followed through quickly and thoroughly with satisfactory resolutions.

EMPLOYMENT HISTORY

1983-now	Dist. Sales Manager	L.B.HEINE TRUCKING CO. - Hayward CA
1981-83	Accounts Executive	C.F. AIR FREIGHT CO. - South San Francisco CA
1975-81	Accounts Executive	EAST TEXAS MOTOR FREIGHT - So. San Francisco CA
1973-75	Sales Representative	AMERICAN INDUSTRIES INC - San Francisco CA
1968-73	Head Teacher	JEWISH COMMUNITY CENTER - St. Louis MO

EDUCATION

B.S., Education - Ohio State University
Sales/Marketing courses at UC Berkeley,
City College, SF and San Francisco State

SALES

196

VRENY ZURICH

314 Glenellen Avenue
San Francisco CA 94118
(415) 555-2331

Her earlier work and business degree from Switzerland are mentioned, without going into detail.

Objective: Position as small-store manager, department manager, or salesperson preferably dealing with quality shoes, handbags and accessories.

Highlights of Qualifications

★ 18 years successful experience in shoe sales.
★ Extremely reliable, hard working, and honest.
★ Establish excellent relations with customers, building loyal repeat business.
★ Work well in a team, with people of all ages.
★ Well organized and thorough in completing projects.

SALES EXPERIENCE

Direct Retail Sales

• Successfully sold high-fashion, high-quality men's and women's shoes at worldfamous shoe stores: Joseph Magnin's, Charles Jourdan Boutique and Denver's, in San Francisco; and B. Altman's in New York City.

• Achieved position of top salesperson at Charles Jourdan Boutique.

Customer Services/Customer Relations

• Developed loyal customer base and increased sales volume through personal attention to customers:
  - maintained detailed record of individual customers' buying habits and preferences;
  - contacted customers to notify them of special sales and new merchandise shipments;
  - sent thank-you notes for patronage, and cards on special occasions.

Managing/Organizing

• Consistently maintained clean, attractive shopping area and well organized stockroom, assuring that merchandise was accurately replaced in stockroom.

• Managed supermarket near Zurich, Switzerland, supervising and training 15 employees, filling in at all positions, and handling store opening, bookkeeping, buying and promotion.

EMPLOYMENT HISTORY

1985-present	**Salesperson**, shoes	DENVER'S FINE SHOES - San Francisco
1975-84	**Salesperson**, shoes	CHARLES JOURDAN at Joseph Magnin - San Francisco
1968-75	**Salesperson**, shoes	JOSEPH MAGNIN - San Francisco

plus earlier store management in Switzerland.

EDUCATION & TRAINING
Degree in Trade and Business, Switzerland

SALES

ELEANOR T. KENNEDY

809 Laurel Drive
San Francisco CA 94123
(415) 202-6164

Objective: Position as Sales Representative

HIGHLIGHTS OF QUALIFICATIONS

★ Experience in sales, handling entire western region of U.S.
★ Enjoy a challenge; work well under pressure.
★ Self-motivated, goal-oriented and well organized.
★ Readily inspire the confidence and trust of customers.

PROFESSIONAL EXPERIENCE

Sales Management
- Managed and operated western regional office:
  - resolved customer problems, serving as liaison with the home office;
  - sold directly to major corporations such as Hewlett-Packard, McDonnell-Douglas, Hughes Aircraft, Los Angles Times;
  - developed extensive database of potential clients through contacting agencies, educators, vocational rehabilitation administrators, corporate managers;
  - followed up on referrals and leads, and established new customer contacts, to arrange product demonstrations.

Direct Sales
- Demonstrated and sold a wide range of products for the blind and visually impaired:
  ...speech output devices   ...braille printers   ...braille output devices
  ...optical character readers   ...electronic mobility aids.
- Made cold calls and field visits to new customers, significantly increasing accounts.
- Sold travel packages to a broad range of clients acquired through individual contact, coordinating vacation itineraries, reservations and ticketing.

Presentation & Training
- Delivered group presentations at national and regional conferences, addressing professionals in the field of blindness.
- Designed and presented workshops throughout the Western U.S., training special educators, vocational rehabiliation counselors, administrators and individuals, on the use of computer products for the blind.
- Planned and implemented individualized travel skills programs for low vision and blind veterans, including their family members.

WORK HISTORY

1/86-present	**Western Regional Sales Rep**	Manufacturers of Computer Products for the Blind Redwood City, CA
1983-85 *	**Outside Sales Consultant**	Travel Design Inc. (*part time) Mt View CA
1981-85	**Blind Rehab Specialist**	Veterans Admin. Medical Center, Palo Alto CA
1975-80	Full time Student	
"	**Program Specialist** summer	Easter Seals Foundation, Inkster MI
"	**Park Technician** seasonal	Everglades Park, FL; Rocky Mt. National Park, CO

EDUCATION

M.A., BLIND REHABILITATION - WESTERN MICHIGAN UNIVERSITY, Kalamazoo MI
B.S., THERAPEUTIC RECREATION - EASTERN MICHIGAN UNIVERSITY, Ypsilanti MI

SALES

DENNIS BRINKLEY
987 Lakemead Way
Redwood City CA 94062
(415) 901-6001 work
(415) 511-6887 home

Objective: Trainee in real estate appraisal.

HIGHLIGHTS OF QUALIFICATIONS

★ Self motivated, mature, focused and persistent.
★ Successful in mastering skills through hands-on experience.
★ Proven ability to reach accurate, objective conclusions
  involving a great deal of data and variables.
★ Skill in identifying the real goal, and finding ways to
  achieve it within available time, resources and conditions.

RELEVANT SKILLS & ACCOMPLISHMENTS

Knowledge of Real Estate, Finance & Economics
- Completed AIREA course in Principles of Real Estate Appraisal.
- Mastered real estate laws and procedures, earning California licensure in real estate sales.
- Authored an abstract on the impact of banking and money on macroeconomics; predicted
  the necessity for American companies to merger with foreign competitors to survive.

Analysis of Value & Feasibility
- Appraised the feasibility and cost effectiveness of company's proposed expenditures:
  -plant improvements -major purchases of equipment -property and equipment leases ,
  -contracts -new facilities -equipment and service upgrades.
- Transformed a chaotic book warehouse into a highly efficient and cost-effective operation:
  -assessed the current conditions, traffic flow, and turnaround time for processing goods;
  -developed theories to best utilize available space and manpower to increase production
  -implemented and modified these new ideas until the desired results were achieved;
  -results: saved thousands of dollars in labor and freight costs; increased customer satisfaction;
  improved quality of the product; met production deadlines and quotas.

Project Planning/Management
- Successfully managed the start-up of a local TV station:
  -assessed needs of community through public and private meetings;
  -found local talent and trained volunteers for all aspects of TV production;
  -supervised production of final programming.
- Developed scholarly journal from initial concept to actual production and distribution,
  learning all aspects of magazine production in the process.

EMPLOYMENT HISTORY

1985-present	**Comptroller**	ACE BOOK DISTRIBUTORS, Brattleboro VT
1984-85	**Operations Manager**	ACE BOOK DISTRIBUTORS, Brattleboro VT
1977-78	**TV Production Manager**	BRATTLEBORO COMMUNITY TV (concurrent w/below)
1975-83	**Editor/Writer**	ZAHRA PRESS; DIWAN PRESS, London & San Antonio TX

EDUCATION & TRAINING

B.A., Social Sciences - UNIVERSITY OF CALIFORNIA, BERKELEY
Real Estate Sales License, California
Course in Real Estate Appraisal Principles, AIREA

POTPOURRI

199

LINDA DURKEE
1219 Shafter Ave.
Oakland CA 94609
(415) 694-3336

Objective: Position as Real Estate Appraiser.

HIGHLIGHTS OF QUALIFICATIONS

★ Committed to developing expertise in real estate appraisal;
   currently enrolled in Real Estate Appraisal course.
★ Direct experience assessing the condition of a building.
★ Skill in researching and comparing market information.
★ Talent for mathematical computation and data organization.

RELEVANT EXPERIENCE & SKILLS

Research/Comparison
- Researched and contracted to purchase skilled labor, building appliances and materials, as owner/manager of a rental triplex.
- Researched commercial sources of gems, metals and related products from various manufacturers to determine best combination of price and quality.

Data Organization & Computation
- Maintained detailed financial and material records for jewelry business, documenting: ...gross income ...expenses ...inventory ...sources and comparative costs of materials.
- Recorded rental operating costs and computed annual expenditures to assure profitability.

Real Estate Knowledge
- Purchased and managed a triplex rental unit:
   -conducted a comparative search of properties in Oakland and Berkeley
   -completed course for owners on home repair
   -handled minor plumbing and electrical problems
   -researched on construction, foundations, earthquake precautions.
- Studied Appraisal and Principles of Real Estate.

WORK HISTORY

1973-present	**Jeweler/Manager/Mfg./sales**	LINDA DURKEE JEWELRY DESIGN, Bay Area
1978-present	**Property Manager** part-time	BUILDING OWNER & MANAGER, self-employed
1965-72	**Sales/Administrative Asst.**	DAYTON POOL & SUPPLY CO., Dayton OH

EDUCATION & TRAINING

Psychology major - OHIO UNIVERSITY, Athens OH

Real Estate Related Courses
- Principles of Real Estate   • Accounting I
- Real Estate Appraisal, currently enrolled

MARGARET LESTER
1919 Richardson Lane
Hayward CA 94541
(415) 256-1990

Margaret got advice from a pro in her chosen field about what to put on her resume (See "Info Interviewing," page 305.) Note that she itemizes the tools she can work with.

Objective: Position as real estate appraiser trainee.

HIGHLIGHTS OF QUALIFICATIONS

- Personal experience in real estate and home maintenance.
- Sharp, quick learner; willing to get involved.
- Effective working alone and as a cooperative team worker.
- Strength in analyzing, researching, organizing, and problem solving.
- Reliable and hard working; thorough in completing projects.

EDUCATION

Master of Arts, Education, 1976 - HOLY NAMES COLLEGE, Oakland CA
Standard Teaching Credential, Elementary, 1972 - HOLY NAMES COLLEGE
Bachelor of Arts, Sociology, 1972 - HOLY NAMES COLLEGE

WORK EXPERIENCE

1978-present	**Branch Manager**	UNIVERSAL SAVINGS BANK - Oakland CA
1973-1978	**Elementary Teacher**	OAKLAND PUBLIC SCHOOLS
1970-1972	**Acting Asst. Manager and Sales Clerk**	GOLDEN STATE BOOK CO. Oakland CA

RELEVANT SKILLS & EXPERIENCE

Writing & Communication
- Wrote bank and bookstore correspondence; developed detailed school curricula.
- Completed studies in "Effective Business Writing" and "Communication Skills for Business."
- Authored 50-page paper documenting research project on the importance of language.
- Advised and counseled bank customers on new accounts and services available.
- Conducted personnel training meetings on procedural changes and product information.

Math & Finance
- Computed interest on savings accounts; trained other staff in computations.
- Calculated daily cash receipts and prepared deposits for bookstore and bank.
- Handled a wide range of customer banking products and services:
 -savings accounts -IRAs -CDs -account loans -loan insurance -financial inquiries.

Research & Organization
- Conducted in-depth research for master's thesis project on language:
 - searched microfilmed records of previous studies;
 - surveyed periodicals for articles and studies on the subject;
 - administered a controlled test to identify the effects of learning in native language as compared with learning in secondary tongue;
 - organized and compared statistical data to develop final analysis of the project.
- Traced detailed history of client bank records to resolve customer service issues.

Tool Skills
Office: microfilm, computer terminals, PC, calculator, copy machine.
Home: power drills, skill saw, table saw, T-square, sander, buffer, auto, pick-up, van.

Real Estate
- Researched real estate market areas extensively, on financial and desirability criteria.
- Performed home maintenance, including:
 -wall papering -painting -wall patching -landscaping -insulating
- Purchased two homes, sold one.

EMILY GEORGE
2440 Parker Street
Berkeley CA 94704
(415) 544-2378

**Objective: position as designer or illustrator, working with
clothing, jewelry, interiors, graphics, or displays.**

Highlights of Qualifications

★ Creative artist with 12 years experience in clothing design.
★ Successfully designed and marketed Emily George Artwear,
   my own line of high fashion women's clothing.
★ Sharp, well organized, hard working; able to meet deadlines.
★ Dedicated to highest quality work.
★ Able to manage and implement a project from initial design
   concept through final production.

PROFESSIONAL EXPERIENCE

Product Design
• Designed appliqued and hand painted women's jackets for quality clothing market, including
  - Neiman Marcus/Beverly Hills   - Liberty House of Hawaii   - White Duck
  - Marriott Hotel Gift Shops   - La Costa Resort   - Maison Mendessolle
• Exhibited and sold original clothing and accessory designs at:
  - American Craft Council Crafts Fair - San Francisco 1985
  - Palo Alto Celebrates the Arts, 1985
  - Pacific Fashion Institute Benefit Fashion Show 1983-84 (by invitation)
  - Oakland Museum Natural Crafts Fair 1982-83
  - Oakland Museum History Guild Needlework Exhibition 1985.

Graphic Design
• Designed advertising mailers for my clothing design business: directed photo sessions,
  designed layout, wrote copy, selected typestyle and paper, coordinated with printer.

Display, Merchandising, Sales
• Designed and built convertible and portable display booth for craft fairs:
  - prepared scale drawings; purchased fabric, wood and hardware materials;
  - supervised construction and painting; arranged merchandise display.
• Created window displays and in-store displays for The Soft Touch Boutique.
• Set up special displays of new and sale merchandise in working studio setting.
• Developed and maintained customer mailing list.
• Negotiated with manufacturer's reps to handle my designs as independents, and at Los
  Angeles Fashion Mart.

Materials: Planning & Purchasing
• Researched sources and bought fabrics and notions at trade shows, warehouses, specialty
  wholesalers, and through manufacturers' representatives.
• Coordinated the selection of fabrics and findings, and the customizing of materials, for each
  season's line.
• Budgeted materials purchase, based on projected season sales and calculations of quantities
  needed. Established business credit with manufacturers and factors.

- Continued -

EMILY GEORGE
page two

WORK HISTORY

1976-present	**Designer/Owner**	EMILY GEORGE ARTWEAR, Berkeley
1974-75	**Partner/Designer**	THE SOFT TOUCH BOUTIQUE, Lafayette
1971-73	**Clothing Designer**	Self-employed, custom/contract design and sewing
1969-71	**Library Assistant**	UC BERKELEY, Bancroft Library
1967-69	**Musician/Violist**	SANTA BARBARA SYMPHONY ORCHESTRA
1967-68	**Retail Sales**	ROBINSON'S DEPT. STORE - Santa Barbara

EDUCATION

B.A., Music; performance emphasis: Viola - UC SANTA BARBARA, 1969
Private Pilot's License - Oakland, 1979

Additional studies:

CCAC Extension	Life Drawing 1982
	Botanical Illustration 1984
	Painting & Color 1984
Pacific Basin School for the Textile Arts	
	Beginning & Intermediate Silkscreen 1985-86
Pacific Fashion Institute	Pattern Drafting 1977
	History of Costume 1977
	Fashion Illustration 1977
Fiberworks	Color Theory 1978
	Soft Sculpture 1979
UC Extension	Small Business Management 1976

JOYCE STROEBECH

578 Willow Drive
Walnut Creek CA 94598
(415) 902-1228

One of two versions of Joyce's resume: this one focuses on production and design. For another, see page 176.

Objective: Position as Product Assistant for ESPRIT Accessories

HIGHLIGHTS OF QUALIFICATIONS

- Enthusiastic team member whose participation brings out the best in others.
- Production experience in manufacturing textile products, including purchasing materials, pricing products and inventory planning.
- Resourceful problem solver who is good at details.
- Proven success at developing new products with broad market appeal.
- Highly committed to the ESPRIT philosophy and eager to support it.

PRODUCTION AND DESIGN

- Developed and produced fabric accessories, children's clothing and soft sculpture toys for retail market:
  -Purchased raw materials
  -Determined retail and wholesale prices of products
  -Processed purchase orders and invoices
  -Shipped and delivered merchandise, meeting deadlines
  -Maintained inventory and kept bookkeeping records
- Ordered and distributed wholesale fabric and notions for 150-member textile artists' guild:
  -Set up and kept bookkeeping and tax records; processed invoices.
- Controlled inventory, collected sales records, received merchandise, and processed invoices for retail store, as manager of Miscellaneous Inc. Gifts.

MARKETING AND SALES

- Established national market for my original gift line, expanded wholesale accounts from 4 to 22 stores.
- Increased sales in several departments of fabric store by combining merchandise to create fashion jewelry display.
- Sold clothing, gifts, cosmetics and fabrics at retail level.
- Developed good client relations on both wholesale and retail levels.

MANAGEMENT

- Managed gift shop and supervised 8 employees.
- Administered wholesale buying co-op for 150-member textile artists' guild. Increased sales and variety of merchandise.
- Planned and directed meetings, activities and field trips for community organization of 180 parents and children. Increased membership by 50%.

WORK HISTORY

1979-present	**Designer/Owner/Wholesaler**	FIBER DESIGNS - Walnut Creek
1986-present	**Fabric & Craft Sales**	FABRIC HEAVEN - Pleasant Hill
1976-78	**Assistant Cosmetician**	RUNYON'S DRUG - Walnut Creek
1974	**Assistant to Decorator**	MOBILIA FURNITURE - Houston TX
1969-71	**Gift Shop Manager**	FYNELINE GIFTS INC. - Warren, OH

EDUCATION

B.A., Home Economics: Interior Design & Textile Art - UNIVERSITY OF HOUSTON

REBECCA VANESS
2707 Benvenue Ave.
Oakland CA 94606
(415) 313-0854

Objective: Position as Production Assistant
with a clothing manufacturer, wholesaler or design house.

HIGHLIGHTS OF QUALIFICATIONS

- Experience with all aspects of garment production.
- Hands-on knowledge of sewing and pattern development.
- Effective and experienced sample room supervisor;
  special talent for bridging communication barriers.
- Proven ability to assume increasing responsibility.
- Committed to maintaining exacting standards.

RELEVANT EXPERIENCE

Production/Engineering
- Coordinated sample room activity:
  -maintained wide variety of sample yardage to meet current and on-going needs of merchandisers and engineering department;
  -monitored and replenished supplies;
  -maintained records of all lines in production for referral of merchandisers.

Supervision/Project Coordination
- Balanced workflow of pattern makers, sample makers, cutter, and merchandisers according to established deadlines and production considerations.
- Promoted cooperative and productive working environment:
  -assessed needs and abilities of each person;
  -maintained an overview of each project;
  -supported staff by assuming appropriate responsibility.
- Negotiated and established realistic deadlines.

Quality Control
- Inspected garments, checking for:
  -correct seam construction, finish stitching and trims
  -appropriate packaging   -fabric quality.
- Measured first-production and counter samples, comparing with specifications.

EMPLOYMENT HISTORY

> She explains what "Bay City" is about.

1985-present	**Design Room Assistant**	BAY CITY UNIQUE CREATIONS (private label design firm)
1978-85	**Boutique Seamstress**	Self-employed, part-time
1976-78	**Cutter/Seamstress**	DAY'S CUSTOM UPHOLSTERY, Spokane WA
1974-76	**Seamstress/Designer**	Free-lance, concurrent w/travel in Europe
1973-74	**Boutique Seamstress**	NAPOLEON & JOSEPHINE'S boutique, Berkeley

Language skills: familiar with Spanish, French, Greek, German

WENDY V. GILLROY
900 Valleyview
Sausalito, CA 94965
901-2662

Objective: Position as project coordinator, product developer, or client services representative, with a local manufacturer.

Highlights of Qualifications
★ Demonstrated success in planning and completing large, complex projects.
★ Technical expertise in the applications of manufacturing materials.
★ Exceptionally creative in design, utilization and problem solving.
★ Outstanding skill in researching all aspects of material and design data.
★ Effective in public presentation of products and services.

PROFESSIONAL EXPERIENCE

Project Planning, Coordinating
• Designed prototype playground for installation in 14 public parks in Atlanta GA: developed manufacturing schedules, coordinated subcontractors and completed all 14 installations in four months.
• Served as owner's representative on multi-million dollar construction projects for City Savings:
 - initiated specifications and developed contracts for each project;
 - developed project budgets and schedules; coordinated tenant leasing.
 - supervised and coordinated all construction and administration matters.

Product Design / Technical Expertise
• Developed unique play environment for handicapped children, based on their physical skills and limitations, and incorporating innovative uses of conventional materials.
• Researched and studied technical properties and applications of many construction materials: ...metals ...wood products & preservatives ...plastics & vacuum forming

Public Relations / Client Services
• Delivered informational presentations on community resources, using slide shows and talks.
• Developed promotional and advertising materials for my own design & construction business.
• Served as college PR assistant, writing press releases for all campus activities.
• Consulted with clients to assess their design wants and needs; then produced custom designed furniture and individualized interiors.

EMPLOYMENT HISTORY

1984-present	**Project Manager**	CITY SAVINGS BANK - San Francisco
1976-83	**Owner/Manager**	GROUNDS FOR PLAY, INC. - Atlanta GA
1975-76	**Art Critic**	ATLANTA GAZETTE - Atlanta
1970-74	**Student**	ATLANTA COLLEGE OF ART - Atlanta

EDUCATION
B.A., Art History - Goucher College, Baltimore MD
B.F.A., Sculpture - Atlanta College of Art, Atlanta GA

KATHERINE BRUNSWICK
4980 - 16th Street, Apt. 6
San Francisco CA 94114
(415) 151-5887

Objective: Position as Production Assistant with film company

HIGHLIGHTS OF QUALIFICATIONS
★ Production Assistant for television series.
★ Production Coordinator for independent film company.
★ Assistant to Producer, Mill Valley Film Festival.
★ Experience in radio production at university radio station.
★ Degree in Art History, with emphasis in art and graphics.
★ Lifelong exposure to film and television industries.

RELATED EXPERIENCE

FILM/TELEVISION
Silver Productions, ABC-TV:
• Assisted in office supervision for producer and production coordinator.
• Copied and distributed script.
• Coordinated transportation for cast and crew members.
• Oversaw communication between Oakland and LA offices.
• Assisted Casting Director and Location Manager.

Farquart Film Productions, as Production Coordinator:
• Scouted locations, acquired filming permits, obtained props.
• Organized catering, chauffeuring, flight bookings, and accommodations.
• Supervised crew, talent, musicians, extras, clientele.
• Wrote and distributed press releases.
• Assisted Art Director; designing/building sets, lighting pick-up shots.
• Photographed promotional stills.

FILM-RELATED
At Mill Valley Film Festival, as Production Assistant:
• Developed and coordinated special children's film series.
• Organized and assisted with operational tasks of film institute office.
• Planned and implemented operational model for Special Events Department.

COMMUNICATION/MEDIA
At KALX Radio, as news writer, anchor and reporter:
• Engineered and anchored a weekly newscast.
• Investigated and reported on student rallies and campus activities.
• Taped live, on-air radio reports of the 1984 Democratic National Convention.
• Trained and supervised incoming staff members.

VISUAL ARTS/DESIGN
• Acted in, directed and coauthored independent short 8mm film projects
• Published photographs in small LA newspaper and university newspaper.

WORK HISTORY

1987-present	**Production Asst.**	SILVER PRODUCTIONS, ABC-TV - Oakland CA
Fall 1986	**Production Coor.**	FARQUART FILM PRODUCTIONS - Berkeley CA
Fall 1986	**Production Asst.**	MILL VALLEY FILM FESTIVAL - Mill Valley CA
1985-86	**Producer**	KALX Radio - UC Berkeley
Spring 1986	**Tutor, Algebra**	WILLARD JR. HIGH - Berkeley CA
1982-1986	**Full-time student**	UC Berkeley and University of Oregon

EDUCATION
B.A., Art History - University of California, Berkeley 1986
Universita di Firenze - Florence, Italy 1983

LYNN M. SHEFFIELD
6023 Dover Street, #B
Oakland CA 94609
(415) 699-8000

Objective: Position with a radio or TV station involving programming and/or announcing.

HIGHLIGHTS OF QUALIFICATIONS

★ Extensive experience in the performing arts; successfully wrote and recorded songs.
★ Lifelong commitment and involvement with music.
★ Resonant speaking voice; accomplished singer.
★ Excellent writing skills in both music and lyrics.
★ Sociable, personable, communicate easily with a wide range of personalities.
★ Talent for generating creative ideas and organizing projects.

PROFESSIONAL EXPERIENCE

Creativity & Performing Skills

• Successfully wrote and performed 4 songs on a major record label, as member of ISIS, a pioneering and nationally recognized women's band. ("Breaking Through," United Artists)

• Recorded extensively with other professional musicians:
  ...sang (and performed in concert) with David Amram, classical and jazz composer, recording "No More Walls" on RCA Victor;
  ...sang and played saxophone with Archie Whitewater; recorded an album on CHESS RECORDS;
  ...played saxophone on Malvina Reynolds' album, "Magical Songs for Children."

• Performed solo, as singer/song writer and guitarist, in East Coast clubs.

Organizing/Coordinating

• Coproduced theatrical dance shows for Bay Area audiences, as business partner in RAINBEAUZ PRODUCTIONS.

• Advised college faculty on modernizing their curriculum and classroom technique using video and sound, as educational consultant for Thirteen College Curriculum Program.

• Organized and coordinated a European tour for the Howard Johnson sextet:
  ...arranged travel   ...contracted for payment   ...interpreted in German.

EMPLOYMENT HISTORY

1980-present	**Bus Operator**	GOLDEN GATE BRIDGE DISTRICT, San Rafael CA
1976-80	**Piano Tuner**	SELF-EMPLOYED, Forestville CA
1976-80	**Bookkeeper/Accountant**	PARTNER, BOOKKEEPING SERVICE, Forestville CA
1969-76	**Musician & Music Teacher**	SELF-EMPLOYED, New York City
1967-69	**Educational Consultant**	CURRICULUM RESOURCES GROUP, Newton MA

EDUCATION

B.A., Liberal Arts - SARAH LAWRENCE COLLEGE, Bronxville NY
A.M., Regional Studies/Middle East - HARVARD
Ph.D. Near Eastern Languages & Lit./Social Relations - HARVARD

POTPOURRI

MARTHA KRAEMER
1991 Greenhaven, Palo Alto CA 94303
Home (415) 256-0121 • Work (415)452-0057

Objective: Production position in special TV programming

HIGHLIGHTS OF QUALIFICATIONS
★ 10 years' experience in TV news broadcasting.
★ Graduate degree in documentary film making.
★ Effectiveness in managing and directing others.
★ Ability to develop a wide range of community contacts.
★ Coproduced highly rated news magazine.

PROFESSIONAL EXPERIENCE

Writing & Producing
• Coproduced daily syndicated news magazine, "PM":
  - generated and researched story ideas   - interviewed potential story sources
  - scouted filming locations   - wrote scripts for 8-minute productions
  - directed production crew on location   - supervised editing.
• Produced 13-min. show for United Way's "Project Match" on issues of housing for the elderly.

Reporting & Interviewing
• Developed contacts and stories, specializing in politics, health and education.
• Developed and researched feature stories reflecting community interests.
• Covered fast-breaking news stories.

Film and Videotape Editing
• Edited videotape for 13-minute United Way promotional program.
• Edited videotape for "PM" news magazine shows.
• Filmed and edited stories for local nightly news show.

Technical Expertise

One way to highlight your technical skills.

• Developed working knowledge of...
  - Videotape editing equipment: Sony, JVC, RCA
  - Videotape camera equipment: Hitachi, JVC, Sony, RCA, Ikigami
  - Videotape recording equipment: Sony-BVU, JVC, RCA
  - Film editing equipment: guillotine splicer, hot splicer, 16mm flat bed
  - Film camera equipment: Bell & Howell, CP-16, Bolex, Beleau, Frezelini

BROADCAST HISTORY

1987-present	Teaching Assistant	STANFORD UNIVERSITY Communications Dept.
1986	Creative Director	OSAKA PRODUCTIONS - El Paso TX
1984-85	Producer	KVIA-TV (for "PM" Magazine) - El Paso
1981-83	Photographer/Reporter	KGGM-TV - Albuquerque NM
1980	Interim News Director	K102 RADIO - El Paso
1976-79	Reporter/Photographer	KTSM-TV and RADIO - El Paso
1973-76	Reporter/Anchor	KELP-TV - El Paso

EDUCATION

A.M., Documentary Film Making, 1985 - Stanford University
B.S., Education (English; Journalism) University of Texas, El Paso
Professional Affiliation: National Association of Hispanic Journalists

POTPOURRI

209

REBECCA NEWBURG
1901 Connecticut Ave.
South Orange, NJ 07079
(201) 909-3886

Objective: Film production manager or assistant, in an agency or production house.

HIGHLIGHTS OF QUALIFICATIONS

★ Special talent for inspiring creative excellence on a shoestring.
★ Proven track record of producing & directing award-winning projects.
★ Dedicated, professional attitude; mature and willing to work.
★ 9 years experience; working knowledge of all phases of production.
★ Practical grounding in the business and sales aspect of the industry.

RELEVANT PROFESSIONAL EXPERIENCE

Broadcast Production
- Produced and directed strip shows, weekly news magazine, live and tape specials, and difficult remote location shoots: -white water rafting -big game hunting -wilderness.
- Produced/directed investigative documentaries: i.e., youth detention, jail conditions, illegal aliens.
- Working knowledge of audio, 16mm, double system, studio, ENG, tape & film editing, mixing.

Film & Theatre Directing
- Directed summer repertory theatre at University of Idaho.
- Created and directed Children's Theatre for Idaho Parks & Recreation Dept.
- Directed 30-minute avant-garde dramatic feature film, "Cheesecake."
- Directed Radio Free Comedy, a professional New York-based improv group.

Producing & Production Management
- Developed sources of funding for film and tape projects, involving packaging, proposal writing, identifying and securing funding sources, capitalization, corporate sponsorship and trade-outs.
- Managed all aspects of a project: story development, budget, hiring, securing services.

Marketing, PR, Sales
- Developed relationship with corporations for sponsorship of Monarch Productions.
- Successfully secured national sponsors for Miss American Teenager Pageant of New Jersey.
- Built sponsorship, through successful cold-calling, for a major cable magazine and cable TV.

WORK HISTORY

1986-now	**Executive Assistant**	BURKE & POWERS ADVERTISING - NYC
1984-85	**AA, Corporate Communications**	CENTRAL CITY BANK, Private Banking Div, NYC
1982-83	**Marketing Rep**	NETWORK 4 ADVERTISING - So. Plainfield NJ
1981-82	**Production Manager**	CBS CABLE DIVISION - NYC
1977-81	**Producer/Director**	IDAHO PUBLIC TELEVISION NETWORK - Boise ID
1974-77	**Associate Producer/Director**	WJCT-TV - Jacksonville FL

EDUCATION, TRAINING & AWARDS
M.P.P., Communications Policy - University of California, Berkeley 1974
B.A., Political Science, honors - University of California, Berkeley 1970

Film Production Awards
Idaho State Broadcasters - Best Documentary 1979 & 1980
Idaho Press Club - Best Documentary 1979 & 1980
Sigma Delta Chi - Best Short Subject 1980
Pacific Mountain Network - Best Short Subject 1980

ROGER LANCASTER
9870 Sixty-first St.
Oakland CA 94609
(415) 491-0098

Objective: Entry level position as news grip with a TV station.

HIGHLIGHTS OF QUALIFICATIONS

- Cooperative teamworker in setting and achieving goals;
  personable, outgoing, approachable and communicative.
- Good eye for photography; experience with VCR cam/recorders.
- Strong interest in the field of TV reporting and camera work.
- Dependable, available, eager to learn, willing to work hard.

RELEVANT EXPERIENCE

Teamwork
- Served as waiter for exclusive party-yacht service, coordinating with coworkers on meticu-
  lously timed dinner cruises:
  -met deadlines for finely detailed preparations;
  -served 4 courses within strict time constraints, maintaining high quality and attention to detail.
- Participated in weekly meetings of a collective, taking into account everyone's opinions and
  priorities in working out problems.

Camera work
- Filmed 20 two-minute opinion interviews of Laney College students, operating a JVC
  cam/recorder.
- Additional experience handling a cam-recorder for personal use.

Project Organizing
- Assisted with order filling and customer services at Center for Local & Community Research:
  -organized a wide range of data (including computerized info) to develop special interest
    mailings;
  -answered phone inquiries, provided information, and referred customers to other sources of
    information in their field;
  -filled mail order for books and pamphlets available from our company.
- Entered and sorted accounting data on a computer for a small accounting firm, successfully
  learning new procedures and following through without supervision.

EMPLOYMENT HISTORY & EDUCATION

1986-present	**Waiter**	HORNBLOWER PARTY YACHTS, San Francisco
1985	**Dishwasher**	HORNBLOWER PARTY YACHTS, San Francisco
1984-86 *	**Clerical Assistant**	CENTER FOR LOCAL & COMMUNITY RESEARCH, Berkeley
		(networking/info center for nonprofit organizations)
1984*	**Accounting Assistant**	CARLENE COLE, ACCOUNTANT, Berkeley
	* part-time	

Berkeley High School Graduate, 1985

ADRIENNE MENDOZA
2900 Ashby Place, #4
Berkeley CA 94705
(415) 887-8779

Objective: entry level position in property management.

HIGHLIGHTS OF QUALIFICATIONS

- Resourceful; skilled in analyzing and solving problems.
- Easily develop rapport with clients and tradespeople.
- Proven ability to learn quickly.
- Experience in maintaining accurate records.
- Familiar with repair and construction terminology.

RELEVANT EXPERIENCE & SKILLS

Project Organizing/Problem Solving
- Organized and maintained Job Placement Program for over 1200 students annually.
- Coordinated large campus Job Fair introducing students and employers:
  -arranged for rooms and publicity;
  -solicited participation of hundreds of employers.
- Successfully gained the confidence of resistant clients in numerous situations (employers, parents, students) through:
  -consistent clarification of policies;
  -listening to their point of view;
  -negotiating workable compromises.

Client Information; Negotiations
- Provided complex contractual information to prospective employers of university students under work-study program, interpreting federal and state employment regulations.
- Conducted field visits to campuses throughout the State, introducing computerized career information system to counselors and administrators:
  -submitted detailed cost statements on lease of software and system installation;
  -trained staff in computer terminology and use of the system.

Reporting, Record Keeping
- Oversaw reporting on student job placement program:
  -calculated matching fund amounts;
  -developed and maintained filing system documenting activity on 1000 student jobs;
  -monitored job placement activity to assure compliance with program guidelines.
- Documented extensive policy and procedure information, providing students with clear program guidelines and relieving staff of time-consuming verbal explanations.

EMPLOYMENT HISTORY

1982-present	**Placement Interviewer**	FINANCIAL AID OFFICE, HAYWARD STATE UNIV.
1980-82	**Service Rep.**	COMPUTER SYSTEMS INC., San Jose
1976-79	**Counselor**	GOODWILL, San Jose

EDUCATION
M.A., Rehabilitation Counseling - SAN JOSE STATE UNIVERSITY, 1976
B.S., Child Development - SAN JOSE STATE UNIVERSITY, 1972

MARK KILLORIN

1219 Parker Street
Albany CA 94706
(415) 425-0632

Objective: Trainee in Real Estate Property Management

HIGHLIGHTS OF QUALIFICATIONS

★ Experienced landlord and apartment complex manager.
★ Licensed in real estate sales.
★ Certificate in Real Estate from Diablo Valley CC.
★ Lifelong exposure to family real estate business.
★ 10 years experience in retail sales.

RELATED EXPERIENCE

Management

- Managed 18-unit apartment complex:
  - -loan collections
  - -yard work, maintenance
  - -monitor parking
  - -tenant complaints/requests
  - -screen & research potential tenants
  - -install appliances
- Managed warehouse: verified accurate delivery, enforced strict receiving rules, prepared work assignments for night crews, designed and maintained a workable schematic for warehouse stock.
- Assistant Manager substitute:
  - -supervised 35 clerks
  - -prepared complex merchandise orders
  - -entered transactions on computer
  - -performed detailed bookkeeping
  - -resolved customer and employee disputes

Real Estate

- Researched and purchased two income properties (a single-family dwelling and a duplex), both generating profit.
- Developed expertise in all aspects of real estate financing.
- Assisted in accounting: loan recording and loan collections.
- Performed market analyses and square-foot analyses for property appraisals.

Sales

- Completed comprehensive course in Real Estate Sales at Diablo Valley College.
- Sold retail products and developed excellent customer rapport for 10 years.
- Participated regularly in team competition for creative marketing displays in a retail store.
- Studied sales reports & reorganized retail stock displays to maximize sales volume.

EMPLOYMENT HISTORY

1975-present	**Warehouse Manager**	P&S PRODUCE MARKET, Oakland
1983 summer	**Asst. Manager**	P&S PRODUCE MARKET, Oakland
1977-1978	**Office Assistant,** part time	E.J., KILLORIN Co., Real Estate Loans, Berkeley

EDUCATION & TRAINING

A.A. degree, Business Administration - Diablo Valley College, Pleasant Hill
Real Estate Certificate Program, DVCC |
Real Estate Licensing Program, Anthony Schools, Oakland

RICHARD C. FLORES
4849 Montana Blvd.
Pleasant Hill CA 94523
(415) 692-1413

Objective: Position in Property Management with Wells Fargo

HIGHLIGHTS OF QUALIFICATIONS

★ Extensive knowledge in all phases of new construction, remodeling and property maintenance.

★ Thrive on opportunity to apply technical knowledge and analytical skills in projects involving people at all levels.

★ Two years experience in residential property management.

★ Outstanding ability to communicate with subcontractors in their language.

★ Trained by one of the area's most reputable, construction firms.

PROFESSIONAL EXPERIENCE

Construction Planning, Scheduling, Cost estimating

• Completely redesigned my own home, adding on 1000 square feet of improvements, complying with all codes, acquiring permits, drawing up plans and scheduling subcontractors.
• Worked on construction of large commercial building and over 150 custom homes.
• Remodeled several residential properties, consulting with homeowners, selecting materials and estimating costs within their budgets.

Management & Supervision

• Scheduled and monitored subcontractors (plumbers, electricians, sheetmetal workers, roofers) for large scale custom home development project, in absence of foreman.
• Trained dozens of carpenter apprentices and new employees of park service.

Monitoring Services/Tenant & Public Relations

• Handled tenant complaints and arranged maintenance services as landlord of a single-family unit.
• Interviewed prospective tenants, made credit checks, drew up rental contracts.
• Effectively provided public information on recreation and nature, and enforced and interpreted park user guidelines, as park ranger.

WORK HISTORY

1978-present	**Journeyman Carpenter**	M.G. ROBERTSON CO. Walnut Creek (residential home building)
1974-1977	**Park Ranger**	PARKS & RECREATION DEPT - Sacramento Co.
1973 summer	**Recreation Leader**	SACRAMENTO COUNTY
1972-1973	**Asst. Manager**	SAMBO'S RESTAURANT - Sacramento
1970-1972	**Park Aide**	MT. DIABLO STATE PARK - Diablo CA (summers)

EDUCATION & TRAINING

B.S., Environmental Resources - California State University, Sacramento 1975
Fundamentals of Real Estate Practice - currently enrolled, DVC
Carpenter Apprenticeship Program - completed 1982

AMY BUCHANNON
2700 Polk Street
San Francisco CA 94109
(415) 551-2866

Objective: Position as Graphic Designer's Assistant / Pasteup Artist

Highlights of Qualifications
- ★ Creative and artistic sense in graphic design.
- ★ Learn quickly; interpret information accurately.
- ★ Enthusiastic, energetic; excellent at working in a team setting to meet deadlines.
- ★ Three years experience in graphics design and layout.
- ★ Working knowledge of pasteup techniques, mechanicals, ruling and assembly of type.

GRAPHIC DESIGN EXPERIENCE

Graphic Design
- Created calligraphy for businesses and individuals, as free-lance calligrapher:
  - selected character styles appropriate to the assignment;
  - produced original and adapted designs for ornamentation and borders;
  - designed wide variety of products: ...brochures ...poems/sayings for framing ...information signs ...certificates ...invitations   ...fliers
  - designed and produced Book of Records for Pyramid Productions, involving calligraphy of 300 names of customers and officers, and ornamentation.
- Designed logos for community group, retail store, and professional therapists.
- Designed successful brochure for Narendra Bulow, bodywork therapist, choosing type, colors and materials consistent with desired image.
- Produced portfolio book illustrating basic production and design skills.

Pasteup
- Pasted up brochure of services for Surfaces Beauty Salon, involving calligraphy, photo reduction and pasteup.
- Pasted up mail order catalog for Emerald Priestess retail store.
- Pasted up many fliers for community organizations and small businesses.

Client Contact
- Consulted with graphics clients throughout production:
  - assessed clients needs and wishes;
  - advised on creative and technical options for achieving desired image;
  - showed comps for clients' approval.

EMPLOYMENT HISTORY

1986 to present	**Student and**	ACADEMY OF ART, San Francisco
"	**Graphic Artist**	free-lance
1985	**Receptionist**	ABOUT FACE & BODY salon, San Francisco
1985	**Graphic Designer**	EMERALD PRIESTESS, books & crystals, Berkeley
1983-84	**Student**	LANEY COLLEGE, Oakland

EDUCATION

Current student - ACADEMY OF ART - San Francisco
-Figure Drawing   -Silk Screening -Graphics Design: Materials, Tools & Techniques
LANEY COLLEGE: -Basic Design -Layout & Design -Lettering & Layout
FEATHER RIVER COLLEGE: Art History

215

BARBARA MONET
1219 Palo Alto Blvd.
Oakland CA 94609
(415) 653-2211

Objective: Graphic production position
with a publisher, print shop, or publications department

SUMMARY OF QUALIFICATIONS
- 4 years experience as a graphics production artist.
- Familiar with the complete process of print production
  from first customer contact to bindery finishing.
- Able to organize and complete a complex project efficiently.
- Committed to high quality production and constantly sharpening skills.

RELEVANT EXPERIENCE

Production Organization
- Organized production of two 64-page yearbooks; did complete paste-up and assisted with type setting and stripping.
- Produced first issue of a 32-page quarterly newsletter, including organizing of manuscript, proofreading, layout and paste-up.
- Coordinated production of 16-page monthly newspaper: arranged schedule with type setter and printer, specked miscellaneous heads, managed last-minute production decisions.
- Acquired an overall understanding of small newspaper publishing by working in each production area:
  -paste-up artist -office worker -news editor/coor. -proofreader -production coor.

Technical Skills
- Pasted-up a wide variety of camera-ready art, from basic business cards and letterheads, to more demanding jobs such as posters, brochures and booklets involving color, screen tints.
- Prepared paste-ups in close coordination with print shop stripper to assure highest quality and greatest efficiency.
- Operated reproduction camera for 2Ó years, preparing stats, negatives & half-tones.
- Did page layout of monthly newspaper for three years.
- Advised clients at a type setting shop on cost estimates for type setting and paste-up, type style availability and appropriateness, and feasibility of their proposed project plans.

WORK HISTORY

1984-present	**Production Artist**	MIRO GRAPHICS CENTER - Berkeley
1983-84	**Paste-up Artist**	MARTINSEN LITHOGRAPHERS - Richmond
1981-84	**Production Artist**	WOMAN monthly newspaper - Alameda
		(range of editorial and production positions)
1980-81	**Asst. Manager/Cook**	RISTORANTE ITALIA - Oakland
1976-79	**Cook**	WHITE SWAN Restaurant - Chicago

EDUCATION & TRAINING
B.A., Humanities - UNIVERSITY OF CHICAGO
Graphics Arts - LANEY COLLEGE, Oakland

GREGORY BYRON
2705 18th St. #7
San Francisco, CA 94110
(415) 212-3551

Objective: Entry level position in multi-image production company.

EXPERIENCE

Print Media
- Operated graphic arts camera for print shop.
- Created concepts and layouts, specified type, and completed mechanicals for posters, brochures and books.
- Managed production department of high quality book publishing company, supervising typography, stripping, printing, colating and binding.

Photograghy and Audio-Visual
- Shot still photographic documentation for an oceanic research expedition.
- Developed a university-sponsored research project visually documenting eight innovative American communities.
- Completed introductory training in a computer graphics paint system, multi-image optical graphics, and multi-image programming.
- Currently working on free-lance multi-image productions.

Exhibits
- Designed and built sculptures and exhibits using variety of media.
- Fabricated and installed trade show exhibits for a high-tech silicon valley corp.
- Achieved expertise at commercial display silkscreen technique.

Writing, Editorial Organization, and Promotion
- Self-published a book documenting history and demise of controversial high school.
- Researched, organized and wrote a course catalog for a new academic major at UC Berkeley.
- Taught editorial, printing, and publishing techniques to architecture students.

WORK HISTORY

1984-present	**Exhibit builder**	Raychem Corporation, Menlo Park, CA
1984	**Free-lance Graphic Designer**	Berkeley and San Francisco
1983	**Photographer, Electrician**	Institute of Ecotechnics - Santa Fe, NM
1980-82	**Project Manager, Fund-raiser**	Ecological Design Group, UC Berkeley
1979	**Production Manager**	Northland Press Book Publisher Flagstaff, AZ
1976-78	**Paste-up Artist, Cameraman**	Nowells Publications, Menlo Park, CA

EDUCATION & TRAINING

Technical Arts/Graphics - College of San Mateo, 1978
Sculpture - Northern Arizona University, 1979
Environmental/Visual Design - UC Berkeley, 1980-82
Computer Graphics - Academy of Art College, Fall 1984
Multi-Image Production - Artists in Print & Assoc. for Multi-Image, 1986
Member: Northern California Chapter Association for Multi-Image

LYNNE CHARNEY
1990 Spruce Street
Berkeley CA 94703
(415) 245-8032

Job Objective: Design/production position in publications or advertising.

SUMMARY OF QUALIFICATIONS

★ Sharp, innovative designer, in both B&W and color applications.
★ Experienced in all aspects of graphics, from client needs assessment through camera-ready art.
★ Effective in organizing large projects & coordinating with outside vendors.
★ Communicate clearly and sensitively with clients and colleagues.
★ Degree in fine arts, plus 10 years professional experience.

PROFESSIONAL EXPERIENCE

Design / Illustration
• Designed and coordinated promotional materials for J. Miller Dance Theatre over a five-year period:
  -posters -announcements -ads -fund-raising package -business stationery
• Conferred with small business people and performing artists to clarify their graphic identity, target audience and written copy.
• Created dynamic, commercially successful designs in unique colors for printed silk fabrics; designed highly effective logo and brochure for Cazadero Jazz Camp.
• Designed custom T-shirts, applying my expertise in designing with type.
• Illustrated high-tech manuals, advertisements, stationery, brochures, and geological maps, featuring both technical detail and artistic expression.

Production / Organization
• Coordinated and produced 500-pg catalog for Whole Earth Access Store, involving:
  -page layout -type spec-ing -pasteup -camera work -supervising an assistant.
• Produced camera ready boards for several books and catalogs, including pasteup, page layout, camera-work, proofing, and type spec-ing.
• Created variety of camera-ready art for business cards, letterheads, brochures, posters, ads, magazines.
• Developed full color art work, with overlays, for scientific slide presentations.

EMPLOYMENT HISTORY

1979-present	**Graphic Designer**	Self-employed - Oakland
1985	**Graphics Tech./Drafter**	CHEVRON USA - San Ramon
1984-85	**Production Artist**	FIFTH STREET DESIGN - Berkeley
1981-84	**Fabric & Clothing Designer**	LYNN CHARNEY HAND PRINTED SILKS, Oakland
1973-84	**T-Shirt Designer**	MARY & JOE's SPORTING GOODS - Albany
1974	**Teaching Asstistant**	CALIFORNIA COLLEGE OF ARTS & CRAFTS
1970-72	**Pasteup Artist**	THE MINES PRESS - New York

EDUCATION & TRAINING
B.F.A. - California College of Arts & Crafts, Oakland
Studies in drawing, print making, design - New York University
- Portfolio available upon request -

POTPOURRI

ANN VOORHEES
530 Battery Street
San Francisco CA 94111
(415) 503-6365

Objective: Position as staff attorney with a government agency or professional organization.

HIGHLIGHTS OF QUALIFICATIONS

★ Superior legal knowledge and skill, combined with a creative
  talent for using them to best advantage.
★ Work well under pressure and thrive on challenging projects.
★ Equally effective working independently or collaboratively.
★ Committed to high ethical standards in the legal profession.

REPRESENTATIVE ACCOMPLISHMENTS & EXPERIENCE

Legal Expertise
• Worked as attorney with total responsibility for cases in a broad range of legal areas, including:
  ...probate   ...estate planning   ...family law
  ...civil litigation   ...property   ...tax   ...criminal law.
• Successfully completed all requirements for certification as Specialist in Family Law.
• Maintained superior expertise and knowledge in the field by keeping current on all cases and
  legislation in family law and related areas.
• Refined and improved legal skills through frequent continuing education programs.
• Serve regularly as Judge Pro Tem, Mountain Superior Court, Domestic Relations Mandatory Settle-
  ment Conferences.

Collaboration & Project Management
• Successfully managed a private law practice, training and supervising support staff and handling
  all accounting, billing and administration.
• Collaborated with court officials and interested professionals in writing and developing a videotape for use in the courts, to educate parents and facilitate resolution of custody and visitation
  disputes.
• Coauthored legislation, with other interested professionals, addressing training needs and job performance standards for city employees in sensitive positions.

EMPLOYMENT HISTORY

1981-present	**Attorney/sole practitioner**	Private practice, San Francisco
1979-81	**Associate Attorney**	SMITH & CRANSTON, attys., San Francisco
1978-79	**Legal Researcher**	Self employed independent contractor
1978	**Associate Attorney**	BERNARD FILMORE, Esq., Palmdale CA
1976-77	**Legal Intern/Law Clerk**	JUDGE MILTON SEBERT, Los Angeles Municipal Court Law & Motion Dept.
		JUDGE JOHN L. HARRIS, Culver City Municipal Court;
		LA DISTRICT ATTORNEY CONSUMER FRAUD UNIT;
		LEGAL AID SOCIETY OF LOS ANGELES

- Continued -

EDUCATION & CERTIFICATION

J.D., UCLA School of Law, 1977 - Admitted to practice December 1977
M.A., History - University of California, Los Angeles 1972
B.A., History - University of Illinois, Chicago, 1970
Certified Family Law Specialist, 1985

PROFESSIONAL AFFILIATIONS

•Executive Committee of Family Law Section, Los Angeles Bar Association
•Video Subcommittee, Los Angeles Bar Association
•Queens Bench   •Women in Criminal Justice   •California Women Lawyers

GAIL SORRELS

1280 Walnut Street #105
Berkeley CA 94709
(415) 499-3806

Objective: Position as Legal Legislative Advocate

HIGHLIGHTS OF QUALIFICATIONS

★ Demonstrated ability to forge links between diverse community groups.
★ Experience drafting and tracking state legislation.
★ Extensive experience as case advocate on patient rights, tenant rights and welfare rights.
★ Excellent writing, research and speaking skills.

RELEVANT EXPERIENCE

Political and Community Organizing

• Prepared outline/draft of proposed legislation on housing discrimination (SB772), introduced by Senator Petris. Conducted lobbying and tracked progress of bill.
• Organized efforts within and between California Network of Mental Health clients, East Bay NOW, and Gray Panthers, to oppose anti-rent control bill.
• Conducted voter education regarding an oppressive welfare initiative (Proposition 41).
• Supervised the implementation of phone trees for candidates, ballot initiatives, & referenda.
• Coordinated efforts by the Alameda County Network of Mental Health clients to improve the City of Berkeley's Section 8 Housing policies and procedures.
• Conducted consciousness-raising training groups relating to women with disabilities.

Case Advocacy

• Served as authorized representative of a client denied SSI:
  -submitted a formal reconsideration document for case review;
  -gathered medical & psychological documentation from physician, neurologist, social worker.
• Researched and summarized facts in preparation for client's deposition on wrongful death.
• Represented two disabled veterans in cooperation with Nevada VFW Commissioner.

Communications

• Spoke before professionals, organizations, & women's groups on epilepsy, mental disability, substance abuse, and disability rights, representing CNMHC, NOW and Epilepsy League.
• Wrote successful speeches, press releases, promotional fliers, and feature articles for candidate seeking and winning Board of Education office.
• Edited promotional material for small advertising agency.

Administration and Management

• Developed job descriptions, screened resumes and interviewed job applicants.
• Facilitated monthly public policy meetings of California Network of Mental Health Clients.
• Prepared agenda for CNMHC public policy meeting in concert with public action coordinator.
• Supervised dissemination of minutes/agenda to committee members in a timely manner.

WORK HISTORY

1981-present	Paralegal	JOHN LARKIN, attorney, Oakland CA
1984-85	Public Policy Chair	CALIF. NETWORK OF MENTAL HEALTH CLIENTS, Sacramento
1982-85	Paralegal	In pro-per; landlord's breach of contract case
1979-80	Community Resource Developer	EPILEPSY LEAGUE, Contra Costa/Alameda Co. 1977-81
	Peer Counselor/lay advocate	ADA MARIE LODGE, Coulterville CA, and
	"	CREATIVE LIVING CENTER, Berkeley
1971-84	Student	Wm.Patterson College, NJ; Antioch Univ. West, SF

MICHAEL OLIVER
1888 Winthrop Ave.
Berkeley CA 94709
(415) 303-6987 home
(415) 411-2627 messages

Objective: Position in law office as clerk, research assistant, or writer/editor.

HIGHLIGHTS OF QUALIFICATIONS

★ Exceptional command of language.
★ Dedicated professional attitude; mature and willing to work.
★ Diligent, punctual, and extremely well organized.
★ Extensive management experience.

RELEVANT EXPERIENCE

Research, Writing & Communication Skills
- Researched and wrote a manual for volunteer training at Ohlone Alcohol & Drug Services.
- Briefed numerous cases for Media Law and Criminal Law courses.
- Chaired meetings concerning house policy and finance for student co-op.
- Wrote job descriptions and annual reports, as Job Coordinator at Moyer House.

Management/Project Coordination
- Managed incoming accounts, coordinating successfully with both management and staff to increase production at large industrial laundry.
- Supervised work crews assigned to community jobs projects:
  ...trained personnel   ...developed work schedules   ...estimated and bid job costs.
- Oversaw kitchen, finance, and maintenance managers, as student co-op President.

Legal Experience
- Co-facilitated drug diversion therapy group (an alternative to incarceration) for Alameda County.
- Counseled clients with drug-related criminal histories, at residential treatment facility.
- Currently serving 3rd term as Administrative Committee Representative for student housing co-op, responsible for adjudication of complaints against the organization.

WORK HISTORY

Current	Full-time student	UNIVERSITY of CALIFORNIA, BERKELEY
1986 summer	**Writer/Facilitator**	OHLONE ALCOHOL & DRUG SERVICES, Ohlone
1984-1985	**Job Coordinator**	MOYER HOUSE INC, Residential Treatment Facility, Oakland
1983	**Resident/Counselor**	MOYER HOUSE INC, Oakland
1981-83	**Finance Manager**	MUMFORD HALL Student Residence, Berkeley
1982 summer	**Co-Manager**	ACME LAUNDRY, Chatham MA
1977-81	**Summer Laborer**	ACME LAUNDRY, Chatham MA

EDUCATION & LEGAL TRAINING

B.A. in progress, Rhetoric Department - UNIVERSITY OF CALIFORNIA, BERKELEY

Law-Related Courses:
• Criminal Law •Legal Philosophy   •Media Law

- References available upon request -

RANDOLPH STROUGH
7900 Piedmont Ave.
Oakland CA 94618
(415) 412-4553

Objective: Position as paralegal

HIGHLIGHTS OF QUALIFICATIONS
- Strong analytical, writing and research skills.
- Solid grounding in litigation skills.
- Conscientious and thorough with detail.
- Equally effective working independently and in cooperation with others.

LITIGATION SKILLS

Writing
- Drafted interrogatories, declarations, and memoranda of law in handicap discrimination case.
- Drafted pleadings, discovery documents, client and demand letters, memoranda of law, and motions with points and authorities, in paralegal course work.

Research
- Performed research in handicap and sex discrimination cases:
  -motion to compel   -application for preliminary relief in U.S. District Court
  -response to motion to strike.
- Investigated public records in handicap discrimination case.
- Researched federal evidentiary questions in construction litigation case.
- Compiled case law on Sixth Amendment ineffectiveness of counsel in criminal appeals.

Trial Preparation
- Organized documents for trial and assisted in revising jury instructions in sex discrimination case.

CLIENT CONTACT
- Interviewed Legal Services clients, and represented them in administrative hearings.
- Interviewed immigration clients and assisted with INS forms, at Centro Legal La Raza.

WORK HISTORY

1985-present	Student, paralegal	SAN FRANCISCO STATE, Certificate Program
1986	**Paralegal Intern**	EMPLOYMENT LAW CENTER, San Francisco
1985-86	**Fund-raiser/Educator**	CITIZENS FOR A BETTER ENVIRONMENT, Berkeley
1984-85	**Youth Counselor**	YOUTH HOMES, Walnut Creek
		(residence for disturbed adolescents)
1981-85	**Circulation rep**, part time	EXPRESS PUBLISHING CO., Berkeley
1980-85	**Baker** concurrent w/above	INTERMOUNTAIN BAKERY, Berkeley
1979	**Circulation representative**	IN THESE TIMES PUBLISHING CO., Chicago
1975-78	**Program Assistant**	UNIVERSITY OF CALIFORNIA, Berkeley
1973-74	**Paralegal**	BERKELEY NEIGHBORHOOD LEGAL SERVICES

EDUCATION, TRAINING & AFFILIATIONS
Paralegal certificate 1987, San Francisco State (GPA 3.6)
Graduate studies in History - University of Rochester 1975
B.A., History - University of California, Berkeley 1974
Member, San Francisco Association of Legal Assistants 1987

POTPOURRI

223

RICHARD T. GRIFFON, JR.
5700 Riverview Street
Albany CA 94706
(415) 389-4111

Objective: Legal assistant or paralegal, with a law firm

HIGHLIGHTS OF QUALIFICATIONS

★ Fast, accurate reader; extensive proofreading experience.
★ Able to summarize written material concisely.
★ Adept in organizing and integrating a number of documents
   into a coherent whole.
★ Skilled in editing; able to write clear, precise prose.
★ Experienced with word processing.

PROFESSIONAL EXPERIENCE

Editing & Proofreading
• Proofread articles written for economic trend forecasting newsletter.
• Served as Associate Editor of college newspaper; wrote articles, proofread articles submitted.
• Edited informative human interest magazine serving 5000 readers of Army Aviation Group.

Writing & Word Processing
• Wrote weekly reports detailing community action projects of Army battalions.
• Authored film reviews for small weekly newspaper.
• Wrote narration for local cable TV documentaries; wrote screenplay for 3 amateur films.
• Typed 130-page screenplay using WORDSTAR word processing program.

Project Organization
• Supervised and coordinated the editorial direction and content, and specific writing assignments,
  of reporters for military publication.
• Organized the production of half-hour TV documentaries:
  -made arrangements for acquiring equipment
  -scheduled interviews and on-site video taping.

EMPLOYMENT HISTORY

Current	**Full-time student**	GRADUATE THEOLOGICAL UNION - Berkeley CA
1982-86	**Telephone Order Rep.**	ESPRIT clothing retailer/mail order - Portland ME
1980-81	**Production Asst./Writer**	PORTLAND HUMANITIES COMMITTEE - Portland ME
		(TV production house)
1978-79	**Cameraman**	Free-lance work for Cable TV Co. - Portland ME
1977-78	**Houseparent**	BAXTER SCHOOL FOR THE DEAF - Falmouth ME
1976-77	**Travel and freelance writing**	EUROPE
1975-76	**Proofreade/Photographer**	RINFRET & CO, economic forecasters - NYC
1973-75	**Student**	NEW YORK UNIVERSITY - studying film production

EDUCATION & TRAINING

M.A. pending, Theology & the Arts - Graduate Theological Union - Berkeley
M.F.A., Film Production - New York University - New York City
B.A., English Literature - Baker University - Baldwin, Kansas

BRADLEY FRENCH
P.O. Box 900
San Rafael CA 94915
(415) 459-2008

Objective: **Writer/Photographer/Editorial Assistant position with
a newspaper, magazine, PR firm or book publisher.**

HIGHLIGHTS OF QUALIFICATIONS
- Successfully published writer, editor and photographer.
- Enthusiastic and committed; a go-getter who doesn't
  quit until the job is done right.
- Effective problem solver; thorough researcher.
- Well organized and focussed in coordinating projects.

PROFESSIONAL EXPERIENCE

Writing & Editing
- Wrote feature articles for national magazines, including ALL ABOUT BEER, as Northern
  California field editor and photojournalist.
- Wrote KQED Beer Festival Guide for S.F. FOCUS Magazine's July 1986 issue.
- Created and published a local specialty newsletter for home brewers/collectors:
  -pub and book reviews   -local events and openings   -new products and recipes.
- Selected, proofread and copy edited manuscripts for Stonehenge Books.

Photography
- Published photographs for:
  -Magazines: produced product shots, location and personality photos, for ALL ABOUT
   BEER Magazine.
  -Newspapers: photo series on Ann Rice, well known local author in FICTION MONTHLY;
  -Book: **The Elitch Gardens Story,** published by Rocky Mt. Writers Guild, Boulder CO.
  -Slide show: Sierra Club's national slide slow, "The Ultimate Environmental Issue."
- Photographed models for glamour and fashion for Vannoy Talent Agency.

Publishing & PR
- Implemented successful marketing campaigns for Jack London books at Star Rover.
- Headed promotion and PR department for Stonehenge Books, Denver book publisher:
  -arranged media interviews for new authors; initiated a new weekly radio program
   featuring interviews with Stonehenge authors;
  -organized book signing publicity events in area book stores;
  -wrote press releases and submitted review copies to book columnists;
  -developed mail order book promotion directed toward special interest groups.

RELEVANT WORK HISTORY

Current	**Writer/Photographer**	FREE-LANCE; most recent assignments for: NETWORK MARKETING, PRACTICAL WINERY, AMATEUR BREWER
1982-86	**Field Editor, No.Calif.**	ALL ABOUT BEER MAGAZINE - Anaheim
1983-85	**Book Sales Rep.** (concurrent with above)	STAR ROVER HOUSE, book publisher - Oakland
1981-82	**Book Sales Coordinator**	DETERMINED PRODUCTIONS, S.F. books/toys/gifts mfg.
1980-81	**Editing/Marketing Asst.**	STONEHENGE BOOKS, book publisher - Denver

EDUCATION
- KIIS Broadcasting Workshop, Hollywood CA • FCC 3rd Class License
B.A., Anthropology - ARIZONA STATE UNIVERSITY, Tempe AZ

GARY AMUNDSEN
4414 Curtis Street,
Berkeley CA 94702
(415) 255-0457

Objective: Position as EDITORIAL ASSISTANT with Chevron Information Technology Co.

HIGHLIGHTS OF QUALIFICATIONS

★ Successfully transformed "CHOBIZ" (Chevron HQ employees' magazine) improving its overall appearance and readability, while reducing costs.

★ Skilled and experienced editor; dependable, industrious and creative.

★ Adept in getting the most accomplished using the fewest resources.

PROFESSIONAL EXPERIENCE

Editing Publications

- Initiated a sharp new look to CHOBIZ, transforming it from a low interest, unorganized throwaway to a highly organized, visually stimulating monthly:
  - created a system for maintaining accurate updated mailing list of 7500 names;
  - coordinated layout and overall design in collaboration with design consultant;
  - introduced the use of photo-typesetting, strengthening the overall appearance and readability of the paper, reducing costs, and simplifying proofreading.
- Coedited in-house quarterly publication on Chevron Resources, THE PROSPECTOR, coordinating improved graphic design and reducing production costs.

Writing, Technical Writing & Copyediting

- Edited scores of articles in company publications for clarity, grammar, and style.
- Authored original articles & reports: editorials, feature articles, budget proposals.
- Wrote technical report documenting detailed start-up and management of a new business venture.
- Researched and wrote a report on computer graphics for cost and feasibility of in-house application.

Project Organization & Coordination

- Persuaded club leaders to write feature articles for company publication.
- Effectively negotiated the quick response and cooperation of a subcontractor to correct a recurrent mailing list problem, significantly saving time and money.

EMPLOYMENT HISTORY

1980-present	**Sr. Draftsman/Design**	CHEVRON RESOURCES - San Francisco
1985	**Editor,** company publication (concurrent with position above)	CHEVRON RESOURCES - San Francisco
1979-80	**Laboratory Technician**	CHEVRON RESEARCH CO. - Richmond
1977-79	**Purchasing Clerk; Lab. Asst.**	CHEVRON RESEARCH CO. - Richmond
1972-77	**Graphics Artist**	FREE-LANCE; SELF EMPLOYED

EDUCATION & TRAINING
B.A. Fine Art; Minor: Botany/Biology - Cal State Hayward 1977

Additional technical skills and education:
Word processing, time-sharing, graphic art, computer graphics, computer programming
Courses: Computers for Management, Fortran IV Programming, Purchasing, Technical Writing

MARY MORIARITY
Freelance Research - Editing - Collaborative Writing
901 Union Street #70 • San Francisco CA 94133
(415) 206-6162, call collect

Objective: Freelance work with books, articles and brochures
- Copyediting • Creative/developmental editing • Acquisition editing
- Research and interviewing services for authors and writers
- Collaborative writing • Reading and evaluating book manuscripts

QUALIFICATIONS

★ Strong commitment to excellence in the printed and published word.

★ Demonstrated skill in developmental editing and copyediting.

★ Over 10 years' experience coordinating library research services.

★ Skill in assessing information needs for collaborative writing projects.

★ Lifelong professional career evaluating and purchasing books for the public.

REPRESENTATIVE ACCOMPLISHMENTS

Copyediting, Creative & Developmental Editing
- Currently serving as series editor for books on health and nutrition; copyedited first book in the series.
- Developed and copyedited a book on color in interior design, working with author, publisher and illustrator to organize and refine the manuscript.
- Collaborated on writing and editing projects under contract with public relations firm:
  -personnel manual for a food manufacturer
  -brochures explaining services of a medical professional group.

Research & Interviewing
- Researched and compiled subject bibliographies for 3 books currently under production.
- Interviewed restaurant owners and members of ethnic cultural associations for book on regional cooking and history.
- Managed reference services for the county library:
  -supervised staff   -interviewed reference patrons and formulated research strategies
  -coordinated research networking services with San Joaquin Valley Information System.

Book Evaluation & Purchasing
- Evaluated manuscripts and produced reader's reports for two book publishers.
- Administered book acquisition budgets for city public library and for county library.
- Evaluated and selected books, using **Publishers' Weekly, Library Journal, Kirkus, Booklist,** book reviews in **New York Times, Los Angeles Times, San Francisco Chronicle**.
- Wrote weekly book review column for community newpaper.
- Analyzed public reading tastes and consulted with publishers' representatives to stock and manage retail bookshop.

- Continued -

POTPOURRI

227

SUBJECT INTERESTS & RESEARCH EXPERIENCE

- Self-help; psychology; sociology; women's studies.
- Medicine; health care; sexual relationships; marriage; parenting; aging.
- Parapsychology; erotica.
- Literature; fiction; mysteries; biography; letters; diaries.
- Bookselling; writing; publishing; book collecting.
- Food; cooking; restaurants; fashion; personal style.
- History; California; England.

EMPLOYMENT HISTORY

1986-present	**Editor**	FREELANCE, San Francisco and Central Valley
		...Martin-Moore Press, book publisher
		...Dooley & Associates, public relations firm
	Manuscript Evaluator	...Hitchcock Press, mystery publisher
1985-86	**Student**	Full-time studies at UC Berkeley Extension
1975-84	**Librarian III, Coordinator of County Reference Services**	OTSEGO COUNTY LIBRARY, Oneonta NY
1972-75	**Librarian II, and Asst. City Librarian**	ONEONTA PUBLIC LIBRARY, Oneonta NY
1970-71	**Librarian I**	ONEONTA PUBLIC LIBRARY, Oneonta
1968-69	**Library Assistant**	ONEONTA PUBLIC LIBRARY, Oneonta
1964-68	**Owner/Manager**	VALLEY OAK BOOKSHOP, Oneonta

EDUCATION, CERTIFICATION & TRAINING

B.A., Sociology - Stanford University, Stanford CA
Publishing & Editing Certificate - UC Berkeley Extension

Specialized Training Courses:
Publishing & Promoting the Cookbook, UCLA
On-line Reference Service, San Jose State University
Basic Data Processing, College of the Sequoias
Interpersonal Skills for Library Management, UC Davis
Collecting, Evaluating & Investing in Books, UC Davis

In the Employment History, Mary presents her various freelance jobs in a tidy package, and at the same time gets a lot of information across.

REBECCA BRIDGES

94 Silver Street
San Francisco CA 94133
(415) 909-3665

Objective: Position as Editorial Assistant/Researcher in publishing

HIGHLIGHTS OF QUALIFICATIONS

★ Keen perception for extracting important data.
★ Proven successful in research writing.
★ Innovative in designing and carrying out projects.
★ Strong skills in interviewing and developing rapport.
★ Highly motivated to achieve set goals.

PROFESSIONAL EXPERIENCE

Writing & Editing
- Authored Policy and Procedures Manual for the office of County Elections Manager:
  - Observed and documented manual office procedures and workflow in detail.
  - Interviewed employees to determine job description and time allocations for various tasks.
  - Analyzed data to establish procedural inefficiencies; made recommendations for improvement.
- Composed official correspondence to the constituents of State Assemblyman, Richard Lehman.

Researching/Analysis
- Researched and analyzed Mexico's macroeconomic policy in relation to foreign investment; presented synopsis of the 40-pg. report to graduate economic seminar.
- Conducted political research on constituent case needs for elected state official.
- Collected data regarding computer industry trends to advise and place computer professionals during job transition.

Project Management
- Managed a 6-month MBA recruiting project for Wells Fargo:
  - Screened resumes, contacted and selected 150 qualified applicants for further interviews.
  - Developed a successful new system for processing qualified MBA candidates nationwide.
  - Presented written recommendations for project improvement.
- Founded and organized a professional development organization, Women in Political Science.

EMPLOYMENT HISTORY

Current	**Word Processer**	BAY TEMPORARY SERVICE - San Francisco
1987	**Student**	San Francisco State
1982-86	**Retail Sales**	CREIGHTON DEPT STORE - San Francisco
1981	**Staffing Coordinator**	WELLS FARGO BANK - San Francisco
1980	**Technical Search Counselor**	HOWARD CORPORATION - San Jose
1979	**Procedures Analyst Intern**	FRESNO COUNTY ELECTIONS DEPT. - Fresno

EDUCATION

B.A., Public Administration/Economics, 1979 - California State University
Graduate work in economics - San Francisco State University

CAROLYN M. CLARKE
115 Washington Blvd.
Sacramento CA
605-4777

The layout helps focus, with simple clarity, on advancement in Carolyn's most recent job.

Objective: Position as editorial assistant in book publishing

HIGHLIGHTS OF QUALIFICATIONS
★ Lifetime interest in books; willing to learn all aspects of publishing.
★ Substantial experience in writing, rewriting, and editing.
★ Well organized and thorough in completing complex projects.
★ Committed to high quality production and attentive to details.

RELEVANT EXPERIENCE

Project Coordination
• Developed and implemented in-service training for savings and loan employees:
  -set training schedules   -selected trainees   -determined curricula needs
  -wrote training materials (quizzes, case studies, work sheets)
  -wrote presentations   -conducted training sessions.
• Administered and coordinated daily operations and long-term planning of retirement plan program involving 160,000 accounts and $560 million in deposits:
  -hired, trained, and supervised staff of six;
  -consulted with marketing, legal, and computer departments on proposed policy and procedure changes;
  -developed promotional strategy to maintain competitive edge in customer services;
  -researched federal legislation to assure continued compliance with new laws.

Editing and Publishing
• Developed glossary of terms, quick reference guides and employee workbooks to be used by 200 branch offices of City Savings and Loan.
• Wrote, edited, and published weekly procedural bulletins for company employees.
• Designed and/or redesigned content and layout of retirement plan forms and booklets.

EMPLOYMENT HISTORY

1983-present	**CITY SAVINGS AND LOAN** - Retirement Plans Department - Sacramento CA **Retirement Plans Administrator** 1986-present **Special Projects Coordinator** 1985 **Research Assistant** 1984 **Customer Service Specialist** 1983	
1978-82	**Salesperson**	COFFEE EXPERIENCE, Sacramento CA MULLIGAN'S PHARMACY, Davis CA
1975-77	**Secretary**	GENEVA ENGINEERING CO, Sacramento CA DR. W. MARTIN medical office, Sacramento CA

EDUCATION & TRAINING
B.A., Political Science 1982 - University of California, Davis
Knowledge of Spanish, French, Norwegian, Swedish
Coursework in: English literature; English composition; Scandinavian literature

CARLENE DOONAN
2731 Southgate Dr.
Berkeley CA 94702
(415) 525-9934

Objective: Position as apprentice baker, with opportunity for quality training and increasing levels of responsibility.

HIGHLIGHTS OF QUALIFICATIONS

★ Work hard, learn fast, willing and able to assume responsibility.
★ Passion for food; commitment to producing highest quality products.
★ Experience with successful retail design and display.
★ Good team player; work well with all kinds of people.

RELEVANT EXPERIENCE

Cooking Knowledge
• Studied with master chef, Ken Wolfe, learning:
  -principles and techniques of food preparation
  -importance of quality and freshness of ingredients
  -chemistry and effects of combining ingredients
  -coordinated timing of food preparation
  -innovative approaches to traditional cooking principles
  -balancing flavors within a dish and within a meal.

Coordination/Teamwork
• Maintained and supervised a balanced flow of inventory for theatre food concession and for retail gift store:
  -monitored sales including seasonal fluctuations
  -researched to determine best prices, by phone and at trade shows
  -assured correct stocking and display.
• Coordinated timing and priority of tasks, as store manager.
• Worked in a finely tuned sales team to expedite customer services.

Speed/Accuracy
• Handled large volume of customers in minimum time, selling theatre tickets and selling retail merchandise.
• Accurately counted, recorded and deposited cash receipts for retail store.
• Prepared puff-pastry dough in cooking class, consistently completing in record time.

EMPLOYMENT or WORK HISTORY

1978-present	**Store Manager**	MIASMA gift/novelty store, Berkeley
1975-78	**Asst. Manager**	MIASMA gift/novelty store, Berkeley
1974-75	**Theatre Manager**	RENAISSANCE-RIALTO THEATRE GROUP, Berkeley
1973-74	**Clerk/Counter Sales**	RENAISSANCE-RIALTO THEATRE GROUP, Berkeley

EDUCATION & TRAINING

Liberal Arts - Laney College 1972-75
Classes in Cooking Principles, with Ken Wolfe, Master Chef

DAWN ELLSWORTH

1415 Montgomery St.
Oakland CA 94611
(415) 548-2223

Objective: Gallery Assistant or gallery sales position

HIGHLIGHTS OF QUALIFICATIONS

★ Demonstrated ability to communicate knowledgeably with clients about specific artists, styles, techniques and media.
★ Able to represent a studio or gallery in public presentations.
★ Effective in sales through enthusiasm for the product.
★ Planned, managed and supervised events for up to 1,000 people.

RELEVANT EXPERIENCE

Conservation & Museum Services
• Conserved works of art and documents at private conservation studio, involving:
 ...washing...cleaning...flattening...mounting...matting...framing...aesthetic restoration.
• Evaluated damage to art pieces and documents & proposed individualtreatments.
• Selected appropriate museum-quality ph-balanced materials to frame and mat both old and new pieces.
• Researched and compiled the provenance of recently acquired paintings at SFMMA.
• Inventoried and registered museum's permanent collection for future catalogue.

Art Media & Design
• Developed working experience with wide range of media and techniques:
 ...glass ...painting ...textile design ...pastel and graphite.
• Designed and produced new stained glass pieces, and restored old stained glass.

Communication/PR/Presentation
• Assembled and presented slide show on art history and restoration techniques.
• Advised art clients of inventory and pricing; made appointments for sale closings.
• Answered technical and historical inquiries from potential clients by phone & letter.

Management & Coordination
• Coordinated and supervised 5-50 staff members for catered events: delegated staff assignments; mediated between party hosts, guests and staff; handled complex logistics for all equipment.
• Trained waiters and waitresses at a newly established restaurant.

WORK HISTORY

1985-now	Party Manager	MARSHALL CATERING - Oakland
1983-1985	Conservation Asst.	KAREN ZUKOR (conservator of art on paper), Oakland
1983-1984	Painter	FRALEY STUDIOS (carousel restoration), Oakland
1982-1984	Waitress	GRIFFON RESTAURANT, Berkeley; LITTLE JOE's, S.F.
1980-1981	Full-time student	UC Santa Cruz
1979-1980	Glass Designer	Self-employed - Los Angeles

EDUCATION & TRAINING

Museum Management & Exhibition Design, JFKU Cntr for Museum Studies (now)
Italian restoration techniques, Inst. of Art & Restoration; Florence, Italy 1984
B.A., Fine Arts (Painting & Print Making) - UC Santa Cruz, 1981

DENISE FRANCIS
6200 Skyline Blvd.
Oakland CA 94611
(415) 754-5151

Objective: Position as cruise staff member working directly with passengers, such as activity director, hostess, gift salesperson, tour escort, deck steward, masseuse.

HIGHLIGHTS OF QUALIFICATIONS

- Enthusiastic, loquacious, fun loving and personable.
- Outstanding leadership and organization skills.
- Honest and reliable in keeping commitments.
- Relate easily and openly with all ages and types.
- Successful work experience in activity directing, child care, nursing, massage, house care and sales.

RELEVANT EXPERIENCE

Activities Directing
- Planned and supervised special event parties for 100 people, including weddings, bon voyage parties, birthdays:
  -designed floral and food arrangements   -installed table and wall decorations
  -planned menu   -coordinated schedule   -supervised outdoor play activities.
- Successfully involved convalescent adults in healthful activities, persuading them to participate in coffee hours, arts-and-crafts activities, and exercise.
- Supported the health and happiness of home-bound patients through assistance with entertainment, personal care and recreation.

Communication/Needs Assessment
- Completed classes in psychology, assertiveness and interpersonal communication.
- Assessed and worked with physical and emotional stresses of clients, as massage therapist, child care attendant and home health attendant in geriatrics.
- Taught a highly popular class in massage therapy.

Promotion/Sales
- Developed friendly, supportive, give-and-take relationships with coffee shop patrons, building a loyal base of repeat customers.
- Promoted and sold merchandise in a variety of settings:
  -flower shop   -coffee shop   -gift shop   -cocktail lounge.

EMPLOYMENT HISTORY

1983-present	**Home Health Attendant**	Independent contractor - Oakland
1983-84	**Floral Designer**	SIEFERT'S FLORAL - Oakland
1980-86	**Masseuse & Teacher**	Independent contractor - Oakland
1981-83	**Assistant Manager**	THE IRIS, arts gift shop - Berkeley
1979-81	**Assistant Manager**	THE COFFEE MILL - Oakland
1976-78	**Punchpress Operator**	KELLER STOVE - Columbus OH
1974-76	**Nurses' Aide**	WORTHINGTON (Ohio) CONVALESCENT HOME

EDUCATION, TRAINING, CERTIFICATION
Merritt College, Oakland - 1981-86 ongoing degree studies.
Certified: Activities Director, Nurse Assistant, Floral Designer
Certified Masseuse - Massage Institute, San Francisco
Certified Independent Travel Agent - Tivoli Travel School, San Francisco

DOLORES L. WALKER

59 Orchid Drive
Mill Valley CA 94947
work (415) 644-9889
home (415) 389-4698

Objective: Position as commercial leasing agent for Charter Commercial Brokerage

HIGHLIGHTS OF QUALIFICATIONS

- Outstanding ability to build trust and deal effectively and persuasively with people.
- Adept at tuning in to clients' priorities to assure accurate needs assessment.
- Proven successful in negotiating and renegotiating profitable contracts and leases.
- CEO of a $17 million business. Ten years executive experience.
- Highly motivated toward achievement and surpassing prior goals.

PROFESSIONAL EXPERIENCE

Sales & Marketing
- Increased annual sales from $11 million to $17 million in 3 years.
- Initiated new marketing unit to improve organizational image & raise development funds.
- Persuaded board of directors to adopt a 5-year plan, after history of crisis oriented management.
- Assessed needs of departments, units and individuals to improve working environment.

Business Contacts
- Developed extensive potential client base through business contacts with attorneys, bankers, professional organizations, entertainers' agents, merchants, alumni.

Contract Negotiation
- Successfully renegotiated long-standing unfavorable contract with major vending contractor:
  - increased commission schedule 40%
  - removed exclusivity clause
  - improved level of services significantly, responding to needs of campus community.
- Negotiated contracts with wide diversity of businesses:
  - bank - food service -entertainment -hair salon -travel center - stationery store
- Maintained rapport and professional effectiveness with vendors under conditions of political diversity and ever changing demands.

Facilities Management
- Coordinated provisions for facilities of major service and commercial complex:
  - bldg. maintenance -custodial services - energy management program -HVAC systems

EMPLOYMENT HISTORY

1982-present	**Executive Director**	Associated Students Univ. of California (ASUC) - Berkeley
1975-82	**Asst. Exec. Director**	" " "
1968-75	**Office Manager**	UC San Francisco, Materiel Management Dept.
1965-67	**Sales**	Self-employed specialty clothing distributor

EDUCATION & TRAINING

Business and Legal studies - Armstrong University, Berkeley
Classes in Psychology, Financial Accounting, Fund-raising
Completed licensing course in Anthony School of Real Estate.
Xerox Professional Selling Skills System III

DONALD OLSON
Private Investigator
License No. AQ 011950

457 Hawthorne Avenue
Hayward, CA 94546
(415) 821-7809

HIGHLIGHTS OF QUALIFICATIONS

★ 17 years professional experience in law enforcement; extensive contacts in law enforcement field.

★ Extensive specialized training in all aspects of investigation, including fire cause, fraud and surveillance.

★ Experience in police internal affairs and preparation of civil liability cases, requiring objectivity and integrity.

★ Persistent, thorough and prompt in completing projects.

★ Excellent communication and interrogation skills; reputation as one of the best interviewers on staff.

RELEVANT PROFESSIONAL EXPERIENCE

Investigation
Conducted hundreds of complex investigations of major crimes, in 6 years as HPD Detective.
- Prepared detailed **investigative reports**, resulting in criminal prosecution and conviction.
- Successfully **elicited confessions** for such crimes as homicide, robbery and arson, applying communication and interrogation skills.
- Investigated **complaints against police** officers, internally and externally generated, during 2-year assignment as Internal Affairs Sergeant reporting directly to Chief of Police.
  - Prepared civil liability defense claims against individual police officers & city of Hayward.

Case Management
- **Managed investigative projects** independently, applying sharp analytic and problem solving skills, exhausting all available leads.
- **Planned, organized and supervised** inter-jurisdictional recovery system dealing with crimes of burglary and possession of stolen property.
  - Developed and coordinated a task force of police officers from several communities.

Security Consultation
- **Developed** original Crime Prevention **Program** for city of Hayward:
  - Conducted security evaluation surveys, both residential and commercial, providing solutions to security problems.
- Provided retail **security management** for Sears, Hayward, auditing cash flow and credit receipts, and monitoring employees, to maintain internal and external loss-theft control.

EMPLOYMENT HISTORY

1986-present	PRIVATE INVESTIGATOR	OLSON INVESTIGATIVE SERVICES, Hayward
1982-87	SERGEANT	HAYWARD POLICE DEPARTMENT
1986-87	Detective Sgt.; and Acting Superintendent /Animal Control Bureau	
1984-86	Internal Affairs Sgt.	
1982-84	Patrol Division Sgt.	
1976-82	DETECTIVE	HAYWARD POLICE DEPARTMENT
1969-76	POLICE OFFICER	
1972-74	SECURITY AGENT, part-time	SEARS ROEBUCK CO, Hayward
1968-69	MACHINE OPERATOR	HERRICK IRON WORKS, Hayward
1966-68	PETTY OFFICER, 3rd Cl.	U.S. NAVY; honorable discharge

- Continued -

POTPOURRI

INVESTIGATIVE & MANAGEMENT TRAINING

Completed advanced **investigative training** in a wide range of specific crimes:
- Robbery Investigation - San Jose State
- Burglary Prevention Seminar - Cal State/Long Beach
- Auto Theft School; Advanced Auto Theft - Dept of Justice, Sacramento
- Homicide Investigation - Justice Training Center, Sacramento
- Homicide Investigation - Hayward Police Dept.
- Arson for Profit - State Fire Marshall, Columbia Jr. College
- Advanced Arson Investigation - State Fire Marshall, Columbia Jr. College
- Internal Affairs Investigation - Cal State/Long Beach
- Recognition & Apprehension of Narcotics and Drug Offenders - Hayward Police Dept.

Completed courses in **technical and management skills:**
- Evidence Technician and Photography - Bahn Fair Inst. of Scientific Law Enforcement
- Investigation School - Los Angeles Police Dept.
- Stress Management - Cal State/Long Beach
- Family Violence and Child Abuse - Chabot College
- Performance Appraisal - Hayward Police Dept.
- Defensive Tactics - Hayward Police Dept.

EDUCATION

B.S., Administration of Justice; minor in Sociology - SAN JOSE STATE
A.A., Administration of Justice - CHABOT COLLEGE, Hayward

California Police Officer Standards Training:
Basic, Intermediate, Advanced, Supervisory Certification

References available on request.

Don's professional independence is clear at the top of the resume. Note that even though his resume covers two pages, the entire work history and skill assessment is complete on page one.

HELLMUT DIETRICH
333 - 65th Street, Oakland CA 94609
(415) 699-4742

Objective: Position in import-export business using background in freight handling

HIGHLIGHTS OF QUALIFICATIONS
- Experience in office work with a major freight company.
- Competent in operating computers and programming.
- Skilled supervisor; able to motivate others and handle conflict.
- Sharp and creative in solving problems.
- Diplomatic and effective with customer relations.

RELEVANT EXPERIENCE & SKILLS

Warehouse/Freight/Dispatching
- Supervised the loading and unloading of goods, assuring that items were handled with care and placed accurately in warehouse.
- Initiated improvements in teamwork efficiency in freight warehouse, by clarifying areas of responsibility and promoting communication between office and warehouse.
- Developed and updated time schedules and delivery tours for truckers.

Computer Skills
- Familiar with use of personal computers and printers.
- Customized commercial computer programs to meet special needs.
- Wrote complex programs in BASIC using direct disk access to retrieve lost data.

Customer Service
- Handled inquiries and complaints of 3 major manufacturing customers, as warehouse superintendent at a large freight company in Munich.
  -took orders for freight service and provided complex pricing information;
  -resolved problems involving shipping delays and damage.

Coordination/Teamwork
- Successfully coordinated community projects involving previously conflicting groups, overcoming hostility and mistrust by identifying common interests and goals.
- Organized public educational/entertainment events, involving arrangements for location, insurance, contracts, security, advertising/promotion.
- Negotiated with city agencies for financial support of community programs.

EMPLOYMENT HISTORY

1987	Travel and relocation to the Bay Area.	
1984-86	**Student**	University of Tübingen, Germany
1979-83	**Display Builder**	S&E Stark Promotional Display Co. - Ostfildern, Germany
1976-78	**Teacher**	Jr.High School; Elementary School - Osfildern, Germany
1973-75	**Teaching Asst.**	Pädagogische Hochschule College - Esslingen, Germany
1972-76	**Student**	Pädagogische Hochschule College - Esslingen, Germany
1970-71	**Social Worker**	City of Schwäbisch Hall, Germany
1969-70	**Warehouse Supv.**	Anton Glatz Freight Co. - Munich, Germany
1966-69	**Warehouseman**	Hohl Freight Co. - Michelfeld, Germany

EDUCATION & TRAINING
B.A., Social Work (German equivalent) - University of Tübingen, Germany
Teaching Credential (German equivalent) - Pädagogische Hochschule College
Classes in: Bookkeeping, correspondence, transportation, business and math.

JO ANNE BURGESS

1266 San Gabrielle Ave.
Oakland CA 94619
(415) 282-6900

Objective: Union Representative / Business Agent; Labor Organization Administrator

HIGHLIGHTS OF QUALIFICATIONS

- Committed to workers and their needs.
- 12 years experience in union organizing, contract negotiations and grievance handling.
- Exceptional ability to communicate with members, and articulate the union's demands to management.
- Demonstrated effectiveness in sizing up a situation and getting the job done.

PROFESSIONAL EXPERIENCE

Contract Negotiations
- Effectively negotiated scores of contracts in:
  - transportation companies - dairies, bakeries and food industries
  - financial institutions   - hospitals and health maintenance organizations
- Handled all aspects of negotiations:
  - ascertained the needs of the membership through meetings and surveys.
  - formulated proposals designed to resolve identified problems, needs and demands.
  - served as chief negotiator working with rank and file committees.
  - drafted and finalized contract language.

Grievance Handling & Contract Enforcement
- Represented hundreds of grievants covered by diverse contracts.
- Prepared and presented grievances for arbitration.
- Monitored contract agreements thru on-going contact with shop stewards and members.
- Represented members in dealings with state and federal agencies.

Organizing Workers
- Directed, planned and strategized successful organizing campaigns with rank and file committees.
- Prepared programs and presentations; spoke at info meetings, rallies and demonstrations.
- Authored and edited many organizing leaflets and brochures.

Administration / Management
- Coordinated a small union office, implementing the directives of union officers, executive board, committees and members: collected and posted dues; responded to inquiries; wrote, typed, laid-out, copied and distributed leaflets; advised volunteers; processed mass mailings.
- Supervised and directed the field work of 4 union representatives in absence of the Senior Union Representative.
- Developed strategies for the union's participation in strikes and strike support activities, in conjunction with other labor organizations.
- Prepared press releases and handled media relations to publicize union activities.

WORK EXPERIENCE

1976-present	**Union Representative**	Office and Professional Employees Union, Local 29, Emeryville CA
1972-76	**Union Organizer and Office Secretary**	American Federation of State, County and Municipal Employees, Local 1695, Univ. of California, Berkeley

BARBARA McCLOSKY
1721 Washington Street, Apt. 2
Ann Arbor, Michigan
(313) 521-7080

Objective: Information specialist, resource manager, or comparable position with an environmental consulting firm.

Summary of Qualifications
- Special talent for quickly and accurately locating needed information.
- Successfully designed & created an Environmental Resource Library.
- Degrees in Librarianship and Conservation Resource Studies.
- Ten years professional experience in information management.

PROFESSIONAL EXPERIENCE

Information Needs Analysis/Advising
- Matched up people and information, providing faculty, students and professionals from a broad range of disciplines, with specific resources:
  - books on resource management, environmental policy, development, assessment and methodology;
  - audiovisual materials: audio tapes, video tapes, and slides on environmental topics;
  - bibliographies, periodicals;
  - reports of governmental agencies, educational institutions and nonprofit organizations
- Developed highly valued personalized networking and information service, known for reliability, resourcefulness and helpfulness;
  - provided job referrals, internships and volunteer placements, leads on experts in the field.

Research & Writing
- Researched and authored a Library Guide to Information on the Environment.
- Coauthored Students' Guide to Audiovisual Materials on Campus.
- Wrote and edited campus and alumni newsletters on information resources and environmental issues.

Data Management
- Conducted thorough assessment of information systems of other libraries, and incorporated the most appropriate features of each.
- Designed specialized catalogs and indexes for quick access to a variety of research materials.
- Continually revised and upgraded library systems to meet changing information needs.

JOB HISTORY
1986-present   **Assistant Director**, Natural Resources Intern Program, Ann Arbor MI
1973-85   **Director, Environmental Resource Center.**, University of Michigan, Dept. of Environmental Studies

EDUCATION
B.S., Environmental Studies - University of Michigan, Ann Arbor
M.A., Librarianship - San Jose State University

LOREN GREENE
1415 Pine Ave.
Richmond CA 94805
(415) 776-3009

Objective: Position as Summarizer for Barron's Legal Services

HIGHLIGHTS OF QUALIFICATIONS
- Enthusiastic and dedicated professional.
- Strong analytical skills.
- Ability to work independently and as a cooperative team member.
- Effective at translating complex technical information into easily understood language.

PROFESSIONAL EXPERIENCE

ANALYSIS & EVALUATION
- Developed and implemented new policies to address issues in all areas of small hydropower development.
- Formulated policy recommendations, incorporating information gathered from various departments at PG&E.
- Researched utility rate-setting procedures for Wisconsin Citizens' Board.
- Documented 20th century US land use and energy policy strategies.
- Designed database procedures, accommodating information needs of PG&E employees.

WRITTEN & VERBAL COMMUNICATION
- Prepared written reports, correspondence and policy papers for PG&E, articulating complex issues and recommending positions.
- Wrote database users' guide for PG&E employees.
- Produced summary reports on California hazardous waste litigation.
- Advised private developers on policies affecting their proposed alternative energy projects.

MANAGEMENT & SUPERVISION
- Served as project liaison between developers and the PG&E system.
- Implemented regulatory requirements, monitoring hydro projects and documenting developer compliance.
- Participated in planning and implementing of prairie restoration project.
- Supervised staff of 10 field canvassers in community outreach techniques.

WORK HISTORY

1986-present	**Resource Analyst**	PACIFIC GAS & ELECTRIC - Walnut Creek CA
1986-present	**Legal Aid**	LEGAL ASSISTANT SERVICES - Orinda CA
1984-85	**Project Assistant**	UNIV. OF WISCONSIN ARBORETUM - Madison
1982	**Field Manager**	CITIZENS' UTILITY BOARD - Madison WI
1981	**Legal Intern**	STATE UNIVERSITY of NEW YORK, POTSDAM
1980	**Library Assistant**	STATE UNIVERSITY of NEW YORK, POTSDAM

EDUCATION
M.A., Political Science - UNIVERSITY OF WISCONSIN, Madison - June 1987
Area specialty: Environmental Policy

POTPOURRI

240

MICHAEL WONG
1914 Twelfth Avenue
San Francisco CA 94122
(415) 688-0900

Objective: Position as Community or Governmental Relations Representative

SUMMARY OF QUALIFICATIONS

★ Over 8 years experience in community relations work.
★ Graduate degree with emphasis in public administration.
★ Effective & persuasive with all segments of the community.
★ Skilled and thorough in analyzing problem situations and finding creative solutions.

PROFESSIONAL EXPERIENCE

Management & Administration
- Evaluated overall program effectiveness and employee performance; established policy for Humboldt Housing Action Project and University Activities Center.
- Trained and supervised volunteers and paid employees in counseling & fund-raising.
- Developed and implemented a successful marketing campaign (where others had repeatedly failed), introducing new students to local business services.

Community Relations
- Advised and offered technical assistance to United Way agencies on fund-raising, budgeting, program planning.
- Served, by appointment, on Housing Committee charged with analyzing local housing crisis and providing follow-up recommendations.
- Coordinated successful special event and direct mail fund-raising for local city council members.

Communications
- Wrote general press releases and PSAs for voter registration drive.
- Chaired meetings of up to 100 people.
- Acted as liaison between student government and campus community, coordinating meeting times, places, and agendas.

EMPLOYMENT HISTORY

Fund-raiser	ROGERS-WILLIAMSON PARENT COUNCIL, Sierra CA	1983-present
Planning Intern	ARCATA PLANNING DEPARTMENT, Arcata CA	1982-83
Sales Manager	ASSOCIATED STUDENTS, Humboldt State Univ, Arcata CA	1982-83
Retail Sales	REDWOODS UNITED, Eureka CA	1982
Researcher	NATIONAL INSTITUTES OF HEALTH, Eureka CA	1979-80

EDUCATION

M.A. Social Science, Humboldt State University, Arcata CA
Emphasis in Public Administration (thesis in progress)
B.A. Social Science, Humboldt State University, Arcata CA

COMMUNITY & VOLUNTEER EXPERIENCE

- United Way, Bay Area and Humboldt County - Allocations Team Member.
- Board of Directors: Humboldt Housing Action Project; University Activities Center
- Chairperson: Student Legislative Council, Humboldt State University.
- Member of Arcata Housing Task Force (appointed by City Council)
- Coordinator, voter registration drives.

RICHARD JENNINGS
8009 Mountain Blvd.
Oakland CA 94602
(415) 111-6887

Compare this with Richard's other resume on page 158.

Objective: Entry level position as fire fighter, municipal fire department.

HIGHLIGHTS OF QUALIFICATIONS
- Excellent relations with the public and the community.
- Committed professional, constantly upgrading training.
- Able to function at top performance throughout a 24-hour shift.
- Proven ability to respond immediately and confidently in emergencies.
- 3 years experience as a paramedic; 5 years as emergency medical tech.
- Mature lifestyle, compatible with emergency work.

RELEVANT EXPERIENCE

Crisis Evaluation & Response
- Effectively evaluated thousands of emergencies, for example:
  -auto accidents requiring treatment before transport
  -heart attacks (80 Code Blues this year, with approximately 20% save rate)
  -family interventions (treating family members with respect and sensitivity)
- Adapted immediately to changing circumstances in medical emergencies, setting priorities and constantly reevaluating them.

PR, Community Relations
- Educated the public on the role of emergency medical services, through demonstrations, lectures and small group talks.
- Taught public CPR classes; served as volunteer medic for public events; trained nurses and hospital employees in trauma skills at Eden Hospital.
- Served as liaison between paramedics, hospitals and fire department:
  -mediated communication problems among professionals;
  -provided monthly training updates for the firemen I worked with;
  -provided follow-up medical information on cases jointly handled.

Medical Teamwork
- Highly skilled in all basic medical emergency techniques:
  -taking blood pressure and pulses -wound management
  -splinting fractures   -CPR
  -applying oxygen   -patient assessment
- Led ambulance team, as Crew Chief for Bay Medical Services.

Training & Quality Assurance
- Selected for and served on Paramedic Peer Review Committee at Eden Hospital, monitoring paramedic response to improve treatment of patients.
- Trained new paramedics in the field portion of their state-required training time, focusing on communication and decision making skills in medical emergencies.
- Evaluated new 911 provider paramedics on the job, as Alameda County paramedic evaluator, assuring they understand the protocols and the skills, and perform to county safety standards.
- Wrote training manual for new medics employed by Bay Medical Services.

- Continued -

EMPLOYMENT HISTORY

1985-present	**Paramedic Crew Chief**	BAY MEDICAL SERVICES, Berkeley/Oakland
1984	**Paramedic**	KING AMERICAN AMBULANCE, San Francisco
1982-84	**EMT-1A**	ALLIED AMBULANCE, Oakland
1977-81	**Warehouseman/Driver**	GOOD GUYS; SAUSALITO DESIGN; PACIFIC FLOORING
1976-77	**Clerk Typist**	PMI MORTGAGE INSURANCE, San Francisco
1974-76	**Day Care Driver**	EASTER SEAL SOCIETY, San Francisco

EDUCATION & SPECIALIZED TRAINING

B.A., Sociology - SAN FRANCISCO STATE UNIVERSITY
A.A., Criminology - San Joaquin Delta College, Stockton

Paramedic Training; EMT-1A Training - City College of San Francisco
Basic Life Support & Advanced Cardiac Life Support Certificates - Amer. Heart Assoc.
Ambulance Driver's License - Advanced Airway Management Training
Additional courses in Anatomy, Physiology, Chemistry, 1985-86

POTPOURRI

243

ROBERT LAWSON
39770 Magee Way
Castro Valley CA 94546
(415) 221-6869

Objective: Position as service writer for an auto manufacturer

HIGHLIGHTS OF QUALIFICATIONS

★ Outstanding talent for assessing people's needs.
★ Proven ability to gain customers' confidence and trust.
★ Business acumen in balancing public relations with profitability.
★ 8 years experience in automotive diagnosis and repair.

RELEVANT EXPERIENCE

Needs Assessment/Public Relations
• Generated large volume of repeat business from satisfied customers, maintaining excellent relations through good repair work and sensitivity to clients' overall needs.
• Developed a keen perception for both the spoken and unspoken needs of customers, providing adequate technical information and advice for decision making, and restoring customers' sense of "being in control."

Technical Knowledge
• Repaired foreign and domestic cars for 8 years, specializing in:
-electronic fuel injection   -SU carburetors   -engine rebuilding.
• 5 years experience in heavy machinery operation and repair.
• Completed 2 years training in automotive repair at Chabot College.

Business Management
• Started up a successful restaurant business, including leasing/remodeling building, hiring/supervising staff, providing day-to-day management.
• Established and managed auto repair business, handling all aspects.

EMPLOYMENT HISTORY

1985-present	**Owner/manager**	ROBERT LAWSON FIXES CARS - Davis
1984-85	**Mechanic**	ALL AROUND AUTO REPAIR - Davis
1981-84	**Owner/manager**	ROBERT LAWSON FIXES CARS - Davis
1980	**Mechanic**	WINTERS GARAGE - Winters
1978-79	**Mechanic**	J & J AUTOMOTIVE - Davis
1972-77	**Machine Operator**	BOSTROM BERGEN METAL PRODUCTS - Oakland
1970-72	**Partner**	ALL ONE NATURAL FOODS - Hayward

EDUCATION & TRAINING
Economics, U.C. DAVIS and HAYWARD STATE, 1980-present
Certificate in Auto Mechanics - CHABOT COLLEGE, 1978
Additional Training
Electrical Systems; Tuneup - GENERAL MOTORS TRAINING CENTER
Electronic Ignition; Infrared Diagnosis - SUN PRODUCT TRAINING, San Jose

STEPHEN R. HONDA
788 Manada Ave.
Oakland, CA 94612
(415) 890-6443

Objective: Position as real estate analyst/researcher for a major development firm

HIGHLIGHTS OF QUALIFICATIONS
★ Extensive experience in gathering, analyzing and presenting
   real estate statistics.
★ In-depth knowledge of California economic growth trends.
★ Adept in developing sources for a local demographic profile.
★ Strong desire to establish a career in real estate development.

REAL ESTATE EXPERIENCE

Research & Analysis
• Documented vacancy rate in Oakland neighborhood: made door-to-door survey in a high density neighborhood to determine the vacancy rate in the area.
• Researched local condominium prices for the city of Concord:
  -visited and viewed new condominiums in the community;
  -gathered accurate information on current market prices and made comparison to those proposed by developer seeking municipal assistance.
• Designed and implemented a state-wide survey of city-funded rental rehabilitation programs:
  -searched files to identify cities with rental rehabilitation programs;
  -designed questionnaire to identify and describe those programs with displacement protection;
  -wrote comprehensive report summarizing the programs featuring protection.
• Researched legal procedure for transferring property management responsibility of abandoned rentalproperties; published results in Renters' Resource Manual.

Writing & Presentation
• Mapped results of apartment vacancy survey, and made a formal presentation to city council.
• Wrote detailed report advising City Attorney on procedure for complex land transfer and write-down for Section 8 rental development.
• Authored concise information bulletin on city of Concord Mortgage Assistance Program.

EMPLOYMENT HISTORY

1984-present	**Classroom teacher**	Oakland public schools; Richmond public schools
1983	**Office Manager**	Pacific Car Rental - Oakland
1981 summer	**Administrative Asst.**	Concord Community Development Dept.
1980-1982	**Full-time grad student**	Columbia University - NYC
1980	**Researcher/Writer**	Task Force on City-owned Property - NYC
"	**Library Clerk**	UC Berkeley
1979	**Housing Advocate**	Oakland Citizens Committee for Urban Renewal
1978 summer	**Housing Intern**	Calif. Dept. of Housing & Community Development

EDUCATION
Completed Graduate course work in Urban Planning, COLUMBIA UNIV., NYC
B.A. - Geography - UC BERKELEY

STEPHEN O. RAVENSTAD
2928 Derby Street
Berkeley CA 94703
Home: 667-1233
Office: 890-5444

Objective: Position in corporate protocol, communications or special projects, with Pacific Gas and Electric Company

HIGHLIGHTS OF QUALIFICATIONS
★ Able to represent the company in an eloquent and professional manner.
★ Well versed in current social, political and economic events.
★ Articulate speaker; excellent interpersonal skills.
★ Dynamic talent for problem resolution.
★ Bachelor's Degree in Economics.

PROFESSIONAL EXPERIENCE

Teaching/Training
• Trained professional and clerical staff members in administrative and purchasing methods and procedures.
• Taught basic medical procedures to student aides serving injured athletes.
• Conducted excursions for young adults to social events, guiding them on correct etiquette.
• Taught business typing to high school students.

Communication/Negotiation
• Successfully facilitated complex technical communications between scientific staff and suppliers.
• Established extensive network of professional resources as ULI purchasing agent.
• Drafted business communications, memorandums and supportive documentation for purchasing.

Project Management
• Coordinated residential construction project:
 - hired and supervised architect
 - prepared documentation for building permits
 - coordinated scheduling of subcontractors
 - sought competitive bids and negotiated contracts with subcontractors
 - researched and negotiated for construction financing

EMPLOYMENT HISTORY

1978-present	**Procurement Administrator** and **Contract Negotiator**	University Labs, Inc., Berkeley
1977-78	**Project Manager**	Reardon Construction Co., San Francisco

EDUCATION & TRAINING
B.A. Economics (emphasis in Industrial Organization) - UC Berkeley

SUSAN G. HOLMES

9000 Le Conte Avenue, Apt. 78
Berkeley CA 94709
(415) 244-6161

Objective: Position as Pastoral Minister, assisting in care of parish family.

HIGHLIGHTS OF QUALIFICATIONS

- Effectiveness in recruiting, motivating, placing, training and recognition of parish volunteers.
- Strong commitment to adult Catholic education, and success in teaching adults.
- Ability to deal with diverse individuals and groups, including minorities.
- Strong background in Carmelite and Ignatian spirituality, and interest in providing for the spiritual needs of individuals.
- M.Div./M.A., May 1987.

RELEVANT EXPERIENCE

Counseling & Pastoral Service
- Provided general pastoral counseling, as:
  - hospital chaplain intern.
  - interviewer for RCIA Program & responsible for recommending advancement of Catechumens.
  - member of House of Prayer team; provided consultation as needed.
  - minister to bedridden, convalescent hospital.
  - member in group process and group spiritual direction in parish prayer group.
- Counseled for Suicide Prevention hotline of Alameda County.
- Served as Lay Minister of the Eucharist for: eucharistic liturgies; prayer group; bedridden.
- Interviewed in parish census and survey to assess needs in Parish Council effort.

Religious Education
- Planned 1-year RCIA Program as member of Core Team: set calendar, evaluated sessions, prepared liturgies.
- Directed children's religious education programs:
  - made teacher development a priority;
  - coordinated sacrament classes;   - selected new texts;
  - relocated teaching facility;   - monitored class content and teaching.
- Designed/presented classes for CCD parents and teachers, on sacraments, teaching methods.

Worship
- Planned eucharistic liturgies
  - Sunday parish liturgy, for 2 years
  - children's liturgies, on several special occasions.
- Conducted Communion Services at Convalescent Hospital and in parish as Eucharistic Minister.
- Planned evening of recollection for CCD teachers.

Administration
- Served on Parish Council, both as college student rep and at-large rep.
- Managed reservations calendar and retreatants' quarters for House of Prayer.
- Coordinated 2 Religious Education programs, including:
  - managing and training 40 volunteer teachers and aides; active recruitment of minorities;
  - liaison among 3 Chaplains and a Sunday School Superintendent;
  - inventorying materials and light budgeting;
  - establishing on-site audiovisual and reference library.

- Continued -

SUSAN G. HOLMES
page two

MINISTERIAL HISTORY

1986-87	Chaplain Intern	Samuel Merritt Hospital - Oakland CA
1985-86	Director of Religious Education	Naval Station Chapel, Treasure Is., San Francisco CA
1984-85	Core Team Member, RCIA Program	Saint David's Parish - Richmond CA
1983-84	Crisis Counselor	Suicide Prevention & Crisis Intervention, Alameda Co.
1981-82	Acting Guest Master	Carmelite House of Prayer - Oakville CA
1979-80	Lay Minister of the Eucharist	Holy Spirit Parish & Elmwood Conv. Hosp.,Berkeley
1978-80	Core Member, Prayer Group	Holy Spirit Parish, Berkeley CA
1972-75	Member & Chair, Liturgy Committee	Holy Spirit Parish, Berkeley CA
1972-73	Member, Parish Council	Holy Spirit Parish, Berkeley CA

EDUCATION

1983-87 **M.A.** in Theology - Dominican School of Philosophy & Theology (at GTU) - Berkeley CA
1983-87 **M.Div.** - Dominican School of Philosophy & Theology (at GTU) - Berkeley CA
(strong emphasis in scripture, moral theology and social justice,
New Code of Canon Law, sacramental theology, liturgy and homiletics)
1970-72, 1974-76 **B.A.**, Ancient History & Archaeology (honors) - Univ. of California, Berkeley

COMMITTEES

1986-87 Member, Planning Committee, Workshop on Sexual Abuse for Ministers (Berkeley 1/87)
1984-85 Member, Lay Student Committee, Dominican School of Philosophy & Theology (at GTU)

AWARDS

1986 Mickey Award (Scholarship - Essay Competition) Graduate Theological Union, Berkeley

- References available upon request -

POTPOURRI

248

TERESA FERNANDEZ
3556 Eighth Ave.
San Francisco CA 94118
(415) 808-6578 E-mail No. 90X8

Objective: Position as wardrobe assistant or supervisor with a movie company or TV soap.

HIGHLIGHTS OF QUALIFICATIONS
- Able to handle a multitude of details at once, under pressure and deadlines.
- Effective in managing dressing room environment with diplomacy and authority.
- Well organized, punctual, resourceful; can be counted on to get the job done.
- Successful experience in wardrobing for international rock tour.
- Works equally well as a team member or independently.

RELEVANT EXPERIENCE

Managing Dressing Room
As wardrobe mistress for a rock group of 7, traveling throughout the US, Canada and Europe:
- Monitored dressing room environment to assure safety, efficiency and privacy:
  -hosted backstage guests and business associates of the band;
  -assured proper security during shows;
  -cleared dressing rooms of unauthorized people before/after/during shows.
- Coordinated with caterers on delivery and set-up of contracted food and beverages, assuring that contract agreements were kept; advised caterers on special dietary needs.
- Checked and maintained towel supply for dressing room and stage.
- Supervised physical exercise class for the band.

Appointments/Logistics
- Scouted directions at each new gig, and advised band members on location of showers, rest rooms, dressing rooms, dining facilities, stage locations, production office, promoters' and reps' names and office locations.
- Located hairdressers and masseurs on the road and arranged on-site appointments.

Costume Maintenance
- Selected and laid out costumes for concert appearances.
- Maintained costumes:
  -pressed stage costumes with electric iron and portable steamer;
  -spot cleaned clothing; polished shoes; cleaned and repaired jewelry;
- Packed wardrobe cases for daily transit, handling clothing, accessories and makeup.

Bookkeeping, Shopping, Errands
- Located and bought stage accessories: shoes, belts, gloves, stockings, hats, jewelry.
- Bought and replaced makeup and toiletries; kept detailed records of purchases.
- Located facilities in different cities each day, for laundry, dry cleaning and shoe repair.

EMPLOYMENT & EDUCATION HISTORY

1985-now	Wardrobe Mistress	ROADHOUSE, rock band - New York City
7-9-86	Wardrobe	BILL GRAHAM FILMS, "A Night at the Filmore" HBO filming
1984-85	Freelance Designer Asst.	EUGENE STEPHENS DESIGNS leather accessories - NYC
1984-86	Freelance Designer Asst.	SUZANNE WORTHINGTON quality womens wear - NYC
1983-84	Designer's Rep	OLIVIERI OLIVIERI women's clothing/accessories - NYC
1981-82	Retail Sales/Bookkeeping	a women's boutique; a film/video supply store
1978-82	Student & apprentice in acting & writing comedy for stage & video; +parttime jobs	

B.A., Art, with honors - SAN FRANCISCO STATE UNIVERSITY

PART TWO

Questions & Answers:

25 Tough Problems
and resumes that illustrate solutions

#1. HOW CAN I DEAL WITH GAPS IN MY WORK HISTORY?

GENERAL GUIDELINE: Make a POSITIVE, unapologetic statement about what you WERE doing.

Look at the resumes below for ideas and solutions to this problem:

#2. WHAT IF I HAVE HARDLY ANY PAID EXPERIENCE?

Look at the resumes below for ideas and solutions to this problem:

#3. WHAT IF I STAYED AT ONE PLACE A VERY LONG TIME?

Look at the resumes below for ideas and solutions to this problem:

#4. WHAT DO I DO WITH MY SCRAMBLED-UP WORK RECORD?

Look at the resumes below for ideas and solutions to this problem:

Page 22, Marla—explains the nature of the business where it's not obvious

Page 167, Fran—consistency in layout makes for clarity

Page 190, Judy—a good compromise, where a lot of explaining is needed

Page 227, Mary—free-lance jobs presented in a compact paragraph

Page 230, Carolyn—creative layout makes it seem less confusing

#5. WHAT ABOUT JOBS I HELD MANY YEARS AGO?

Look at the resumes below for ideas and solutions to this problem:

Page 120, James—previous jobs as stevedore, ship rigger, etc.

Page 132, Tudy—prior years: variety of positions

Page 197, Vreny—plus earlier store management in Switzerland

#6. WHAT CAN I DO ABOUT AN EMBARRASSING JOB IN MY WORK RECORD?

Look at the resume below for ideas and solutions to this problem:

Page 187, Jerry—"truck driver" becomes "transportation," (a compromise in form)
For more discussion of this, see "when to break the rules," page 297.

ANOTHER EXAMPLE: Dolores was embarrassed at the name of her old workplace, "Uncle Bunnie's Incredible Edible," considering her relatively dignified current objective. But the experience was too important to omit, so we took liberties and changed the name of the workplace to "U.B.I.E. Restaurant," like so:

| 1985 | Night Manager | U.B.I.E. RESTAURANT—Rockridge CA |

GENERAL GUIDELINE: Don't put things on your resume that could undermine your desired image.

#7. HOW DO I SHOW PART-TIME JOBS WHILE I WAS IN SCHOOL?

Look at the resume below for ideas and solutions to this problem:

Page 77, Estelle—uses "summer" or "weekends" to explain

Page 83, Stephen—helped his father in the summer

Page 87, Anthony—shows that his work history is concurrent with schooling

#8. HOW DO I GET RID OF THIS "JOB HOPPER" LOOK ON MY RESUME?

Look at the resume below for ideas and solutions to this problem:

Page 133, Veronica—11 entries cut down to 8

#9. WHAT IF MY LAST WORKPLACE HAS A NONDESCRIPTIVE NAME?

The names of some businesses give no clue to what they are about, so merely listing them in the Work History doesn't give the reader enough information.

Look at the resumes below for ideas and solutions to this problem:

Page 29, Rita—Seventy-Seven, Inc. = Hawaii real estate development
Page 68, Gelia—Shoreline Shipping, Inc. = international cargo shippers
Page 205, Rebecca—Bay City Unique Creations = private label design firm

#10. WHAT IF MY OLD JOB TITLE UNDERSTATED MY ACTUAL LEVEL OF RESPONSIBILITY? WHAT IF MY OLD JOB TITLE DIDN'T INDICATE WHAT I REALLY DID?

If you were called "Administrative Assistant" or "Secretary" but in fact you had Office Manager responsibilities, then you could describe yourself fairly and ACCURATELY as "Office Manager."

(Important note: Remember, if the job was in the recent past and you intend to use your old boss as a reference, you will need to graciously let him know what you're doing and why, so he can back you up on this.)

ANOTHER EXAMPLE: In some major universities and government jobs, hundreds of people all have the same job title ("Senior Clerk," "Administrative Assistant," "Program Assistant"), which is actually a PAYROLL title. On the resume, it helps to add a job-descriptive title along side it. (Student Academic Advisor/Principal Clerk)

#11. WHAT IF I DON'T HAVE A DEGREE (OR IT ISN'T RELEVANT) BUT I DID TAKE SOME CLASSES?

Look at the resumes below for ideas and solutions to this problem:

Page 45, Mary—shifts emphasis from her degree to her on-the-job training

Page 78, Joy—spells out her recent business training

#12. WHAT IF I DON'T QUITE HAVE MY DEGREE OR CREDENTIALS YET?

Look at the resumes below for ideas and solutions to this problem:

Page 47, Patrice—MFCC Intern Registration Pending

Page 94, Lynne—listing the academic major, where there's no degree

Page 119, Fereshteh—eligible for equivalent U.S. credentials

Page 165, Elizabeth—Graduate studies in expressive arts, in progress...

SOME OTHER SOLUTIONS WHEN THE DEGREE IS INCOMPLETE OR NOT RELEVANT:

In the HIGHLIGHTS section, you could say:

- Graduate degree in Career Development pending at JFK University.

or

- B.A. in Anthropology; elementary teaching credential pending.

In the EDUCATION section, you could say:

- B.A. due 4/88, Accounting—Golden Gate University

or

- M.A. candidate, Career Development, JFK University (anticipated 6/88)

#13. WHAT ABOUT NAMES THAT AREN'T CLEARLY MALE OR FEMALE?

Look at the resume below for ideas and solutions to this problem:

Page 186, Hollis—adding her middle name, "Ann"

ANOTHER EXAMPLE: For Lee Krieger we would use "Ms. Lee Krieger."

GENERAL GUIDELINE: Don't leave people in doubt. Even though it may be irrelevant to the job, readers are uneasy when they can't tell from your name whether you are a man or a woman.

#14. WHICH ADDRESS SHOULD I USE, COLLEGE OR HOME, TO MAKE SURE PEOPLE CAN REACH ME?

List BOTH addresses, one on the left at the top of the resume, and one on the right. You can also add "Call collect" after the phone number. (Or maybe you also need a phone answering machine?)

#15. WHAT IF MY JOB OBJECTIVE IS COMPLICATED TO DESCRIBE?

Look at the resume below for ideas and solutions to this problem:

Page 116, Christiane—making it simpler and clearer through spacing and layout

#16. WHAT IF I HAVE SEVERAL CURRENT JOB OBJECTIVES, OR I NEED A MORE GENERIC RESUME TOO?

Look at the resumes below for ideas and solutions to this problem:

Page 19, Janet—easy to make this resume "generic"

EXAMPLES of two or three different resumes for the same person:

Page 34, Carol—personnel analyst
Page 55, Carol—program specialist/generic
Page 135, Carol—program development, elderly
Page 158, Richard—EMT Supervisor
Page 176, Joyce—marketing/sales
Page 204, Joyce—clothing design/production
Page 242, Richard—fire fighter, entry level

GENERAL GUIDELINE: It is much more effective to use several focused variations than to use one "generic" resume to cover a wide range of job possibilities.

#17. HOW CAN I MENTION MY LONG-TERM GOALS?

Look at the resume below for ideas and solutions to this problem:

Page 114, Charles—presents both current and future job objectives

Or, as this high school student expressed it:

> "Current Objective: Part-time entry level position in Bookkeeping
> 1988 Objective: Full-time Bookkeeping position after high school graduation"

#18. HOW CAN I AVOID TELLING MY AGE WHEN I'VE WORKED FOR 30 YEARS?

You can mention SOME but not ALL of your experience. For example, even though you may actually have 25 years' experience as a teacher, it is ALSO honest (and may serve you better) to say in the HIGHLIGHTS section:

- Fifteen years' experience in public school teaching.

  or

- Over 15 years' experience in public school teaching.

The same principle holds true in the Work History section: *you don't HAVE to include ALL of your work history:* you can go back only as far as necessary (say 10-15 years) to document a substantial (but not TOO substantial!) record of employment. Eventually you'll have to deal with age discrimination, but at least you'll have a chance to get your foot in the door FIRST.

#19. WHAT'S A GOOD WAY TO LIST
TECHNICAL SKILLS OR SPECIAL KNOWLEDGE?

Look at the resumes below for ideas and solutions to this problem:

Page 109, Pamela—chemists' instruments
Page 201, Margaret—home maintenance tools/skills
Page 209, Martha—video/film equipment

#20. HOW DO I KNOW WHAT SKILL AREAS
TO PUT ON MY RESUME?

Look at the resume below for ideas and solutions to this problem:

Page 201, Margaret—good results of 'Informational Interviewing'

#21. IS IT OKAY TO MAKE A MORE
PERSONAL STATEMENT ABOUT HOW I WORK?

Look at the resumes below for ideas on this issue:

Page 151, Ken—describes his professional approach and techniques
Page 120, James—master teacher tells just what he does to help kids learn

#22. WHAT IF I PREFER
A CHRONOLOGICAL TYPE OF RESUME?

Here are some examples of combining the best features of functional resumes with the
best features of chronological formats:

Page 32, Anne—accomplishments, then job content in chronological order
Page 57, Deborah—again: two jobs each described from the skill perspective
Page 114, Charles—most recent job described in functional detail
Page 125, Michele—two overlapping jobs, each broken down by skills

#23. HOW DO I TRANSLATE MY MILITARY BACKGROUND TO CIVILIAN?

Look at the resumes below for ideas and solutions to this problem:

#24. HOW IS A RESUME DIFFERENT IF I WORK FREE-LANCE, OR AS A CONSULTANT?

These people are seeking a professional affiliation, rather than employee status:

#25. HOW DO I PRESENT MY EDUCATION AND WORK HISTORY IF I'M FROM ANOTHER COUNTRY?

Look at the resumes below for ideas and solutions to this problem:

Sample "Highlight" Statements

The examples of "Highlight" statements on the following pages were drawn directly from the resumes in this book. The job seeker's current job objective is added (in parenthesis) where helpful.

"Highlights" can address any of the subjects below, but you should **USE ONLY THE FOUR OR FIVE MOST PERTINENT,** remembering that Brevity and Punch are the magic words here.

> Obviously there's a lot of overlap in these rather arbitrary groupings. The author welcomes ideas that increase the usefulness of this kind of data.

Examples of "Highlight" Statements

Accomplishment or Success

- Outstanding record in recruiting, training, and motivating employees. (management)
- Consistently rank among the top 5 sales reps in the company. (outside sales rep)
- Proven ability to get any individual into the best shape of their life.
    (fitness consultant)
- Successfully published photographs in national and regional magazines.
    (photography)
- Completed over 50 assignments in 37 countries to the clients' complete satisfaction.
    (planner, international investment projects)
- Successfully implemented a personal financial plan that allowed a quality early
    retirement. (financial planner)
- Number One ranked salesman for 4 straight years. (electronic sales rep)
- Earned an Outstanding Achievement raise at MacDonald's.
    (entry level position in bookkeeping)
- Designed and implemented highly successful employee training programs.
    (personnel analyst)
- Managed extremely successful retail stores. (retail store manager)
- Successfully transformed employee magazine, improving its appearance and
    readability while reducing costs. (editorial assistant for Chevron)
- Planned, managed, and supervised events for up to 1,000 people.
    (gallery assistant)
- Succeeded in only 6 months, to educate myself in real estate and implement a highly
    profitable real estate investment. (apprentice financial planner)
- Designed 5 courses, and all materials, to train over 500 adults in job search techniques.
    (trainer, human resources)
- Proven track record of producing and directing award-winning projects.
    (film producer/director)

Background

- Lifelong exposure to international diplomacy.
    (director, international visitors' service)
- Native familiarity with European and Middle Eastern culture, politics & economy.
    (translator, Arabic/English)

- Sharp insight into the subtleties of both Spanish and English, with extensive background in both cultures.
- Lifelong exposure to family real estate business. (trainee in real estate sales)
- Grew up in the corporate world where selling is a way of life.
  (cruise sales rep trainee)

Commitment—values

- Committed to bringing about real, practical results in people's lives. (psychotherapist)
- Highly committed to the Esprit philosophy and eager to support it.
  (creative design for Esprit clothing)
- Self-confident; committed to financial success in sales. (outside sales representative)
- Deeply committed to my clients' well being (therapist/social worker)
- Deep commitment to supporting the world of film and art.
- Committed to the challenge of providing quality and cost-effective construction for
  public housing. (Housing Authority rehabilitation officer)
- Commitment to professional growth and development in financial services.
  (financial consulting)
- Commitment to work that furthers the growth and wholeness of individuals.
  (human services program director)
- Sincere commitment to children's enjoyment and skill in reading.
  (educational sales, publishing)
- Compassionate, professional approach and commitment to service-oriented work.
  (physical therapy aide)
- Enthusiastic and committed to professional excellence. (career counselor)
- Committed to high quality education for young children.
  (preschool/primary grades teacher)

Commitment—motivation and enthusiasm

- Strongly self-motivated, enthusiastic and profit oriented. (sales rep)
- Enthusiastic, creative, willing to assume responsibility.
  (production coordinator)
- Master classroom teacher who loves teaching.
  (high school teacher, social sciences)
- Thrive on consulting with clients, helping them get what they want.
- Highly motivated to achieve set goals.
- Lifelong consuming interest in natural history research and photography.
  (photography/research)
- Strong motivation to help others live life fully. (social service program manager)
- High energy coupled with enthusiasm and dedication to the arts.
  (civic arts association director)

Communication

- Exceptional communication and interpersonal skills; effective negotiator. (international trade)
- Skill in clearly interpreting and explaining regulations. (program analyst)
- Outstanding person-to-person communication skills. (program assistant)
- Outstanding communication and presentation skills.
- Excellent communicator: able to draw people out and put them at ease. (educational sales)
- Communicate well with a wide range of personalities. (special events planning)
- Effective in public speaking and media presentations. (PR, marketing, sales rep)
- Accomplished public speaker and presenter.
- Excellent mediator, moderator, facilitator. (member relations manager)

Creativity or intelligence

- Creative flair in putting on events; thorough in handling details. (hospitality/special events planning)
- Creative idea generator.
- Exceptional talent for creating design solutions that are both artistically innovative and commercially successful. (lighting designer)
- Innovative educator, not afraid to try something new. (high school math teacher)
- Sharp business acumen with extensive background in both the Orient and the U.S. (foreign trade)
- Sharp, innovative, quick learner; proven ability to adapt quickly to a challenge. (public relations)

Credentials or training

- Credential in Financial Planning at UC Berkeley. (financial planner)
- Trained by one of the area's most reputable construction firms. (property management)
- Licensed clinical social worker; 10 years' professional experience. (psychotherapist)
- Specialized courses in finance, economics, and investment. (financial planner)
- Graduate degree in clinical psychology; training in family mediation. (divorce mediator)
- Solid theoretical grounding in psychology and education. (teacher/counselor, children's social services)

Culture and language

- Readily transcend cultural and language differences. (international trade)
- Effective and knowledgeable in working with cultural/social differences.
  (preschool teacher)
- Bilingual in English/Spanish
- Firsthand experience with worldwide range of cultures.
- Familiar with European and Middle Eastern culture, politics and economy, through
  study, extensive travel, and lifelong native residence in the Middle East.
  (translator, Arabic/English)
- Excellent command of both English and Arabic languages.
  (translator, Arabic/English)
- Sharp insight into the subtleties of both Spanish and English, with extensive background in two cultures.

Experience

- Extensive public service experience in not-for-profit organizations.
- Four years' professional practice with large and small firms.
  (campus planner, architecture)
- Extensive experience in business forecasting and planning. (chief financial officer)
- 5 years' experience counseling individuals, couples, and families
  (therapist/social worker)
- 8 years' professional engineering experience. (senior engineer)
- 9 years' experience; working knowledge of all phases of production.
  (film producer)
- Over 15 years' financial management experience in manufacturing. (CEO)
- 18 years' experience in shoe sales.
- Extensive contacts in the arts/entertainment field.
  (public relations with an arts organization)
- CEO of a $17 million business. Ten years' executive experience.
  (commercial leasing agent)

Interpersonal relations

- Work cooperatively with a wide range of personalities. (customer service rep)
- Special flair for relating with a wide range of people, organizations and businesses.
  (outside sales)
- Exceptionally adept at developing rapport with people. (financial planner)
- Demonstrated ability to forge links between diverse community groups.
  (public interest legislative advocate)
- Sincerely enjoy helping people. (customer support/office support)

- Skilled in resolving conflicts and promoting harmonious relationships (school teacher)
- Exceptional communication and interpersonal skills; relate warmly with people, generating trust and rapport. (translator/interpreter in Spanish)
- Diplomatic and tactful with professionals and nonprofessionals at all levels. (foreign trade)
- Skilled in handling the public with professionalism and sensitivity. (social services)
- Communicate with children and parents with warmth and diplomacy. (children's mental health counselor)

Leadership and management

- Ability to prioritize, delegate, and motivate. (program director/coordinator)
- Successful in building and managing a highly effective staff. (CEO)
- Management talent for "seeing the whole picture."
- Sensitivity in integrating a wide range of program priorities. (program director)
- A born leader; effectively handled position of major responsibility on a continuous path of professional advancement. (marketing management)
- Proven record of dependability with increasing responsibility. (office management)
- Inspires and supports others to work at their highest level. (manager, member relations)
- Talent for picking the right people for the job. (management services officer)
- Able to pull together and manage all aspects of a complex project. (marketing management)
- Outstanding record in recruiting, training and motivating employees. (management)
- Effective in promoting a positive, productive work environment. (director, nonprofit agency)
- Outstanding leader with proven record of accomplishments.

Professionalism and poise

- Readily project a professional, fashionable image. (fashion sales rep)
- Extremely sociable, able to put clients at ease. (sales rep)
- Poised and competent as a professional business representative. (international trade)
- Skilled in handling the public with professionalism and sensitivity. (social services)
- Personable, articulate; professional in appearance and manner. (office administrator)
- Poised and professional with both top management and support staff. (PR, customer services)

Reputation and credibility

- Proven ability to gain customers' confidence and trust. (customer service rep)
- Readily inspire the trust and confidence of clients.
  (merchandise sales/client services)
- Excellent professional reputation among city building inspectors, architects,
  subcontractors, builders. (Housing Authority rehabilitation officer)
- Excellent references from past employers and teachers.
  (clerical position in a bank)
- Industry reputation for professionalism and competence.
  (food and drug/quality control management)

Self-management

- A decision maker; well organized, resourceful, and work well independently.
  (outside sales rep)
- Extremely dependable in completing projects accurately and on time. (accounting)
- Results-oriented professional who doesn't take No for an answer.
  (public relations, marketing)
- Equally effective working in self-managed projects and as member of a team.
  (public relations)
- Can be counted on to get the job done, without supervision.

Skills and effectiveness in a variety of areas

. . . ORGANIZATION
- Excellent organization, communication, and writing skills.
- Strong skills in organizing work flow, ideas, materials, people.
  (production coordinator)
- Adept in organizing and integrating a number of documents into a coherent whole.
  (legal assistant)

. . . ASSESSMENT
- Sharp and creative in problem solving and needs assessment.
  (office administrator)
- Outstanding skill in assessing clients' needs for rehabilitative services. (therapist)
- Special talent for assessing and improving office systems.
  (program manager, social services)
- Able to accurately establish priorities and adapt quickly to changing needs.
  (office support)
- Adept at tuning in to clients' priorities to assure accurate needs assessment.
  (commercial leasing agent)
- Able to pinpoint problems and initiate creative solutions. (program analyst)

...SALES

- Effective in persuading others through my enthusiasm for good ideas and products. (educational sales)
- Special talent for motivating and influencing people. (sales rep, PR, marketing)
- Sold directly to major decision makers in industry and medical sector. (marketing rep, health care)
- Successful in generating new business and enlarging client base. (marketing manager, medical/health care)

...COMPUTER RELATED

- Exceptional ability to quickly master new software and apply its full range of capabilities. (software support)
- Skill in refining and translating researchers' goals into computer languages. (university research services)
- Highly skilled in precision writing for special educational applications. (computer education)

...ET CETERA

- Effective in developing programs and reaching project goals.
- Special talent for inspiring creative excellence on a shoestring. (film producer/director)
- Specialist in developing self-worth and self-esteem. (psychotherapist)
- Finely tuned sense of color and its uses. (fabric designer)
- Special talent for coordinating colors, textures, and fabrics. (clothing design)

Special knowledge or technical expertise

- Well versed in California State Tenant/Landlord laws. (housing counselor)
- Knowledgeable and experienced in low income housing finance and development. (housing counselor)
- In-depth knowledge of California economic growth trends. (real estate analyst/researcher)
- Familiar with the scope and quality of Civic Arts programming. (director, civic arts association)
- Knowledge of word processing systems. (office support)
- Experience in restaurant and country club environments. (hospitality/special events planning)
- Technical expertise in the applications of manufacturing materials. (product developer, manufacturing)
- Working familiarity with the Bay Area. (merchandising display for a manufacturer)
- Sharp insight into the subtleties of both Spanish and English, with extensive background in two cultures. (translator and interpreter in Spanish)

- Expert troubleshooter in both manufacturing and packaging.
    (industrial quality control manager)
- Extensive experience with new construction, remodeling, and rehabilitation.
    (housing rehabilitation)

Teamwork

- Easy to work with; a cooperative and supportive colleague.
- Work equally well as a team member or independently.
    (wardrobe assistant, movie company)
- Equally effective working in self-managed projects and as member of a team.
    (public relations)
- Able to work collaboratively in a team effort.
    (counselor, substance abuse treatment program)
- Excellent at working in a team setting to meet deadlines.
    (graphic design/pasteup artist)
- Enthusiastic team member whose participation brings out the best in others.
    (design team)
- Effective working alone and as a cooperative team worker.

Work style

- Take pride in achieving the best possible results. (retail store manager)
- Dedicated, professional attitude; mature and willing to work.
- Sharp eye for details, while maintaining the project overview.
- Keen perception for extracting important data.
    (editorial assistant/researcher in publishing)
- Thrive on organizing complex projects and following through to completion.
    (social service mgr)
- Resourceful and committed, can be counted on to get the job done.
- Self-starter; highly motivated, ambitious and goal oriented.
    (sales rep, marketing, PR)
- Thrive in a dynamic and challenging environment.

...SENSE OF HUMOR, COMPOSURE
- Able to maintain a sense of humor under pressure. (foreign trade)
- Remain calm and work well under demanding conditions.
    (management, nonprofit organization)
- Able to handle a multitude of details at once, meeting deadlines under pressure.
    (TV wardrobe assistance)

Important Tips
about the "Highlights"

TIP #1:
DON'T CONFUSE "HIGHLIGHTS" STATEMENTS AND ONE-LINERS.

These "juicy highlights" are NOT the same as the one-liners which go in the skill section of the resume. The "highlights" appear at the top of the resume ("Highlights of Qualifications") and are unsupported generalizations; the one-liners appear in the Experience section and are explicit action statements of fact that illustrate skills and back up (support) the highlights, making them credible. Mixing these two together will confuse the reader and weaken the resume.

TIP #2:
CUSTOMIZE THE "HIGHLIGHTS" FOR EACH SITUATION.

The "Highlights" section of a resume outlines the four or five "juiciest" things to be said about this job seeker, *for this particular job objective*. These four of five juicy statements would change when the job objective changes, just as they'd be different for someone else applying for the same job.

TIP #3:
CHECK FOR APPROPRIATENESS TO THE CURRENT JOB OBJECTIVE.

When you use motivational statements in the "Highlights," remember that "profit oriented" is fine in the sales field and "compassion" is fine for the therapy role, but each one may be inappropriate on the other resume, even though both may be true of the job seeker. You need to remind people of this all the time: "It may be true about you, but it's not necessarily relevant to this objective."

TIP #4:
REFLECT THE JOB SEEKER'S PERSONAL STYLE.

It's critical that these Highlights be expressed in words that accurately reflect the personality of the job seeker, not of the career counselor! This section of the resume offers the employer a strong clue to the personality and motivation of the job seeker, so be sure it reflects THEM. Try out phrases and repeatedly ask, "Does this sound like you?" —"Would you use this word?"—"How does this feel to you?"—"Are you comfortable with the way it's expressed?" Remind them it's THEIR resume and needs to be in their words.

Cover Letters

Guidelines for Cover Letters:

1. ADDRESS SOMEONE IN AUTHORITY
   (who has the authority to hire you)

2. SHOW THAT YOU'VE DONE YOUR "HOMEWORK"
   (and you know about THEIR priorities and concerns).

3. CONVEY YOUR ENTHUSIASM AND COMMITMENT

4. BALANCE WARMTH AND PROFESSIONALISM

5. PRESENT SOMETHING UNIQUE ABOUT YOU

6. BE APPROPRIATE, YET STAND OUT

7. BE SPECIFIC ABOUT WHY YOU'RE WRITING

8. TAKE THE INITIATIVE ON THE NEXT STEP

9. REMAIN BRIEF AND FOCUSED

13 Sample Cover Letters:

6200 Skyline Blvd.
Oakland CA 94611
(415) 754-5151

Subject:
Cruise staff application

Dear Personnel Director,

Because of my combined interest in travel and working with people
of all kinds in a stimulating, unconventional environment, I am
applying for a cruise staff position with your firm.

My personality and skills are especially well suited to this work, as
you'll note in the attached resume. I have years of successful
experience working with many different types of people, of all ages,
and have sincerely enjoyed my work.

I would especially like to point out my strengths that are most
relevant to the cruise field:
-strong in leadership and organizational skills
-sensitive to the needs and feelings of others
-personable, enthusiastic, and dependable.

I am 30, in fine health, and available for an extended cruise
commitment.

I would look forward to hearing from you at your earliest
convenience. I can be reached at 754-5151. (If I'm not home,
please leave a message on my answering machine.)

Sincerely,

Denise Francis

1776 Twelfth Ave.
San Francisco CA 94118
(415) 212-6822

August 12, 1987

Manager
Sales Department
P.O. Box 57346
Hayward CA 94545

Dear Manager,

This is in response to your ad in Sunday's Examiner/Chronicle, seeking a salesperson. I was excited when I read your ad since I've had a long-time interest in food sales, and your product line sounds particularly appealing to me.

In the course of my recent career research, I spent some time interviewing and accompanying a sales rep for a well known cookie and snack food manufacturer; from that experience I discovered that I have the personality, aggressiveness, and persuasive manner required in this line of work.

I would be delighted to talk with you in person about this position, and look forward to hearing from you soon. I may be reached at 212-6822, where my answering machine can take your message if I'm out.

Sincerely,

Donna Cole

Gerald Davis
7600 Miracle Road
Napa CA 94558
(707) 899-6000, work
(707) 899-4710, home

the ad's inside address

_____

_____

Dear Selection Committee,

In response to your ad in the _____newpaper of October ___
for a _____, I am enclosing my resume for your consideration.

As you will see, I have extensive and successful professional
experience, as Vice President with my current employer, Calnap
Tanning Co.

Due to economic conditions in the marketplace, our company is
ceasing operations, and I am now looking for a new and challenging
opportunity in sales and marketing.

I would enjoy talking with you in person to discuss your needs and
how much skills would best benefit your organization. I look forward
to hearing from you soon.

                                        Sincerely,

                                        Gerald Davis

272

JERRY WILCOX
Montecito Ave.
Pleasanton CA 94566
(415) 943-0104

to

_____

_____

_____

I am enclosing a copy of my resume for your consideration. and would like to call your attention to the areas of skill and achievement in my background that are most relevant.

I am an achiever, with 7 years experience as a highly successful salesman. I've always set high standards and consistently achieved my goals. I am highly motivated and would be a top salesman for whatever company I represent.

I'm confident in my sales ability, and have already proven myself in the areas of increasing territory sales and building customer loyalty, as shown on the attached resume.

I look forward to hearing from you soon and having the opportunity to discuss your needs.

Sincerely,

Jerry Wilcox

JOHN BRIDGES
97 Foothill Lane
Berkeley CA 94705
(415) 990-3466

Mr. Dwight Fontain
Chief Executive Officer
Genentech Inc.
460 Point San Bruno Blvd.
South San Francisco CA 94080

Dear Mr. Fontain,

It was a pleasure to attend the Genentech Shareholders Meeting last week.

After the meeting I introduced myself to you and expressed my excitement at following the company as a shareholder and now my desire to work directly for Genentech.

During the question period I asked if the company had any plans for the treatment of breast cancer. The treatment of this disease and others by the activation and restoration of the immune system with the immunoregulatory drugs created at Genentech is of particular interest to me.

I would be thrilled by the opportunity to contribute to the work the company is doing in this field.

Enclosed is my resume which you kindly requested. Thank you very much for your interest and I look forward to hearing from you soon.

Sincerely,

John Bridges

JOYCE STROEBECH
578 Willow Drive
Walnut Creek CA 94598
(415) 902-1228

Marilyn Sneider
Advertising Director, ESPRIT
900 Minnesota Street
San Francisco, CA 94107

Dear Ms. Sneider:

I recently visited the ESPRIT offices in San Francisco and was immediately impressed by your positive and aesthetic environment for creativity. I especially connected with the inspirational messages mounted on the walls. Since then I have read many articles about ESPRIT and talked to several people about the company, including Jean Livingston in the International Dept. I am very impressed with your Real People ad campaign and its strong impact of color, simplicity, personality, and energy.

I knew from the beginning that I wanted to support the ESPRIT movement, to be a dedicated and integral part of the company. I believe very strongly in the ESPRIT commitment to individual style, fitness, fun, and originality.

I have many skills and experiences gained from my years of work in design, retail and wholesale, and management, as outlined in my resume. I have a good color sense, an eye for coordinating fabrics, fashions, and accessories, and a playful attitude. I'm a resourceful investigator, creative problem solver, and a strong motivator. I like to research new trends, analyze information, and discover new inspirations. I believe my experience and enthusiasm will make me a valuable team member helping ESPRIT continue to grow and inspire.

I would like to talk to you in person and discuss where my skills would benefit you the most. I am looking forward to hearing from you soon. The best time to reach me is between 9 AM and noon, at 902-1228.

Sincerely,

Joyce Stroebech

JOYCE STROEBECH
578 Willow Drive
Walnut Creek CA 94598
(415) 902-1228

John Lorenzo
ESPRIT
900 Minnesota Street
San Francisco CA 94107

Dear Mr. Lorenzo,

I was very excited to learn that ESPRIT is opening retail stores in the Bay Area. The Esprit Look has a very dynamic impact when a complete collection is presented in one environment, as it is at your Union Square Macy's store-within-a-store. I would like to contribute my special skills and energy to this new, challenging venture and work very hard to help it succeed.

I have known from my first exposure to ESPRIT that I wanted to support the ESPRIT movement and be a dedicated and integral part of the company.   I have researched ESPRIT'S unique approach to fashion, advertising, marketing and design. My lifestyle and my values fit with ESPRIT'S commitment to individual style, fitness, fun and originality. I am eager to inspire people to be spontaneous, whimsical and adventurous through ESPRIT'S fashions and philosophy.

I have worked in many levels of retail and wholesale, from sales to management to production. I am also a textile artist with a special talent for coordinating colors, fabrics and accessories. I am a creative problem solver, an enthusiastic and energetic motivator, and good at details. I strive for excellence and originality in everything I do.

I would like to talk to you in person and discuss where my skills would benefit you the most. I am looking forward to hearing from you soon. The best time to reach me is between 9 AM and noon, at 902-1228.

Sincerely,

Joyce Stroebech

276

MARSHA RIFENBERG
12 Sherwood Avenue
Oakland CA 94611
(415) 797-2131

===

Selection Committee
P.O. Box 4992-788
Walnut Creek, CA 94596

Re: Manager, Human Resources Development position

Dear Selection Committee:

The greatest satisfaction in my current assignment in an engineering
company is derived from the management consultation and support I provide.
Whether the issue is a job performance problem, policy/procedure
interpretation or management/employee development, I enjoy working with
management to explore new ways of motivating people. I also enjoy the
results!

I have designed, delivered and evaluated management trainings. The focus of
these trainings has been understanding and consistent use of company
policies and procedures, as well as motivational techniques.

The enclosed resume describes my experience and skills.

I look forward to the opportunity to meet with you regarding your Manager,
Human Resources Development position.

                                        Sincerely,

                                        Marsha Rifenberg

677 Williams Lane
Castro Valley CA 94546
(415) 663-9144

September 15

Mr. R. L. Montrose
Department K
Glick, Schilling & Martin Co.
1934 Drawbridge Road
McLean VA 22102

Dear Mr. Montrose,

In response to your ad in the San Francisco EXAMINER on Sept.14, I am enclosing my resume for your consideration.

I was particularly attracted to your position because of my interest in international affairs and travel, and the opportunity to use my language skills and international working experience in developing a more broadly based career.

As you will notice on my resume, I have an excellent command of both the Arabic and English languages, as well as international exposure through my career, travels and self education.

I believe I would be a good candidate for your position as translator, and look forward to hearing from you soon.

Sincerely,

Nabil T. Rama

Attached: Resume and letter of reference

Richard T. Griffon Jr.
5700 Riverview Street
Albany CA 94706
(415) 389-4111

Office Manager
Law Firm

Dear Manager,

After talking with a friend who is a lawyer, I was encouraged to seek work as a legal assistant, a position that has interested me for some time. My purpose in writing is to determine whether a legal assistant position is available or may become available with your firm soon.

As my resume illustrates, I have extensive experience and skills that are relevant to this position. I would very much appreciate the chance to come in and talk with you further about your personnel needs either now or in the near future.

As a professional creative writer, I'm interested in finding a job that calls for the writing and editing skills I've developed. I look forward to hearing from you soon.

Sincerely,

Richard Griffon

RICHARD JENNINGS
8009 Mountain Blvd.
Oakland CA 94602
(415) 111-6887

James Lawler
Director of Operations, Alameda County
Bay Medical Services
780 San Joaquin Street
Oakland CA 94604

Dear Mr. Lawler,

I was very pleased to learn of the opening for the Alameda County Field Supervisor-Operations position.

In my 18 months as a paramedic with Bay Medical Services I believe I have demonstrated independence and initiative in developing plans to resolve problems I encountered on the job.

I enjoy participating in the operational functions of BMS as a Crew Chief and Relief Field Supervisor.

I look forward to an opportunity to take on more responsibility in this organization and I see the position as a chance to further contribute to the development of paramedicine and to Bay Medical Services as an organization.

I have enclosed a copy of my resume and would like an opportunity to interview for this position.

Sincerely,

Richard Jennings

TERESA FERNANDEZ
3556 Eighth Ave.
San Francisco CA 94118
(415) 808-6578 E-mail No. 2238

October 12

Kathy Nishimoto
Manager, Wardrobe Dept.
CBS-TV
7800 Beverly Blvd.
Los Angeles, CA 90036

Dear Ms. Nishimoto,

In late October I will be in Los Angeles checking out job possibilities in my field of wardrobe, since I will be moving to the area soon.

I would particularly like the chance to meet with you to discuss the possible use of my skills and experience at CBS. I'm especially enthusiastic about working with soaps such as "Capitol" or "The Young and the Restless", the show I love and never miss.

You will see on my enclosed resume that I've successfully handled full responsibility for the wardrobe of a band of 7 people doing live performances around the world. I've also had experience with wardrobe for film and video.

When I arrive in L.A., I'll call your office and ask whether an appointment can be set up. If you wish to call me before then, you can reach me either by E-mail or by phone, as noted above.

Sincerely,

Teresa Fernandez

Dear So and So at Apple,

I am inspired to contact APPLE because of your reputation as a company with a unique and refreshing management approach, one that I highly respect. Also I understand that you have an opening for a Fitness Director.

In my own career development, the greatest satisfactions have come from exploring entirely new ideas for creating the workplace of the future, where the needs of management and staff are integrated to get the job done. I believe that innovative approaches are absolutely necessary to the survival of corporations in today's market place. As an example, a corporation's support of their employees' fitness and health is consistent with the growing awareness and need for corporations to reduce health insurance costs.

My particular expertise is in managing with information systems to identify a wide range of programs that create the most efficient and profitable working environment. As you have discovered and so ably demonstrated, such an environment is healthy for both the organization and the employee.

I strongly feel that my talents in strategic planning and innovative program design, coupled with a clear understanding of the dynamic nature and functions of organizations, could be valuable to APPLE in achieving its corporate goals.

A copy of my resume is enclosed; I will call your office in a few days and request an appointment to talk with you in person about our common interests in these areas.

Sincerely,

Cathryn Naiman

Tips for Career Counselors

(others may eavesdrop!)

A Resume is not
a Career Obituary!

A lot of resumes LOOK about as thrilling as an obituary! They are dead and boring, and there isn't a shred of evidence that the person is an alive, exciting, enthusiastic, committed human being.

Why IS that? Why do people think this document has to be so DULL??

Maybe it's because they think their WORK was dull? In many cases, of course, their past work WAS dull; but even so, there were always aspects of it that were fulfilling and interesting, perhaps the informal times when they helped out a coworker or the creative times when they came up with a new way to get a small piece of the job done more efficiently.

As a counselor, you may have to DIG to get at those illustrations of creativity and aliveness that were there in a client's otherwise uninteresting work history. You can tell you are using the right technique when you see the client "light up" and get excited in describing what they did on the job. They'll sit up straighter, talk faster, maybe smile, and be surprised at what's coming out. They'll say, "Yes, that was really fun and it made me feel good. BUT, that had nothing to do with my job. I wasn't even supposed to be doing it."

But keep on pushing them and get them to tell you WHAT THEY ENJOYED DOING, WHAT GAVE THEM A SENSE OF SATISFACTION AND ACCOMPLISHMENT, regardless of whether it had anything to do with the job they were hired to do. That way, you'll get at their REAL SKILLS, because it's invariably true that people get a sense of enjoyment and gratification when they're using their highest level of skills.

It's also true that they may not YET have figured out how to get PAID for using their highest level of skills. But if you have any serious commitment to your profession, it's your business to support them in finding out what their real strengths are as Step One, and NOT to support their belief that work usually has to be a drag. One proof of your success in this would be a resume that's alive and interesting because it reflects the client's real personality, priorities, and giftedness.

So keep asking your client over and over:

"What did you do   ...that you loved doing?

     ...that used your highest level of skill?

     ...that you want to do again in your new job?"

And you'll get the material for an exciting resume — decidedly NOT a Career Obituary!

Client "Homework"

to clarify the current objective

Very often a new client will not be certain about what kind of work they are currently going after. In that case I give them some simple "homework" to bring to the session.

The actual homework:

1. MAKE A LIST OF ALL THE <u>JOB TITLES</u> YOU CAN THINK OF that describe the kind of work you want to do in your NEXT job; or in other words, what might they call the job you think you want?

    (The key phrase here is "your NEXT job," as distinguished from "your ideal job," because our function at this point is not Career Counseling, but producing a tangible product, right now, related to a goal we are now going to articulate.)

2. MAKE A LIST OF ALL THE <u>WORKPLACES</u> YOU CAN THINK OF that might hire people for this kind of work, e.g.,
    - specific employers ("Bank of America") and/or
    - general descriptions of workplaces ("a large bank")

I specify JOB TITLES and WORKPLACES rather than "skills you'd like to use" or "characteristics of the work scene" because I want the job hunter to begin to move out of the realm of generalities and actually picture themselves in Real Live Jobs. I also recognize that my role is not Career Counseling; they have to have some notion of where they're going, for my resume-writing services to be appropriate. If they can't come up with one real-live job they could do next, then I send them back to their Career Counselor!

The criteria for doing the homework:

a) Don't spend more than 15-20 minutes on the entire homework; don't make a big deal out of it. (This keeps them from getting obsessed over their indecisiveness.)

b) Don't strive for consistency or accuracy. What we really want here is an intuitive, "fast-and-dirty" list, a "first-hit" response. (The counselor will help prioritize later; hearing a few of their peripheral interests helps the counselor get a better perspective of the desired job, especially regarding the level of responsibility the person is seeking, and some of the skills they hope to use.)

c) If possible, get somebody else to write things down while you think out loud.

Working with the homework:

Our resume session starts at the computer screen, typing in the client's name, address, and phone number. Next on the agenda is to enter an explicit job objective. To make sure it's accurate, I now ask the client for the homework they brought, and type it onto the screen. I use a "page 2" for this, already set up in advance, in the format below.

Sometimes people will list job titles and workplaces side by side, even though I asked for two separate lists. Whatever they bring, I type up the two lists in such a way that we can move things around, creating groups of similar job titles and similar workplaces.

> NOTE: When homework has one or two "off-the-wall" things included in the lists, I usually enter them and then set those items aside for the client's future consideration. Remember that, at any point in time, we are harboring the seeds of a FUTURE career objective (as well as a number of interests that may NEVER be manifested in our work lives), and these of course will show up on the lists.

Here's the homework that Marty, a young college graduate, brought in today:

JOB TITLES	WORKPLACES
financial analyst	
customer service/customer relations	
political analyst	
political specialist	
demographer	
geographer	
travel agent?	
politician?	
author	
intelligence	
defense research	
stockbroker	
history professor (or international relations)	
historian	
journalist	
banking	
real estate	
astronaut?	
lobbyist	
	special interest group
	international bank
	foreign service
	something in foreign policy

We did some prioritizing and discovered that right NOW Marty is most interested in the financial area, so we highlighted and grouped all the finance-related job titles he had listed, and then moved that group to the top of our work page:

JOB TITLES	WORKPLACES
<u>1st priority, now</u>	
customer service/relations	**international bank**
banking	
stockbroker	
financial analyst	
<u>2nd priority:</u>	
interest group rep	
lobbyist	special interest group
political analyst (foreign policy)	foreign service
political specialist	
demographer	
geographer	
travel agent?	
politician?	
intelligence	
defense research	
journalist	
real estate	
<u>maybe later:</u>	
author	
history professor (or international relations)	
historian/professor	
astronaut?	

I experimented with composing a tentative job objective that incorporated MOST of what was implied by the job titles and workplaces, asked Marty's reaction, and then modified it several times until it felt right to him.

Stating the Job Objective is particularly tricky. A guideline I share with clients is this: "What we want is something that is FOCUSED ENOUGH and yet BROAD ENOUGH… focused enough to really tell people clearly what you want to do in the immediate future, yet broad enough to incorporate most of the options you want to keep open."

It's a fine line to walk, but it's critical to strive for that just-right balance. On the other hand, don't get hung up in agonizing over it; remind the client of this maxim:

> "It's not so important WHAT you choose;
> but it IS essential THAT you choose."

And show them the handout called "Commitment" on page 306. When my clients insist on "keeping their options open" (meaning avoiding stating a job objective) I work hard at convincing them that their strategy won't work and persuade them to settle on the best compromise that is both FOCUSED ENOUGH and BROAD ENOUGH.

In Marty's case, this was the objective that seemed to fit that description best:

OBJECTIVE: Position in financial analysis or customer services with an international financial institution.

However, by the time we completed the resume, I noticed there was no direct experience we could call "financial analysis," and got Marty's agreement to add "entry" to the job objective, which then read:

OBJECTIVE: Entry position in financial analysis or customer services with an international financial institution.

Lastly, he decided to drop "international" from the objective because he realized that it wasn't critical to his choice. We ended up with:

OBJECTIVE: Entry position in financial analysis or customer services with a major financial institution.

I reminded Marty that if he found a terrific, specific job he wanted to apply for, he should change the objective to read their job title/their firm, for example:

OBJECTIVE: Junior analyst position with Bank of America.

A note about perfectionism

My policy is to let clients know in advance that I charge modestly for future changes they may need, strongly encouraging refinements and making them affordable. That frees us from the pressure to "be perfect" during the resume-writing session. I find this policy to be a great relief for both of us, allowing us to work creatively without inhibiting experimentation. We KNOW we can change it tomorrow if it doesn't look so great in the next morning's light!

Helping Job Hunters
Find the Right Words

People often "go blank" when trying to write a resume—even self-confident, articulate people.

Here are some "tricks" I use to jog their memory and spark their imagination. These apply to the "One-Liners," the Skill Areas and the "Highlights of Qualification" statements, when clients can't think of what they've done or what their strengths and skills are:

1.   I ASK, "HOW DO YOU STAND OUT FROM SOMEONE WHO'S MEDIOCRE?" or "Suppose there were four other people who were just as qualified as you, what could we say about you that makes you *different* from the others, that would give the employer a reason to choose YOU to interview instead of them?"

2.   I ASK THEM TO TELL ME <u>EXPLICITLY</u> WHAT THEY DID.
If they have told me about an accomplishment or an activity, in a very general way, for example . . .

"When I got there the warehouse was a mess, you couldn't find anything, but now it's much better."
. . . then I probe with questions like:
"HOW did you accomplish that?"
"What was YOUR PART in making it better?"

3. I GENTLY CHALLENGE THEM WITH THE QUESTION "SO WHAT?" to get them to identify the *relevance* of the information.

When you're getting "just the bare facts" out of your client ("I made a design for a new bridge"), ask this provocative question (gently), *"So what?!"* immediately paraphrasing it with, "What's the So-What about that? Was it special? Was it bigger or better or cheaper or innovative or cost-effective? Did it work? How did you *know* it was any good?"

Then they'll say, "Well, nobody ever DID that before! I was the *first one who ever did that . . .*" And then you take that as a clue for how to liven up the one-liner. ("Designed the *very first* bridge across the bay . . .")

OR they'll say "Well . . . actually there was nothing special at all about it . . . it was kind of a flop in fact," In which case you're next question could be, "Did you *enjoy* it, was there any satisfaction in it?" and they'll probably say "No," *so you leave it off the resume.*

> REMEMBER: *There is no point in documenting skills the client never enjoyed using and doesn't really want to use again.* You'd only be helping them get *another* job they don't like, and that's not doing them a service.

4. I PRESENT AN IMAGINARY SCENARIO TO GET THEM LOOKING AT THINGS IN A FRESH NEW WAY.

Here are some scenarios I use:

• FRIEND AND EMPLOYER AT LUNCH

"Imagine that your closest friend and colleague (who respects your work and thinks you're great) just happens to be best buddies with the employer where you want to work next, and the two of them are chatting over lunch one day. Your friend thinks you are just *perfect* for the employer's job opening, and is telling him why he thinks so, in five short punchy statements . . . what would your friend be saying about you?"
This scenario gives us material for the Highlights of Qualifications.

• FIRST DAY ON THE JOB

"You've found a job that's just perfect for you and you applied for it . . . along with several other applicants, four of whom were just as qualified as you. The company liked your resume and you were among the five interviewed for the job. All five people were in fact okay for the job . . . all being well qualified, bright, and experienced. BUT, *they chose you.* At the interview you hit it off fine with each of the people you talked to, especially with the person you'd be reporting to on the new job. Somehow you were just yourself, enjoyed the interview, felt confident, weren't attached to whether you got the job or not, but DID convey your interest and enthusiasm. So it went very well — they really SAW you, they tuned in to the very things you most appreciate about yourself and they liked what they saw — so they said "Yes" and you said "Yes.""

"Now you're working there, this is your first day, and you're having lunch by yourself and smiling as you think back on the interview with satisfaction that the interviewers *truly* saw and appreciated and valued those best qualities of yours . . ."

"SO . . . WHAT WAS IT THAT THEY SAW? *What were those outstanding qualities* that are so true about you and so very relevant to this job?"

> NOTE: I particularly like using this scenario, because the client often "lights up" and seems to benefit from visualizing success. This scenario takes awhile to describe, but it WORKS.

• YOU'RE THE EMPLOYER (variation on above)

"If YOU were doing the hiring, and somebody JUST LIKE YOU came along, and you just had this TERRIFIC INTERVIEW with them where you REALLY SAW who they were, what was special about them, what they could offer your company, *what was it that you would have seen?*"

• VISITING EXPERT

"Pretend you're the Visiting Expert in your skill area and your business is to REVEAL YOUR SECRETS OF SUCCESS to the eager novices. You have to tip them off about the things you've discovered and practiced, the subtle awarenesses and sensitivities you've honed and polished to get where you are."

"What kinds of things would you be telling them? ('Look, if you want to be THE BEST in this business, you've got to . . .' THAT kind of thing."

Once they've noticed what specific things they do that make them GOOD at their line of work, you can DESCRIBE THAT ON THE RESUME! Make it into a very focused one-liner or two-liner (or a "compound one-liner")

• THE TOTAL KLUTZ

"Supposing someone else had a job just like yours, and they were a *total klutz* . . . they were a *complete disaster*, they DID EVERYTHING WRONG! What would they be doing? How would they be messing up?"

This works fine when a client is stuck and *can't think positively;* I go in their direction and let them think negatively, then turn everything around to its opposite, ending up with a picture of what it takes to do an excellent job (and often times this is actually what they DO on the job).

• THE PERFECT JOB

"If you could design your absolutely PERFECT JOB, out of any combination of stuff you've already done and felt good about . . . what would that be like?"

• THE TRAINING MANUAL

"Pretend you've been assigned to write the training manual for your job . . . You have to describe very clearly exactly what the employee is supposed to do, and how to do it excellently."

If it's a training manual for being a teacher, for example, you have to tell them the SECRET of superb teaching."

• TYPICAL DAY ON YOUR NEW JOB

"Picture yourself on a typical day, at your new job . . . you're *enjoying* yourself, you're busy, you're involved, *you're using your top level of skills*. Now what, exactly, are you doing? What are you working on? What's YOUR PART in it?"

This helps identify the *skills* the job hunter really wants to use.

An idea/invitation to counselors

NOTICE your own successful techniques . . . LISTEN to yourself as you work, and when you hear yourself saying or doing something that works, jot it down (a key word or two will suffice, and won't interrupt the flow of your session) and then write it out in more detail as soon as you have time.

If you'd like to share these techniques with other readers of this book, please send them to the author and we'll include them in future editions.

Collaborating with the Reader's Brain

to make a good impression

People (including employers) don't like to feel stupid. They get annoyed and frustrated when ideas are presented in a confusing way. Your challenge, then, in developing the resume, is to take advantage of this fact and GO TO ANY LENGTH TO MAKE THE INFOR-MATION TRANSPARENTLY EASY TO GRASP, thereby bringing the reader over to your side.

Keep in mind what happens internally when a person first encounters a resume: the first thing they have to do is mentally answer the question, *"What's this thing doing in my hand?"* (Hopefully, there's a statement of the person's Job Objective at the top, to answer THAT question!)

Then, more or less unconsciously, they will scan the page very quickly to get a feel for *how it's organized,* and their brain will respond to its communication clues and techniques.

Then, IF they're still interested, they'll read for *content,* going first to what's most interesting to them, and what's relevant.

Here are some ways to COLLABORATE with the reader's brain in its tasks:

● The <u>KEY WORD</u> of the <u>MAIN POINT</u> OF EACH STATEMENT should appear at or near the beginning of each line. First, this helps the reader quickly scan for general content (which is what the reader will try to do anyway). Second, it assures that you make the right point, deliver the right "so what."

For example, the impact of the third point in the resume excerpt that follows could vary considerably according to the way the words are arranged. What the job hunter *wanted* to highlight was her willingness to take the initiative in finding funding sources. So she led off with the words "Initiated contact . . ."

Public Relations/Marketing

- *Lobbied for* job-training programs, assisting legislators in developing first drafts of youth training bills and keeping them informed of CRP's progress and developments.

- *Secured* national *recognition* from National Arbor Foundation, for CRP's "Tree Project," named an "exemplary education project" in 1982.

- *Initiated contact with* potential funding *sources* (local, county and state governments, and community agencies) to promote training programs of Circuit Rider Productions.

But notice how the focus and impact changes when she rearranges the words to lead off differently:

"Contacted all levels of government . . ." would focus on her familiarity with local, county, and state governments.
"Promoted training programs . . ." would call more attention to her experience promoting programs.

● ADDRESS THE "SO WHAT?" QUESTION IN THE READER'S MIND BEFORE IT EVEN OCCURS TO THEM.
This point is extremely important because people put things on a resume and mistakenly assume that the reader will figure out its correct significance. There are two hazards in that assumption:

1. The reader may arrive at a totally different conclusion from what you had in mind.

2. The reader may not have the time, or the inclination, to figure out what you meant.

Claudia's resume has some good examples of addressing the "So What?," incorporating the relevance right along with the statement:

- Delivered product presentations to corporate employees during work hours, increasing customer base of our nearby retail store.

- Developed outstandingly effective network of resources and support for Community Arts Festival, resulting in a lavish, "smash hit" fund-raiser.

- Set up an advertising department for a restaurant in Eugene OR, successfully initiating its new image as a community cultural center.

To change the emphasis, Claudia could have rearranged the words in any of these one-liners. The first one, for example, might read:

- Increased customer base of a neighborhood retail store by delivering product presentations to nearby corporate employees during work hours.

IMMEDIATE COMPREHENSION is the big advantage this kind of resume has over the old-fashioned, long-winded resume that told everything in gory detail. With that old resume, the reader's job was to take all that stuff in, crank it around in their mind, and then figure out what it meant to them. Today's employers don't have time for that. So what we're doing here is "predigesting" the info for them, so they can see immediately what it means to them.

● HELP THE READER ORGANIZE HIS THOUGHTS through careful use of formatting graphics:

—"BULLETS" (•) help the reader see how many individual statements he's about to read, and where each different thought begins and ends (as opposed to paragraphs, where a number of thoughts and illustrations may be run together).

—**Boldface,** Underlining, and CAPITALIZING need to be used sparingly and consistently to help a reader organize the ideas. He may not even consciously realize it but his brain will notice, for example, that   —all the **skill areas** are boldface,
                           —all the job titles are underlined,
                           —all the WORKPLACES are in caps.
This makes scanning-for-information extremely productive. (see resumes on pp. 301-304)

—COLUMNS similarly help the reader quickly grasp things, especially in the chronology of the work experience. Notice the extensive use of this technique in all the resumes in this book. See how the columns, coupled with consistent underlining and CAPITALIZING, make it a snap to get a clear overview of a person's job history.

—SPACING can play a big role in comprehension.
Notice the different impact of these two arrangements of the same data, from Tudy's resume:

- Counseled individuals at JFK University Career Center, covering:

   ... test interpretations   ... job search skills

   ... resume preparation   ... interviewing techniques

   ... networking skills   ... researching potential employers.

- Counseled individuals at JFK University Career Center, covering test interpretations, job search skills, resume preparation, interviewing techniques, networking skills, and researching potential employers.

More examples of the same technique, from other resumes:

- Counseled as primary and family therapist in short and long term treatment for adolescents, adults, couples and families using a range of methods:

   —Psychodynamic   —Transactional Analysis   —Family Systems   —Values Clarification.

- Trained individuals, applying programs of diet and exercise to achieve various goals:

   ... weight reduction   ... body-fat reduction   ... weight gain.

- Organized the logistics of speaking engagements and investment seminars:
   —location   —catering   —seating   —literature   —speakers   —travel   —RSVP calls.

—COMPOUND ONE-LINERS maximize action-impact.
These are statements that begin with action verbs
...AND are broken up graphically into sub-statements
   ...which in turn ALSO begin with action verbs. For example:

- Led disaster-recovery team, successfully restoring full business functionality after the county government's computerized system was destroyed by flood:
  —coordinated complex scheduling at four different private firms offering emergency use of their facilities on a time-as-available basis;
  —resolved problems caused by differences in software releases and configurations;
  —delivered payrolls and monthly and quarterly financial reports on time;
  —maintained effectiveness over an extremely demanding 5-month period.

- Created a highly successful program for hospital chaplains which dramatically decreased on-the-job stress: (program still in operation five years later)
  —identified and interviewed the potential participants located at 39 hospitals;
  —designed a program addressing the 3 concerns uncovered in the survey, namely:
     ...training and education   ...clarification of values   ...burnout prevention;
  —developed a program budget and submitted it for Diocesan approval;
  —designed evaluation tools to assure staffing and program effectiveness.

HERE IS A GOOD VARIATION when you have ONLY ONE COMPLEX OR DETAILED
EXAMPLE to illustrate a skill area:

Management

Currently managing a $3.5 million project for the US Navy, in collaboration with a major construction firm:

- Succeeded in the first 6 months, in marketing $650,000 in additional needed effort, despite widespread cutbacks in federal funding;

- Created order out of chaos by instituting general office procedures and filing systems, computer operational logs, and instructions, where none previously existed;

- Developed professional staff from 4 to 17, justifying additional positions to client, writing job descriptions, and hiring and training staff.

—TOPIC HEADINGS immediately answer the question, "What's this item generally about?"

Simply listing one-liners under APPROPRIATE topic headings (skill areas) is *the simplest formatting trick that most resume writers don't take advantage of.*

Bend the Structure,
Break the Rules,
Get Feedback,
etc.

- ## BEND THE STRUCTURE, NOT THE PERSON!

The structure or outline of a person's resume is like a frame for a picture of them. If the structure doesn't fit them, please don't bend the person out of shape to fit the structure; instead, bend (or redesign) the structure!

- ## WHEN TO BREAK THE RULES

Consistency in form is one of the most useful Communication Rules, and I honor it about 99% of the time because it helps in conveying a message to the reader quickly. But 1% of the time I break the Rule of Consistency because I need to in order to avoid conveying the wrong message or creating an image that does not serve the job-hunter. Jerry's work history, in the "Problems" Section, page 187, illustrates an instance of appropriately breaking the rules.

- ## GET FEEDBACK TO MAINTAIN TOP QUALITY WORK

For maintaining excellence and integrity in your resume work, remind your clients to get feedback on the effectiveness of the resume (ie, *when* they used the resume, *did it work to get an interview?*).
AND ask them to TELL YOU the feedback they got, so you can continuously upgrade your service. (Remember to thank them.)

- ## "AGING" A RESUME FOR 24 HOURS

A resume needs to "shake down" a bit; after it's completed, it should be considered as only a "draft" for at least a day or two, until the owner has "slept on it" and some knowledgeable others have looked it over and given feedback.
This is a good reason to have it word processed in the first place, (and NOT to make a lot of copies in the second place) so one doesn't get attached to its initial form.

• DON'T GET SING-SONG-Y

Make sure the cadence or rhythm of one-liners doesn't get too sing-song-y, for example:

   —Revised, edited, and updated . . .
   —Created, implemented, and monitored . . .
   —This, that, and the other . . .

Break up rhythm, or you'll put the reader to sleep!

• TWO-PAGE RESUMES

Two-page resumes are far more effective than OVERCROWDED one-page resumes. However, so the reader can still view the whole resume at once (without flipping pages over), and to minimize risk of page 2 getting lost or ignored, use the guidelines below.

1. Write "continued" at the bottom of the first page.
2. Write your full name and "page two" at the top of page two.
3. Don't staple the pages together.
4. Don't print the pages back-to-back on one page.

A Resume Business
on the Macintosh

For anyone else wishing to combine Resume Writing and the Macintosh computer, here are some notes on my experience.

HARDWARE AND SOFTWARE

The most basic Macintosh setup is adequate for a resume business; my original 128k Mac and ImageWriter printer were fine, except that I always wanted (and still want!) a full-page-size screen. Working on-screen for a long time is stressful on the eyes, so I never do more than one resume a day (that's about 3+ hours).

I use the Microsoft WORD program rather than MacWrite, because I like the ease and flexibility for getting very refined vertical spacing. For example, I change the spacing below paragraph headings (such as "WORK EXPERIENCE" and "HIGHLIGHTS") to a fraction of a line ... perhaps 3/10 or 4/10 or even 2/10 of a line ... depending on the space available on the page. This flexibility also makes it possible to squeeze in one more line when necessary, on an otherwise full-to-the max resume.

I finally designed a TEMPLATE, or Resume Format document, including all the tab-settings, font changes, and other features I routinely use for a resume, and begin each session using a copy of that template.

PRINTING: IMAGEWRITER VS LASERWRITER

After nearly three years on the Mac, I still use the ImageWriter most of the time, because I don't own a LaserWriter and trucking off to the Copy Center to use one is a nuisance. (I'm experimenting now with putting a client's resume on a floppy disk and sending the *client* to a Copy Center that offers LaserWriter consulting services.)

Also, I actually like the ImageWriter fonts beter; they're more interesting and distinctive. The LaserWriter output is maybe TOO high-tech for most people? (Times change, though ... and quickly. Plain old typewriters were good enough a few years ago, and now even my excellent IBM Selectric is considered a dinosaur!)

TYPESTYLES (FONTS)

At first, I found that "Geneva" was the best font to use because it was clean, clear, and uncluttered looking, *and* it was possible to get a terrific amount of words on the page using it. BUT when reproduced on a copy machine, the closely spaced letters could get muddy.

Then I discovered a font called "Clean" which resolved that problem. Then I *rediscovered* "Montreal" font, which is very attractive, though less economical of space. Finally, I came across "Boston II," which is probably the sharpest in terms of printed clarity. Each of these favorite fonts appears on one of the following 4 resumes, all printed on the Apple ImageWriter printer. All the other 200 resumes in this book were re-formatted and re-printed on the Apple LaserWriter so we could get consistent camera-ready copies ... *but* I do not mean to suggest that it's necessary (generally) to print on a LaserWriter. About 95% of my clients use their ImageWriter-printed resume and it works fine.

One font rarely has everything I need. A typical resume has text in 10 pt "Boston II," but the "stars" in the Highlights are from "Zapf Dingbats"/10 pt, and the "bullets" are "Geneva" 10 pt. If there's a fraction in the text, say an address of 10½ Downing St. the fraction (only) may come from "Clean." And if there's a percent sign, it can't be in "Montreal" but it's okay in "Geneva."

I am still looking for the Ultimate BestFont, that's as pretty as "Montreal," as clear as "Boston II" and "Clean," as space-conserving as "Geneva," and that has perfect stars, bullets, and fractions! If you find it, PLEASE let me know!

CLIENT RECORDS FILING SYSTEM consists of:

- COMPUTER RECORDS
  —a computerized copy, on disk, of each version of the resume, plus the "screen notes" and "homework" that we worked from originally.
- PAPER RECORDS or "hard copy"
  —a 4" × 6" filecard for each client, with brief on-going notes about our interactions; clipped to the back is a folded-to-fit copy of the latest resume, for scribbling on when they call back with revisions and updates.
  —a notebook of "hardcopy" originals, "Master Copies" filed alphabetically; each copy is dated because several versions may accumulate over time.

HANDY RESOURCES I DEVELOPED

—A notebook of Xerox copies of the Master Resumes, reorganized by Job Objective. (to show to clients when working on resumes with similar objectives)
—A supply of expendable sample resumes to send home with people who need to do some extra work to finish up.
—A supply of sample Cover Letters to refer to for good basic phrases.
—A supply of hand-outs to send home with people:
...fliers and business cards about my business (clients pass them on to friends)
...info sheets explaining "Informational Interviewing" and "Prioritizing"
...information sheet summarizing Prime Local Resources: good copy centers, word processing people, business libraries, career counselors, career centers.

HANNAH CORTLAND
1990 Grand Avenue
Berkeley CA 94703
(415) 220-1990

The following 4 pages show what my clients' resumes actually looked like originally, produced on the Apple ImageWriter (before "Laser-izing" for this book). This one is done in a font called "Montreal."

Objective: **Bookkeeper/receptionist position, with emphasis on accounts receivable, office coordination, scheduling, computer data entry**

Highlights of Qualifications
- Exceptionally responsible, diligent and thorough.
- Fast learner with a wide range of practical skills.
- Special talent for office organization.
- Excellent verbal and written communication skills.
- Thrive on challenging tasks in a busy office.

RELEVANT EXPERIENCE

Bookkeeping
- Computed and prepared monthly billings for over 100 employment agency clients, achieving a record of exceptional accuracy.
- Maintained records of daily income, and prepared agency's bank deposits.
- Calculated payroll deductions: state/federal taxes, disability, social security.
- Developed monthly Financial Report for Board of Directors of Athena House.

Office Coordination/Scheduling
- Created an efficient filing system for Here's Help Employment Agency, transforming haphazard records into readily retrievable form.
- Coordinated wide range of logistics for office functions:
  -supervised repairs of office equipment   -performed minor repairs & maintenance
  -researched sources/selected new office equipment   -ordered supplies.
- Scheduled screening interviews of job applicants; filled in for Office Manager.
- Responded by mail to employer requests for insurance related information; devised form letter for responding to inquiries from potential job applicants.
- Designed and produced promotional brochure for employment agency:
  -edited text   -arranged for typesetting   -laid out graphics.

Computer Data Entry
- Accurately entered personnel data for over 1000 applicants, using customized computer program; updated and maintained each applicant's records.
- Taught myself computerized word processing and basic spread sheet, and taught other employees to use business programs.

EMPLOYMENT HISTORY

1985-present	Receptionist/Bookkeeper	HERE'S HELP employment agency, San Francisco
1980-84	Housekeeper	Self-employed - East Bay clients
1978-80	Bookkeeping trainee	ATHENA HOUSE residential treatment, Santa Rosa
1977	Accts.Payable/Cashier	COMMUNITY MARKET COOPERATIVE, Santa Rosa
1976	Produce Buyer	OUR SMALL PLANET RESTAURANT, Santa Rosa

EDUCATION
Interdisciplinary Studies - Sonoma State University 1974-77

ELIZABETH LEONARD
340 California Street
Sacramento CA 95818
(916) 881-7213

This resume is printed in my current favorite ImageWriter font, called "Clean."

Objective: position in public relations, public affairs or promotions

HIGHLIGHTS OF QUALIFICATIONS
- 5 years successful experience in public relations.
- Special talent for persuasion and problem solving.
- Ability to relate easily with all kinds of people, in acting as company representative.
- Skilled in writing PSAs and promotional material.
- Well organized and self-motivated.
- Creative, energetic, positive and hard working.

RELEVANT EXPERIENCE

Public Relations/Problem Solving
- Successfully handled PR problems for cable TV company, gaining the cooperation of previously resistant homeowners, for installations on their property:
  - established friendly communication and identified homeowners' specific objections;
  - negotiated creative solutions acceptable to both our company and homeowners.
- Resolved restaurant's PR problem involving customer injury, demonstrating genuine concern for the customer, taking responsibility for medical costs, and successfully retaining the good will and business of the customer.

Promotion
- Promoted campus entertainment events: -wrote PSAs and ads
  -implemented creative promotional ideas -designed and distributed fliers.
- Sold program advertising space for a fund-raising musical event, raising money for Stanford Children's Home.
- Promoted special seasonal offerings for a gourmet vegetarian restaurant:
  -proposed new entrees -designed menu -designed & distributed discount coupons.
- Currently developing a 60-second TV spot to raise funds for a local charity.

Project Management/Organization
- Coordinated programming and scheduling for a live radio talk show on KGNR:
  -contacted public figures and ordinary citizens to set up specific schedule;
  -wrote up biographical material and proposed questions, for radio anchorman;
  -followed up to confirm appointments just prior to show time.
- Managed Mum's in Sacramento, an 80-seat restaurant:
  -hired, supervised and scheduled employees -monitored customer satisfaction.

EMPLOYMENT HISTORY

1985-present	Construction Coordinator	SACRAMENTO CABLE TV - Sacramento
1983-85	Restaurant Manager	MUM'S RESTAURANT - Sacramento
1983-84	Producer Intern (concurrently)	KGNR RADIO - Sacramento
1984 spring	Public Relations Intern	STANFORD CHILDREN'S HOME - Sacramento
1980-84	Student	CAL STATE UNIVERSITY, SACRAMENTO

EDUCATION
B.A., Communication Studies - CALIFORNIA STATE UNIVERSITY, SACRAMENTO

JUDITH R. LIPPETT
1403 Acacia Road
Oakland CA 94610
(415) 213-4646

This resume is printed in the early-Macintosh default font, called "Geneva."

Objective: Position as Sales Representative with Gallo Sales Co.

HIGHLIGHTS OF QUALIFICATIONS
- Sincere enthusiasm and enjoyment of sales.
- Successful record in securing repeat commitment from clients.
- Easily communicate and develop rapport at all levels of interaction.
- Designed & managed direct mail & phone campaign that raised $100,000.
- 3 years increasingly responsible professional experience. College degree.

SALES RELATED EXPERIENCE

Customer Relations
- Developed a strategy for maximizing new and repeat commitments from donors:
  - Identified donors' values, interests and priorities through personal contact and research.
  - Collaborated with volunteer solicitors to develop effective presentations.
- Developed long-term relationships with donors, increasing contributions:
  - Maintained project reports, and ensured continued donor satisfaction.
  - Resolved client problems related to staff and procedural errors.

Sales and Promotion
- Developed promotional material:
  - written brochures   -two video tapes   -monthly newspaper articles.
- Planned and organized public relations events: concerts, dinners, receptions.

Project Management
- Successfully maintained the continuity and direction of a $7.4 million fund-raising project under several changes of management style.
- Recruited 25 fund-raising volunteers by persuading them of the value and satisfaction of participation.
- Facilitated biweekly planning meetings on campaign strategy and progress, to reaffirm volunteers' commitments.
- Trained and supervised small office staff in general support procedures.
- Supervised and coordinated 88 individual local fund-raising campaigns throughout the Bay Area.

WORK HISTORY

1982-present	<u>Administrative Director</u>	EPISCOPAL DIOCESE OF CALIFORNIA, San Francisco
	<u>Asst. Campaign Director</u>	"
	<u>Campaign Coordinator</u>	"
1981-82	<u>Admin. Law Paralegal</u>	CONTRA COSTA CO. LEGAL SERVICES, Pittsburg CA and
	" "	WELFARE RIGHTS ORGANIZATION, Chico, CA

EDUCATION
B.A., Political Science, with highest honors - CSU, Chico
Minor: Business Administration

-References available upon request-

LORI W. VERNON
97 Del Mar Blvd
Oakland CA 94611
(415) 982-9065

This resume is printed in an easy-reading font called "Boston II."

OBJECTIVE: Position as Administrative Assistant

HIGHLIGHTS OF QUALIFICATIONS

- Special gift for getting along with all levels of staff.
- 5 years responsible experience in administrative work.
- Bachelor's Degree in Education.
- Can be counted on to get the job done, without supervision.

RELEVANT EXPERIENCE

Computer Use & Data Processing

- Entered all data for Levi Strauss employee contributions to United Way on an IBM-PC, retrieved data, and ran spreadsheet reports.
- On WANG word processor, composed correspondence and reports, merged letters, addressed envelopes.
- Edited reports and correspondence on IBM Displaywriter documents.

Administrative Support Projects

- Managed office for 6 weeks while all other staff worked at Olympics.
- Compiled complex financial computations and verified eligibility for "matching funds" for over 400 nonprofit agencies throughout the country.
- Coordinated accurate placement of thousands of pieces of office furniture and equipment in major corporate relocation project.
- Arranged transportation for United Way agency visits for 400 employees.

Supervision & Training

- Trained new employees in equipment use, cashiering, food preparation.
- Monitored attendance of student teacher aides.
- Oriented substitute teachers on school policies and schedules.
- Advised coworkers on various procedures of WANG word processing.

EMPLOYMENT HISTORY

1984-present	Admin. Coor., United Way Campaign	ALDOUS CORPORATION, SF
1983-84	Admin. Asst., Olympic Marketing	LEVI STRAUSS & CO., SF
1982-83	Counter Salesperson	CALIF. BAKING CO, Piedmont
1981-82	Levi Plaza Relocation Team Asst.	LEVI STRAUSS & CO., SF
1979-81	Assistant to Principal	Piedmont Unif. School Dist.

EDUCATION

B.S., University of Texas, Austin TX – Elementary Education

Informational Interviewing

"INFORMATIONAL INTERVIEWING" is career counselor jargon for the process of systematically RESEARCHING A CAREER FIELD through a series of in-person, workplace visits with people already employed in similar jobs. It is one of the most valuable career development tools.

SOME MAJOR BENEFITS OF INFORMATIONAL INTERVIEWING ARE:

1. It DEMYSTIFIES the field or position you're interested in, —making it possible for you to speak more knowledgeably about what you want to do, and
   —helping you decide whether this is really an appropriate career choice.
2. It provides you with explicit JOB DESCRIPTION INFORMATION that you need in developing a sharp and focused resume, and a source of CONSTRUCTIVE CRITICISM if you've brought a draft resume with you.
3. It contributes VALUABLE PERSONAL CONTACTS for your job search networking, which is the time-tested, surest route to a good job.

SOME GUIDELINES ABOUT INFORMATIONAL INTERVIEWING:

1. DON'T CONFUSE IT WITH A JOB INTERVIEW; be clear, honest, and unambiguous about your motive or agenda, and stick to the agenda of just getting career information, not fishing for a job opening.
2. MAKE AN EXPLICIT APPOINTMENT for a short period of time (say 20 minutes); be on time, and leave on time.
3. ARRIVE THOROUGHLY PREPARED with the questions you want answered.
4. LEAVE WITH AT LEAST TWO REFERRALS to other people in the field that you can talk to in the same way.
5. TAKE DOWN NOTES IMMEDIATELY after the interview, recording everything you learned.
6. SEND A THANK-YOU NOTE right away.
7. KEEP WELL-ORGANIZED RECORDS of your informational interviewing process.

HOW DO YOU FIND PEOPLE TO INTERVIEW?

1. Ask your friends and acquaintances,"Who do you know who works at a job SOMETHING LIKE the one I'm looking for?" Then ask THEM, "Who do you know who works at a job JUST LIKE the one I'm looking for?" That's the commonest, most direct way; another is:
2. Check with a local career counseling center . . . a nonprofit agency or a community college placement center for leads on people available for informational interviewing.

FOR MORE ON INFORMATIONAL INTERVIEWING (and why you shouldn't CALL it that), see:
* *What Color Is Your Parachute*, R. Bolles, latest edition.
* *How to Get a Job in the San Francisco Bay Area*, J. Beach 1983 edition, pages 41-42.

Commitment

Until one is committed there is hesitancy, the chance to draw back, always ineffectiveness. Concerning all acts of initiative (and creation), there is one elementary truth, the ignorance of which kills countless ideas and splendid plans: that the moment one definitely commits oneself, then Providence moves too. All sorts of things occur to help one that would never otherwise have occurred. A whole stream of events issues from the decision, raising in one's favour all manner of unforeseen incidents and meetings and material assistance, which no man could have dreamt would come his way.

I have learned a deep respect for one of Goethe's couplets:

**"Whatever you can do or dream you can, begin it.
Boldness has genius, power, and magic in it."**

W.H. Murray

Prioritizing Grid

The resume writing process (indeed, the whole job hunt) can get hopelessly bogged down when we lose track of PRIORITIES. To help keep things straight and minimize this hazard, use the Prioritizing Grid repeatedly for every issue along the way by making lists and then ranking things in the order of their CURRENT importance to you. For example, you could prioritize the skills you want to use; the working conditions or desirability factors of pay/location/advancement/autonomy, etc.; YOUR OWN PERSONAL NEEDS AT ANY POINT IN TIME. ("I need some money NOW," "I need a day off, NOW," or "I need to get my priorities straight, NOW.") It actually takes only a few minutes.

Notice that priorities can and do change daily! Then, BE SURE YOUR JOB SEARCH ACTIVITIES LINE UP WITH THESE IDENTIFIED PRIORITIES, so you can at least make some progress each day on THAT day's top priorities. (Note: FIRST make a dozen photocopies and save this page for an original.   —YP)

ITEMS TO BE RANKED:

1. _____   6. _____

2. _____   7. _____

3. _____   8. _____

4. _____   9. _____

5. _____   10. _____

Compare the items above, one pair of items at a time. Pick ONE from EACH of the pairs, and circle your choice below. When you can't decide, just pick one; it will all come out in the wash.

1 or 2	1 or 3	1 or 4	1 or 5	1 or 6	1 or 7	1 or 8	1 or 9	1 or 10
	2 or 3	2 or 4	2 or 5	2 or 6	2 or 7	2 or 8	2 or 9	2 or 10
		3 or 4	3 or 5	3 or 6	3 or 7	3 or 8	3 or 9	3 or 10
			4 or 5	4 or 6	4 or 7	4 or 8	4 or 9	4 or 10
				5 or 6	5 or 7	5 or 8	5 or 9	5 or 10
					6 or 7	6 or 8	6 or 9	6 or 10
						7 or 8	7 or 9	7 or 10
							8 or 9	8 or 10
								9 or 10

Then summarize below. Count up and enter below . . . how many times did you circle #1?,   #2? etc.

#1 ____   #2 ____   #3 ____   #4 ____   #5 ____   #6 ____   #7 ____   #8 ____   #9 ____   #10 ____

(When there's a tie, look back and see which from that pair you chose earlier, and rank it higher.)

FINAL RANKING (for today): Copy the items over again, but now list them in the order of THEIR PRIORITY (for today)

1. _____   6. _____

2. _____   7. _____

3. _____   8. _____

4. _____   9. _____

5. _____   10. _____

On Getting Things Done:

The "Well Begun" Motivator

By Terrie Osborn

My life has been influenced by a long list of philosophies and adages, including "Think positively;" "A bird in the hand is worth two in the bush;" and one of my father's classics, "You can lead a horse to water, but you can't make him tie his shoes."

One of my favorite recurring themes, however, has been one first spoken of by Julie Andrews when she portrayed Mary Poppins in the film of the same name. In this scene, Mary Poppins was faced with the overwhelming job of motivating her young charges to clean up their playroom. Pulling a powerful ace from her English nanny's sleeve, Ms. Poppins clued the children in on what could actually be one of Life's Major Secrets when she told them: "Well begun is half done."

Well begun is half done. These words had a magical effect on the playroom of young Michael and Jane. At the utterance of this simple phrase, scattered clothes, toys and books miraculously rose up off the floor, flew around the room and settled appropriately into closets and drawers. In no time at all, the messy room became neat. Michael and Jane were delighted by this new approach. Clearly, Mary Poppins had power. Such power did not pass by me unnoticed.

I am an every-day-type procrastinator/perfectionist. I am often unable to accomplish anything because, first, I wait until the last minute, and then second, I have no time to perform the task with the high degree of perfection I demand of myself. Rather than do a less than perfect job, I do nothing . . . unless I manage to bring to mind the Poppin's philosophy: Well begun is half done.

Begin it well, I tell myself, which mostly means to just BEGIN. Period. I can always find a long list of reasons to put off the task: It's unpleasant; I'm tired; I'd rather read/watch TV; or, my favorite, I just don't feel like it.

I can recognize pure and simple procrastination, though. I know as well as anybody that tasks cannot accomplish themselves, that they wait with endless patience for the doer to get around to them. I also know that the tasks don't suffer if they don't get done, although I generally suffer if I don't do the tasks.

Many valid excuses can be found. But, in spite of the soundness of such excuses, a little voice speaks in my head with a thought I cannot ignore. "Well begun (it says) is, you know, . . . "

O.K.! Who can argue with that little voice? Procrastination is one thing, but the little voice has the last word. I look at my watch. It's three o'clock. I'll take One Hour, starting right Now, and apply it to this (stupid) project (that I don't want to do.) I flash to Mary Poppins standing in the playroom. "Well begun," I hear her tidy voice saying, parrot-head umbrella in hand, "is half done. Spit spot!"
It always works.
The phrase implies that to simply get started means actually eliminating half of the project. Such a good deal! Just starting wipes out half the task!

I have also discovered a hidden surprise to the Well Begun adage. Once the project is started, one of two things generally happens: I become so interested, and the task reveals itself as so engrossing, that I have the energy, and, lo and behold, the time, to complete the task . . . or, and this never ceases to amaze me, the project takes LESS time than I thought it would! An unwritten law says procrastinated projects require more time than tackled projects actually end up needing.

I have used the phrase unconsciously now for so long that it amuses me to trace it back to Mary Poppins. Perhaps the film was created by a director hoping to influence his own children. He influenced me, at least. Now: if I could only figure out what that "chim chiminy cheree" thing meant.

This article appeared in Vermont's *Country Courier*, 1/23/87. Reprinted with permission of the author, Terrie Osborn, a Stowe, Vermont resident and student of writing and journalism at Johnson State College.

How to Use This Index

The Index is in three parts

● An index of the **JOB OBJECTIVES** that appear at the top of each resume in this book. Look in the *Job Objectives Index* for your *future desired job* ...

        if you want to see a resume written by somebody else looking for that same kind of job

        if you need help identifying the skills used in that line of work

● An index of **WORK HISTORIES** as they appear in the Employment or Work History section of the resumes in this book. Look in the *Work Histories Index* for your *current* or *past jobs* ...

        if you can't find the words to describe what you did on your job

        if you need help in identifying the skills you used in your job

        if you want to see what career directions other people took, who once had a job like yours

Look in *both* the **Work Histories** and the **Job Objectives Indexes** ...

        if you want to find resumes that describe jobs or skill areas *similar* to the ones you are trying to describe

        if you're looking for clues about what some other people's jobs were like

● An index of **GENERAL SUBJECTS,** listing *anything else* you might want to look up, that isn't in the other two indexes.

GENERAL SUBJECTS INDEX

JOB OBJECTIVES INDEX

WORK HISTORIES INDEX

Note: This listing of **work histories** incorporates *some* references to a job-hunter's unique **educational background** (e.g., "language studies") in cases where *that* was a major source of the skill "one-liners" on the resume.

TOM POOLE, OAKLAND

About the Author

DAMN GOOD RESUME SERVICE ● 540-5876

The author works in Berkeley, doing one-to-one resume counseling and writing, on a Macintosh computer. She also teaches and supervises a team of Damn Good Resume Writers-in-Training. Job hunters living in the San Francisco Bay Area can call the number above for information or an appointment.

WORKSHOPS FOR JOB HUNTERS

Yana also presents one or two-hour Workshops on Resume Writing at:

● career development centers ● job fairs ● corporate training programs
● schools ● educational conferences ● association meetings.

If you would like her to speak to your group, please call. Or write:

YANA PARKER, P.O. Box 3289, Berkeley CA 94703.

HELP FOR NEW RESUME WRITERS

Yana provides support and training in the Business of Writing Resumes, helping job counselors, entrepreneurs, retirees, and others to explore the career potential of full-time or part-time Resume Writing.

● Saturday and Weekend Workshops in the Bay Area
● National Newsletter ● Phone consultation.

Call (415) 540-5876 or write to the address above.

THE DAMN GOOD RESUME GUIDE

by Yana Parker

Author of "The Resume Catalog"

Here is the short-and-sweet, step-by-step, authoritative guide to resume writing. It is clear, concise, and highly readable. Simple enough to grasp in one sitting, the basic ideas work for everybody: executives, students, blue-collar workers, housewives. And employers LOVE this resume style because everything they need to know about the job hunter (and nothing more) is *there*, super-easy to find.

Despite its irreverance (or because of it?) this little how-to book has become "required reading" for job-hunters, counselors, and career centers across the country. Following up on the Guide's great success, The Resume Catalog emerged as a companion volume, presenting 200 more examples of the foolproof model described in Damn Good Resume Guide.

The two resources belong side-by-side on every job hunter's desk top.

"Of the many resume books available here's one that can be recommended wholeheartedly."
—*Kliatt Paperback Review*

". . . all summed up here in a few highly readable pages."
—*Co-Evolution Quarterly.*

8-1/2 X 11 inches   80 pages $6.95 paper

When ordering directly from the publisher, please include $1.00 for each book's shipping and handling.

TEN SPEED PRESS
P. O. Box 7123
Berkeley, California 94707